CAREERS
IN FOCUS
Family and Consumer Sciences

◆ BUSINESS AND MARKETING ◆ ARTS ◆ SCIENCE AND TECHNOLOGY ◆
◆ EDUCATION AND COMMUNICATION ◆ HUMAN SERVICES ◆

Lee Jackson

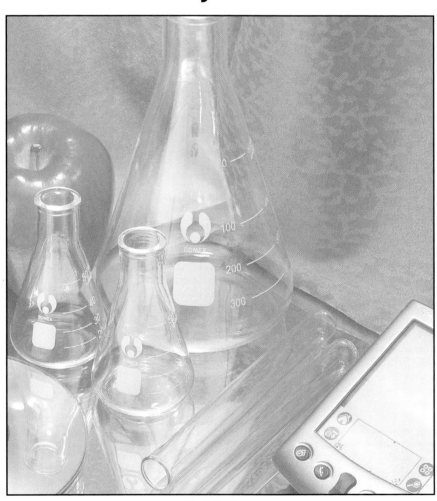

Publisher
The Goodheart-Willcox Company, Inc.
Tinley Park, Illinois

Library of Congress Catalog Card Number 2001040873

ISBN-13: 978-1-56637-882-6
ISBN-10: 1-56637-882-6

5 6 7 8 9 0   03   06

Library of Congress Cataloging-in-Publication Data
Jackson, Lee.
    Careers in focus: family and consumer sciences : education and communication, science and technology, human services, business, art / by Lee Jackson.
        p. cm.
    Includes index.
    ISBN 1-56637-882-6
    1. Vocational guidance. 2. Occupations. 3. Work and family.
4. Family services. 5. Consumer goods. 6. Job hunting. I. Title.
HF5381.J33   2002
650.14--dc21   2001040873
                                                CIP

Introduction

Careers in Focus: Family and Consumer Sciences offers guidelines for succeeding in the world of work. It surveys key careers and shows you how to develop job skills to achieve success in any field. You will also look at how work impacts individuals and families.

This book helps you understand yourself and your career goals. Finding a satisfying career begins by identifying your personality traits, interests, aptitudes, and skills. Knowing what to look for in a career and where to find career information is discussed. You will learn how future job trends may affect you.

Skills necessary for job success are emphasized. These include basic skills in reading, writing, math, computer, and learning-to-learn skills. Other skills necessary for the workplace include communication, personal management, group effectiveness, and leadership. Improving these important abilities will give you an advantage in the job marketplace.

This book will show you how to use effective job-seeking skills. Good job interview techniques are summarized. Points in evaluating job offers are given. Knowing what to expect will help you prepare for those first days on the job. Positive work habits and attitudes influence your job performance and help you be a better employee.

The last section of the book focuses on careers in many areas of family and consumer sciences. Selected careers are identified in business, education and communication, human services, science and technology, the arts, and entrepreneurship. Profiles of men and women in jobs related to these fields are provided throughout Part 4. You may gain inspiration and guidance by reading about people who have successful and interesting careers in family and consumer sciences.

This is an important and exciting time in your life! There are many decisions you will need to make in the months that lie ahead. Reading this book will help you make decisions about your future education and career plans.

About the Author

Lee Jackson, CFCS, taught family and consumer sciences in Wisconsin and Missouri middle and high schools for over twenty-five years. She also served as technical consultant to a professional magazine and wrote articles on child development, parenting, nutrition, fashion, and finance. Lee's entrepreneurial spirit and special interest in foods and nutrition inspired her to write and publish several cookbooks and guides to nutrition and physical fitness. She received her B.S. degree in Home Economics Education from the University of Wisconsin-Stout and her M.S. degree in Education from Northwest Missouri State University. Lee lives in Maryville, Missouri.

Contents in Brief

Contents

Part I
Preparing for a Career

Chapter 4

Preparing for a Career in Family and Consumer Sciences 68

Part II
Developing Personal Skills for Job Success

Chapter 5

Basic Skills for the Workplace 88

Chapter 6

Communication Skills 106

Chapter 7

Understanding Personal Management Skills 120

Chapter 8

Group Effectiveness and Leadership Skills 134

Part III
Achieving Job Success

Chapter 13

Job Evaluation and Change 221

Part IV
Family and Consumer Sciences Careers

Introduction to Family and Consumer Sciences Career Clusters 236

Chapter 14

Careers in Business and Marketing 238

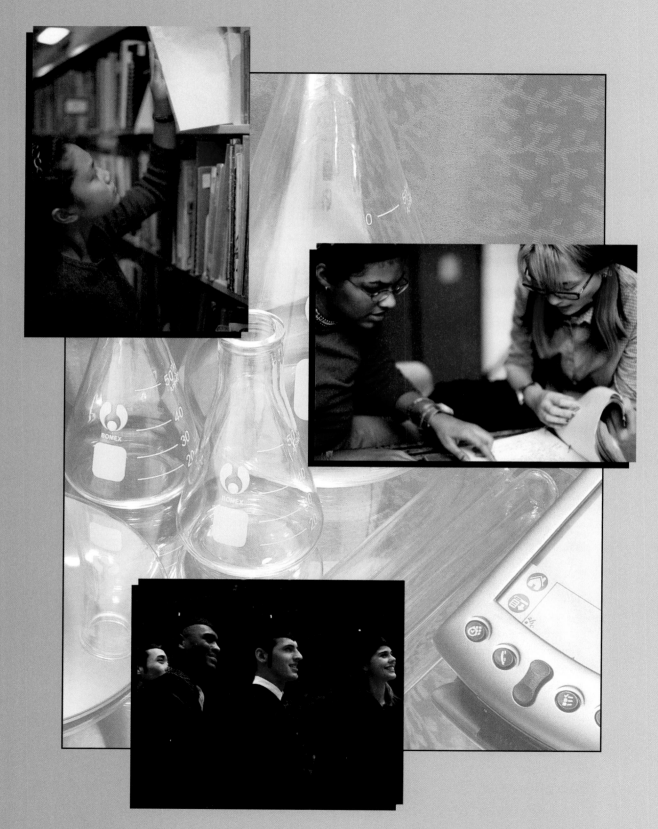

Part I
Preparing
for a
Career

1 Thinking Ahead— Work and the Family

After studying this chapter, you will be able to
◆ explain the meaning of work.
◆ differentiate between a job and a career.
◆ describe the role of a homemaker.
◆ state reasons for working.
◆ examine how family structures affect career choices.
◆ describe the impact of work on the family.
◆ list practices helpful in managing multiple personal, family, and career roles.

Terms to Know

work	outsourcing
career	stepfamily
job	extended family
wage earner	childless family
career ladder	dual-career family
homemaker	single-career family
work ethic	family life cycle
stereotype	management
self-esteem	resources
family	flextime
nuclear family	job sharing
single-parent family	support system

Choosing your career is an exciting decision. Throughout this text, you will be exploring many new and interesting job opportunities. Looking at different career options helps you determine what type of life's work you may like. In the next few years, you will make decisions that will affect your future. Already you have imagined many different kinds of work for yourself. Soon you will be a part of whatever work you choose, carrying out your role in the real world.

Young people today have many career options. Of all the job choices, which will you select? Why will you choose that type of work? Why work at all?

Most people spend an average of forty years in the workforce. Careful planning and preparation must go into career decisions. This requires a basic understanding of yourself. Knowing your special skills and interests will help you decide what is right for you. See 1-1.

1-1 Good career decisions are based on knowing what you want to do with your life.

Making money is the key reason that most people work. However, many factors besides money affect what people do and why they work. In this chapter, you will examine some of these factors. Your career and the type of work you do have a great impact on your personal and family life. You will also read about the effects of career decisions on family roles.

◆ The Meaning of Work

How would you define the term *work?* Work is one of those words having different meanings for different people.

Some people define work as paid employment. Under this definition, parents are not working when they care for their own children. However, parents who are paid to look after someone else's children are considered to be working.

Many people have jobs and get paid for the work they do. However, a lot of people work in the home and other places without getting paid. Housekeepers are paid to perform the same cleaning tasks that most homemakers do without pay. Volunteers do not receive money for organizing fund-raising events; professional fund-raisers do. These examples evoke an interesting question: Are tasks still considered work if people don't get paid for doing them?

When work is defined as an activity that produces something of value, you get closer to the meaning of work. The homemaker then is indeed working. The volunteer's many hours involve work. The mother and father who are caring for their children are also working.

What you consider work may be play to others, 1-2. For instance, if you had to design a cover for a booklet on careers, you might get very frustrated with the task. Someone else might say, "Oh, that will be easy. I like doing that." Without much effort, he or she would create an interesting cover. To you, sweeping the floor may be work, but give a child a broom and dustpan and watch the dirt fly! That is not work, but fun!

School may mean work to you. Because you have responsibilities and jobs to do, it is similar to the workplace. You must be in classes at certain times. You have work to do at school and at home. Getting everything done is sometimes difficult. When a job is completed, there is a sense of satisfaction.

Virginia Division of Tourism

1-2 Is this work or is this play? Some people play golf and get paid for doing it; others play for recreation.

A Job or a Career?

In this book, the terms *work, career, job,* and *wage earner* will be used often. You should understand the differences among them. As stated earlier, a practical definition of **work** is any activity that produces something of value. A **career** is a planned sequence of work in a field, industry, or profession. A career is a series of related jobs that have a common skill, interest, and purpose. A **job** consists of a task or group of tasks performed as a part of work. It is a way to earn a living.

You may change jobs several times in your life without changing careers. Once you change the direction of your skills, interests, and motivations, you change careers. A **wage earner** is a person who works and is paid for those services.

A career involves planning, preparation, and training. For instance, you might prepare for a career in the food service industry. You could choose from hundreds of jobs in this career field, such as a caterer, restaurant manager, or dietitian.

A career usually progresses through a number of stages. One job often leads to another. You might begin with an entry-level job requiring minimal skills. With training and experience, you can move up to higher positions. This progression of advancement in a career is called a **career ladder.** Each new position represents a rung on the ladder. Higher-level jobs involve added responsibilities.

You might remain in the same career field your entire life. However, career changes are common in today's workforce. The average person changes jobs seven to ten times. Likewise, the norm is three to five different careers in a lifetime. You, too, will probably change your career path several times during your life.

Homemaking as a Career

As an adult, you will probably be responsible for making and managing a home for yourself and perhaps for others. A **homemaker** is any person, male or female, who contributes to the comfort and safety of the home and the well-being of the family members. Homemaking has typically been considered a female role, but males are homemakers, too. You may work outside the home for many years, but you will always be a homemaker. See 1-3.

Homemaking is the creation and maintenance of a wholesome family environment. Homemakers perform a wide range of jobs, from home management and organization to professional and scientific tasks. A homemaker must organize the work to be done, plan a budget, and produce goods and services. This is similar to work in paid employment.

1-3 A homemaker performs many types of services that make family living more satisfying.

Have you thought about homemaking as a career? Perhaps you would say, "No, you don't make any money taking care of the home." It is true homemakers don't get paid for their work. Nevertheless, their work in the home is very valuable.

According to some estimates, homemakers spend between 62 and 67 hours per week on household work. See 1-4. If a homemaker were paid even minimum wage, the pay would be over a thousand dollars a month. However, if a paid employee did the work in the home, the costs would increase significantly. Some estimates indicate that hiring housekeepers, bookkeepers, interior decorators, gardeners, taxi drivers, and other specialized personnel would cost over $80,000 per year!

Percent of Time Full-Time Homemakers Spend on Household Tasks per Week

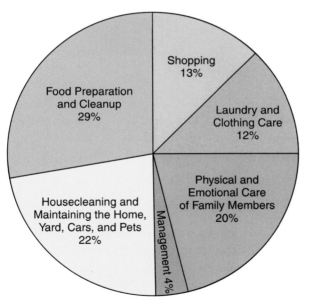

1-4 The most time-consuming task of the homemaker is food preparation and cleanup. The amount of time spent managing may be understated because management is often a part of other activities.

Sometimes a person chooses to become a full-time homemaker at certain stages in life. For example, while children are young, one parent may choose to stay home while the other works. The first parent, then, returns to work when the children start school. After retirement, that person may become a full-time homemaker again.

The number of full-time homemakers is decreasing. More and more families find they need two incomes to survive. Consequently, many choose to be two-income families throughout life in order to live more comfortably.

What would your life be like if nobody performed homemaking tasks in your home? How would you be affected if nobody cooked, cleaned, or did the laundry? Would you make enough money to hire someone to do these tasks for you? Even if you could afford to hire help, you still should know how to do these basic jobs. Otherwise, how will you set standards for a job well done by the people you hire? Homemaking skills are important in the management of home and family life.

You can learn home management skills from many sources. Perhaps the best way is to take an active part in jobs around your house now. Taking high school courses in areas of family and consumer sciences will also expose you to many duties and organization skills needed for running a household.

◆ The Reasons People Work

If you had enough money to live comfortably, would you still consider working? Your first thought might be "Of course not. I would go to the beach or the mountains, travel, and never, ever work!" Upon further consideration, though, most people would admit they would want some kind of meaningful work. People are motivated to work for a number of reasons. Many of these reasons are discussed on the following pages.

1-5 The American work ethic suggests that hard work will bring rewards.

Work Ethic

In the early 1900s, working hard and being industrious were the accepted ways of getting ahead. Through hard work and a great amount of ambition, businesses could be started from scratch. Business owners who failed could start over. Laziness, tardiness, and idleness were not tolerated in the workplace. *Doing an honest day's work for a fair day's pay* became associated with the American work ethic. A **work ethic** is an individual's or society's attitude or belief about work. See 1-5.

The American work ethic has changed somewhat over the years. Hard work and perseverance have been replaced by other job expectations. Today's workforce wants a job challenge. Workers expect to have a chance for self-expression. They feel they should be well *compensated,* or paid, for their labors. They want work that is important to them.

Social Needs

Work meets social needs. Work gives people a chance to interact and be with others. Many social relationships are formed at work. The workplace has always been a place to meet people, talk with them, and establish friendships. Many people form friendships at work that carry over into their nonworking hours.

Work provides a sense of belonging. People feel they are part of an organization, company, or team. There is a sense of being connected to a common cause or goal.

Psychological Needs

Work contributes to a person's identity. When you first meet people, you do not have a good mental picture of who they are. You may make some initial judgments about them from their clothes, hairstyles, or what they say. You do not really know much about them until you find out what they do. Maybe you learn that a person is an office assistant at the high school or handles horses for rodeos. This gives you a better picture of the person. A person's work forms a part of his or her identity since everyone doing similar work shares some characteristics.

When thinking about this, be careful not to stereotype people based on their work. A **stereotype** is a fixed set of beliefs about a particular group of people. You may have certain stereotypes about careers, such as carpentry, teaching, or nursing. Remember no two people are exactly alike, even if they do have a career in common.

Work also provides self-esteem. **Self-esteem** is the feeling you have of your own self-worth. A healthy self-esteem means you recognize and value your own unique talents and abilities. Having a job can help you feel good about yourself. As an employee, you feel you have something to offer your employer. Your talents and skills benefit others. To be working is evidence you are needed and valued.

Financial Needs

Work provides a source of income. Most people work because they must have money to pay for items they need to survive. Through income earned from work, people buy what they need. Their income allows them to pay for food, clothing, and shelter. They can save money for major purchases and future needs.

Independence

Work provides independence. Teens often work in order to have their own money. See 1-6.

Kentucky Fried Chicken (KFC) Corp.

1-6 A teenager's first job symbolizes independence.

It provides financial freedom. "This is my money. I can do what I want with it," is a remark commonly heard. Young people who have jobs don't need to depend on their families as much for spending money.

Physical and Mental Outlet

Work provides a physical and mental outlet. Work allows individuals to be actively doing something. They have someplace to go and feel as if they have a purpose in life. Many people would feel lost or isolated if they did not work to use their talents and abilities. Work also occupies the mind. When you concentrate on work, personal problems and worries seem less troublesome. Work often absorbs your attention even during nonworking hours.

As you can see, work fulfills many important needs. Many societies are organized around work. Work provides a framework for the way people choose to live.

◆ The Meaning of Family

As mentioned, work often affects a person's thoughts and activities during nonworking hours. In other words, work has an impact on your personal and family life.

A **family** is a group of two or more persons who reside together in a household. They are usually related by blood, marriage, or adoption. Members have some of the same goals and values. They share the responsibility for decisions and resources. They have a commitment to each other over time.

Changing Family Patterns

Changing economic and social needs have caused American families to change over the years. Means to provide for these needs have also changed. Some of the major changes occurring in families are listed here.

◆ More women of all ages are gainfully employed. See 1-7. By 2005, the number of women in the labor force will likely rise above 61 percent. For men, the number will drop to 73 percent.

◆ Today, the majority of mothers with young children are in the labor force. This includes 60 percent of those with children under age three and 70 percent of those with children between ages three and five. This trend is expected to increase.

◆ With the increase in divorce and separation, more children are living in single-parent homes. Nearly 30 percent of families are headed by single parents, affecting over 25 percent of American children.

◆ More people are living alone. This is a trend observed among adults of all ages.

◆ The number of two-career families is increasing. Often both parents must work to make ends meet financially, which presents special challenges for spending family time together.

◆ Families are smaller and tend to live apart from other relatives. This means there are fewer close family members to turn to in times of need.

◆ Elder care is a growing concern as seniors live longer lives, often distant from other family members. Finding dependable care for seniors while the adult children are at work is a special challenge to those unable to pay high nursing home costs.

Family Structures Affect Career Choices

The common family structures are nuclear, single-parent, blended, extended, and childless. You may live in several different family structures in your lifetime. While each is different, no one structure is better than another. Each can provide a happy and positive setting for growth and development. Each structure may affect the type or kind of career you choose.

1-7 The changing social and economic needs of families brings women of all ages into the job market.

Gerber Products Company

1-8 Fewer nuclear families exist today than in the past.

The **nuclear family** consists of a father, mother, and their children living together. This is often referred to as the traditional family. In early times, this was the norm of family living. Now the number of nuclear families has declined sharply to only seven percent of households, 1-8.

A single-earner in a two-parent family has become the exception rather than the rule. Either the wage earner must hold a high paying job or the family must make allowances for a reduced lifestyle.

Single-parent families are families who have a mother or father as the head of the household. The children live with only one parent. The children do not always live with the mother, as was the case in years past. Today, many fathers have custody of their children. Sometimes both parents have custody of the children. Work arrangements must be adjusted when one parent assumes the total caregiver role. Children also must adjust to the changing situations and work roles within each household. This structure, too, can provide a happy, positive setting for family members. See 1-9.

1-9 Single-parent families share closeness and commitment. The members work together to achieve their goals.

Balancing work life and family life is very challenging. This is especially difficult when others care for young children while the single parent works. Some single parents find nontraditional work so they can spend more time with their children. *Nontraditional work* can be defined as work done outside the typical working hours of nine to five. Many companies hire workers to perform tasks for their business outside the business environment. This type of work is called **outsourcing**. Often the work can be done at home.

A **stepfamily** is a household where two families are united through marriage. It brings persons from previous marriages together under one roof. This type of family is becoming more common. The couple may each have one or more children. Living with stepparents and stepchildren requires new adjustments. Through cooperation and understanding, these families can provide many rich, new experiences for all members. (Sometimes media sources call these families *blended families.*)

In addition, a stepfamily must often deal with the special work demands of people who likely have more established careers. Career choices may depend on which parent and family will move to the other's location. Both parents may need to rethink their career directions as they make decisions in the best interest of their expanded family.

In the **extended family,** several generations of a family live together. Sometimes an aging grandparent comes to live with the family. Other times, a young adult with a child may move back into the parental home. These types of families have a ready support system in times of trouble. They are there to offer help when needed. Working hours are easier to manage if child care is available through family members.

Childless families are couples without children. Some couples choose not to have children. They may feel that they are not prepared to be parents. They do not want to be responsible for others' lives. Some who planned to have children may find they cannot

have children of their own. This family structure has much more freedom of career choice, work hours, and work location.

Defining Families by Work Patterns

Each type of family structure will encounter different problems concerning work and the family. Whether one or both parents work makes a big impact on family life.

Dual-Career Families

In a **dual-career family,** both the mother and the father are employed outside the home. This family system has several advantages. In addition to having more financial security, both spouses develop their own identities related to their work. Each spouse is able to meet his or her career challenges. Children in these families often are more independent because of their increased responsibilities.

The dual-career family also has its disadvantages. Care of children becomes one of the most difficult problems these families face. See 1-10. Parents must decide how they will coordinate their work and parenting roles. Job transfers become more complicated in dual-career families. A couple may have trouble finding desirable careers for both workers in the same geographic area.

Single-Career Families

In a **single-career family,** only one parent is a wage earner. The other parent has the responsibilities of caring for the home and family. A family may choose this arrangement, or it may be the result of circumstances. A family may choose to have only one parent work because the children are young. They may feel that one wage is sufficient for their lifestyle. This arrangement may also occur when one parent is unable to find work.

The employed parent's work often influences how much he or she can help with parenting

1-10 Raising children is a joy and a challenge.

and homemaking duties. Many mothers and fathers are away from home for long periods. They cannot spend as much time in parent and homemaker roles. They may feel that providing an income is their main family responsibility.

Some parents who stay in the home feel they are missing out on what is going on in the working world. They may feel isolated and trapped in their homes. Others find fulfillment in caring for their home and family. They feel good about providing nourishing meals and making their home life better and more organized. Individuals have different views on their place in the working world versus their place in the home.

Many times the single-career family is a single-parent family. Single parents must fulfill the roles of both wage earner and homemaker. This can be very challenging for some. Single parents must develop skills to juggle their added responsibilities.

Single Living

Being single is a common lifestyle in the United States. According to the latest census,

38 percent of Americans over 18 are single, up from 27 percent in 1970. Many people are single because they delayed getting married or decided never to marry. Other singles include the widowed and those who are divorced or separated. A longer life span has also contributed to more elderly living alone.

Single adults work to earn a living and provide for themselves and, perhaps, other family members. Their lifestyles may give them more freedom to travel. Job transfers may be less complicated. Single people usually develop a vast network of friends and maintain close relationships with their families.

The Family Life Cycle

Often decisions about whether to work outside the home and what type of work to do are based on the stage of the family life cycle. The stages of change that families pass through as they expand and contract form the **family life cycle.** Each of the six stages involves decisions concerning employment and career choice. Three of the stages are marked by the presence of children at home. See 1-11.

As stated earlier, no family fits into a perfect mold. The following is a description of how a family might progress through the following life cycle stages:

◆ beginning
◆ childbearing
◆ parenting
◆ launching
◆ midyears
◆ aging

The first stage in the family life cycle, the *beginning stage,* starts with marriage. It continues until a child is born. During this stage, a married couple learns to live together as husband and wife. The spouses must consider each other's needs and use give-and-take as they make adjustments in this stage.

Often, both spouses are working in this stage. Each must learn to support the other in his or her work and in their marriage. They may be saving to buy a house or other large

1-11 This family is in the parenting stage—the time between the childbearing stage, when children arrive, and the launching stage, when they leave to begin independent lives.

purchase. Some hope to have children and want to provide for them.

The *childbearing stage* begins with the birth of the first child and lasts until the birth of the last child. The focus of the couple shifts to the care and concern of the children. Many more demands affect the couple's time and energy. This stage may be viewed as confining by some, but most find it a time of fulfillment.

During the *parenting stage,* parents must decide whether to continue working or stay home with the children. This decision will be based partly on finances. With the arrival of their firstborn, family expenses increase and continue to rise. Deciding to live on one salary may mean tightening the family budget. If they have car and house payments, usually both must work. If one parent does stay home, he or she may miss the environment of the workplace.

This stage of the family life cycle brings other economic and social challenges. It generally covers the children's educational years, a busy and expensive time in the life of most families. Parents need to recognize the needs of each of their children during this stage. Children may be busy with school, lessons, sports, and other activities. Some may have part-time jobs.

Parents may be at their peak earning power during the latter part of the parenting stage. They are helping children with education and expenses while funding their own retirement plans. They might move to a bigger house as the children grow. This would mean a larger mortgage with bigger house payments.

Sometimes this stage is a time when parents become dissatisfied with their jobs. They may seek a change in their life or their jobs. Smaller paychecks may be routine before a new business or career is established. This could create financial difficulties for the children as well as the parents.

In the *launching stage,* the children leave home to pursue their own careers and goals. Life quiets down considerably. When the last child leaves home, there may be a big void in the life of the parents. This requires an adjustment in living style or family relationships. With the children gone, the couple can redirect their attention toward each other and their marriage. They must now relate to their children as adults, 1-12. They may have grandchildren to enjoy. The couple may also be caring for elderly parents during this time.

The *midyears stage* might bring more financial freedom for a couple. They may both be earning an income. Perhaps the mortgage on the house is paid. Living expenses are generally less expensive than earlier in life. The couple might concentrate on increasing their savings for retirement and putting retirement plans into sharper focus. For some couples this, too, can be a difficult time. One or both partners may have lost their jobs due to industry changes or company reorganization. A new job might need to be found. It is often difficult for older people to find new jobs at their previous salary levels.

1-12 The launching stage arrives when children form lives that are independent from their parents.

The *aging stage* lasts from the time of retirement until the death of both spouses. Traditionally, age 60 to 65 was considered retirement age. However, those who are successful in their careers, and enjoy what they do, are often unwilling to retire just because of reaching a certain age. With the population living longer and in better health than a generation ago, financial incentives now exist for people to remain in the workplace until age 70.

For those who do retire from their jobs, this is a time of more freedom and different concerns. For some couples, this may be the time when they travel or start new hobbies. Other couples wonder whether they will be able to adjust to retirement. This is especially true if they were not active and involved in many activities before retirement. They may suddenly have too much time on their hands. Their health may be more of a concern, too.

No longer having regular income from wages creates financial difficulty for some retired couples. They might worry that their investments will not provide enough income to support them. Since they don't need a lot of the space, they may move to smaller houses or apartments to save money.

Although many retired people continue to do some type of work, they generally place less emphasis on making money. They may work at jobs that give them fulfillment but not much pay. Many retirees begin volunteer or part-time work.

◆ Impact of Work on the Family

Just as families have changed, the work roles within those families have changed. Years ago, most women did not work outside the home. Women were expected to stay home and take care of the family, while men worked to earn money. Each spouse performed a specific role. Now people perform *multiple roles*. That is, they combine two or more work and family roles. Sometimes they are both parent and worker. At other times, they are consumer and family member. Individuals today assume many roles as they function in society. See 1-13.

Today, almost half of all women work full-time. Most women, single or married, will stay in the work force about as long as men. Many work because of economic necessity. That is, they must work to pay the bills.

In two-career families, most of the household chores are still done by women. However, families are realizing the responsibility for household tasks must be shared. In many families, fathers, mothers, and older children all share the work of maintaining a home.

Role Sharing

In many families, there is no division of "women's" versus "men's" work. Each spouse does what needs to be done.

Often spouses may reverse roles and do work that is generally done by the other person.

McCormick/Schilling Spices

1-13 Many people balance the multiple roles of employee and family member.

In *role sharing,* jobs such as meal preparation or financial bookkeeping are done by both.

Role sharing is easier to accept for people who saw their parents share roles. For example, men whose fathers shared household chores may find it easier to do housework than those whose fathers did not. Role sharing is also easier for children to accept if they see role models in the community. They may say, "Brock's daddy was feeding the baby," or "Shanda's mother was changing the tire on the car." They can then more readily accept these changes in their own families.

Role sharing is also common in the working world. More women are working in jobs that were once considered male jobs, 1-14. Men are finding openings in jobs traditionally held by females. Except for a few special cases, all jobs are open to both men and women. This is called *equal opportunity.* Society as a whole believes that men and women are entitled to the same opportunities in the workplace.

1-14 Today many women are working in jobs once considered men's jobs.

Challenges of Families and Work

Changing roles in the workplace have created new challenges for families. High stress, financial problems, more responsibilities, and less free time are issues families face. These issues may influence how working parents perform on the job.

High Stress

Many parents find it stressful to meet the demands of family and work. Working mothers with young children find it especially difficult to cope with their combined roles. Men also experience the stress of balancing home life with a career.

Financial Problems

Mothers may prefer to stay home with their young children but must work to make ends meet. Sometimes a wife has a higher salary than her husband, so she keeps working while he stays home with the children. This can cause conflict in some families. Single parents may find there is not enough money for their families. Many single-parent families experience very serious financial problems.

More Responsibilities

With more women working, all family members must share household tasks. The husband may question why he has to do the laundry or vacuuming. This is the result of changes resulting from the increased demands on each family member. The cooperation of all family members is needed in the home. Some may feel, however, that family obligations interfere with their jobs.

If both parents work, more is expected of the children in terms of household chores and duties. Some children find this hard to accept. "Why do I have to mow the lawn while Justin can play football?" some may ask. Teens may question why they must help prepare or clean up after meals, while others their age have little or nothing to do.

Lack of Time for What Is Considered Important

Work may demand a great deal of the parents' time. There may not be much time to spend with their family, in leisure activities, or by themselves. If a job keeps them away from home a great deal, parents feel they are missing out on their children's growth and development, 1-15. Many single parents receive little moral or physical support from others in their roles as parents. Single parents often must deal with limited or inadequate time for getting everything done.

Effect on Job Performance

Job performance may be affected by how the family reacts to the other challenges mentioned. Some job behaviors that may be influenced by family concerns include: tardiness, absenteeism, low productivity, fatigue, and inability to work overtime.

Virginia Division of Tourism

1-15 Individuals must allow time in their schedules for what they think is important for them and their families.

◆ Balancing Work and the Family

When family members have many demands on them, they may have difficulty balancing their career, personal, and family roles. Balancing work and family requires wise management of time and energy. Family members need to find time to meet personal needs, as well as family needs.

Some parents may turn down promotions if it means working on weekends and not spending time with their children. Some even change jobs or the direction of their careers if the demands are too great. Martin had a high-paying job in a large company. "It was a very grinding job," he said. "If you worked 20 hours a day, management wanted to know why you didn't work 21 hours." Martin's company did not seem concerned about his health or family

time. He resigned that position and chose to work at a less demanding job for much lower pay. Like many families, Martin and his family had to make adjustments to reach their personal and family goals.

In order for families to manage their multiple roles at work and at home, they need to use their skills and available resources. This requires management. **Management** can be defined as using resources to get what you want and need. **Resources** are everything you have or can use to reach a goal. For instance, your school is a resource. It helps you complete your studies for graduation. See 1-16. Your ability to read well or do math are human resources that come from within yourself. To be a good manager means you use what you have to get what you want.

Managing multiple roles can be difficult. Families must learn to use resources to cope with the stress and strain. Management skills

1-16 Your school is a valuable resource. Here you not only learn about the world and people in it, but you learn to interact with others.

help them balance their work schedules and their home life. Some of these management skills are discussed below.

Prioritizing Goals

In this first step of management, you and your family decide what is most important. Then you determine how to reach these goals. Suppose you have a goal to make more time for studying. Look at what needs to be done after school. Decide what must be left undone in order to have time to study. Your mother may tell you the dishes must get done, too. You conclude that if the dishes and studying are both to get done, watching TV must go.

Managing Time and Energy

Time and energy are important resources. Everyone has 24 hours in a day, but each individual spends this time differently. Often a person's energy level varies throughout the day. It is affected by diet, amount of sleep, age, and activities. Families need to find time for the activities they consider important. By planning their time and providing proper food and adequate rest for their family members, they can work to reach their goals.

Sometime employers provide programs that help employees better manage their time. One type of program, called **flextime,** permits flexibility in work hours. Generally, individuals can choose from among different starting and ending times, but all employees work the same number of hours. This program lets people adjust their work schedules around family demands.

Job sharing is another helpful alternative offered by some employers. This means two people split the amount of time they work. Together they make sure the job gets done but divide the work hours to their convenience. Families find they can accomplish their goals better when they have more control over their time.

Making Trade-Offs

Sometimes families adjust by making *trade-offs,* or giving up something in favor of something else. This is done to create increased benefits in a future lifestyle or level of personal fulfillment. For example, a lower standard of living may be accepted while one parent is in college. The family may be willing to compromise now so the education can provide self-fulfillment and a better future. Often families cut down on movies and other extras for several months in order to take a nice vacation. See 1-17.

Getting Outside Help

Families may choose to hire someone to help with child care or housework. This allows family members to have more time for other activities. Outside help can be beneficial to the whole family.

Sometimes employers provide programs that make reliable child care available for employees while they are at work. A few companies provide an on-site child care facility. Others may offer special coupons, redeemable at local child care centers. Some companies also provide similar programs to help employees in need of reliable daytime care for aging seniors.

Developing a Support System

A **support system** is any group of people who help with the care of the family, especially in difficult times. In years past when families lived closer to each other, grandparents or other relatives provided these services. Neighborhoods, too, were a source of support. Now, with families often living away from relatives and not knowing neighbors, support systems are sometimes difficult to find.

However, some families do have family, friends, and neighbors who provide the kind of supportive help they need. Various community

1-17 Many families pay for the family vacation by cutting back on extras throughout the year.

groups, schools, and businesses have set up programs to provide a network of care. Sometimes networks of working families take turns in caring for others' children. Establishing friendships with people who share similar stressful circumstances often makes the load easier to bear. A support system of concerned individuals is important to families.

Families use a number of management skills to provide a satisfying home life. They use the resources at their disposal. Management is vital to successful families.

Summary

Work is defined differently by different people. Most people work for money, but they also expect to get self-satisfaction from their jobs. Work contributes to self-esteem. Many people enjoy the social relationships that are established in the workplace. Activities may be considered work to some, but play to others.

Besides a career outside the home, you will probably have a homemaking career. A homemaker is anyone engaged in the care of the home and family. A homemaker produces goods and services through activities in the home.

The typical traditional family is changing. These changes, with their different roles and responsibilities, have created challenges for families. Changes in family life also affect changes in the work life and career choices of spouses. Family members must work to balance their family, community, and wage-earner roles. Balance can be achieved by managing resources to meet goals.

To Review

1. Give an example of an activity that may be considered work to some people but not to others.

2. Explain the terms *work, job,* and *career.*

3. Name five roles of a homemaker.

4. Compare work ethics of 50 years ago to today.

5. State four reasons people work.

6. How can work help your self-esteem?

7. List four major societal changes that have affected families.

8. What are the common family structures?

9. What is one of the major problems facing dual-career families?

10. What event in the expanding stage of the family life cycle causes a couple to decide whether both should work outside the home?

11. List the stages of the family life cycle.

12. What unexpected occurrences may affect retirement?

13. Give an example of role sharing.

14. Name five ways families can better manage their multiple roles.

To Do

1. Interview a variety of people who are employed and write a report on your findings. Try to interview a female head of household, a male head of household, a dual-career family member, and someone close to retirement. Ask the following questions:

    ◆ Why do you work?

    ◆ How many years have you worked?

    ◆ What do you like most about working?

    ◆ What do you like the least about working?

    ◆ How long do you expect to work?

    ◆ How do you manage your home and job responsibilities?

2. Write a paragraph about your feelings concerning the changing roles of men and women, both in the workplace and at home.

3. Find an article about work in a magazine or newspaper. Summarize the major points of the article in a one-page report.

4. In small groups, brainstorm examples of role sharing in the workplace and at home.

5. Debate the statement: A woman's place is in the home.

6. Role-play the various stages of the family life cycle. In each of the stages, present a family's major concerns about money and working.

2 Deciding What Is Right for You

After studying this chapter, you will be able to
◆ identify your interests, aptitudes, and abilities.
◆ state how interests, aptitudes, and abilities relate to career choices.
◆ describe how personality characteristics influence career choices.
◆ explain how personal priorities and goals relate to choosing a career.
◆ describe ways personal health affects career choices.
◆ analyze how a career choice can impact various aspects of lifestyle and personal priorities.

Terms to Know

interest	peer
aptitude	culture
ability	lifestyle
personality	standards of living
personal priorities	goal
self-actualization	standards

"This is a dream job! I'm doing what I enjoy and I'm getting paid for it!" Have you ever heard anyone say this? Maybe you've heard others say, "I really don't like my job. I wish I could do something else."

How do some people find jobs suited to their individual likes while others are unhappy? How can you know which career could lead to a successful work experience? See 2-1.

Choosing a career is not a decision to be made for you by your best friends, your parents, school counselors, or anyone else. They may give you guidance, but only you can decide what you want to do. The more you know about yourself, the better able you will be to find a satisfying career. Only then will you be able to say: "This is what I want to do. My job is a part of me. I like it!"

2-1 Activities that absorb your spare time might become part of your work environment.

Knowing your personal interests and identifying your aptitudes and abilities can help you find suitable career choices. Determining the personal priorities important to your life will guide you in selecting a career. Finally, setting goals will give direction to your life. This chapter will guide you in a self-evaluation. It will help you decide on a direction for your career.

◆ A Look at What Interests You

A good place to begin in your search for the right job is to identify your interests. **Interests** are those areas that attract your special attention. Listing your interests will help you determine what kind of jobs you would most enjoy. Think about what subjects and activities most appeal to you. Perhaps clothes or cars are high on your list of interests. Maybe you are interested in art, music, animals, or sports. You might enjoy writing a paper for English or getting the boat in proper working order. Computers, hobbies, or TV programs may provide you with hours of entertainment and fascination.

Your life experiences have provided you with many opportunities to explore various interests. As you encounter new experiences, you may discover new interests. Therefore, your interests are likely to change as you get older. You may find yourself drawn to some interests more than others. Identifying areas of high interest will help you decide a career direction.

Hobbies and Activities

Your hobbies and leisure-time activities indicate strong interests and areas of knowledge. Hobbies are more than pleasant pastimes. They are often springboards toward a job that challenges you. For example, someone who likes to read may want to someday work in a library or own a bookstore. Hobbies of model building or sewing may lead to careers in airplane design or clothing design.

Think about what sports or extracurricular activities interest you. One way to learn more about your interests is to try new activities. This might mean joining clubs and organizations and participating in their work. Are you in band, choir, or any school or community organization such as Family, Career, and Community Leaders of America (FCCLA) or 4-H? Do you volunteer in your community?

Before Darrie joined FCCLA, he had no interest in working with the elderly. Darrie did not live near his grandparents nor did he have any close relationships with older people. When his FCCLA chapter chose to work with the elderly in the nursing home, Darrie volunteered to adopt a grandparent. Much to his surprise, he found he worked well with this age group and enjoyed spending time with them. Darrie discovered new abilities and interests that he might pursue in a future job.

Your interest areas may reveal important facts about you. What do you enjoy doing in your free time? The activities and surroundings you enjoy will help you select a career area, 2-2. As you think about your interests, consider how they might relate to various careers.

I Like to
◆ work alone
◆ work with people
◆ work with animals
◆ instruct others on what to do
◆ work with facts and figures
◆ copy words or pictures
◆ analyze why events happen
◆ tend to items, such as gardens or plants
◆ control how items work
◆ work indoors
◆ work outdoors
◆ live in the country
◆ live in a small town
◆ live in a medium-size city
◆ live in a large city

2-2 What do you enjoy most? You may find your interests change as you get older.

◆What Are Your Aptitudes?

Knowing what your interests are can help identify work that you may enjoy. It is also important that you have an aptitude for that work. An **aptitude** refers to a natural talent for a certain physical or mental skill. It is your inborn capacity to perform well in a particular area.

Having an aptitude for a certain skill means it will be easier to perform that skill well. For example, a person who has an aptitude for creative work might find success as a designer or artist. Someone who has an aptitude for working with his or her hands might be very good as a carpenter, automotive technician, or watch repairer.

Discovering your talents will help you consider your career options. For example, if you have a flair for using words and ideas, you might think about a career in journalism. If you have an ear for music, you may look into becoming a band instructor or a dance teacher. Choosing work that makes use of your aptitudes can bring happiness and success in the career world. Realizing your aptitudes is helpful in choosing a career, 2-3.

◆Making the Most of Your Abilities

While you might have an aptitude for a certain skill, you might not have the ability to perform the skill. Having an **ability** means you are capable of performing a certain skill. You are born with certain aptitudes, but abilities must be developed. Abilities are learned through training and practice. For instance, you may have an aptitude for finger coordination and dexterity, skill in using your fingers. However, keyboarding or piano playing ability comes from practice. A cartoonist should have a natural drawing talent, but without practice this skill will not be developed fully. What skills have you developed through training and practice?

Aptitude Identification
General Intelligence
◆ Understand instruction.
◆ Reason and make judgments.
◆ Make good grades in school.
◆ Use memory skills.
Physical Dexterity
◆ Move fingers rapidly and accurately.
◆ Move hands quickly and easily.
◆ Coordinate hand or finger movements with eyes.
Verbal Perception
◆ Understand and use words.
◆ Understand relationships between words and ideas.
Clerical Perception
◆ Detect mistakes in written material.
◆ See differences in written material.
◆ Record details accurately.
Motor Coordination
◆ Coordinate hands and fingers with eyes.
Numerical Perception
◆ Solve problems.
◆ Use figures.
Spatial Perception
◆ Comprehend three-dimensional forms.
◆ Recognize and match various forms.
◆ See relationships in space.
Artistic
◆ Discriminate between colors.
◆ Put colors together creatively.
◆ Demonstrate an ear for music.

2-3 Use the descriptions listed above to help you identify your areas of aptitude.

Sometimes it is helpful to identify your weaknesses as well as your strengths. What weak points do you have that would stop you from doing certain jobs? Think of a situation you dislike, fear, or dread so much that you would rule out any occupation requiring it. For instance, some people dislike repetitious work, doing the same thing hour after hour, day after day. Many people are afraid of speaking in front of a group. Others dislike doing hard physical work, such as carrying or lifting.

Your fears and dislikes are sometimes due to lack of ability. These feelings may subside once a skill is developed. For instance, Sue had a fear of public speaking. She overcame her fear by taking speech courses. With training, she became a successful demonstrator for a toy company. Even if a job situation sounds undesirable, do not cross it off your list immediately. A job initially associated with adverse circumstances can still work out well.

Learning what aptitudes and abilities are required in a career can help you decide if it is right for you. You may not have the aptitude or ability to learn skills needed to be successful in some careers. If you are "all thumbs" and want to be an automotive technician, another career might be a better choice for you. On the other hand, if you really want to pursue a certain career, you may

need to work harder to develop some of your abilities. See 2-4.

◆ Your Personality

Recognizing your unique personality traits and characteristics is helpful in finding satisfaction in your job. Each individual has a distinct **personality**, a combination of behavioral and emotional traits. Your personality is evident in the way you think, act, and speak.

Personality traits that may influence the type of job you seek include
- quiet
- shy
- outgoing
- aggressive (is forceful)
- dominating (likes to be in charge)
- submissive (prefers to follow someone else's lead)
- energetic
- friendly

Different work requires certain personality traits. A job that involves working alone on projects would not be good for someone who works

2-4 Data entry would be a good job choice for someone with an interest in computers and the aptitude of finger dexterity.

better in group settings. Likewise, a quiet person who likes to work alone would not be happy working in a fast-food restaurant. An aggressive and dominating person would probably be more comfortable in a leadership role. Choosing a job to suit your personality will make you more comfortable and happy. See 2-5.

◆ Your Personal Priorities

Your career choice should match your personality as well as your personal priorities. **Personal priorities** are objects, beliefs, or principles that are important to you. They give direction to the way you act, think, and feel. Personal priorities are those characteristics you rank most important in your life.

You are not born with personal priorities. Personal priorities result from past experiences. They are learned from people and situations around you. Your personal priorities have made an impact on you, influencing what you consider important today. They are guides to the choices you make.

People have different backgrounds and experiences. Therefore, one person's personal priorities may be different from another's. You may not always agree with the personal priorities of others, but you can learn to respect them.

Personal priorities fall into two main groups. Tangible personal priorities can be seen or touched. Your family and financial success are tangible personal priorities. Intangible personal priorities cannot be seen or touched. They are beliefs or principles such as honesty or religion. The chart in 2-6 lists a number of tangible and intangible personal priorities that teens may have.

You may find that some of your personal priorities will change over time and new ones will develop. New understandings and knowledge tend to alter ideas and beliefs. Your personal priorities at age 16 may not be the same as those at 26. However, your deep-seated personal priorities will likely stay with you throughout life. For example, if you were raised to respect fairness and honesty, these personal priorities will probably remain with you.

Some personal priorities will be more important to you than others. Consciously or unconsciously, your most important personal priorities will guide the career decisions you make. If compassion is one of your personal

Union Pacific Corporation

2-5 Spending long hours on the road as a long distance truck driver might suit someone who likes to work alone and has a great deal of stamina.

Personal Priorities	
Tangible	**Intangible**
Family	Patriotism
Diploma	Honesty
Children	Intelligence
Friends	Love
Money	Good health
Clothing	Individuality
Artwork	Independence
Hobbies	Creativity
Sports	Recognition

2-6 Some personal priorities will be more important to you than other personal priorities.

priorities, you may choose a health-related occupation or law enforcement. If education and new experiences are among your personal priorities, you may want to teach. Some personal priorities relate more directly to some careers than others, 2-7.

Your personal priorities might affect where you live, with whom you associate, and what you do. Having a career that takes these into consideration can provide a better match between work and personal life.

Many factors influence your personal priorities. These include human needs, your family, peers, culture, society, and media.

Human Needs

Every human being shares the same needs. Abraham Maslow, a noted psychologist,

Suggested Careers to Match Personal Priorities	
Family	Teacher, social worker, child care worker, counselor, minister
Creativity	Architect, interior designer, writer, photographer, artist, design engineer, image consultant
Education and Knowledge	Researcher, teacher, librarian, editor, college professor, school principal, historian, scientist, motivational speaker
Adventure	Pilot, tour guide, astronaut, diplomat, travel agent, detective
Money	Lawyer, surgeon, stockbroker, corporate executive, building contractor, banker
Independence	Caterer, freelance writer, artist, business owner, rancher, farmer, publisher
Recognition	Professional athlete, musician, actor, politician, television reporter
Service to Others	Nurse, doctor, firefighter, veterinarian, law enforcement agent, funeral director, minister, counselor, family financial consultant
Beauty	Interior designer, jeweler, cosmetologist, manicurist, fashion designer, cosmetics salesperson, artist, landscaper

2-7 Your most important personal priorities will guide the career decisions you make.

grouped human needs at five levels. He explained that needs at one level must be met, at least in part, before moving to the next level. Although their decisions and actions will reflect this progression, most people are not specifically aware of it.

The most basic level of needs includes food, clothing, shelter, air, water, space, and sunshine. These are called *physical needs.*

After basic physical needs are met, you work to meet your safety and security needs. Feeling safe from crime and accidents helps you feel secure. You also need to be financially secure, having enough money to provide for your basic needs.

Once safety needs have been addressed, you need love and acceptance. You need to feel that you belong, that you have the approval of others. You need to feel that family and friends care about you. In turn, you show care and love toward them.

At the next level are your needs for esteem. These are met through the respect you give yourself and the admiration you receive from others. Self-esteem is your sense of personal worth. When you feel you have value as a person, you can expect others to respect you.

Self-actualization is the highest level of need. This is the need to be everything you are capable of becoming. If you are fulfilling your goals and are happy and content with yourself, you are said to be self-actualized. See 2-8.

You never completely fulfill all your needs at any level. You will continue to have needs at all five levels throughout your life.

Your needs impact your personal priorities. People place the greatest value on their basic needs. Once these needs are met, more value can be placed on higher-level needs. For instance, your friends are one of your personal priorities. Their approval of you helps meet your need for love and acceptance. However, suppose your basic need for food had not been met. If you were starving, you might be willing to risk losing your friends' approval by stealing food. In that situation, your value of food would be greater than acceptance by your friends.

Family and Peers

Family is probably the most powerful force in the formation of a person's personal priorities. Parents help their children learn moral personal priorities when they teach right from wrong through their words and actions. The personal priorities of learning and education are taught when parents encourage their children to do well in school. Parents' love and concern give children a sense of belonging, another family priority.

During the teen years, your peer group may become a strong influence on your personal priorities. **Peers** are people your own age. Even with peer influence, personal priorities learned as a child tend to remain with you throughout life.

Culture

The culture in which you live strongly influences your personal priorities. **Culture** refers to the beliefs and customs of a racial, ethnic, religious, or social group. Diverse historic, political, and religious backgrounds helped to shape people of many different cultures.

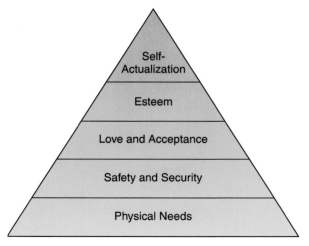

Maslow's Hierarchy of Human Needs

2-8 Maslow's Hierarchy of Needs identifies five areas of human needs.

Your cultural heritage and background result from learned behaviors and beliefs passed from one generation to the next. Your family helps you learn about your culture and about the society in which you live.

Personal priorities concerning relationships and family behaviors are often grounded in culture. In some cultures, parents have the primary responsibility for caring for their children. In other cultures, grandparents, aunts, and uncles take an active role in rearing children.

Cultural patterns may involve the holidays celebrated, clothing worn, food eaten, type of music or art enjoyed, spiritual beliefs held, and other factors. For instance, women in Indian culture wear *saris*. Families in Jewish culture celebrate *Hanukkah*. People in Ethiopian culture eat a spicy stew called *wat*. See 2-9.

Cultural patterns affect career choice. For example, if your family has a long history in a particular line of work, you may picture yourself in that job setting from an early age. Farming, ranching, or operating a small store or restaurant are examples of industries influenced by strong cultural patterns.

You will want a career that is not in conflict with your cultural practices. For example, suppose your cultural dress consists of special headwear, clothing, or accessories. If a job requires wearing a uniform, it may present some uncomfortable choices—either not wearing the cultural items during work, or trying to merge them with the uniform. In a similar way, you may feel uncomfortable about a career requiring working on a certain day if you have been raised to devote that day to spiritual matters.

Bear in mind there are many careers that pose no conflict with your cultural practices. It is best to pursue a career from among these choices.

Society

Individual personal priorities are also influenced by what is happening in society. With modern-day communications, people are affected by what happens throughout the world as well as in their own country. Learning of another country's lack of freedom may cause people to value their freedom more. The impact of earthquakes, floods, droughts, and terrorist attacks is felt worldwide. Such disasters affect the importance people place on personal safety.

Other societal issues that affect people's personal priorities concern the environment, politics, and the state of the economy. Environmental concerns include air pollution, food safety, water contamination, deforestation, endangered species, and waste management. Focus on these issues causes some people to have a greater appreciation for the environment, 2-10. Other societal concerns affect such personal priorities as freedom of choice, civil rights, and public programs.

North Carolina Division of Travel and Tourism

2-9 This woman is helping to preserve the traditional dress and handicrafts of her culture.

North Carolina Division of Travel and Tourism

2-10 Water pollution is just one of many environmental concerns that may affect one's personal priorities concerning natural resources.

Mass Media

Television, movies, radio, the Internet, newspapers, and magazines influence personal priorities in various ways. Through the media, people are made aware of value-ladden social issues throughout the world. They are presented with advertising messages that certain products will completely satisfy various needs and wants. These messages impact the personal priorities people place on those products. People are also shown images of celebrities in the media. These images influence the value people place on wealth and social status.

Personal Priorities Impact Career Choices

Your personal personal priorities affect your career choices. Suppose creativity is one of your personal priorities, and you want to be a sculptor or painter. You know that the life of an artist will not pay well until you get established. You may choose to work at another well-paying job and paint on a part-time basis. On the other hand, some artists will consent to a lower standard of living while they develop their talents. They place more importance on developing their skills than on making money.

You will want to choose a career that suits your personal priorities. This means you will need to know what your personal priorities are. Look again at the chart of personal priorities in 2-6. Which of the items listed are important to you? Also, think about how you spend your time and your money. This can give you a good indication of your personal priorities. You would not invest a lot of time and money on items that are not important to you. Suppose you spend a lot of time volunteering at a recycling center. It would indicate that the environment is one of your personal priorities. If you spend a lot of money on sports equipment and competition, that might show a high regard for exercise and good health, 2-11.

If you have trouble identifying your personal priorities, you might want to talk to your guidance counselor. He or she can have you take a survey that will help you recognize what is important to you.

◆ Your Health

Health habits formed over your lifetime will help or hinder your employability and productivity in the workplace. Personal health is an individual responsibility. Each person must make the necessary decision and commitment to lead a healthy lifestyle. Poor habits such as smoking, staying inactive, skipping meals, or eating foods with poor nutritional value will not make positive contributions to personal health.

There are many advantages to being healthy when applying for a job. Your personal level of health affects how you look, act, and

Virginia Division of Tourism

2-11 The way you spend your time and money is an indication of your personal priorities.

feel. It affects your attitude and work performance. Employers want their employees to be positive reflections of their work. They want employees who are healthy and productive.

Your health stems from your inherited factors but also from what you do to keep yourself healthy. There are lifestyle habits or behaviors that tend to make a difference in the health of people. They are called *lifestyle factors* because they relate to the way people live.

Employers hesitate to hire an individual with health problems. Such employees often present a hardship to fellow employees who may need to do their unfinished work. Individuals with obvious disabilities often have difficulty seeking gainful employment. Many chronic and acute illnesses may limit job possibilities.

Consider how your career might affect your physical and mental health as well. Some careers are dangerous and place you in risky situations. Heavy equipment, great heights, or exposure to toxins are examples of job risks. Sometimes a person's work is very stressful, as when pressing deadlines occur frequently. Some people work well under stress while others do not. If stress reduces the quality of your productivity at work, it will probably affect your lifestyle as well. See 2-12.

◆ Your Lifestyle

In addition to your personal priorities, your lifestyle affects the kind of job you will choose. **Lifestyle** is the way you choose to live. People may not always have the same lifestyle throughout their lives. You probably have some idea of the type of lifestyle you would like to achieve in the near future. Answering a few questions will help you determine the kind of lifestyle you seek.

Where Do You Want to Live?

Being able to live where you want is important to most people. You may want to live in a certain part of the country, such as near the ocean or mountains. Perhaps you want to live in a big city. Maybe a secluded cabin is more to your liking. Abbie wanted to

Factors Affecting Lifestyle
◆ Amount of rest and sleep obtained
◆ Quality and quantity of food eaten
◆ Frequency of physical exercise
◆ Exposure to unsafe products, such as tobacco, alcohol, and drugs
◆ Your general health
◆ Frequency of mental stimulation
◆ Amount of money you make
◆ Family relationships
◆ Your personal priorities

2-12 These are the most common lifestyle factors, but there are others such as peer pressure and family expectations.

get a job in a large city. She had always lived in a small town and wanted to experience city life. Her friend, Sara, enjoyed living in a small town. She wanted to find a job in a community like the one in which she grew up.

The career you choose will affect where you are able to live. Some jobs are not available in small towns. Some types of work can be found only in certain parts of the country. You will need to choose a career that will allow you to live where you want to live.

Whom Do You Want to Share Your Life?

The kind of family structure you hope to have will affect your lifestyle. Will you choose to get married or stay single? Do you want to have children? Will yours be a single-career family or will you and your spouse both work?

Some people place great importance on maintaining close ties with their families. They enjoy spending time with family and friends and want to be near them. If you value family life, you will want regular and reasonable work hours. You may not want a job that requires frequent travel. If closeness of family is important to you, you will also want a job that allows enough time off for you to be with your family. Some people choose to work in a home business so they will be close to their family, 2-13.

Part of Abbie's motivation for moving to the city was that she wanted to be away from her family. Although she loved them, she wanted to be out on her own. She planned to remain single for a few years and establish an independent lifestyle. Starting her career in a large city would allow her to meet this goal. Sara, on the other hand, felt she would really miss her family and friends if she moved too far away. In addition, Sara planned to be married soon. She and her fiancé wanted to start a family in a few years. Starting her career in a small town would allow Sara to rear her children near their grandparents.

2-13 Wanting time to spend special moments with your family will influence your career choice.

What Possessions and Experiences Are Important to You?

Perhaps you want to someday have a cabin by the lake or a home in the mountains. Perhaps you want to spend as much time traveling as possible. Perhaps you dream of raising a large family. What kind of career is needed to make those dreams come true? Your job should pay enough for you to be able to buy what is important to you.

You must think about the costs involved in fulfilling your desires. This will help you assess your income needs. If your needs are simple, finding a high-paying job may be less important to you. However, some people want a large family or enough money for the finer things in life. They will look for a job that pays more, 2-14.

2-14 If expensive recreational items are important to you, you will want a career that allows you to buy them.

Your Standard of Living

The income needed to support your lifestyle will affect the kind of career you choose. What standard of living do you expect to have? A **standard of living** is the lifestyle or type of living that people have due to the quantity and quality of services they can afford.

Many factors influence the standard of living, but income is most important. Other factors may include past experiences, positions held in the community, and expectations. Exposure to the media is another important factor that promotes the desire for more goods and services. Satisfying that desire raises the standard of living.

Obviously, different jobs pay different amounts of money. A teacher does not make as much money as a lawyer. You will need to investigate the earning potential of careers that interest you. This will help you determine whether those careers will meet your needs for income.

A person's career choice will influence his or her standard of living. Generally, higher paying jobs lead to a higher standard of living. This assumes finances are managed well.

◆ What Are Your Goals?

Many people have a tendency to let situations happen rather than take control of their lives. Thinking and planning for the future will lessen your chances of drifting through life without a direction. Setting goals for yourself is one way to take charge of your life. **Goals** are the aims you want to reach.

Most people have a number of goals for their lives. Each of those goals could shift and change as their needs and wants change. For instance, your initial goal might be self-employment. However, you decide to get experience first by working for somebody else. Later, you enjoy that job so much that you decide to change your goal. You choose to advance in the current job instead of owning your own business.

Working toward all your goals at the same time is seldom possible. Ranking your goals in order of their importance will help you plan for them. Decide which goals you want to work toward first. This will improve your ability to attain what you want. Chanci wanted to go to nursing school, but she also wanted to have her own apartment. She couldn't afford to pursue both goals at the same time. Therefore, she decided to get her nursing degree first, and then her own apartment.

Goals should be realistic and attainable, or able to be reached. Suppose you want to be a singer, but you don't have any musical ability. This is an example of a goal that is neither realistic nor very likely to be attained. To be attainable, a natural aptitude and a musical ability would need to be present. Realistic, well-defined goals give you a clearer picture of how to get to where you want to go.

Short-Term and Long-Term Goals

People tend to think of goals in time frames, such as short-term goals and long-term goals. *Short-term goals* are goals you want to achieve in a short time. You might achieve these goals within a day, a week, or a few months. Getting an *A* on your test, buying a jacket, or learning a routine are examples of short-term goals.

Long-term goals take longer to reach. These are goals that may take a year or more to reach. Graduating from college, buying a house, and raising a family are long-term goals. See 2-15.

What you want to accomplish is a combination of short-term and long-term goals. Short-term goals can help you reach your long-term goals. Suppose you have a long-term goal to buy a computer next year. You might set short-term goals to save a certain amount each month for the next 12 months.

Standards

Goals need to be measurable so you can judge whether they have been reached. One way of measuring goals is by standards. **Standards**

are means used to determine if you have reached your goals. When you set standards for goals, you can see more clearly how you are progressing. In a simple example, suppose your goal is to make your bed. Your standard for a well-made bed is to have smooth sheets and blankets that hang evenly on both sides. If your bed looks neat when you have finished making it, you have met your standard and reached your goal.

Deadlines are one type of standard. Having a completion date for goals will help keep you focused. Deadlines also give you a way of evaluating your progress. If you are a newsletter editor, you may set a standard of publishing four editions per year. When the year is up, you can evaluate your progress by the number of newsletters published. When you have reached a goal by the deadline, you can take pride in your accomplishment.

U.S. Department of Agriculture

2-15 Carla's long-term goal is to be a horticulturalist. Her short-term goal is learning to grow and identify plants in a greenhouse.

Setting Career Goals

Major businesses define what they want and what direction they will take by setting goals. They then list ways of achieving those goals. Successful people use this same approach to choose and advance in careers.

When making career choices, consider your short-term and long-term goals. Think about your future and what you would like to accomplish. Suppose your goal is to become a cosmetologist. Your first short-term goal might be to examine various cosmetology programs. Your next short-term goal might be to take high school classes related to the training programs.

You will measure your career success by your standards. Are you happy with your work? Do you feel that you are doing the best job you can? Do you feel challenged in your work? Are you being paid what you are worth?

Have you achieved the level of responsibility you are seeking? Answering yes to these questions indicates that your job is meeting your standards. Keep in mind that if you work for someone else, you must also meet his or her standards.

Setting Lifestyle and Retirement Goals

Retirement is probably not on your mind, but perhaps having a nice car or wardrobe is. No matter what possessions you desire in life, they will cost money. Buying them will require working and planning. Developing a habit of saving money while young is the key to reaching your goals. Contributing regularly to a savings account will also help you develop financial responsibility, 2-16.

2-16 Contributing regularly to a savings account is a habit to develop as soon as you start earning money.

Although your first goal is to get a good job, you will need to prepare for the possibility of losing that job. If you have money saved, you will be able to stay in your apartment, make your car payments, and join friends for dinner while job hunting. Three to six months worth of living expenses in a savings account is considered a good cash "cushion."

It is never too early to start investing for future long-term goals such as retirement. In Chapter One, you learned that some stages of the family life cycle are costly periods for families. High expenses make it difficult to save for retirement. For that reason, young people are advised to start saving early. Investing just $25 a month from the age of 21 will probably yield more than $216,000 in 40 years. (This yield assumes an 11 percent return, which is the stock market's historical average since 1929.)

Planning for retirement must take into account the way you want to live. These are details you won't know for some time. Once you envision your future lifestyle as you best can, then you will need to estimate what your expenses might be. Often people figure 75 percent of current costs as a general guideline for their retirement budget. However, be aware that people are overly optimistic about how far their money will stretch during retirement.

Financial planning affects both your current and future standard of living. Spending all your money now may bring great comfort and happiness, but at considerable risk to your future. Whether single or in some stage of the family life cycle, financial planning is essential for a more secure future.

Summary

Learning about yourself helps you decide what career might be right for you. Looking at your interests will help you determine what kind of jobs you might most enjoy. Identifying your aptitudes will assist you in finding work involving tasks you can perform with ease. Considering your abilities should help you decide if you would be willing to get the training for a chosen career. Listing your personality traits will allow you to choose a career in which you are comfortable.

Deciding what career is right for you also involves thinking about your personal priorities. Your personal priorities are what are important to you. Since your career should be important to you, your career should match your personal priorities.

Your chosen career should allow you to live where you want to live. Your career should allow you to share your life with the people who are important to you. It should also provide financial returns that enable you to meet the needs of your chosen lifestyle. A healthy lifestyle will help you to better enjoy your work and home life.

You can define what direction you want to take in your career by setting goals. Choosing a career serves as a long-term goal. Then you can set short-term goals for training and education to help you reach your long-term goal. You will measure success by your standards of career satisfaction.

To Review

1. Why is it important to consider your interests and abilities when choosing a career?

2. Why are some of your interests different this year from your interests two years ago?

3. Name two careers suitable for people who have an aptitude for solving math problems.

4. List three of your abilities. Name one career that could be related to each of these abilities.

5. List three personality traits that may influence the type of job a person chooses.

6. List three factors that influence personal priorities.

7. Why are personal priorities important to consider when choosing a career?

8. What factors influence lifestyle?

9. Why are goals important to consider when choosing a career?

10. Name a long-term goal and three short-term goals that would help you achieve it.

To Do

1. From hobby magazines available, find examples of hobbies that were turned into jobs or careers.

2. In small groups, list five extracurricular activities available at your school. Discuss possible careers that each extracurricular activity might support.

3. Select a job that interests you. In a paragraph, explain why it is a good choice, based on your interests, aptitudes, abilities, personality, and personal priorities.

4. Interview two people in different careers. Use these questions as a guide: Why did you choose your career? What has been the most satisfying part of your career? What has been the most difficult part? If you could start over again, what would you do differently? What advice would you give someone in preparing for a career? Write a summary of your findings.

5. Cut out five advertisements from the help-wanted section of your newspaper. Mount each on paper. Beside each advertisement, list the personality traits a person would need to work satisfactorily in that job.

3 Learning and Deciding About Careers

After studying this chapter, you will be able to
- describe factors to consider when investigating careers.
- identify sources of career information.
- summarize future job trends.
- describe the career preparation process.
- list the steps in the decision-making process.
- apply the decision-making process to career choices.

Terms to Know

fringe benefits
computer literacy
technology
volunteer work
internship

transferable skills
decision-making
   process
human resources
nonhuman resources

You have done some preliminary thinking about your aptitudes, abilities, and personal priorities. Now you are ready to find out more about specific careers and how they can match up with your personal qualities.

"There are so many career possibilities out there," you may say. "How will I ever find one that is best for me?" Most people have many interests and abilities and could succeed in several careers. The more you learn about careers, the better able you will be to make a decision and plan for your future, 3-1.

In this chapter, you will learn what factors to consider when investigating careers and where to find that information. It is important to look at future job trends, too. You will look at ways to prepare for careers that interest you. Then you will take a look at the decision-making process and how to use it to make career decisions.

What to Consider When Making a Career Decision

Before starting to research careers, you will want to know what to look for and how to use that information. You can then relate it to your interests, aptitudes, abilities, personal priorities, and other personal data. When considering different careers, keep the following points in mind.

Job Duties and Responsibilities

What are the specific activities to be performed in this career? You will want an idea of the variety of tasks you might be expected to do. For example, if you choose a career in fashion writing, you need a keen sense of fashion. You must be able to spot newsworthy fashion trends. You will also conduct research and gather information about the latest and newest styles. Other responsibilities include writing

Marcia Nelsen

3-1 Using a career counseling center at your school can help you make decisions about your future.

under deadline pressure and keeping up with changes in the industry. See 3-2.

Another example is in the area of furniture design. In this field you must use technical knowledge of materials, be creative, sketch designs, and be able to picture the finished product. Understanding the basics of furniture construction such as measuring, selecting materials, and using finishing techniques will be important to know.

Once you learn the general duties and responsibilities of a job, you will be better able to evaluate it in terms of your interests, abilities, personal priorities, and personality traits. Then you can decide if you want to investigate that career field further.

Job Prospects

Is this a growing career field? What is the projected outlook for this occupation? Find out how many jobs will be available when you are ready to enter the job market. Will there be few openings and much competition? Will this occupation still exist 10 or 20 years from now? Employees in a field that is projected to decrease are more likely to be faced with job transfers and layoffs.

3-2 If you want to operate your own restaurant, you will need knowledge of food preparation and food service. You should also have the ability to work well under pressure and with many different personalities.

Being aware of career trends can be helpful in finding a job with a stable future. Studying the job market will help you plan for a career with a potential for growth.

Improving skills and expanding your work experiences are the best ways to build job security. People who obtain the skills that will be in high demand are making the best preparation for the future. They will have no difficulty finding a place in the workforce. Also, they will find it easier to adapt and change to another work environment

Skills, Education, and Training Needed

Do you have the abilities needed for this career? Does it require skills you feel you could master? Some jobs require higher skill levels than others. These usually require more education and training.

What kind of training and education will be required? The amount of education and training required would depend on the kind of career you choose. A few occupations require very little education. Most occupations require a high school diploma. In addition, other occupations may require specialized training. This training can be obtained at a business or technical school or community college. Highly skilled or professional careers require a college education. Some may even require training beyond college, 3-3.

Knowing the amount of education and training required can help in making career decisions. If you have a specific career in mind, you'll be able to start planning for that training now. If you don't plan to continue your education after high school, look for a job that requires only a high school diploma.

3-3 Some employers provide on-the-job skill training to keep their employees up-to-date.

Salary and Fringe Benefits

Income is a factor to consider in your career choice. How much money does the career pay? Find out the starting salary range. Also find out what experienced workers earn. The starting salary is not as important as what you can expect to make as your career advances. What is the future earning potential of this career? Could you support yourself on the amount earned? If you had a family, could you support it?

How important is the amount of money you make? Would you choose a career based only on the salary? Making a great deal of money often requires making some personal trade-offs. Depending on your personal priorities, you may or may not be willing to accept some trade-offs.

Jobs that require more education and training often pay more. Jobs with specialized skills are also on the higher end of the salary scale. In the last decade, the average earnings of college-educated males ages 24 to 34 went up 10 percent. The incomes of men with only high school diplomas fell nine percent.

What types of fringe benefits does the company offer? **Fringe benefits** are financial extras, such as paid vacations, sick leave, health insurance, and retirement plans. The benefits vary from employer to employer. Because they represent payments you would otherwise need to make yourself, they are valuable additions to your paycheck.

Location and Work Environment

You will want to know whether jobs in your chosen field are commonly available. Will you work in one place or travel to many sites? As you learn about careers, make note of the work location and environment. For instance, food stylists do most of their work on location in photo studios, restaurants, or test kitchens, 3-4. Interior decorators often work out of their own offices, in stores, and in clients' homes.

Think about where you want to work. Maybe you have always dreamed of living in a big city. Perhaps you prefer small town or

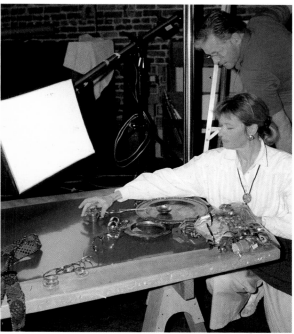
Stevie Bass

3-4 A food stylist might work in a test kitchen or other locations to prepare food shots.

country living. Midsize towns and cities offer their unique advantages, too. You will want to find out if the type of job you are interested in is offered in the location you desire.

What are the environmental conditions related to this career field? Would the job environment be harmful to your health? Environmental conditions refer to the surroundings in which you work. For example, you may prefer to work in a quiet office setting versus a busy, noisy environment. Some work outdoors in good and bad weather. Others work in clean, atmosphere-controlled settings. Think about what type of environment you would prefer when choosing a career.

Cost of Living

The cost of living is the amount of money it takes to live in a community. It includes such costs as housing, food, clothing, and others. When the cost of living changes, it is due to increases or decreases in the cost of commonly purchased goods and services. When the cost of living rises, you need more money to pay bills. Consequently, you have less spendable income.

Costs vary from region to region depending on the economic conditions of the area. You will want to know the cost of living in the area where you plan to work. You will also want to know how it compares with the stated income of the job. In some areas of the country, incomes are high because of a high cost of living. In other areas, jobs that appear low paying may result in more spendable income because the cost of living is low.

Room for Advancement

Is this a field in which you can begin at an entry-level position and advance to higher levels? When thinking about a career field, consider the possibilities for advancement. Find out if the job would allow you to move ahead. Would you be doing exactly the same work for as long as you are there? Usually, with more advancement come more responsibility and an increase in pay.

How would you feel if you did the same type of work day after day? Many people consider this a dead-end job and would prefer moving up the career ladder. Some people with extremely hectic family lives, however, may prefer a relatively routine job. As a general rule, young people starting their career should seek one with as many advancement opportunities as possible.

Rewards of the Career Field

Jobs can offer workers many rewards. Some examples are a high salary, pleasant working conditions, convenient hours, emotional satisfaction, and adventure. Would the career you are considering offer any of these? By again reviewing your personal priorities, interests, and life goals, you can see whether this career field would be personally rewarding to you, 3-5.

These are the main areas to research when learning about different careers. As you investigate, see how different careers suit you. Changing your career direction several times during the research process is not uncommon. You will probably alter your plans as your interests broaden. Keep the above areas in mind as you investigate new possibilities.

3-5 One of the rewards of office work is a clean, comfortable work environment.

◆ Resources for Career Information

There are many ways to locate information about possible careers. Knowing where to look and whom to contact can speed up and simplify the process. Talking to individuals, teachers, counselors, and other resource people serves as a starting point in learning more about careers.

Individuals

Begin by talking to your family, friends, and neighbors about their job experiences. These people can serve as firsthand sources of valuable information. Then talk to people who work in the areas that interest you. Find out what they like and do not like about their jobs. Ask them about the educational requirements and advancement opportunities. If your school sponsors a career day, company representatives and others will be present to talk about careers. They can answer questions and provide information about different areas.

Teachers and Counselors

Your schoolteachers and counselors can help you find information about different jobs. Teachers often know what interests you and the subject areas in which you excel. They can provide names of people working in areas of your interests whom you might contact for information. A counselor can direct you to books and pamphlets about careers. Counselors often give tests to find out areas that match your aptitudes. Some schools have vocational counselors who specialize in helping students with career decisions.

Many school counseling offices have computer programs that help students learn about various careers and the schools that provide training. By using these programs, you can look at a wide range of possible career options. This can start you on the path

of career exploration by matching your interests and skills to possible career clusters. *Career clusters* are groups of occupations that are similar. For instance, the *hospitality and tourism* cluster includes the occupations of hotel manager, chef, and tour guide.

Many private career counseling services, career planners, and employment specialists are also available. These specialists use various tests or computer programs to match skills and abilities to specific jobs. However, check their credentials carefully and learn the costs involved before going ahead with the testing.

Research Information

You can also learn about jobs by reading reference material related to jobs and careers. School and public libraries have lots of information about careers. See 3-6. The government publishes three excellent career information guides. These and other references can usually

Apple Computer

3-6 School and public libraries are excellent sources of career information.

be found in your school library or school counselor's office.

The *Occupational Outlook Handbook* describes the occupations that account for nearly 80 percent of U.S. jobs. The handbook lists duties and working conditions of each job plus educational requirements and average earnings. A valuable feature is the description of job trends and the future outlook for job prospects.

The *Dictionary of Occupational Titles* lists over 20,000 different kinds of jobs. It describes work responsibilities and general duties of each job.

In the *Guide for Occupational Exploration*, jobs are matched according to interests and abilities. Appropriate work groups and subgroups are listed for each interest. From this guide, you can match your abilities to the job requirements.

Magazines often run features about different jobs. To find magazine articles on different careers, use the *Readers' Guide to Periodical Literature.* Look up the career in which you are interested. The information will refer you to articles in particular magazines. Your school librarian can help you use the guide.

Magazines such as *Entrepreneurial Woman, Guide to Franchise & Business Opportunities, Entrepreneur, Success,* and *Inc.* focus primarily on different kinds of jobs. These magazines run features on starting or managing a business.

Other Resources

Computer users can also find vast amounts of career information on the Internet. You can try keywords to search for information on any number of career choices. You can find information about the fastest growing careers. You can ask questions or share ideas with those who are interested in the same careers as you.

Be sure to search reliable sites when using the Internet. One excellent choice is the Department of Labor's O*NET System. It was designed to replace the 60-year old *Dictionary of Occupational Titles* with an online database that summarizes all occupational information. O*NET can be used to explore careers, related job skills, and trends. Access O*NET at http://online.onetcenter.org/.

Other sources of occupational information include audiovisuals, such as videotapes, cassettes, and films. Trade unions and professional societies also have information on careers. Information about their names, addresses, and Web sites can be found in reference books in the library. Pamphlet files in libraries are also good sources.

By doing as much research as possible, you will learn more about fields that interest you. You will discover those career areas that would most satisfy your interests and abilities. The more you learn about a career, the easier it will be to make career choices and plan for that career. See 3-7.

Marcia Nelsen

3-7 Counselors display current information about various jobs for students to read and study.

◆ Looking at Future Job Trends

The job market is constantly changing. This could affect your choice of a future career. You will want to prepare for a career that will have job openings—one that is growing and not likely to disappear. It is important to keep up with the current trends to identify the changing markets. Major trends affect the future job scene. By being aware of these trends, you can be in the forefront of job opportunities. The following are major trends that will impact career choices.

Explosion of Knowledge

The last few years have seen an explosion of knowledge and information in all fields. This is especially evident in the sciences. Changes caused by new information will affect many consumer fields, particularly those involving foods, fabrics, housing, and communication.

Increased knowledge has also caused advances in technology. When people think of technology, immediately they think of computers. Computers are so widely used that many people take them for granted. Practically every job involves a computer in some way. Knowing how to operate a computer is an important skill in today's job market. This skill is called **computer literacy.** Computers are used in countless ways that affect all areas of society.

Technology, in its widest sense, means more than computers. **Technology** is the use of ideas, methods, tools, and materials to get things done. Each new discovery causes a ripple effect that creates ever more scientific advances.

Advances in technology cause career options to change, sometimes rather quickly. For instance, buying airline tickets no longer involves the services of a travel agent.

Scanners and bar-coding machines keep track of inventory, thus eliminating the need for clerks. Cash machines operate around the clock, reducing the need for bank tellers. Technology eliminates some jobs, but creates a need for new ones. Demand will increase for people who can design the tools and systems needed to operate the latest technology, 3-8.

More Time at Home

Studies show that people want to spend more time at home. Because of this, they want their homes to serve more needs. The skills of home remodelers and others who can make the house more functional will be in demand.

Consumers will spend more money on home services. More workers will be needed in service occupations to do such tasks as laundry, dry cleaning, housecleaning, and lawn care. Food delivery occupations will increase as consumers demand home-delivered meals in the same way they expect pizzas.

Apple Computer

3-8 Technology specialists are needed in every industry. Often there are more jobs than qualified people to fill them.

More electronic shopping via computers, television, and telephone will be conducted from the home. Shopping on the Internet will become more commonplace. Mail order houses will continue to do well. These trends will greatly affect the retail industry.

The Internet will also be used for working at home, increasing the need for equipment and services for home offices. Growing numbers of people are working at home while connected to the workplace through computers, telephones, modems, and fax machines.

Working Project by Project

A big change in the workplace is the trend to work on a project basis rather than a "full-time employee" basis. One method gaining momentum is that of a free agent. Free agents move from assignment to assignment and company to company. They tend to design their work around their lives rather than having their lives fit a normal work schedule. Free agents are usually self-employed individuals working in an area of their expertise.

Greater mobility in the workplace is even seen among full-time workers. In general, average employment periods are shortening as workers change jobs more often. This is in sharp contrast to 20 or 30 years ago, when workers often stayed with one employer for life. For average workers, this means holding five to eight jobs or more during their career. It also means forever staying alert to new career opportunities.

Emphasis on Healthy Living

People are realizing that good health requires health maintenance throughout life. They know that disease is not just caused by chance or genetics. It is often the result of how people choose to live their lives.

Nutrition and fitness are more than a passing fad. Eating healthful foods and exercising are important lifelong concerns. People of all ages are running and bike riding. Diet, exercise, stress management, environment, and lifestyle choices are all factors in healthy living. Jobs that cater to these interests will increase.

Aging Population

Another important trend is the increasing number of active older Americans. In the coming years, the many people born shortly after World War II will reach retirement age. This is causing rapid growth in the over-65 population.

The aging population will affect every aspect of society. It will present challenges to families, businesses, policy makers, and health service providers. Anyone who gears products specifically to seniors will see a ready market. Seniors are interested in fitness programs, delivery services, traveling, entertainment, and quality health care. Jobs that provide these services will be in demand, 3-9.

Armstrong

3-9 With the population aging, jobs that manage and deliver affordable services to seniors will be in high demand.

Other Population Trends

Following are more trends that will impact the type and location of jobs becoming available in the future.

◆ By the year 2030, minorities will make up the majority of U.S. births. Since preferences vary among racial and ethnic groups, businesses and industries that produce individualized goods and services for these groups will benefit.

◆ Hispanics are the fastest growing racial/ethnic group, projected to account for 18% of the U.S. population by 2005. More information in Spanish will be needed as well as bilingual customer service assistants.

◆ The number of people in the U.S. job market will continue to grow.

◆ The fastest growing U.S. population areas are in the west, especially in the Rocky Mountain States of Arizona, Colorado, Idaho, Nevada, and Utah. Rapid, short-term growth is often caused by migration flows, but birth and death rates also make a difference in some places.

◆ College graduates are more than twice as likely to move to a different state than people who lack a high school diploma. Long distance moves are typically job related. College graduates often have skills valued in the national job market.

◆ In general, a person with a college degree earns more money and has more employment opportunities than a person with only a high school education. High school graduates are entering college in greater numbers than ever. Enrollment is higher for women.

◆ The high school dropout rate is declining. Boys are more likely to drop out than girls.

◆ A record number of young children are in U.S. nursery schools. As more mothers of young children enter the workforce, nursery schools offer a positive solution to the increasing demand for quality and affordable child care.

◆ Enrollment in private schools recently increased to its highest level in 25 years.

Effects of Trends on Occupations

These major trends indicate where the jobs will be in the future. Careers of tomorrow will be client centered and service oriented. This shift to information and service means that greater efforts will be made to serve the needs of individuals and families. Business and industry will need to track family or consumer needs and then adapt products or services to meet those needs.

The jobs of the future indicate a need for people trained in family and consumer sciences. Jobs that should see an increase are those associated with consumer services. Services such as those listed in 3-10 will be among those important to consumers and families.

Careers That Provide Consumer Services Directly or Indirectly
Biochemists
Clothing buyers
Computer support specialists
Consumer information specialists
Desktop publishing specialists
Dietitians
Environmental designers
Equipment designers
Food scientists
Food caterers
Foodservice directors and managers
Furniture designers
Home-health aides
Housing analysts
Kitchen designers and planners
Merchandising analysts
Nutrition consultants
Nutrition research specialists
Personal and home-care aides
Product designers
Research scientists
Space planners
Travel consultants

3-10 These careers will increase services for the consumer.

Economic Factors Affecting Occupations

When consumer demand for products and services is strong, businesses compete to satisfy the demand. This is a sign of a healthy economy, and consumers benefit from a wide selection of choices. On the other hand, if demand slows or stops, companies produce less, lay off workers, and perhaps even close the business.

Several factors can reduce consumer demand. Sometimes a shift in technology makes products or services obsolete, as was the case with steam engines and chimney sweeping. Sometimes new products that perform better and faster take the place of older products, such as the replacement of typewriters with computers. Sometimes, too, if a job layoff seems possible, consumers postpone buying a new house, car, or other expensive item that takes many years to pay.

A drop in consumer demand for a product or service causes an industry to produce less and eliminate some employees. Laid-off workers have less money for buying goods, so a slowdown in one industry can eventually affect others. Thus, the cycle continues. When planning a career, it is important to recognize which types of jobs are likely to remain strong no matter what the economy does, 3-11.

In order to stay employed in a changing economy, workers will constantly update their skills and education. Future jobs will demand more training and specialization. Professional occupations such as teachers, doctors, dentists, and lawyers, will continue to be in demand. Updating of skills and education will be needed to stay in the mainstream of professional careers.

The job market is closely tied to the economy, and the economy is tied to current events. Reading and keeping up with local, state, national, and world news is helpful in predicting job trends. Knowing which way employment trends are swinging will help you plan your future. For example, by watching or reading the news, you would know that U.S.

3-11 People employed in the hospitality and recreation industry are likely to find steady employment in this fast-growing field.

companies try to manufacture their products in countries having low wages. As a result, you would know it is unwise to plan for a career as a U.S. factory worker.

◆ The Career Preparation Process

There are many ways to prepare for a career. Education is one of the most important of these. Part-time jobs are a source of valuable experience. Volunteering is another way to help prepare you for the world of work. Participation in school and community activities is also significant to employers. Many opportunities are available for career preparation, depending on your goals and abilities.

The global economy links our economy to the vast network of economies throughout the world. What is happening in our economy can affect other countries' economy and what is happening in their economy can affect ours. Knowing how our economy and the economies of other countries are growing and developing will help you make better career decisions.

Education and Training

Education is gaining knowledge and skills to live in today's society. It is the development of the special and general abilities of the mind. *Training* is practical education or practice, usually in some art, trade, or profession.

Every educational level can prepare you for a career. This includes high school, college, and occupational training. In high school, you can take courses that teach basic skills for a specific career. For example, Elizabeth wanted to go into the medical profession. She took as many science and math courses as were available. Jerry wanted to work with food. He also took science courses as well as food and nutrition courses offered in his family and consumer sciences classes.

A college or university education is required in certain professions. To receive a college or university degree, four years of study must be completed. Some fields of study require five or six years. If college is part of your career plans, more time and expense will be needed to meet your goals. How much time, money, and effort can you spend on furthering your education and training? A college or university degree often results in a higher-paying job. However, you should be realistic about what you can manage.

Occupational training is another way to prepare for a job. This kind of training prepares you for a job in a specific field. This training can be obtained through vocational or occupational schools, 3-12. Training is also offered through community or junior colleges, trade schools, on-the-job training programs, apprenticeships, and correspondence schools. These will be examined in the next chapter.

Work-based learning programs are offered at both the high school and community college levels. These programs help students successfully make the transition from school to work. They offer on-the-job training to students as

University of Wisconsin-Stout

3-12 Occupational and career training schools help prepare students for the world of work.

they take school classes toward a particular career goal. Your on-the-job experience might be at a hospital, bank, construction site, garage, insurance company, or other place of business. In these programs, you acquire marketable skills while gaining on-the-job experience and earning money.

Gaining Work Experience

One of the most frequently asked questions during a job interview is, "Do you have any experience?" Some companies only hire people with experience. You may wonder how you can get experience if no one will hire you for that first job. This is a dilemma for young people anxious to begin work in their chosen career. Following are suggested ways to gain work experience.

You can volunteer to work at a particular job and, in that way, find out whether you like it. **Volunteer work** is work you do without pay. If you can manage without an income, this is an excellent way to learn skills and gain experience. Your "pay" will be in the form of extra experiences you can list on job applications.

A summer internship is another possibility. An **internship** is a supervised experience in your field of study. For example, as a merchandising intern, you might be supervised by a clothing store manager. You would gain experience in such tasks as ordering and displaying clothes. This might be done with or without pay. If you want to work with children, you might apply for a summer internship as a camp counselor.

Even if you are not able to find a job in your career field, work experience of any type can help you acquire employment skills. Many young people begin working by mowing lawns or babysitting. This part-time work experience will help you learn responsibility and management skills.

Work experiences offer many benefits. Not only do you earn money, but you also gain valuable work skills. Good communication skills, such as listening and following directions, are necessary for any job. In your work experience, you may also learn to relate to customers and develop telephone skills. Depending on the type of job you have, writing skills may also be needed.

All part-time jobs will strengthen your managerial skills. For instance, you will learn to manage your time. How can you get the job done in the time available? Can you do your household chores, study, and still handle this job? Money management is another skill learned and an important part of a job. What will you do with your earnings?

Later when job hunting, you may need references from former employers. Your reputation for doing a good job and being honest and fair will quickly be passed on to others. Any work experience will provide expertise worth listing on a job application.

At-home work experiences are also beneficial. Some students get paid for home duties or chores. Others feel these chores are part of family living and receive no pay. From cleaning your room to doing the dishes, each job requires effort, organization, and follow-through. These same work habits are essential in the career world.

Home responsibilities require many skills that transfer to the workplace. **Transferable skills** are skills that are useful in different work settings. For example, knowing how to plan, organize, and finish tasks on time are examples of skills needed in the workplace. Other examples of transferable skills include knowing how to find information, teaching others, and balancing resources wisely. Accomplishing responsibilities well at home, at school, and in the community can form a solid foundation of skills useful in the workplace.

Participating in School Activities

Many students choose to be active in various clubs and organizations. They may also have paying jobs. These students gain valuable experience in leadership and group activities that will help them in their future careers.

Working with others to achieve common goals provides a sense of commitment. You may be a member of a school club or a social or community group. These groups often work on improvement projects, such as highway or park clean up. Some groups choose to work with preschool children, the elderly, or the disadvantaged. Peer groups, such as Students Against Destructive Decisions (SADD) and Teens Need Teens (TNT), provide students with valuable skills in interacting and relating with others.

Getting along with others is an important skill that can be learned in any setting, 3-13. Often this is far more important than how you perform on the job. A willingness to work in a team setting is critical in any job situation.

Activities such as band, chorus, athletics, or theater arts require a personal dedication to practicing and improving skills. Self-discipline is a big part of this training. Participants must work at improving performance. Competition is often involved. With improvement comes more self-esteem, or a feeling of pride and self-satisfaction

in doing good work. These are the same traits that are important in the job market.

All of these experiences contribute to employability. The same traits and characteristics needed to carry out a successful project are necessary in many job situations. Confidence, responsibility, commitment, and dedication are as important in the job market as they are in working on student projects.

Offering Your Services to the Community

Volunteering your time and energy to charitable programs or community services provides many benefits. You offer a valuable service to another person or group and also gain useful work experience. For example, suppose you handle the children's story hour at the local library. You may find that you really enjoy working with children, reading, or both. This may help you decide whether you would like to work full-time in a child care center or a similar job. You might also learn what children's age group appeals most to you.

University of Wisconsin-Stout

3-13 Working with others on a project helps to develop job skills.

You could volunteer at a hospital, nursing home, library, park district, food pantry, animal shelter, or local charity. When you volunteer in a number of different settings, you get a better idea of what interests you most. As one young person remarked after offering to mow lawns as part of a community park service, "Now I know what jobs I do *not* want to do for the rest of my life!"

Even full-time workers are encouraged by their employers to be more involved in the community. Some companies give workers time off from the job to work as volunteers. Companies see it as a plus for building employee morale and fulfilling their "social responsibility" goals. Volunteers gain new insight into the community, their company, and themselves. Adding new skills to a resume or portfolio is another advantage of volunteering, although this should not be the main goal of people established in their careers.

◆ Making Career Decisions

After a thorough self-evaluation, you can focus more on learning about careers. You are ready to begin looking at your career goals and identifying career choices. What would you like to be doing in 10 years? 20 years? 30 years? What different kinds of jobs or occupations would you like to experience? As you consider a job, do the duties and responsibilities match your interests, abilities, and personal priorities? Do you have the personality traits to feel comfortable in the career?

Most people want a career that is enjoyable and satisfying, 3-14. Perhaps you want to make a lot of money. Maybe you want to serve humankind or make the world a better place. Perhaps you are concerned about the environment and want to do something to preserve it. You will probably consider a number of different work situations in trying to find satisfying career goals.

Apple Computer

3-14 Most people want a challenging and satisfying career.

Career Stages

Adult life often involves many career stages that may occur in a variety of sequences. For example, a person may choose a career as a full-time homemaker in early adulthood and then choose to enter the workforce after the children are in school. A single adult might decide to go to college and then work full-time.

Some people may be involved in more than one stage at a time. For example, self-employed people often extend their skills into community service through volunteer efforts. Career stages that individuals may encounter in adult life include the following:

◆ higher education, career preparation, and training
◆ military service
◆ part-time paid or unpaid employment
◆ full-time paid employment
◆ self-employment (entrepreneurship)
◆ full-time homemaking
◆ community service (volunteer work)

To decide which of these steps to take, use the decision-making process. The **decision-making process** is a logical series of steps used to work through or make a decision. Following the steps in the process is helpful in career selection. You can use the process to decide whether to go to college or a career training school. If you are choosing between two careers or various career areas, these steps can help you make a more careful decision. Following is an in-depth look at these steps and how you can use them to choose a career.

Identify the Question to Answer or Problem to Solve

Use the career making process to look at possible career alternatives. Should you take the higher paying job or the one in which you feel more fulfilled? Should you become a full-time homemaker or stay a full-time student? Should you work in the family-owned business? Do you want to go into your own business or work for someone else? Should you go back to work, even though you have a small child? What type of job will give you enough free time to care for elderly parents? You need to be very specific when identifying the question to answer or problem to solve.

Whenever a decision involves planning for the future, it is helpful to view the decision in terms of goals to be reached. State what you expect to accomplish from the decision you plan to make. Establish what you want to do with your life. What do you dream of becoming or doing? Now is the time to set the course for those dreams to come true!

List all the items you can use to reach your goals. Identify your resources by thinking through the human and nonhuman resources you can use. Your **human resources** are those that come from within you. These include your talents and abilities. Your energy level and your intelligence are other human resources. Help from other people is a human resource, too. Your **nonhuman resources** include material resources, such as the amount of money you can spend on your education. How much time do you want to invest in planning and preparing for your future?

List All Possible Alternatives

The next step toward answering a question or solving a problem is to list your alternatives. Think through all of the options that are available to you. Often an acceptable choice will come into focus if you simply list the alternatives. Being able to choose from several alternatives allows you to view them more clearly. It will help you better see which would be best for you.

Weigh the advantages and disadvantages of each. Based on what you know about yourself, what occupation interests you most? Think about the results or consequences in terms of your interests and skills. Suppose you consider becoming a social service worker. You would list the pros and cons as shown in the chart in 3-15.

See which list is longer or which points seem more important to you as you work through each option. Do this for a number of

Considering a Career in Social Services

Pros

- I like working with people.
- I would have a sense of accomplishment from improving people's lives.
- I feel a sense of responsibility to others since many people have helped me in life.

Cons

- I would work with people on a one-to-one basis; I would rather work with groups of people.
- I would be working inside most of the time; I prefer to work outdoors.
- I may get too involved in the problems of my clients and take their problems home with me.

3-15 There are pros and cons to consider regarding every career.

occupations that interest you. For some, you will have long lists of either good or bad points. Through the process of elimination, you will narrow your choices down to a few. You will probably find at least one potential match, or several potential matches between you and a career. That is good. You do not want to get locked into one field or occupation too soon before you do further exploring. Keeping options open is very important because it can provide more choices later.

Choose the Best Alternative

Now choose the best alternative and make a decision. Which sounds most desirable to you? Imagine yourself going through the daily routine of a person in that occupation. Think about the activities that would occupy your time during your working hours. Do you feel excited about this kind of work?

Before you make a final decision, think about your goals. How will they fit into your life plans? Based on your evaluation and study, choose the alternative that best meets your goals or gives you the best combination of alternatives. Write out your decision if it helps to make it clearer.

Act on the Decision

After choosing the best course of action, carry out your decision. By this time you have considered all your options and the possible results of each. The best choice is easier to identify now that you have thought through each of the steps.

Evaluate the Decision

Reflect on the action you took to see whether your decision met your goals in the most positive way. Evaluation is an important part of decision making. You should evaluate and judge the results of your choice. Sometimes the results are not immediately evident. It may take years to see whether it was a good decision. Some questions to consider about the decision are: Have I made a choice that could result in the best possible outcome? Did it help me reach my goal?

You will continually evaluate your progress and adjust your strategies, if necessary. Sometimes your evaluation may even result in changing your basic career objectives or your long-term goals.

Taking courses directed toward your career decision will give you a clearer picture of whether this was a good choice for you, 3-16. Working in a part-time job in your career area will also help you evaluate your decision. Such was the case with Beth. She thought she wanted to be a nurse—until she actually followed a nurse for a day. She decided she wouldn't like to care for sick people. As a result, she reevaluated her decision and began looking into other careers. In this way she avoided making a costly mistake.

Fisher Price

3-16 By getting on-the-job experience, you can make better career decisions.

Good Career Decision Making

What characteristics are shared by people who have made satisfying career decisions? One characteristic is self-understanding. People who make satisfying career decisions know themselves. They know who they are and what they want from life. They have identified their interests, aptitudes, and abilities. They understand their personalities. They decide what is important to them and then set goals based on these priorities.

They tend to listen to their own calling. This calling might be a strong desire to pursue a specific career. *Child prodigies* have similar tendencies. These are children who have exceptional talents from an early age. Research indicates these children have a burning desire to use their unique gifts. Similarly, no matter what a person's talents might be, there is a desire to want to use them. People who have found satisfying careers have recognized and responded to their inner drives.

People with satisfying careers work hard to reach their goals. If this means getting training, going to school, or working temporarily at a less-than-desirable job, they do it. They realize that success is not immediate. They know it may take time to reach certain goals, 3-17.

A satisfying career choice allows you to become the type of person you desire. When you reviewed the hierarchy of human needs, self-actualization was at the top of the pyramid. To reach a high level of self-fulfillment is to find a satisfying job within your range of abilities and interests. This is what is meant by self-actualization or self-fulfillment.

3-17 It takes time to reach certain goals, such as buying a home.

Summary

By learning more about careers, you can find out which occupations match your personal characteristics. When investigating these careers, find out the job duties and prospects. Learn what skills, education, and training are needed. Ask about the salary, fringe benefits, work environment, and location. Make sure there will be room for advancement.

Information about careers and jobs can be obtained from family, friends, school counselors, and people in jobs that interest you. School and public libraries and the Internet are also important sources of career information. Many excellent career guides are available to help you in your search. When researching trends, keep in mind the current trends that will affect the job market.

You can start preparing for a career now. Obtaining the proper education and training is the first step. You can also gain valuable skills through work experiences. You may have summer or after-school jobs or do volunteer work. Being involved in clubs and activities contributes to employability. Important leadership traits, such as self-confidence, self-discipline, commitment, and perseverance, are strengthened by these early experiences.

Once you have narrowed down your choices of a career, you can use the decision-making process to decide among the options. Good career decision makers tend to understand themselves. They have a strong desire to use their natural talents and abilities. They work to achieve their goals. By using the decision-making process, the chances of working out satisfactory solutions to difficult situations are greatly improved.

To Review

1. What are three examples of fringe benefits?

2. List four rewards that jobs can offer.

3. What are four careers that involve working with people?

4. Name five sources of career information.

5. Which career guide lists working conditions, duties, and future trends of 80 percent of U.S. jobs?

6. List three trends that have an effect on the job market.

7. Which types of careers will grow because of recent trends?

8. List four skills that students can gain through outside work experiences.

9. How can participating in school and community groups contribute to employability?

10. List the steps in the decision-making process.

11. Why is the decision-making process important in career selection?

12. Give an example of an individual in a situation resulting from a hasty career decision and failure to consider alternatives.

13. Give an example of using the decision-making process successfully with an FCCLA experience.

To Do

1. Examine a copy of the *Occupation Outlook Handbook* or search the O*NET at http://online.onetcenter.org/. Write a brief description of two occupations that interest you. List the job prospects for the future in each of the two jobs.

2. Think about the trends that will affect job opportunities. Develop a list of ideas for jobs that would meet the needs of families, singles, or seniors.

3. Contrast an ideal working situation with one that would be undesirable.

4 Preparing for a Career in Family and Consumer Sciences

After studying this chapter, you will be able to
◆ identify the focus of family and consumer sciences.
◆ determine preparation requirements for various levels of employment.
◆ describe postsecondary training and education options.
◆ list the elements of a Tech Prep program and give an example of a secondary and postsecondary Tech Prep program.
◆ give examples of careers in family and consumer sciences that require a bachelor's, master's, and doctorate degree.

Terms to Know

family and consumer sciences
geriatrics
cooperative education
Tech Prep
trade apprenticeship
associate degree
bachelor's degree
baccalaureate degree
field experience
practicum
graduate degree
master's degree
doctorate

As you consider different career areas, you might want to explore careers in **family and consumer sciences,** formerly known as *home economics.* This field is devoted to enhancing the relationships among individuals, families, communities, and the environments in which they function. The core value of the field is to improve the life of individuals, families, and communities.

Professionals in this field are concerned with the strength and vitality of families and the development of policies that support families and communities. They focus on the role of individuals and families as consumers of goods and services. They also focus on the development and use of resources to meet consumer needs.

The family and consumer sciences field includes a broad range of careers that can be divided into the following basic groups:
◆ child development and early childhood education
◆ family studies and human services
◆ consumer and resource management
◆ hospitality, tourism, and recreation
◆ textiles and apparel
◆ nutrition and wellness/food science and technology
◆ environmental design

Within each basic group, you will find many distinct careers. The variety of jobs in this field is continually changing and expanding. A high school diploma may be all that you need for some entry-level jobs, 4-1. Other jobs require you to have more education and training. For example, a two-year college degree is needed to become a Head Start teacher, and a four-year degree is needed to be a dietitian or family therapist. You can prepare for a wide range of careers in business, education, government, and human services. A discussion of the various careers available will follow in later chapters.

You can start preparing for a career in one of these areas in a *secondary* (high school) family and consumer sciences class. Classes are offered in most high schools throughout the United States and Canada. These courses teach skills that help improve personal or family life. They also support community well-being.

◆ Types of Family and Consumer Sciences Programs

Would you like to learn how to prepare different kinds of food? Do you know how to take care of a baby? Do you think you would like to work in a retail store selling clothing? Are you interested in working in a science field? If so, you might be interested in learning more about the two types of family and consumer sciences programs.

You will study the same basic information in both programs. However, each program serves a different purpose.

◆ **General courses.** In these courses, you will learn skills that prepare you to manage a home and handle family responsibilities. The program prepares you for the career stage of *homemaking.* Information learned in these courses can help you improve your economic well-being. In addition, they can help you learn social skills and improve your emotional and physical health. As a result, both you and your family will benefit. Family and consumer sciences courses help you learn how to solve problems and achieve family goals.

4-1 Many marketable skills, such as flower arranging, can be learned in a family and consumer sciences class.

◆ ***Occupational programs.*** Occupational family and consumer sciences programs teach skills that will help you earn a living. Many of these programs include on-the-job experience. Both high school students and adults can take occupational courses in family and consumer sciences. Courses may be found in vocational-technical high schools, area career centers, and other schools.

General courses in family and consumer sciences versus occupational programs are shown on the next page in the chart in 4-2. As you can see, general courses teach skills that will help you and your family. Occupational courses, on the other hand, train you for a career.

Typical Family and Consumer Sciences Courses and Programs		
Subject Areas	**General Courses**	**Occupational Programs**
Child development and early childhood education	Child development Parenting	Child care management and services Child care guidance
Family studies and human services	Family living	Family and community support services Services for the elderly
Consumer and resource management	Consumer education Home management and resource development	Consumer and family economics
Hospitality, tourism, and recreation	Food preparation	Institutional maintenance, management, and services
Textiles and apparel	Clothing and textiles	Textile and apparel design Textile and clothing production, management, and services
Nutrition and wellness/food science and technology	Family and individual health Foods and nutrition	Food production, management, and services Human nutrition
Environmental design	Housing Interior design	Interior design services Environmental design management, production, and services

4-2 General programs in family and consumer sciences prepare students for homemaking, while occupational programs prepare students for employment.

◆ Career Preparation Begins in High School

To be prepared to compete for good jobs, you will probably need special training. There are many opportunities for job training at the secondary and postsecondary school level. *Postsecondary* means any education beyond high school. Many of these training opportunities are known as *work-based learning programs*. These programs combine work experience and school.

Occupational family and consumer sciences programs offer a variety of work-based experiences. In some instances, the work expe-

rience takes place in the classroom. At other times, you receive work experience outside the classroom, sometimes on an actual job.

◆ *In-school laboratory experiences* provide training in classrooms that are set up to resemble work situations. For example, a bakery might be set up in the school. Students would learn some commercial baking methods and retail selling techniques.

◆ *laboratory experiences* are any training that takes place outside the family and consumer sciences department. Students might work in the school cafeteria or a kindergarten classroom. Some programs provide experience at an actual job. The school might arrange for students to receive training in a business or agency in the community.

Any place that relates to work or jobs can provide an opportunity to experience a work environment. A student interested in a career in foodservice, for example, can work at any place that sells prepared food. Working at a fast-food restaurant, family-type restaurant, deli, or other eatery provides actual foodservice experience. Students receive hands-on training at the work site. This helps them see and experience what it is really like working at that type of job.

Several other work-based learning programs are described here through page 74. These are examples of occupational family and consumer sciences programs.

Child Care Services

Many high schools have special child care laboratory facilities within the family and consumer sciences department. In other schools, students rotate to different child care facilities in the community. Whether in a school or community facility, students plan learning experiences to help children, 4-3. Students might prepare nutritional snacks and plan other activities. Activities might include a music experience, an art project, or a counting game. Students gain actual experience that prepares them for a career in child care.

Clothing Production and Services

In a clothing production and services class, students learn sewing skills to make and alter clothes. If available, students receive training on industrial sewing machines. Students learn speed sewing methods and mass production techniques. They might use these skills to mass-produce products for sale or charity. For instance, students might sew puppets for a children's hospital or lap blankets for residents of a nursing home.

Some classes set up an alteration shop to give students business experience. Students, teachers, and community members bring in

University of Wisconsin-Stout

4-3 Working with young children and planning learning activities provide experience for a career in child care.

garments that need simple alterations. Students practice such skills as replacing buttons and taking up hems. Students can also learn and practice customer relations skills.

Running a clothing alteration or production business requires more than technical skills. In classes, students also receive training in business management. For instance, they would learn how to write and follow a financial plan for their business.

Food Production and Services

Some high school family and consumer sciences classes work with the high school cafeteria to provide training in foodservice management. Other schools run bakeries, mini-restaurants, or similar ventures. Students alternate between different workstations to learn the variety of positions. Sometimes students are waiters, short-order cooks, cashiers, and hosts. At other times they bus tables, serve as general managers, or perform other related jobs, 4-4. In this way, they gain more experience. This helps them see more sides of a career in the field.

One high school developed a food catering service as an extended laboratory experience. The experience helped students learn that caterers prepare and serve food for many different occasions. These include daily meal services such as the meals on wheels program for seniors as well as special occasions, such as banquets, wedding receptions, and anniversaries.

Interior Design and Home Furnishings Services

Interior designers, advisors, and consultants focus on making home environments comfortable and attractive. Custom-order

University of Wisconsin-Stout

4-4 With the growing demand for foodservice workers, schools often provide training in foodservice careers.

sewing services provide curtains, draperies, pillows, bed covers, and other items sewn specifically for clients' homes. A furniture upholstering service covers worn furniture, giving it a new look. Furniture refinishing and repair is another specialized service.

Other housing specialists focus on housing as it relates to the coordinated and efficient use of resources. This is why the housing area is sometimes called environmental design. Specialists in this area focus on both the artistic qualities and scientific aspects of the home and its contents.

Family and consumer sciences classes provide training in some of the areas mentioned. Students might plan and sew draperies for the faculty lounge, school offices, or school entrance. Students in these courses might recommend color schemes or rearrange furnishings for an area. If the school has a building trades class that constructs a house, students might plan the color scheme for the entire house. A home furnishing services class may redecorate a house that the carpentry class is remodeling. In this way, both classes benefit, 4-5.

Hospitality and Tourism Services

The hospitality industry is a large and fast-growing field. This is due to more business travel as well as recreational travel by families. The hospitality field includes working in hotels, restaurants, travel, and recreational facilities.

Some employees have little customer contact, such as hotel accounting department personnel, food preparation employees, housekeepers, and hotel maintenance workers. Other employees work as front-end staff. These include restaurant hosts, hotel reservation staff, greeters, and counter attendants. Some people might like employment in the travel and tourism area, either working directly with guests or their arrangements.

Specialized skills as well as skills in customer service and management are needed to work in all hospitality areas. Self-motivation,

University of Wisconsin-Stout

4-5 Students enrolled in a home furnishings and equipment class often have in-school laboratory experience. In some programs, students help decorate a house built by the building trades class.

good interpersonal skills, and the ability to work with coworkers as well as customers and guests are essential for work in this field.

Some secondary schools offer introductory courses in hospitality management. In some cases, schools have cooperative arrangements with local hotels for students to gain first-hand experience in the hospitality area.

Family and Community Support Services

Another fast-growing occupation is that of homemaker/home-health aide. These specialists offer a variety of services to patients in their homes. Basic services may include personal care, housekeeping, shopping, and meal preparation for the elderly or people with disabilities. Those interested in becoming a homemaker/home-health aide receive training in safe food handling, nutrition, and basic health care courses. Because they work in patients' homes, people employed in this type of work must be responsible, trustworthy, and respectful of others' possessions.

Services for the Elderly

Geriatrics is a branch of medicine that deals with the elderly. Since people are living longer, providing care for older adults is another fast-growing career. Some family and consumer sciences classes provide experiences for students to learn about this type of work.

Adult care homes might be simulated in some classrooms. In other instances, students set up a simulated *convalescent center,* where people can go to recover from an illness or injury. Students practice basic health care. They also learn how to change bedding, bathe patients, or help feed them. In addition, students role-play directing recreational activities, such as light exercises. At other times, they practice how to teach patients new games. In this way, students learn how it might feel to work with elderly or sick people. They also gain leadership experience.

Sometimes schools make arrangements for students to work in adult care homes. This is an example of an extended laboratory experience. Students help residents with their meals, grooming needs, or in other areas of service. In this way, students see and experience what it would be like to actually work with the elderly in an adult care facility.

◆ Work-Based Learning Programs in Family and Consumer Sciences

Some work-based learning programs are available only at the secondary level. Cooperative education, also called co-op education, is the best-known example.

Other work-based learning programs in specific career fields begin at the secondary level and include two more years of additional training.

This additional training is often necessary before a full-time job can be secured in a specialized area. Often, secondary and postsecondary education programs are coordinated, as in Tech Prep programs. Students may receive credit at the postsecondary level for high school courses.

These two work-based learning programs are offered in conjunction with family and consumer sciences.

Cooperative Education

Cooperative education is a high school program that helps prepare students for work. It is called cooperative because schools and employers work as a team. Together, both provide students training in a career. Students often attend school for a half-day and work in a local business or industry the other half of the day. See 4-6.

The student, a teacher, and the employer plan an on-site work program. A written training agreement identifies the classroom work and the work-site training to be provided. The teacher, known as the *cooperative education coordinator,* directs the student's training. The teacher works with employers to plan learning experiences for the student. A student's on-the-job training is carefully supervised and evaluated. Students receive school credits for the work experience.

Local retail stores, banks, and offices often work with schools to provide training. Some manufacturers and service industries work with schools to give students training in a job. A student might work in a child care center as a teacher's aide. Another student might work in the foodservice department at a local hospital to prepare for a career as a dietary aide.

A cooperative education program is very beneficial to students who plan to work right after high school graduation. Students learn to set career goals and prepare for the work environment. See 4-7. They learn skills in the classroom and on the job that prepare them for a better job. The program helps students make a successful transition from school to work.

4-6 Besides having a fun job, this student is learning about the foodservice industry.

Tech Prep

Many high school students are not sure if they want to go to college, but they want a secure future. These students may find that Tech Prep meets their needs. **Tech Prep,** or the *Technical Preparation Education Program,* is a secondary and postsecondary program that links academic and technical courses into career preparation. It trains students for a growing range of technical careers. It also provides a strong academic background. The Tech Prep program helps students form solid career goals and prepare for a satisfying, successful job.

The Tech Prep sequence of study often begins in the junior year of high school. Students enter this program after analyzing their personal skills and choosing a career goal. Then a program is designed to prepare them for their career choice. This program includes a common core of math, science, communications, and technology courses. It also includes special courses related to the students' specific interests.

Long John Silvers

4-7 Students gain valuable experience as they learn skills in foodservice and customer relations.

Tech Prep programs are also called $2 + 2$. This is because the programs combine two years of high school courses with two years of higher education. Students may go to a two-year college or enroll in an apprenticeship program. After two years of postsecondary training, students receive either an associate degree or a technical certificate. At this point, students are prepared to enter technical careers in the workforce.

Some Tech Prep courses satisfy approximately half of the requirements of programs at four-year colleges and universities. This leads some students to pursue a four-year degree after completing a two-year program. These students are said to be in a $2 + 2 + 2$ program. After receiving a four-year degree, students are prepared to enter professional careers in the workforce.

Elements of Tech Prep Programs

Tech Prep programs contain three key elements. *Applied academic courses* lay the foundation for employment and lifelong learning. *Technical training* teaches skills required for a specific technical field. *Partnerships* help teachers and counselors make sure their programs are meeting the needs of business and industry.

Tech Prep students take regular high school classes to meet graduation requirements, 4-8. They also take applied academic courses that show students how to use math, science, and English in the workplace. Most students find it easier to learn when they understand how class work relates to their career goals. Some schools have separate classes to teach the applied academic skills required of the Tech Prep. Other schools integrate these skills into their basic courses. In either case, the Tech Prep curriculum can be as challenging as that taken by college-bound students.

Besides taking applied academic courses, Tech Prep students receive schooling in a technical field. Typically, training begins in the junior year. Technical preparation might include the areas of engineering technology or applied science. It might involve the mechanical, industrial, or practical arts. Training might

4-8 Students in Tech Prep programs can easily relate what they are learning in their high school classes to their future careers.

also include agriculture, health, business, or a trade. Introduction to Drafting, Quantity Food Production, and Growth and Development of the Young Child are examples of actual course names.

Business, industry, community organizations, and parents work as partners in the Tech Prep program. They help identify what the student needs to know for success on the job now and in the future. Business and industry representatives usually work with the school to make suggestions for the school curriculum. They also suggest courses that would help the student acquire additional skills.

Benefits of a Tech Prep Program

Both the student and the community benefit from a Tech Prep program. Students are better informed about the workplace and the range of career opportunities. They learn job skills to meet the needs of local and regional employers. In addition, students qualify for jobs that provide higher earnings.

Through a Tech Prep program, students gain confidence in their abilities to use specialized skills. Students learn what behavior is acceptable on the job. They also learn the attitudes needed for working well with fellow employees.

Employers profit because Tech Prep-trained workers can solve problems and communicate well. Training produces workers with the ability to work well alone and in groups. Students, workers, employers, and the community all benefit from the Tech Prep idea of learning for life.

Tech Prep Programs in Family and Consumer Sciences Areas

Tech Prep programs are offered in a number of family and consumer sciences areas. As with other Tech Prep programs, students take applied academic courses. These courses help students see how they would use basic skills in specific family and consumer sciences careers. Students also receive technical training to learn job skills needed in these careers. Partnerships

for family and consumer sciences Tech Prep programs might be formed with a variety of people. An employer in a foodservice business would be a likely partner.

Many states have developed Tech Prep programs for child care occupations. A typical program begins with introductory child care courses in high school. Many of these combine classroom instruction with field experience in kindergarten classes, licensed child care facilities, and child development centers at the high school or community college campus. If the courses are completed satisfactorily, students can earn college credit for them. When these students graduate from high school, they can exit from the program and become assistant teachers in child care facilities, 4-9.

4-9 Many assistant teachers in child care facilities are graduates of Tech Prep programs.

Their other option is to continue the 2 + 2 training at a community college. There they might take such courses as Curriculum Resources; Safety, Health, and Nutrition; Child Growth and Development; Learning Environments, Activities, and Materials; Guidance Techniques; and Administration of Child Care Programs. Upon completion of the program, they would have a two-year degree in child development. They would then be qualified to be assistant or associate teachers in child care centers.

The 2 + 2 Tech Prep program also allows students to continue their postsecondary training at four-year institutions. By taking two more years of college classes, the student could receive a four-year degree in child development or early childhood education. Graduates of these programs can work as teachers in child care programs.

◆ Career Preparation after High School

For many careers, education must continue beyond high school. While education through a Tech Prep program of study at a postsecondary technical school is one option, there are others. Opportunities for career preparation after high school—other than Tech Prep—are discussed here.

A private technical school also provides a postsecondary option. Some students want to continue their training and education by joining the armed forces. Certain careers require one or more college degrees. As you can see, there are many options for further study after high school to gain marketable skills for a career choice. The following discussion will help you understand these options.

Professional Schools

Some schools specialize in training for one field of work. For example, if you would like to be a chef, you study at a culinary school. Other schools specialize in interior design, fashion, cosmetology, or travel. These schools are generally located in larger cities. Schooling involves classroom and actual skill training. When you complete your schooling, you will receive a certificate or diploma. You might be required to pass a test to receive a license.

Trade Apprenticeships

Some students want to learn a specific skill for their career. One way to learn a special skill is through a trade apprenticeship. A **trade apprenticeship** provides concentrated training and practice under the guidance of a skilled artisan. It provides training in a skill and knowledge of a trade while working full-time on the job, 4-10. Training also involves classroom instruction in the skill and related areas. An apprentice needs to learn the entire trade, not only certain parts of it. Therefore, each skill is broken down into separate blocks. As each block is learned, an apprentice's skill level and pay increase. Generally, apprenticeships take three to four years to complete.

4-10 *Apprenticeship training is a valuable method of learning a trade. You work with a master artisan in a skilled field.*

Home-Study and Correspondence Courses

Another way of learning is through home-study courses. These may include correspondence courses, educational television, or tape recordings. Lessons come to you by mail. You complete the study requirements by working at your own speed on the assignments. When lessons are completed, you return them to the sponsoring company for checking. You are also required to pass tests covering the material. The company sends the graded tests back to you with suggestions for improvement. More than 200 companies or institutions offer correspondence courses. One home-study course is interior decorating.

Postsecondary Vo-Tech or Technical Schools

Many areas have regional schools with postsecondary programs offering six-month to two-year programs of study. Some of these schools are called *vocational-technical (vo-tech) schools* or *area career centers*. Some might be called *technical centers, technical institutions,* or *technical colleges.* All of these schools offer similar programs.

Vo-tech schools provide broad training in a skill or a trade. Many vocational training programs focus on business or retail training. Vo-tech schools also offer training in technical areas. Programs teach practical knowledge of a mechanical or scientific subject. Again, programs stress career preparation for gainful employment. See 4-11.

Vo-tech schools often provide the last two years of a 2 + 2 Tech Prep program. Students take formal education courses and receive training in a skill. This helps prepare them for employment. Some programs also meet the labor needs of a local community. The length of the training period varies depending on the type of program. Often, programs are offered under the categories of business, family and consumer sciences, home economics, or applied technology.

Most postsecondary schools are public, or run by the state or community. They are generally reasonable in cost. Some technical schools are privately owned and, therefore, more expensive. Both public and private schools offer night and Saturday classes. Postsecondary vo-tech schools have flexible entrance requirements. High school students can often attend classes. Other students, whether they have graduated from high school, can also attend classes.

If you consider attending a private technical school, be certain it is accredited. This means that the school meets certain educational standards. Consequently, when you graduate, you are qualified to work in your chosen profession and to take advanced courses. Check the placement policies of private

Typical Occupational Family and Consumer Sciences Courses in Postsecondary Vo-Tech Schools
Baking
Child care services
Day care operation
Family day care
Fast-food operation
Floral art and design
Food and resort management
Food preparation assistant
Foodservice
Home furnishings services
Home health care aide
Home management
Institutional foodservice
Quantity food preparation
Sewing production methods
Short-order cook
Tailoring

4-11 These courses are common in six-month to two-year programs.

technical schools. Some of these schools charge you a fee when you find work.

Postsecondary vo-tech or technical schools award certificates or diplomas but usually not degrees. Many of the credits earned will transfer to a college if you decide to work toward a four-year degree. Some four-year colleges may require you to take review or additional courses before admitting you.

Community and Junior Colleges

Today, most of these colleges are known as community colleges. Junior and community colleges have two types of programs: one offers preparation for a career, while the other provides the first two years of a four-year college program. Some students complete two years of community college and then transfer to a four-year college. The Tech Prep program also links with a junior or community college for the last two years of training.

Most community colleges can prepare you for a job in data processing or computer technology. You might also prepare for work in the building trades, television production, hotel or restaurant management, child care management, retailing, or interior design. Many types of career programs are generally offered. These programs are often based on the needs of the local community's job market.

Junior and community colleges award two-year degrees. They also award certificates. See 4-12 for some typical programs in the area of family and consumer sciences.

Military

The military provides training in many career areas. Education is available at little or no cost to the student. In return, students must commit a certain length of time to the branch in which they are training. Military students must also conform to a strict, disciplined life. Some students study at a military college for their four-year degree.

Colleges and Universities

Colleges and universities are institutions of higher learning for high school graduates, offering four-year programs leading to college degrees. Some of these schools also offer programs for more advanced degrees.

College Entrance Requirements

Students desiring a four-year college degree start their career planning in high school by taking college preparatory courses. School counselors and advisors work with students and parents to plan a high school program of study.

Typical Family and Consumer Sciences Career Preparation Programs in Junior and Community Colleges

Baking
Catering
Chef training
Child care management
Clothing and textiles
Clothing manufacturing
Clothing production
Costume design
Culinary arts
Dietary technology
Dress design
Dressmaking
Early childhood development
Fashion arts
Fashion merchandising
Food and hospitality
Food sanitation
Food technology
Foodservice
Gerontology
Hotel-motel management
Long-term care administration
Restaurant management

4-12 These courses are common in two-year programs in the family and consumer sciences area.

Most colleges have certain requirements for admission. In their senior year, high school students who are college bound will take either the ACT or SAT test, or both. *ACT* stands for American College Testing. The *SAT* is the Scholastic Aptitude Test–College Board. Both are college entrance examinations.

Scores that you receive on these tests might determine whether some colleges admit you. Scores received on the tests are also used for placement in some college classes. A high score may admit you to courses above the introductory level. The ACT and SAT scores are also used when awarding scholarships.

College Programs in Areas of Family and Consumer Sciences

All family and consumer sciences programs at the college or university level prepare you for a career. Look in college and university catalogs for programs in the area of family and consumer sciences. They have different titles. You may find programs listed under Family and Consumer Ecology, Family and Consumer Sciences, or Human Ecology. Also check for Human Environmental Sciences or Family Science. All programs have as their base of study the improvement of individual and family life.

Some colleges and universities offer two-year programs, after which students receive a certificate or an **associate degree.** Preparing students to manage a child care facility is an example of a two-year program. The programs also serve as a step toward a four-year degree. College credits usually transfer into four-year degree programs.

Most college programs lead to a four-year **bachelor's degree.** This degree is also called a **baccalaureate degree.** Students receive a basic education and also take courses in their area of career interest. Colleges and universities require a certain number of credit hours for graduation. When students complete their studies, they receive a bachelor of science (B.S.) degree or a bachelor of arts (B.A.) degree. See 4-13.

A bachelor's degree in an area of family and consumer sciences will prepare you for various professional jobs. You might work in the design field, either as an interior designer or fashion designer. Retailing or marketing are popular areas of interest with many jobs available. There is great demand for people with

4-13 A bachelor's degree will prepare you for a higher-paying, professional career.

degrees in child care. Working as a nutritionist in business or industry requires a bachelor's degree. High school family and consumer sciences teachers need broad college preparation in the field. Many careers in the communications field require skills learned in family and consumer sciences classes. These include jobs such as editors, journalists, television writers, and computer programmers. Most higher paying positions require college degrees.

Selecting a Major Area of Study

A number of concentrations, or major areas of study, are available in the family and consumer sciences field. Names will differ slightly at different colleges and universities.

Areas of study you might choose include the following:

◆ child development
◆ clothing and textiles
◆ consumer education
◆ dietetics
◆ family and environmental resources
◆ fashion merchandising
◆ foods and nutrition
◆ hotel and restaurant management
◆ household equipment
◆ housing and interior design
◆ parenting and family life

A college catalog includes descriptions of many programs of study. It lists general and specific course requirements for each program. One section of the catalog includes course descriptions. Look through various programs of study to learn what courses you need to complete for different majors. This will help if you are undecided about a major. It will also help you make certain that this is the area of your interest, 4-14.

Decide what field you want to pursue. This is the area in which you will specialize. *Specialization* is when you concentrate your studies in a certain area of interest. Students usually take general preparation courses the first two years of college. A few courses might be in your area of interest. In the last two years, you take more courses in an area of

specialization. Check the college catalog for the number of credit hours required in your major area of specialization.

Field Experience or Practicum

In some programs students receive part of their education off-campus through a field experience. A **field experience** allows students to work in a job related to their career goal. The job is in an area related to their major. Another name for field experience is a **practicum.** For example, a student majoring in foodservice might work as an assistant manager of foodservice in a hotel. In this way, the student gets a better understanding of the challenges and job potential in the hospitality area. Students in education, on the other hand, practice-teach (student-teach) in a school setting for a period of time before completion of their studies. Students receive credit for knowledge learned while performing a field experience.

Talbots

4-14 Training for a fashion merchandising career will provide many possibilities for employment.

Certification

In addition to a B.S. or B.A. degree, professionals in some fields need special training. Some types of work require that you have a license. Many professionals need *certification*. To be certified, professionals must meet specific education requirements. They must have a certain level of experience in a field. In addition, they must pass special exams required by local, state, or federal agencies.

A teacher, for example, must have a state teacher's certification or a teacher's license. The certification or license can be obtained only by people with a bachelor's degree and several other qualifications. These include having a major in a specialized area, completion of a course in education methods, and student teaching experience.

Other professionals might need different kinds of certification. The American Association of Family and Consumer Sciences certifies professionals in family and consumer sciences. Professionals in the field use the initials *CFCS* (Certified in Family and Consumer Sciences) after their names. In order to stay certified, these professionals need to keep up in their field. They do this by regularly taking additional courses or training.

Graduate Schools

A **graduate degree** is schooling beyond the bachelor's degree. Master's degrees and doctorates are graduate degrees. Typical positions that generally require a graduate degree are listed in 4-15.

A **master's degree** requires a certain number credits at the graduate level. The degree generally takes about two years to complete. About 150 schools in the United States offer master's degrees in family and consumer sciences areas.

A more advanced degree is called a doctorate. A **doctorate** requires approximately

Family and Consumer Sciences Careers Requiring a Graduate Degree
Behavioral scientist
Education director
Extension specialist
Family therapist
Nutrition chemist
Nutrition director
Quality control director
Research and development director
Textile chemist
Therapeutic dietitian
University professor

4-15 These careers generally require education beyond a bachelor's degree.

two years of study beyond a master's degree. The names of the degrees differ, depending on the course of study. You might receive a Ph.D. (Doctor of Philosophy), an Ed.D. (Doctor of Education), or another degree. Less than 50 colleges and universities offer a doctorate in areas of family and consumer sciences.

◆ The Future

There are many kinds of jobs available in family and consumer sciences. This is one of the biggest advantages of a career in this field. Most careers easily adapt to the needs of today's changing society. A degree, certificate, or special training in this field can open the door to many different careers, 4-16.

A degree in family and consumer sciences prepares students to serve society. All professionals in the field contribute to the quality of home and family life. They are aware of the needs of families. No matter what type of work they do, they help individuals and families meet the needs of society today.

4-16 Working at home is an option chosen by some parents who have young children.

Current trends show a number of areas that will provide new jobs related to family and consumer sciences. These include the following

◆ researching market trends, customer preferences, and satisfaction levels
◆ developing improved products and services
◆ informing the public
◆ providing customer services or counseling
◆ working in family and community service agencies
◆ managing operations
◆ teaching or conducting research in a variety of settings

These trends will affect the type of jobs available in the coming years. They can also guide you in your career decisions.

Summary

Family and consumer sciences programs are involved with improving the relationships among individuals, family, community, and their environments. There are two types of courses in family and consumer sciences programs. Some teach students the skills to help individuals and families, while others prepare students for employment.

Various programs offer school-to-work experiences at the secondary school level. Many of these programs provide either in-school laboratory experiences or extended laboratory experiences. Cooperative education offers students supervised, on-the-job experience.

Many high school courses and programs prepare students for entry-level jobs. Students who have chosen a specialized career might continue their studies in a professional school. They might decide to study as an apprentice. Home-study and correspondence courses also offer opportunities for further study and training in areas related to the family and consumer sciences.

The two-year Tech Prep program of study, started in secondary school, can be continued at the postsecondary level. Vo-tech or technical schools and community colleges offer two-year programs in many family and consumer sciences areas. Upon completion of their studies, students receive a certificate, diploma, or an associate degree.

Four-year colleges and universities prepare students for many careers. Undergraduate programs at these institutions lead to a bachelor's degree. With further training and education, students can earn advanced degrees, such as a master's or a doctorate degree. Graduates in family and consumer sciences programs are prepared to work in a wide variety of challenging careers.

To Review

1. What is the primary focus of family and consumer sciences?

2. What is the primary purpose of general programs in family and consumer sciences?

3. What is the primary purpose of occupational programs in family and consumer sciences?

4. Explain the difference between an in-school laboratory experience and an extended laboratory experience.

5. What is cooperative education?

6. Explain the basis of Tech Prep education. How does Tech Prep education help many students get a better job?

7. Name four options for further study after high school.

8. Name an area of study in family and consumer sciences that a student might pursue at the college level.

9. What is meant by a field experience or practicum?

10. What is the importance of the ACT and SAT tests?

11. What is the difference between a bachelor's degree and a master's degree?

To Do

1. Assume that you must describe family and consumer sciences to someone who knows nothing about it. Make a list of the major points you would include in your description.

2. Conduct an interview with an employer who hires students from occupational family and consumer sciences programs. Find out from the employer one advantage of hiring these students.

86

Part II
Developing Personal Skills for Job Success

5 Basic Skills for the Workplace

After studying this chapter, you will be able to
- discuss the importance of knowing how to learn.
- identify reading and writing processes needed to perform job skills.
- determine workplace applications of math skills.
- describe computer operation and use.
- explain how competence in using resources, information, and technology affects employability.

Terms to Know

learning style	Computer-Aided
job simulations	Drafting and Design
letterhead	(CADD)
salutation	Computer-Aided
memorandums	Manufacturing (CAM)
e-mail	CAD/CAM
computers	Computer-Integrated
hardware	Manufacturing (CIM)
Read Only Memory	word processing
(ROM)	data communications
Random Access	terminals
Memory (RAM)	networking
software	database

Basic reading, writing, and math skills have long been viewed as necessary parts of formal education. Employers know that employees with strong basic skills are more productive. Having a staff with a mastery of these skills increases the employer's ability to compete in the marketplace, 5-1.

Workers must also have a broad set of workplace skills. With increased global competition, shifting technologies, and emphasis on quality and service, special skills are needed. Being flexible and willing to learn and working as a team member are some necessary skills.

As a student, you are challenged to gain competence in the basic skills of reading, writing, and math. In addition, knowing how to use computers is becoming more and more crucial in the workplace. You should have good communication skills and understand your own personal skills. Group-effectiveness skills, such as problem solving and creative thinking, as well as leadership abilities are also important. These skills will be expected of future employees.

Many workers are coming into the workforce with skills too low for entry-level positions. Employees who lack basic work skills often find it difficult to get a job, make job changes, or advance in their careers. Poor basic skills limit an employee's choices and potential for earning.

Manufacturers in all sections of the country sometimes are unable to find enough skilled workers to meet their needs. Studies

5-1 Today's work roles are changing. Skills once considered adequate are no longer sufficient.

have shown that factories turn away five of every six job applicants due to poor reading and math skills. Some applicants are turned away because they appear to lack the motivation needed to be productive employees.

Employees with good basic skills find it easier to learn higher-level skills. The ability to perform higher-level skills increases opportunities for better jobs and higher pay. Therefore, good basic skills are the keys to greater opportunity and a better quality of life.

It has been predicted that jobs will be restructured about every seven years. New jobs and new ways of performing jobs will continually develop. Employees will shift jobs and accept new responsibilities. Consequently they must constantly absorb new information and quickly recognize how to use it. In today's competitive atmosphere, continual learning is an integral part of any job.

◆ Learning—A Basic Skill

Knowing how to learn is an essential skill for future workers. It is the key to acquiring new skills and sharpening the ability to think through problems. Learning how to learn helps you to acquire all other skills—from reading and writing to interpersonal skills such as leadership. It is the most basic of all skills.

What Are Learning-to-Learn Skills?

Learning-to-learn skills help you understand and use new information quickly and efficiently. How you absorb new information and relate it to different situations is an indication of your learning-to-learn skills, 5-2.

Workers who know how to learn can transfer new knowledge from one job to another.

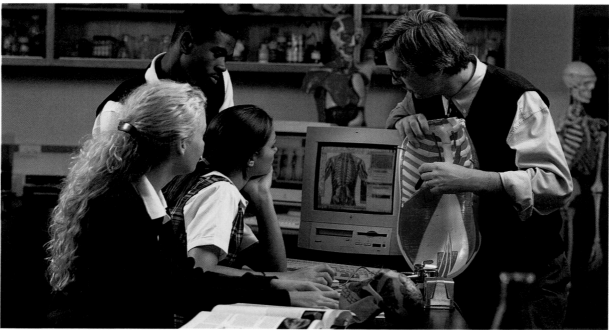

Apple Computer

5-2 Teamwork skills are critical in today's workplace.

They can recall information learned earlier. They can distinguish between important and unimportant information. These abilities are useful in the workplace.

In addition to organizing and applying new information, employees must learn how new training fits into the work of the company. They won't simply learn what needs to be learned; they will understand why it is important. They understand that knowing how to learn can help them improve performance on the job.

From an employer's viewpoint, an employee who knows how to learn is very cost-effective. Less time, energy, and money will be spent on training or retraining these employees. Production increases when employees can apply their learning toward acquiring new skills. See 5-3.

Education and learning is a lifelong process. It does not stop when you graduate, but continues on through life. Studies show that poorly educated workers who are unwilling or unable to learn new skills will only have

low-paying jobs in life, if they find work at all. They will especially have problems finding jobs that pay enough to support a family.

Learning-to-Learn Skills Needed on the Job

- ◆ Recall earlier learned information.
- ◆ Think through problems.
- ◆ Relate and organize information easily.
- ◆ Apply information effectively.
- ◆ Transfer learning from one job to another.
- ◆ Apply knowledge quickly to any job change.
- ◆ Absorb and apply training quickly.
- ◆ Learn particular skills of the job quickly.
- ◆ Distinguish between important and unimportant information.
- ◆ Use strong reading, writing, and math skills.

5-3 The range of skills needed for success in the workplace has greatly expanded.

Steps in Learning How to Learn

The first step in learning how to learn is discovering how you best absorb information. Each person brings a different learning style to the workplace.

Know Your Learning Style

Personal preferences and tendencies that influence learning are an individual's **learning style.** One person learns more quickly by watching and observing others. Another person may prefer to read the directions or an instruction manual. Yet another would rather practice through trial and error.

There is no right or wrong way to learn. Each person has a preferred approach that best meets his or her needs, 5-4.

Individual learning styles affect the ability to process information. Therefore, people learn differently, absorb different information, and apply information differently.

Use Organized Activities

In the workplace as well as in school, organized activities increase a person's ability to learn. Some learn best in settings similar to school such as lectures, where note taking, questions, and answers are common.

Preferred learning strategies may change as employees progress through their careers. Some prefer small group activities, case studies, or job simulations. **Job simulations** are situations that are acted out, or role-played, such as on-the-job experiences. A variety of activities can be used when additional learning is needed to do the job right.

Learning to learn is the foundation on which all other learning rests. Before you can acquire reading, writing, or math skills, you must learn how to learn. It is critical to future success.

5-4 Each person has an individual learning style. Some learn better through lectures, while others learn through reading or working through a situation.

Reading Skills

Reading helps you to be a good learner. Having good reading skills is one of the underlying essential skills for success in the workplace.

The increased use of computerized machinery and other high-tech equipment requires a high degree of reading and comprehension skills. You may need to respond quickly and properly to computer-generated directions and safety warnings. Messages that are transmitted by machine or through written work must also be clearly understood.

On-the-Job Reading

Workers often spend about two hours per workday reading. This includes reading forms, letters, charts, graphs, computer printouts, and faxes. On-the-job reading emphasizes locating information for immediate use. Workers should be able to understand and summarize the information they read.

Reading tasks in the workplace are different from other types of reading tasks. On-the-job reading uses the same fundamental skills that you have learned in school, but it requires more analytical thinking. You must also check to see that you understand job-specific terms used at work and remember the meaning of what you have read.

Information Processing

On-the-job reading processes are generally classified into "reading to do" and "reading to learn." "Reading to do" requires use of short-term memory and limited information processing. An example is locating information to use immediately from printed materials on hand, such as finding addresses in a directory. Another example is knowing how to use a dictionary, thesaurus, manual, and map.

"Reading to learn" involves reading information from a number of sources to make job decisions, solve problems, or troubleshoot.

This requires use of long-term memory and more complex information processing.

Problems Resulting from Poor Reading Skills

Poor reading skills can result in many problems. These include the following:

- increased problems with workers' safety when workers can't read signs or follow directions, 5-5.
- lost work time because instructions must be given orally.
- failure of employees to understand incoming correspondence and orders for goods.
- inability to read training manuals.
- inability to enroll in courses that would upgrade skills because workers cannot follow directions to complete the application.
- inability to perform unfamiliar tasks.

Marcia Nelsen

5-5 Your safety often depends on being able to read and interpret safety signs.

Reports indicate that almost 65 percent of the entry-level workforce over the next decade will read at a fourth- to eighth-grade reading level. Deficiencies in basic reading skills impair a worker's ability to get a good job and perform well in it. This is a growing problem in the workplace.

Improving Reading Skills

By improving your reading skills now, you will be better prepared to summarize information, prepare reports, and perform other job-related tasks. If you have difficulty reading and interpreting, here are some tips that may help you.

Skim over the material to get the general idea or theme. Read the underlined, italicized, and boldface words. Read the groups of words or phrases that give meaning to the article. Determine whether the text contains relevant information.

After you have an idea of what the passage is about, reread it to yourself. Are there any words you don't understand? See if you can get the meaning from the way a word is used in the sentence. Does the word look like any other word you know? This might give you a clue as to its meaning. Perhaps reading further may help in identifying the word or meaning. If you still don't understand a word or phrase, look it up in a dictionary or check the glossary. Ask for assistance if none of these methods help.

Know how to locate information within a text. Be able to use the table of contents, index, appendices, and glossary to locate information. Know where each part is and how to use it.

After you finish reading a section, summarize it to yourself. Information will stay with you longer if you think back and recall what you have just read. This can help you on the job when you summarize information or prepare reports.

Get in the habit of reading. Resolve to spend some time each day reading. This could be your school assignments or other reading.

Reading only for pleasure or relaxation is also beneficial and enjoyable.

Share information with others. Recalling information and telling it to others can be helpful on the job as well as socially. Being able to verbalize what you have read is an important skill. Examine how skillfully you use various types of resources and information, 5-6. Then, determine in which areas you may need additional training and experience.

◆ Writing Skills

Writing clearly and accurately is an essential job skill. Higher professional jobs require very good writing ability. Administrators consistently rank writing skills among the highest priorities they seek in would-be employees.

An employer first judges you and your writing ability by the appearance of your job application and resume. These are important indicators of your overall writing ability. You should fill these out as neatly and correctly as possible.

Source of Written Information
◆ Almanacs
◆ Annual reports
◆ Books
◆ Dictionaries
◆ Encyclopedias
◆ Indexes (or directories)
◆ Information on the Internet
◆ Maps
◆ Periodicals
◆ Telephone books
◆ Thesaurus
◆ Other publications

5-6 Information is presented in many different formats. Most people find it easier to read and understand some formats more than others.

Writing Skills on the Job

The majority of occupational writing tasks involve completing forms and preparing brief memos and letters. Translating messages into a concise, accurate form is a typical on-the-job writing skill. Other job-writing tasks require planning, summarizing, or recording messages or work completed. The competencies needed to perform writing tasks include:

◆ planning, organizing, and revising written thoughts into concise messages.
◆ selecting important or relevant information.
◆ summarizing information and events accurately and completely.
◆ using correct, clear, and readable grammar.
◆ spelling task-related words correctly.
◆ using key technical terms correctly on forms.
◆ entering correct data on forms.

When these tasks are done carefully, the work progresses smoothly. Fewer mistakes are made and less time is lost. See 5-7.

Inadequate writing skills have a negative effect on productivity and product quality. Letters, reports, work orders, instructions, or other materials you may write must be correct and on time. If correspondence must be corrected for errors, production time is lost. Furthermore, a company's image is closely related to the type and quality of its business correspondence. People often judge the company based on the written work received. The image of your company can be reflected by the quality of your work.

Writing Business Letters

Writing is often the first step in communicating with customers. Knowing how to write business letters will help you in your work. The type of business letter you write will determine what you will say and how you will write it. Most business letters are written to request information, merchandise, or service. See 5-8.

Some letters are written to make announcements about events, policies, and procedures; to answer requests; or to express

5-7 Writing helps you think through a situation, analyze information, and make a decision.

appreciation. Sometimes you will need to write "bad news" letters. These are letters written when orders can't be filled, requests need to be turned down, or a price has changed. Try to word these letters as positively as possible.

When writing a business letter, a standard format is followed. This letter is usually placed on the company's stationery. Stationery printed with the organization's name and address is called **letterhead.** The essential parts of a business letter include the following:

◆ ***Return address***. Most companies have their name and address printed on their stationery's letterhead. If you are using a blank sheet of paper, you will type in the address. It is called a return address because the letter will return to that location if it cannot be delivered to the intended address for some reason.
◆ ***Date.*** Type in the current date. It tells the reader when the letter was written. When

ABC Corporation

487 Dewey Lane
Philadelphia, PA 19106

April 16, 2004

Mr. Randall Buyer
Efficient Book Publishers
389 Main Street
Snow Bank, MN 59999-9999

Dear Mr. Buyer:

Please send me one copy of the most recent edition of *Writing for the Fun of It*, by Angie Consultant, ISBN 0-487-15167-3. I am enclosing a check in the amount of $17.95, which includes postage and handling.

Please send it as soon as possible. Thank you.

Sincerely,

Jane E. Lange

Jane E. Lange
Purchasing Agent

5-8 This is an example of a business letter.

you keep a copy for your files, a date will be helpful if you need to refer back to the letter.

◆ **Inside address.** This is the name and address of the person to whom you are sending the letter.

◆ **Salutation.** The greeting that is used before the body of the letter is called the salutation. The most common salutation is "Dear (Mr., Mrs., Ms., or Miss) White." Type a colon (:) after the greeting.

◆ **Body.** This is the main part of the letter.

◆ **Complimentary close.** Most business letters close with "Sincerely," or "Yours truly." Type a comma after the closing.

◆ ***Signature and typed name.*** Your name should be typed four lines below the complimentary close. If you have a business title, this can be typed below your name. Then, sign your name with a pen in the space above your typed name.

◆ ***Reference initials.*** The initials of the sender and the typist should be typed two lines below your name and business title. The sender's initials usually appear in capital letters first, followed by the typist's in lowercase letters. An example would be LMP:ar, or LMP/ar. When typing your own letters, you would not add reference initials.

Business letters should be neat and clean and contain no misspelled words. The computer has made business letter writing much easier. Type the address on the matching business envelope. Make sure it has a return address.

Writing Business Reports and Memos

In writing business reports and memos, plan and organize your information in order to cover the points intended. Determine the relevant material to be included. The points listed below should help you.

◆ Identify your target audience. Who will receive this report? Perhaps it is aimed at the sales team or a committee. Your writing style and format should be appropriate for the intended audience.

◆ Identify your purpose. State why you are writing this report.

◆ Get ideas going and organize thoughts. Start by writing notes or a rough draft of your report. Translate these into a clear, concise form.

◆ Write in an easy-to-read style. Make sure you cover all points and convey the message accurately.

◆ Review what you have written and revise it where necessary. Few people can write a final version on the first try. The few extra minutes it takes to proofread a document can save hours of confusion later.

Business reports are generally written to help others understand a situation. Sometimes they are written to help solve business problems or announce company decisions. Business reports can be classified as formal or informal.

Formal reports are often quite long. They contain a cover, title page, table of contents, introduction, body, summary, and perhaps a bibliography. Graphs, tables, and charts are often included to help clarify complex information.

Informal reports are brief and to the point. Reports of business trends, sales, and work progress are examples of informal reports.

Memorandums, or memos, are informal messages written from one person or department to another in the same organization. They are usually short, dealing with only one subject. Memos can be messages concerning a change in meeting times or reminding others of an event. See 5-9.

Memos are always dated. The sender and receiver's names are written or typed in the *To:* and *From:* sections. The subject is identified and a short written explanation is given.

Writing E-Mail Messages

The Internet offers new modes of communication in the workplace. **E-mail,** also called *electronic mail,* is a message sent from one computer

---

ABC Corporation Memo

Date: December 5, 2004

To: All Employees

From: Yumiko Azel,
               Personnel Manager

Subject: Staff Meeting Change

The December 13 staff meeting has been changed to 10:00 a.m. Please mark this change on your calendar.

5-9 A memo is a short, informal message that usually deals with one subject.

to another. E-mail is very popular because it fills a very simple need—rapid communication. With e-mail, written messages are delivered to one or more people immediately. The content of an e-mail message is usually text, although you can send pictures and other nontext files.

Workplace e-mail is often used in place of a memo. Although e-mail is much less formal than most paper documents, it still should contain correct spelling and punctuation. Make sure your message is clear and easy to understand. Keep it short and to the point. Send it only to those individuals or groups who have a known interest in the topic.

Communicating via e-mail is usually faster than via telephone, but responses are less complete. With e-mail you may get a one-word answer to a message. With a telephone call, you can listen for subtle tones and other clues that enhance the meaning of the message.

Unlike the e-mail you may send to friends from home or school, e-mail at work fulfills a serious purpose. It should never contain gossip, smiley symbols, or abbreviations for common expressions. For example, you would write *for your information* instead of *FYI*, and *by the way* instead of *BTW*.

Electronic messages can be just as permanent as paper documents and may be read by even more individuals. Many people will know you only by what you say and how well you say it. Always be polite in your online communication and never send abusive messages.

Before you receive Internet access in the workplace, you will be asked to follow the company policy regarding its use. Your employer will be able to tell whether you are using e-mail for purposes other than business.

Improving Writing Skills

If you have problems with writing well, it would be helpful to enroll in an English or communications course that requires a great deal of writing. You will learn to organize your thoughts and use logical thinking skills. By practicing your writing and getting feedback from others, you will identify areas that need work.

When writing a long, in-depth paper, an outline is helpful. An outline gives your writing a direction. It helps prevent rambling. Following your outline, write a rough draft of the paper. State your message in the shortest and best way possible. Be concise. Write about the most important points first. Then fill in the details. End with a conclusion or summary. Revise or change what you have written until ideas are clear and supported by facts or examples.

The final step is to edit what you have written. To *edit* means to adjust. When editing, check to see that spelling and punctuation are correct. Also check for grammar usage. If you write with the aid of a computer, it will check and review your work as you write. If you are handwriting your work, can people read what you have written? Do you have good penmanship? These are all-important skills in written communication.

Keeping a journal is good practice for recording experiences, thoughts, and ideas. See 5-10. A journal will help remind you of points

5-10 If you keep a journal, the exercise will sharpen your perceptions and help you express your ideas more clearly.

you do not want to forget. A journal will also give you writing experience. Just as athletes, dancers, skaters, and others must practice their skills every day, writers must also practice.

◆ Math Skills

Workers use math skills to conduct inventories, report on production levels, measure machine parts or specifications, and so forth. Truck loaders use calculations to figure weight allowances. Chemists, chefs, and bakers must measure quantities. Architects, carpenters, and pattern makers also need to know specific measurements. Math skills are central to many jobs, especially cashiers, bank tellers, and engineers.

Workplace Applications of Math Skills

The four fundamental concepts of addition, subtraction, multiplication, and division with single- and multiple-digit whole numbers are used in most jobs. In addition to numbering and counting, higher levels of operation are required in many occupations. Math skills might include

◆ working with mixed numbers, fractions, decimals, and percentages.
◆ measuring time, temperature, distance, length, volume, height, weight, velocity, and speed.
◆ using algebra to solve equations.
◆ using geometry to find area and volume.

The introduction of new technologies demands higher mathematical skills. One such example is the use of statistical process control (SPC). A worker on a food packaging assembly line that uses SPC must use a variety of skills. The worker removes samples from the production line at given intervals. Then he or she must weigh each sample and record its weight to the hundredth of an ounce on a chart. The average weight per package is calculated. This determines whether the weight falls within the allowable range. The employee must perform accurate calculations. Results of this employee's work might indicate whether the line must be shut down for readjustment. Another worker interprets the data and readjusts the line machines, if necessary. Both of these positions require interpretive, decision-making, and problem-solving skills beyond basic computation and measuring. See 5-11.

Often workers have problems knowing which computation to use to solve a particular job problem. Workers may not recognize errors because they do not understand why a specific computation was used. This is especially true if several numerical operations must be used in sequence.

New England Business Service, Inc.

5-11 Math skills are needed in all types of jobs. Data must be interpreted and machines realigned in many production jobs.

The most successful workers know how to interpret numbers. They use problem solving and logical thinking to transfer knowledge about one problem to another. Many entry-level workers must make decisions based on the interpretation of completed computations. If these employees can transfer their learning to their job, they can determine whether a solution to a math problem is reasonable and correct.

Improving Math Skills

If you feel you need to improve your math skills, you could take more math classes in school. You could ask your math teacher or counselor for suggestions on which courses would be more beneficial to you. Your teacher or counselor can also recommend advanced math classes for career areas that interest you.

◆ Computer Skills

It is said that society has entered the Information Age. This is because communica-tion technology has provided access to vast amounts of information. The use of computers is one reason this has occurred.

Computers are electronic devices that store large collections of data and process it. Such data includes numbers, letters, and symbols. The computer can add, subtract, list, compare, sort, and store data. It can also display the data in various charts and graphs.

Computers are an essential tool in business and industry as well as in schools and homes. Living and working in today's society requires a knowledge of how computers are used and what they can do. Knowing how to use them is called *computer literacy.* Understanding and using the terms associated with computers is part of this literacy.

The Use of Computers in Daily Life

Computers are everywhere. They control many functions in homes and business places, 5-12. Touch-pad controls, such as those on microwave ovens, are controlled by computers.

Talbots

5-12 Many businesses rely on their computers to inventory supplies and fulfill orders.

Your grocery store probably has a computer that reads the code on each item you buy. It adds the price to your bill and adjusts the store's inventory for the items you have purchased.

When you go to the library, you may use a computer to access information about a book you want. The computer will tell you about the author, title, subject, call number, and availability of the book. A summary of the book may also be noted.

Personal computers, or PCs, are used in many homes, schools, and businesses. PCs are popular because they perform many information and communication functions.

The Computer System

A look at the major parts of computers will explain how they work. A computer system is made up of hardware and software. These are necessary to operate the system.

Computer Hardware

Hardware refers to the physical equipment itself. This includes the computer and everything needed to communicate with it. Most hardware is made up of four basic parts. See 5-13. These parts are

◆ input device
◆ central processing unit (CPU)
◆ memory
◆ output device

You use an *input device* to enter data into the computer for processing. Many input devices are used with computers, primarily keyboards and scanners. A *keyboard* has a series of numbers, letters, and function keys. As the keys are pressed, electrical impulses are sent to the computer. The computer then converts these impulses into data. A *scanner* can be used to "read" drawings and type from printed pages into a computer. Information can then be viewed on the screen, modified, and stored in a memory system.

Apple Computer

5-13 Various components make up the hardware of a computer system.

At the heart of every computer is the central processing unit (CPU), which processes all the data. The CPU controls the flow of data, storage of data, and the way the computer interprets the data. The program is read by the CPU and transformed into functions.

Each computer has a *memory* that stores information, either temporarily or permanently. Permanent memory is called **Read Only Memory (ROM).** ROM holds the instructions that computers need when first turned on. ROM is programmed at the factory, and its contents cannot be changed.

The remaining memory is **Random Access Memory (RAM).** RAM stores information temporarily as it is being processed by the CPU. Temporary memory is activated only while the computer is turned on. If information needs to be stored for longer periods of time, it can be held on data storage devices. These devices allow information to be saved even when the computer is turned off. Data storage devices used at home include accessory hard-disk drives, floppy disks, or CDs. Storage devices used at work may include these plus more powerful devices such as magnetic tape and special computer terminals.

Computers process information in units called *bytes*. A computer's RAM capacity is expressed in megabytes. A *megabyte* is equal to about one million bytes.

An *output device* allows you to see the data. Output devices include monitors, printers, and plotters. A monitor displays text and graphic images from the computer onto a screen. A *printer* receives information from the computer and prints it out on paper. *Plotters* operate like printers, using pens to create images on paper. Plotters are used for drawings, such as house plans.

Computer Software

The set of instructions that directs and guides a computer is called **software.** These instructions make the computer perform a range of tasks. In the home, people often use PCs to write letters, keep records, play games, and figure finances. Special software is needed for each of these functions. Likewise, businesses use word processing, project management, and payroll programs.

Computer Uses in the Workplace

Companies are replacing many typical ways of doing business with computer-aided technologies. Product development and manufacturing systems have been automated to reduce costs and maintain product consistency.

Computer-Aided Drafting and Design

Computer-aided drafting and design (**CADD**) is used in all aspects of design and manufacturing processes. A CADD system can rapidly do many complex functions. It can draw curves, rotate objects, align them in a design, and make mirror images. It can automatically draw objects to scale or to exact measurements. For instance, pattern makers can use CADD to instantly create the pattern pieces for different sizes.

CADD provides greater quality, accuracy, and speed of creation than traditional paper-and-pencil methods. Instead of viewing drawings on paper in the traditional method of drafting, drawings are viewed on a display screen. Different parts of the drawing can be magnified for detail work. Colors can be used to separate different parts of the design, 5-14. Changing parts of a drawing can be easily done through the use of commands entered into the system. Designs can be tested and analyzed as they are being drawn, rather than taking time and materials to build models first.

IBM

5-14 Computer-aided drafting and design (CADD) rapidly does many functions. Color can be used to separate different parts of the design.

Computer-Aided Manufacturing

Another system that has greatly increased the speed and accuracy of production is **computer-aided manufacturing (CAM).** Machines are set up for manufacturing processes through computer commands. When computer-generated designs are used to run manufacturing equipment, this is called **CAD/CAM.**

Computer-Integrated Manufacturing

When computers are used to control the entire factory operation, the system is known as **computer-integrated manufacturing (CIM).** Loading, processing, removing, and transporting parts through the production line are controlled by the system. This method is fast and leaves little room for human error.

Spreadsheets

Another popular function of computers is managing numbers. By using a spreadsheet, you can put numbers in rows or columns. You can add, subtract, multiply, or divide these numbers any way you want, and instantly see the effect of changes. Some spreadsheets are graphing programs, too. This means they can produce pie charts, bar charts, and line graphs for further analysis.

Word Processing

One of the most useful functions of a computer is managing words through word processing programs. **Word processing** is typing words on a keyboard, viewing and rearranging them on the screen, and printing a *hard copy* or *printout.*

Word processing involves two major steps, editing and formatting. In the editing step, you type in words, arrange them, and check their spelling. Some programs will even analyze your writing for content, style, and grammar. *Formatting* is selecting the shape, size, and general arrangement of words on the printed page.

Desktop Publishing

Desktop publishing software can create professional looking brochures, newsletters, pamphlets, and even books. Word processing and page layout systems make it easier and cheaper to prepare your own material. *Page layout systems* let you decide where pictures will go, and what type and size of print to use. You can also create charts and illustrations to enhance your work.

Data Communications

Data communications is a process that allows computers to "talk" to each other. Information is sent, or transmitted, between terminals over telephone or cable lines. **Terminals** refer to the output and input devices.

Computer terminals can be wired together in-house and connected to a central unit called a *server.* The server provides a means for people to communicate via their computers. This computer communication is called **networking.** For instance, suppose several people need to prepare a report. Each person can individually write a section and network with other committee members. One person can receive all input and prepare the final report. Time and expense will be saved. If computer output needs to be sent longer distances, special devices called *modems* allow the information to be transmitted over standard telephone lines.

Databases

By using your computer and a modem, you can access information from databases across the country. A **database** is an organized collection of information stored in computers. These databases are accessed through information companies or agencies known as *electronic information services* or *online computer services.* Once you subscribe to these sources, usually by paying a monthly fee, you can receive almost any information within seconds.

Databases contain much information for office, school, and home use. You might shop coast-to-coast at hundreds of nationally known stores. The latest news, weather, and traffic reports can be received as events occur. You might access data, transfer it to a software program, or use it to perform a complex analysis.

Learning About Computers

There are many ways to learn about computers. Information is available through computer specialists, school courses, computer clubs, magazines and books, or hands-on experience, 5-15. Looking at computers in local stores can also provide you with more information.

Courses in computer use are available in most schools. Many of these courses provide hands-on experience as well as other instruction. Some schools offer classes on the operation of a specific kind of computer or computer program.

5-15 Computers and word processing programs help you quickly produce your work and refine it.

Computer clubs exist in many localities. Clubs might focus on a specific brand of computers, a software program, or special interest. Clubs are especially valuable for sharing information about problems and solutions.

Many books and magazines are available on various computer hardware and software topics. However, the best way to become computer literate is to actually use one until you feel comfortable working with it. Most young people are eager to use computers and realize the challenge, importance, and fun in using them.

◆ Knowing How to Use Technology Affects Employability

To be prepared for the workplace, you must have the skills that employers need. Knowing how to use technology is one such skill. Most employers rely on copiers, fax machines, telephones, and computers to operate. They expect employees to be familiar with these basic business tools. New employees should be able to fully operate even the most sophisticated versions with some practice.

Employers also expect workers to follow all rules related to using the equipment correctly. These include all rules pertaining to
◆ safety
◆ company policy concerning business versus personal use of equipment and communication links

Employers seek computer literate employers, even for jobs that are not computer focused. They try to hire new workers who know how to handle the following computer basics:
◆ organizing and maintaining personal files
◆ processing information accurately
◆ presenting information in different formats
◆ acquiring data via the Internet quickly

◆ recognizing when equipment is malfunctioning

Perhaps your future job will involve specialized equipment only accessible on the job. In that case, you will be expected to demonstrate your ability to do the following:

◆ use the equipment that relates to your specific job or department

◆ know which tools to use for specific tasks

Remember, you won't be expected to know everything. However, it is assumed that you will have the foundation skill of knowing how to learn. Employers also assume that you will want to excel. See 5-16.

People who are able to use different resources, information, and technology will have an advantage in today's job market, no matter what their field is. These skills increase a person's opportunity to obtain an interesting job with good earnings. People who are open to change and who value lifelong learning also have an advantage. The reason is simple. Technology is advancing so quickly that employers don't them-

Technology Applications
Which of the following can you use with confidence?
◆ Answering machine
◆ Cellular phone
◆ Computer hardware and software
◆ Copy machine
◆ E-mail
◆ Fax machine
◆ Pager
◆ Printer
◆ Scanner
◆ Voicemail

5-16. Knowing how to operate many different technologies will be beneficial to your work.

selves know what tomorrow's tools will be. By staying abreast of today's technology and being ready to learn tomorrow's, you demonstrate a desire to remain an effective worker.

Summary

Much is written about poor reading, writing, and math skills of high school students. Businesses and industry have had to retrain and educate their workers because of a lack of these strong basic skills.

Skills in reading and understanding, writing, following directions, solving problems, and using computers and technology are necessary in the workplace. Mastering these skills will give you an advantage in the working world today.

Workers must be willing and able to learn how to learn. New technologies are changing the ways that businesses and industries operate. A good foundation in the basic skills, computer literacy, and technology application will open the door to more job opportunities.

To Review

1. What are the basic skills needed for the workplace?

2. Describe the relationship between good basic skills and company profits.

3. What is meant by learning-to-learn skills?

4. How are employees with good learning-to-learn skills cost effective to employers?

5. Compare "reading to do" and "reading to learn."

6. List three tips that may help improve reading skills.

7. List five writing competencies needed to perform job tasks.

8. List the four basic math operations.

9. What are the four components that make up the hardware of a computer?

10. What is the difference between RAM and ROM?

11. Name five sources for computer information.

12. How does being able to use different resources, information, and technology affect employment?

To Do

1. Invite a local adult education director to speak to your class about adult illiteracy and what is being done to reduce it in your community.

2. Role-play a situation in which a high school graduate has not learned to read or write well. Act out how this affects the person's life.

3. Ask former graduates how their reading or writing skills have helped them in their work.

4. Make a point to include at least 20 minutes of reading in your schedule each day for a week.

5. Write a business letter to a company expressing your satisfaction with their product.

6. Write a letter to your "Aunt Emma" thanking her for the gift she sent you.

7. Try to identify the many places you have been where computers were being used. Make a list of all the places you remember. State how computers were being used and who was using them.

8. Debate the question: Should a course in computers be required for graduation?

9. Choose one of the computer-aided technology programs to research. Write a two-page report on the topic.

6 Communication Skills

After studying this chapter, you will be able to
◆ demonstrate verbal and nonverbal communication skills.
◆ identify barriers to good communication.
◆ explain assertive techniques for improving communication.
◆ demonstrate good telephone communication skills.
◆ list tips for public speaking.
◆ identify active listening skills.

Terms to Know

communication
verbal
  communication
nonverbal
  communication

inflection
body language
assertive
aggressive

When you are at work, you communicate with many people. **Communication** is the process of interchanging thoughts, ideas, or information with others. As a worker, you will communicate with your supervisors, coworkers, and customers. You will write messages, talk, and listen to others every day. You want to be understood and interpreted correctly.

Being a good communicator means sharing information with others as well as responding to what others are communicating. In order to do this effectively, workers need to understand each other's messages. See 6-1.

In this chapter you will read about ways of sending clear messages through verbal and nonverbal communication. You will also read about good listening techniques. Speaking and listening are the most common forms of communication.

Of the total time a person spends communicating, about nine percent of the time is spent

writing; 13 percent, reading; 23 percent, speaking; and 55 percent, listening. Clearly, speaking and listening are powerful channels of communication. Recent studies on factors for workplace success indicate that *communication skills* rank second, after *knowledge about the job*.

Good communication skills are central to the smooth operation of any business. Workers must relate information to customers and express appreciation for the customers' business. Workers may need to discuss problems with their employer. They might also need to review procedures with a coworker.

Poor communication can be costly to the employer. Problems can arise if an employee doesn't handle customer orders properly. If employees give the wrong information or don't interpret it correctly, it can result in a huge financial loss. The loss can be measured in wasted materials and labor as well as lost customers.

S.C.U. Color

6-1 Strong communication skills are very important in the working world.

◆ Ways of Communicating

You can communicate your message in many different ways. When you talk, you are communicating with others. You may, perhaps, choose to write your message. You may draw to illustrate what you mean. You can use gestures to emphasize or replace words. The way you stand, sit, move your body, or make facial expressions also help relay your message, 6-2.

People communicate verbally or nonverbally. **Verbal communication** involves using words, either written or spoken. **Nonverbal communication** involves ways other than words to communicate your message. Often, verbal and nonverbal communications are combined to relay messages. For example, at a basketball game, the crowd communicates support and praise by clapping (nonverbal) and yelling, "Go team" (verbal).

Verbal Communication

Verbal communication refers to the words you say. The tone of your voice as well as the words you choose make an impact on what you are trying to communicate.

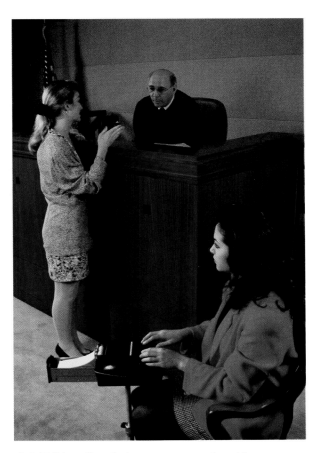

6-2 Talking directly to a person and making eye contact will show that you are interested in communicating.

How You Sound

The voice has certain characteristics, such as shrillness, volume, tone, rhythm, tempo, pauses, and clarity. The voice transmits as much as 38 percent of the meaning in face-to-face interactions. In telephone conversations, the voice transmits 70 to 90 percent of the meaning.

Listen to your voice. How does it sound? A loud voice or rapid speech may make the listener anxious or disturbed. A soft, soothing voice tends to produce a more calming effect on the listener and may even help communication, 6-3. Think about the effect the sound of your voice has on your listeners.

Inflection is the way you use your voice to affect the meaning of the spoken message. When you say "no," the tone of your voice can come across to others as "maybe," a questioning "no?" or a very definite "no!"

Saying "What a weekend I had!" can have at least two different meanings depending on the tone of your voice. It might mean it was a glorious, wonderful weekend. With different voice qualities, or inflections, it could mean it was a terrible weekend. Loudness and tone of voice affects how others interpret your message.

You can use inflections to make your voice more attractive. Inflections can be used for emphasis and interest. You can stress important words and syllables. This gives more meaning to your words.

What You Say

Another way people communicate is through their choice of words. This is the spoken exchange of thoughts, ideas, and messages. It can take place when an individual speaks to another, to a small group, or to a large crowd. Messages are constantly sent and received as meanings are shared through the spoken word.

"What do I say?" In the first few minutes of meeting someone, only about seven percent of a spoken message makes an impact. Most impressions are formed from observing the person's appearance and voice quality. If a good first impression is not made, the receiver may not care to listen. His or her mind may already be made up because of what is seen. The spoken message, therefore, will be lost.

If the receiver finds a person's body language and vocal characteristics appropriate,

6-3 Positive messages are conveyed with a pleasant voice and a smile.

then the words used will be important. At this point, it is worthwhile to evaluate the choice of words.

◆ Are the words appropriate for the situation?
◆ Are the words powerful enough to keep the receiver's attention?
◆ How are thoughts organized?
◆ Are the words used to help share meanings?

The way your thoughts are put into words and expressed is important in communicating. Some phrases or comments encourage speech, while others tend to cut the lines of communication. See 6-4.

Nonverbal Communication

To communicate clearly on the job, you need to understand the effect body language has on a message. Body language refers to body movements such as facial expressions, gestures, and posture used to send messages to others. **Body language** is nonverbal communication. People interpret your message by what they see.

Everything about you sends signals. Body language includes the way you sit or stand, your eye contact, and your reaction to what is going on around you. All this is observed and interpreted by other people. A welcoming smile tells a lot about a person. A smile is universal—you don't even need to know how to speak the other person's language to interpret this message.

People also receive messages about you through other observations. These messages include

◆ your age
◆ your appearance (manner of dress, grooming)
◆ your health and habits (how you move)
◆ the personal space you need

Sometimes other factors enter into body language, such as physical contact, status or power, culture, and gender differences.

Whether you make physical contact with others influences the kind of message they receive. A handshake, a slap on the back, and a hug send different kinds of messages. Also, the distance you keep from the speaker encourages or discourages communication. Try to stay neither too close nor too far away. Find a comfortable distance and watch the nonverbal cues of the speaker as you move toward or away from him or her.

The actions of people in positions of power or high social status send out signals. People may also send messages by their mannerisms or what they wear. A woman in a white uniform in a hospital sends the message that she can help you with a health concern.

Actions have different meanings to people of different cultures. In some Middle Eastern countries, a woman is not permitted to look directly in the eyes of a man unless he is her husband. In the United States it is generally considered rude to not look at an individual when you are talking to him or her.

Statements Encouraging Communication
"Are you saying that . . ."
"Please explain how . . ."
"Tell me about . . ."
"Help me to understand . . ."
"Tell me again . . ."
"Do you mean that . . ."
"Did you say that . . ."

Statements Hindering Communication
"That's dumb."
"I don't want to talk about it."
"You don't know what you're talking about!"
"I don't believe that."
"Nobody understands me."
"That was a stupid statement."
"I don't want to hear about it."
"You don't understand."

6-4 Which of these statements do you use in your conversation pattern?

Gender also has an effect on body language. Gender refers to whether you are male or female. Men and women often react differently to various situations. It is known that women smile more often than men. Women often smile even when the message they are conveying doesn't call for a smile.

Impact of Body Language

Body language helps you communicate more clearly. Be aware of your body movements. Know what impression you are making on others. Then use body language to make the kind of impression you want. See 6-5.

According to experts, your body language makes up 55 percent of the meaning of the messages you send when you first meet someone. Body language includes appearance. Therefore, one key question to ask is: "How do I look?" How you look makes an important impact on those who receive your messages.

When speaking, what is said should correspond with how it is said. Language usage should be consistent with body language and vocal communication. In other words, if you are telling a sad story, you should not be smiling. Knowing how you look and sound and what you plan to say will help increase the effectiveness of your communication. Body language, vocal impressions, and verbal language are vitally important. You will benefit by taking a closer look at your communication methods.

In practicing for a job interview, you might want to role-play shaking hands and other situations with an employer. Videotaping these sessions will help you see how you look to others. You will see the positive points about the way you present yourself and your message. You may also spot some mannerisms or figures of speech that you would like to improve.

You may need to accept certain aspects of your body language while trying to improve others. You can do little to change your age, gender, or physical features. However, you can change your gestures and posture to send clearer messages.

6-5 Your body language—a smile, frown, or gesture—tells a lot about what you are saying.

◆ Creating Barriers

Communicating clearly is not always easy. Sometimes the message is plain and direct. At other times, messages get lost or confused.

Why Messages Get Confused

There are many barriers to good communication. Barriers in communication can cause misinterpretations, misunderstandings, or inappropriate responses. Barriers might result from physical surroundings, personal habits, or opinions. Barrier conditions or situations are not the same for everyone. Try to prevent problems by learning to recognize and identify areas that are barriers for you.

People who are tired or under stress will not be able to respond accurately. These conditions can be barriers to communication. People need to be rested and alert. Also, if people are not comfortable in their surroundings, they will accomplish fewer tasks. Some people can work profitably with background noise and periodic interruptions. For others, this would be a barrier. They need quiet surroundings and cannot work or concentrate otherwise.

When people communicate, they need *feedback*, or response from the other person. Feedback can provide support, approval, or suggestions. Lack of response can be a barrier and stall or stop progress on a project. It might even break up a friendship!

Mixed messages can also develop when people attach different meanings to words. Another person may think you mean something entirely different from the message you are intending to send. You need to make sure everyone is talking about the same thing.

There are other barriers to communication. The way you view others may hinder communication. Sometimes we have difficulty communicating because of the other person's stature, beliefs, nationality, or physical traits. Are you forming opinions without enough information? Do you make snap judgments without enough reasoning behind your decision? Often, it is important to think over your answer before responding. Do you daydream a lot? Do you let your mind wander when someone else is talking with you? These barriers can be overcome by concentrating on the verbal and nonverbal message being conveyed.

Barriers can block communication. They can trigger defensiveness and resentment. Identifying and understanding these problems can help you avoid them.

Removing Barriers

Conditions for fostering good communication must be improved before messages can get through, 6-6. You must do your part to understand what is being communicated. Perhaps by being more rested, you can communicate better. By being nonjudgmental or by staying alert instead of daydreaming, you will communicate better. Noise or uncomfortable seating arrangements make listening difficult. Be aware of your surroundings and try to arrange a comfortable setting. Good communication skills need to be practiced and continually improved.

6-6 Each person must do his or her part in removing barriers that block good communication.

The rest of this chapter focuses on ways to improve communication skills. By following the suggestions given, you can start to remove the barriers in your communication patterns.

Communicating Assertively

Assertiveness is an important part of good communication. Being **assertive** means you state your ideas in a confident and direct manner. You recognize you have certain rights and beliefs and others cannot take advantage of you. By being assertive, you state your wants and needs in a nonthreatening way. See 6-7.

6-7 Assertive communication involves the use of both verbal and nonverbal language to communicate and achieve goals.

Assertive messages usually have the following pattern: "When you _____, I feel _____ because _____." Following are some examples:
- "When you call me lazy, I feel angry because I think I hold up my end of the work load."
- "When you say you'll wait for me and then you don't, I feel left out because then I don't have anyone to walk home with me."
- "When you wear my shirt and don't give it back, I feel upset because it is not there when I want to wear it."

Assertive statements can also inform others of your needs. Statements can begin with: "I need," "I expect," or "I want." For example, you might say:
- "I need to see you in my office."
- "I expect you to return to work promptly after your break."
- "I want this job finished by noon."

Being able to communicate your thoughts, feelings, and experiences is necessary if others are to understand you better and react to you more positively. Assertiveness is having the confidence and the quiet manner of persuading others to your point of view. You work to get what you want without putting others down or hurting them.

Being assertive is different from being aggressive. Being **aggressive** refers to the practice of attacking, as in a battle or combat. Aggressiveness is usually hostile and destructive. An aggressor tries to get his or her needs met at the expense of others.

Assertive skills can be used to accomplish the following communication goals:
- making simple requests
- requesting a change in behavior
- refusing requests
- teaching others
- offering criticism
- expressing opinions
- showing appreciation
- initiating conversations

Making Simple Requests

When you make simple requests, ask for what you want in a direct way. For example, you can say, "Please bring your own supplies when you come to work." Assertive people let other people know what they want done. They feel they have the right to make their wants known to others.

Requesting a Change in Behavior

Getting people to change their behavior is not always easy. You stand the best chance of achieving your goal if you make your request assertively.

Think about what you are going to say to the other person. Focus on the unacceptable behavior and not on the person's personality. Describe the offending behavior and state how it has created a problem. Be firm but not dominating. Tell the person in clear terms how you want his or her behavior to change. Explain the consequences if he or she fails to change.

Making an assertive request means using body language that reinforces your verbal message. The following suggestions for assertive body language will help you get across your request:

- Face the other person squarely, whether standing or sitting.
- Look the other person in the eyes, but not in an aggressive stare.
- Look confident and act with assurance.
- Don't smile if you are angry about something, as this sends a mixed message.

Selecting an appropriate place and time to make your request will affect how well the request is received. A person is less likely to get defensive or feel embarrassed if you talk to him or her privately. You will want to allow enough time to discuss your request thoroughly, without feeling rushed.

After your assertive message has been sent with both spoken words and body language, pause briefly. Remain silent so the other person can absorb what you have said and done.

Respectfully listen to the other person's response to your request. The response to a request for a change in behavior is often defensive. Sometimes excuses are given. Sometimes the person attacks verbally, and sometimes he or she withdraws.

Provide feedback to let the other person know you understand his or her response. Repeat what the other person says concerning how he or she feels. Then restate your request. It may take more assertive messages to change another person's behavior.

Remember, you cannot make a change occur in another person's behavior. All you can do is state your position in a firm, confident manner. Then it is up to the other person to assess his or her behavior.

If the other person agrees to change, clearly state the solution you reach. Make sure you both understand your agreement. End your meeting by thanking the other person for his or her willingness to discuss the issue.

Refusing Requests

Assertive statements may be used to refuse to do something. "No, I can't go with you tonight." Be direct, concise, and to the point when you say "no." Let others know that pleading, begging, or using other manipulative measures will not make you change your mind.

Teaching Others

Assertive statements can also be used to teach others. For example, you might tell a coworker, "When you are working on this machine, wait until this button is lit." When someone is not performing a task properly, you should be assertive enough to correct him or her. You could say, "No, that is not the way to do this. It should be done this way." Listen as the other person responds to your instruction. Be patient, but do not leave the point until you are sure he or she understood your instruction. See 6-8. Effective assertive teaching methods

USMC

6-8 Effective teaching methods give direction and a clear, concise explanation of expectations.

give direction and a clear, concise explanation of the expected outcome.

Offering Criticism

Assertive statements can make criticism productive. Assertive criticism will offer a way to improve. You may say, "Your speech had some good content. However, it could have included suggestions for ways your audience could get involved. Next time, also try using visual aids to help clarify your points."

Expressing Opinions

Assertive statements can be made to express opinions. In the workplace, you should speak up when you feel strongly about an issue. Be ready with valid reasons to back up your opinions. For example, you could say, "I feel we should

appoint Robert to head this committee because of his experience and background."

Showing Appreciation

It takes an assertive person to admit he or she cannot do everything alone. Assertiveness allows a person to say two of the most important words on the job, "Thank you." Always express appreciation when someone has helped you or has done a good job.

Initiating Conversations

Good communicators are willing to initiate conversations. If you find it difficult to start a conversation with someone, you might try to focus on a situation you both have in common. News items and subjects of local interest make good conversation openers. Another approach is to begin talking about yourself. Your comments can involve any situation as it relates to your feelings, interests, or beliefs. Remarks expressed in a friendly manner usually trigger a response from the other person.

◆ Telephone Communication Skills

Using the telephone requires good communication skills. When you use the telephone, you are being judged by your promptness, your tone of voice, and your attitude. At home, your telephone manners will be a reflection of you. At work, your telephone manners can help or hurt your employer. They send a mental picture of you and the company, 6-9.

When the telephone rings, answer it promptly. In most businesses, your employer will tell you what you are to say when answering the phone. For instance, you may be asked to answer by giving the company name. Listen carefully and speak clearly. You should not be chewing gum, eating, or drinking when you answer a call.

6-9 How employees communicate on the telephone can help or hurt their company's business.

Write down the necessary information requested as thoroughly but briefly as you can. Get the name and phone number of the person calling, the name of the person who should receive the message, and the message itself. Recording the date and time is a good practice. Be helpful, pleasant, and courteous. Try never to interrupt the other person.

If you are calling others, have all the information or questions you need to ask organized in your mind or on paper. Thank the person for their time and assistance. If the person called the company, thank him or her for calling. The way you sound on the telephone when conducting business is very important. The impression you give will reflect upon the company.

Speaking Before a Group

As a part of your job, you may be asked to give progress reports about your team's accomplishments. Salespeople may present sales talks to potential customers. You may be asked to make a formal presentation to a group. There are many more occasions when you will be asked to deliver a few informal comments for the whole group to hear. These are examples of another method of communicating you will use in the workplace.

A well-organized speech will have an introduction, body, and conclusion. At the beginning of your speech, give a short statement about your topic and why it's important to the audience. In the main body, cover the key information to share. For the closing, summarize your points.

Always practice your speech beforehand, but do not try to memorize it. Having the outline of your speech written on note cards will help you speak effectively and remember your key points. When you speak, use a normal tone of voice. Speak clearly and distinctly. Enunciate your words. Appear interested and excited about your topic. This is your chance to inform, entertain, or convince others.

Body language is very influential in how others respond to your talk. The first message you convey is often given through your body language. Dress neatly and attractively. When speaking, maintain eye contact with your audience. Use body language to support your message, not cause distractions.

Listening Skills

Employees need to know the importance of listening in their everyday work lives. Employers want employees who will hear the key points that make up their customers' concerns. They want people who can listen to directions and carry them out exactly.

Workers spend over half of their time listening, yet they tend to forget 95 percent of what they hear. Average workers spend about four hours in listening activities every day. They hear for about two hours. They actually listen for about an hour. Listening and hearing are not the same. You hear with your ears, but listening requires the use of your brain. You need to think in order to listen!

Many people have not learned to listen well. They do not hear every word when a person is speaking. Often, they are thinking ahead to what they will say next. Poor listening habits cost employers hundreds of millions of dollars every year. Productivity is lost because of mistakes or misunderstandings. If an order is misinterpreted, the cost of poor listening is an expensive mistake.

Businesses with effective listeners see many benefits. They have more satisfied customers, which increases their sales. Good listening provides a more productive workforce. Through effective listening, more information is gained and fewer mistakes are made. This improves relations with people inside and outside the company.

Reasons for Listening

You will listen more intently if you have a reason. Why is it important for you to listen to the message being given? Perhaps it is to learn information for a grade or a particular process or skill. Maybe you are trying to increase your overall knowledge. Perhaps you are listening to be entertained, 6-10.

There are five major reasons for listening carefully in the workplace. These are as follows:

- listening for content
- listening for emotional meaning
- listening for directions
- listening for long-term understanding
- listening to respond

Listening for Content

In order to listen for content, close attention must be paid to the overall message. What is the main idea? What are the specific details? An example is when a supervisor announces that a meeting has been changed from Friday to Monday. The main idea is the meeting has been changed. The specific details are the time and day of the change.

Listening for Emotional Meaning

Listening for emotions will help you understand the meaning of a message. Think about the

Reprinted with permission from Family, Career and Community Leaders of America

6-10 A good listener looks interested, doesn't interrupt, and concentrates on what is being said.

statement, "All the ants are dead." Someone troubled with an infestation problem might utter this statement with joy. The owner of an ant farm might speak this phrase with sadness. An animal rights activist might say this sentence with anger.

When you listen, ask yourself if the speaker is expressing feelings such as joy, sorrow, fear, hate, or love. Also determine if the speaker is trying to bring out such emotions in you.

Listening to Follow Directions

When directions are given, they must be followed closely. If they are given in steps, remember the sequence in which the steps are done. Taking notes may help you remember the correct directions.

Listening for Long-Term Understanding

Attention and concentration are keys to effective listening for long-term understanding. Concentrate on the main ideas of the message. Focus on the important concepts. First, look for the ideas, then the facts and significant details. Summarize and review the message content. Try to link it to some preexisting information.

Writing down key points will help you refer to the message later.

Listening to Respond

Conversational listening involves two or more people interacting. It requires not only listening but also responding. Speaker and listener roles shift often.

You need to be fully aware of what the other person is saying, 6-11. Let the speaker complete his or her message before responding. This will help you avoid losing the speaker's train of thought as you plan what to say next. You must be a good listener as well as a good responder.

Being an Active Listener

Active listening is much more than just hearing what a speaker is saying. Skilled listeners understand the speaker's message and can respond to it. Active listening involves listening with the eyes and ears as well as focusing in on the feelings of the speaker. The following suggestions will help you become an active listener.

Long John Silvers

6-11 When listening for content, pay close attention to the overall theme of the message.

Ask Questions

Active listeners ask questions if they are unsure of the messages. This is especially important on the job. If you are unsure, it is better to ask questions than to risk doing your job wrong because of a misunderstanding.

Summarize

Listen to the speaker's words. Mentally summarize what the speaker is saying. Restate, or rephrase in your own words, the idea or feeling being expressed. In this way, understanding and acceptance will be communicated.

Give Feedback

Give the speaker nonverbal feedback by nodding and smiling. Also give verbal feedback. You may repeat what the person has said to clarify meaning, "So you're saying you want to meet at noon by the library?"

Feedback is the receiver's response to the message. Feedback makes it possible for the sender to determine whether the message was understood.

Communicate Nonverbally

Indicate by your actions that you are paying careful attention to the person talking. Show your attentiveness by leaning slightly toward the speaker. This shows you are paying total attention to the other person and consider his or her message important. Good eye contact reveals you are interested in what is being said.

Good listening skills enable a person to really understand what another is saying. It is a combination of hearing what the person is saying and staying involved with the person who is talking. Good communication skills are required for effective human relationships at home and at work.

Summary

You share ideas, feelings, and information with others in many ways each day. Good communication skills will help you on the job as well as in all areas of your life. How well your message is sent and received depends on effective use of body language as well as verbal communication. How you look, how you sound, and what you say are important personal communication patterns.

A number of barriers can interfere with the communication process. Removing these barriers will increase the shared understanding of the feelings, thoughts, wants, needs, and intentions of the communicators.

Being assertive is another communication skill. Assertiveness enables you to state your wants and needs in a firm but non-threatening manner. Improving your assertiveness can help you defend your rights and acknowledge your self-worth.

You will need to use good communication skills in all areas of work. Using the telephone requires good speaking and listening skills. If you are asked to speak in front of a group, you need to present your material in a clear, concise manner.

Becoming an active listener will help you on the job. An active listener listens to words and tunes in to the feelings of the speaker. Good listeners understand the speaker's message and can respond to it.

To Review

1. Name two ways of communicating.

2. Give an example of how inflection can change the meaning of a message.

3. Give three examples of nonverbal communication.

4. List two factors in expressing yourself nonverbally.

5. List three barriers to good communication.

6. Explain the difference between being assertive and aggressive.

7. Explain how a business call should be handled.

8. List five major reasons for listening.

9. Give three guidelines for being an active listener.

To Do

1. Write down a word to convey a thought or feeling. (Examples include *happy, shy, frightened, insecure, annoyed, tired, surprised,* and *angry.*) Pantomime to a partner your feelings or mood. What were the nonverbal clues that led him or her to guess correctly?

2. Go to a public place, such as a shopping mall. Remain silent while watching others. Record the nonverbal messages you observe.

3. From magazines, find an illustration that shows several different people in the same picture. Mount the illustration on paper. Label it with the messages the people appear to be sending to each other and to you. What nonverbal gestures or postures are they using?

4. List any listening behaviors you find annoying. Examine your own listening style to see whether you use any of those behaviors.

5. In class or another public place, close your eyes for a few minutes and listen to the sounds around you. List the sounds you hear. Then repeat the listening. This time, listen first for the nonhuman sounds you hear. Then focus your attention only on human sounds, such as talking, whistling, and laughing. Record your results.

7 Understanding Personal Management Skills

After studying this chapter, you will be able to

- define self-concept and self-esteem.
- identify three parts of your self-concept.
- list four ways in which self-esteem affects worker performance.
- analyze ways to improve your self-concept.
- explain the relationship between motivation and goal setting in job success.
- list steps in setting and reaching goals.

Terms to Know

personal manage-
   ment skills
self-concept
productivity

creativity
stress
motivation

Your effectiveness in the workplace is linked directly to your **personal management skills.** These skills include work habits, attitudes, and basic life skills. Punctuality, willingness to work, and good grooming are a few of the specific skills employers seek in their employees. Being able to open a bank account, read a road map, and rent an apartment are personal management skills, too.

Personal management skills are also "job keeping" skills. They will help you hold a job. They may also affect how quickly you advance in your job. Well-developed personal management skills are keys for success in the workplace.

The way you feel about yourself affects your personal management skills. Your motivation and the way you set and reach goals have an impact on your personal management skills, too. This chapter will focus on how these factors can help you better meet the demands of the workplace. See 7-1.

Your Self-Concept

The ideas and impressions you have about yourself are called your **self-concept.** Your self-concept is the way you describe yourself. It is the picture you see of the kind of person you are.

If you have a strong sense of self-worth, you possess a positive self-concept. You are aware of your strengths and weaknesses. You feel good about your strengths. You may not like your weaknesses, but you accept them as part of who you are. You feel good about yourself and are proud of who you are. This positive self-concept gives you a feeling of being a worthwhile person.

A positive self-concept gives you a firm foundation for reaching your full potential in the workplace and in other areas of your life. You are able to accept yourself for who you are and readily take on new challenges. You are confident and in control of your life.

7-1 Employers want employees who know how to get tasks done.

How Is Your Self-Concept Formed?

A self-concept is formed long before a person enters the workplace. It continues to develop throughout life. Your self-concept is based on past experiences and the people around you. The response or reactions you get from your family, peers, and others with whom you associate helps you form most of your self-concept.

Early childhood is the most important time in the development of self-concept, 7-2. The way parents react to and care for their child greatly influences the child's self-concept.

A negative self-concept is likely to develop if children are neglected, unloved, and rejected. Children with negative self-concepts are afraid to try anything new. They often feel worthless. A positive self-concept is likely to develop if children receive love, care, encouragement, security, and guidance from their parents. Other factors that influence a person's self-concept include

◆   number of children in the family
◆   birth order (oldest, middle, youngest)
◆   goals that parents have for the child
◆   family relationships
◆   protective attitudes parents have toward the child

A positive self-concept is more likely to develop if a child grows up in a home where each person is valued as an individual. If your family shows they think you are capable and responsible, this is how you will view yourself.

Fisher-Price, Inc.

7-2 Early experiences in childhood influence self-concept.

Another factor that affects your self-concept is your contact with friends and other people. The way others treat you gives you an idea of what they think of you. If others compliment you on a job well done, you will feel good about yourself. For example, someday you want to be a graphic designer. A local gymnastics instructor needs a special emblem on costumes her students wear for competition. She really likes your designs and asks you to develop an emblem for her students' costumes. She is extremely pleased with the emblem you develop. This helps build your positive self-concept.

Although the core of your self-concept was developed in the early years, it continually changes as you grow, develop, and mature. Your sense of self changes as you respond to new situations and experiences.

Parts of Your Self-Concept

A person's self-concept is made up of three essential parts: self-awareness, self-image, and self-esteem.

Self-Awareness

Your knowledge of your skills and limitations is called *self-awareness*. Self-awareness comes from knowing and understanding yourself.

Self-awareness means that you recognize what you do well. Workers need to have self-awareness concerning their job skills, 7-3. They need to know which tasks they can do well and which they cannot.

If you know your skills, you are more aware of your talents. You also know where your strengths lie and how they relate to your job performance. It is important to recognize your current skills. You also need to know how to use them to prepare for a career or successfully perform a job.

When you have self-awareness, you know your limits. You are able to identify your needs and deal with your personal limitations. You recognize when you need more information or need help with a problem or situation. By being aware of your limitations and needs, you have a better sense of control over your life.

Self-Image

Another part of your self-concept is *self-image*. When you view yourself in relation to others and other situations, you form a mental picture of yourself. This is your self-image.

How you see yourself as compared to how you think others see you provides you with either a positive or negative feeling about yourself.

People who have a positive self-image will not let negative opinions of others affect their confidence. If they act according to their personal priorities, other people's different opinions will not affect their good self-image. If they behave according to workplace ethics, other people's negative feelings will not concern them. These opinions do not change their positive self-image.

A good self-image influences your behavior positively. You will act in ways that maintain your self-respect. You will not let the positive picture you have of yourself be shattered by inappropriate behavior.

A negative self-image hinders a person's ability to achieve. People with a negative self-image will not try new methods for fear of failing. Their confidence level is low. They often feel inadequate and incapable of doing work satisfactorily. This often results in lower production and lower quality work. If you see yourself positively, you will be more confident and secure in your abilities, 7-4.

7-3 Self-awareness, or the ability to know what you do well, strengthens your self-concept.

USMC

7-4 Having confidence in your abilities allows you to do a better job.

You have some control over shaping your self-image. By becoming better at what you do, your self-image will improve. Improving your work performance requires effort. If you feel you need help in doing good work, you can ask your teachers. On the job, you can ask your manager.

Your self-image can also be improved by reminding yourself of all you do well. Look at all your good qualities. Acknowledge your weaknesses and try to improve them if you can. Remain positive and you can probably find a corresponding strength for every weakness.

Even though no one is perfect, try to focus on your good points. Perhaps you are a good student or a loyal friend. Maybe you are a hard-working and conscientious employee. You may have a good sense of humor or a strong desire to complete tasks you begin. You may be surprised at how many good qualities you can find in yourself.

Remind yourself frequently that you are a good person with many important qualities.

You may even need to remind yourself daily of your good qualities as well as the qualities you desire. Soon these desired qualities will become an important part of your individual makeup. By doing this, you will develop desirable ways of thinking, acting, and feeling. You might even have better relationships with others. This will help you in the workplace and in all areas of your life.

Self-Esteem

When you have a positive self-concept, you also have *self-esteem*. Self-esteem is a feeling that you are important, worthy, and valuable. It is the level of confidence and satisfaction you have in yourself. It is an expression of your happiness or dissatisfaction with your self-image.

A high level of self-esteem means you appreciate who you are, 7-5. You respect and take pride in yourself and what you do. High

Virginia Division of Tourism

7-5 People with positive self-esteem believe in themselves. They believe they will be successful in what they set out to do.

self-esteem means you believe you are a capable, significant, successful, and worthy individual. Your self-esteem affects how well you carry out your everyday work.

Self-Esteem and Worker Performance

There is a relationship between workers' self-esteem and their personal management skills. It is reflected in the work they do. It is shown in workers' productivity, creativity, product or performance quality, and even in job hunting.

Productivity

Productivity refers to the amount of work employees do. Workers who feel good about themselves and what they are doing tend to work up to their full potential, 7-6. They do the work assigned to them. They do not slow down the production line or keep others from doing their jobs. Workers who have high self-esteem feel their work is important to the total operation of the company.

Creativity

Creativity is the ability to make or bring into existence something new. Workers with high self-esteem are confident in their ability to solve problems, often through their creativity. They have the ability to visualize ideas or to try different or new methods to achieve their goals. Even if they fail to come up with a workable solution, they do not lose their feelings of self-worth.

Product or Performance Quality

Workers with high self-esteem have confidence in their skills. They are proud of the work they do. They work to the best of their ability. Often, they set high performance standards and strive to surpass those standards. This results in high-quality products and well-performed services.

Advancing in a Career

People with high self-esteem create opportunities for promotion in the workplace. They successfully carry out their work. As they feel more competent and more satisfied, these workers produce better work. They transfer

Fisher-Price, Inc.

7-6 Employees who feel they make a meaningful contribution to the job have a positive outlook on life, their work, and themselves.

learning from one experience to another. They are willing to assume leadership roles and accept more responsibilities. Employers often reward these workers by mentioning their accomplishments to the staff. Pay raises or job promotions may follow.

People with high self-esteem often consider going after a new challenge in the form of a new job. They are not afraid of being turned down because they feel confident about their abilities. Their efforts to keep trying are not hampered. Workers with high self-esteem know that advancing in their career requires effort on their part. They do not feel defeated on the first try. Feelings of self-worth and confidence help workers move forward in their careers.

Your Self-Concept and Self-Esteem

Having a good self-concept is essential for self-esteem. You deal with new problems and people in a positive way. You face new situations with less fear. A feeling of being capable and successful generates a sense of accomplishment. This leads to improved self-esteem.

An employee with good self-esteem takes pride in his or her work. This benefits both the employee and the employer. A positive self-concept and self-esteem lead to competence in the workplace.

◆ How to Improve Your Self-Concept

An important part of your self-concept has to do with how you handle your emotions. Stress, criticism, mistakes, and change in your life affect your emotions. The following ideas should help you handle your emotions as you experience each of these circumstances. Learning to handle your emotions can help you feel better about yourself and improve your self-concept. In turn, you strengthen your personal management skills.

Learn to Manage Stress

Stress is any emotional, mental, or physical tension that people experience. It is your body's response to the demands made on it. Stress occurs in everyday life—in school, at home, and on the job.

Some situations are more stressful than others. A job loss is a very stressful situation. Conflicts with coworkers or supervisors can create stress. Low levels of stress result from minor, everyday events, such as misplacing objects or forgetting appointments. These can be a cause for concern, too.

Some stress is good. Stress can act as a force to motivate people to reach goals. For example, stress can be used to good advantage if it helps a person complete an assignment. Some people like to work under pressure. Stress causes them to get down to business and finish their work.

Much of the stress people experience is negative stress. This kind of stress threatens a person's sense of self-worth and integrity. In addition, too much negative stress on your mind or body can make you physically sick. See 7-7.

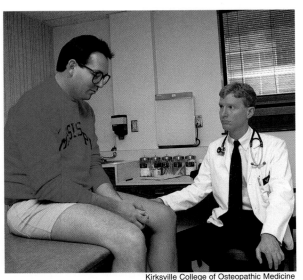
Kirksville College of Osteopathic Medicine

7-7 Physical symptoms that may be associated with severe stress include ulcers, high blood pressure, and a lowered resistance to infection or certain diseases.

Certain workplace conditions tend to contribute to stress. Many workers cite the following as very stressful:

◆ intense pressure to perform
◆ poor working environment
◆ no chance to succeed
◆ changes in workplace rules

No matter what you might do to prevent stress, it will always occur. It cannot be totally prevented, so you must learn how to live with stress in your life. There are various positive ways of managing stress.

Discuss Problems with Those Involved

Coworkers, managers, and other people may be involved in a stressful situation. Many times a problem can be resolved when it is discussed. This is often more effective than letting the problem bother you and not doing anything about it.

Maintain Good Health

Some stressful situations occur when you are tired or not eating properly. Get adequate sleep and rest to let your body relax. To ensure good health, eat a wide variety of nourishing foods. Good health can help your body when you are in stressful situations.

Stay Physically Active

Exercise and take part in activities such as bicycling or running. Play basketball or tennis, go swimming or dancing, or become involved in other physical activities. Fresh air and stimulation of your muscles and nervous system will relieve some of the tension caused by stress. See 7-8.

Find a Way to Relax

Some people find listening to music very relaxing. Others enjoy watching TV, reading, or becoming absorbed in a hobby. Some like to garden or go out with friends. Try to find some type of activity that you particularly enjoy, 7-9. This will help you cope with personal or work-related tensions.

North Carolina Division of Travel and Tourism

7-8 Regular exercise, such as walking, bicycling, or jogging, can aid in managing stress.

7-9 Getting absorbed in hobbies or favorite pastimes helps people relax. Then they can learn to adjust to stressful situations.

Know Your Limitations

By knowing yourself, you will know what you can handle and what you should avoid. Sometimes you are better able to handle certain kinds of stress. Other times even small incidents can be stressful. Learn to recognize when you can handle stress and when it can become overwhelming. This will help you manage stress in a more positive way.

Learn to Handle Criticism

How you handle criticism can affect your self-concept. Being criticized may cause a worker to react with anger and frustration. This may affect his or her self-concept. The worker's productivity may also decline. Such a person may lose promotions or even lose a job because he or she cannot handle criticism.

If a coworker or manager criticizes you or your work, you can use a number of positive responses. You can admit there probably is a better approach to the job. You can acknowledge that you are receptive to the suggestion or comment. You could also ask for more information. Ask the person or persons to clarify the meaning of their statements. In this way you may bring about a clearer understanding of the problem.

Do not let your self-concept be undermined or lowered when someone criticizes you. Try not to immediately defend or fight back. Think how constructive or accurate the criticism is. This will help you maintain a positive self-concept.

Learn to Handle Mistakes

Through your sense of self-awareness, you know you make mistakes. Everyone makes mistakes, but some are more serious than others. Most people try to avoid mistakes and improve their performance. However, they realize mistakes will sometimes happen.

How you handle making mistakes affects your work. You might be so concerned about making mistakes that you cannot concentrate fully on your work. This can cause you to perform poorly on the job.

Making mistakes should not lower your self-concept. Recognize what went wrong and resolve to do better next time. You will feel much better about yourself. Then you will continue to think of yourself as a person of worth and value. You will continue to have a good self-concept, which is important to your personal management skills.

Learn to Adjust to Change

New workers need to make many changes from the classroom to the demands of a job. See 7-10. Time schedules may be different. You might work night shifts or have different working hours than you had during school. The job itself may be difficult to learn. Friendships with

7-10 A person needs skill in learning how to adapt to the new challenges of the workplace.

coworkers are not the same as those of long-time friends. Your life as a new worker will probably be very different from what you experienced in school. It takes time to adjust to these changes.

As an employee, you need to know change is inevitable. It will always occur. In order to work well within the system, you need to adapt to change.

In order to handle change, you must be a flexible worker, able to adjust to new situations. This could mean moving easily from performing one job to another. Sometimes it takes learning a new procedure or new information. Learn as much as you can about the changed environment. In this way, you will be better able to adapt to change.

It takes time to adjust to changes in schedules, types of work performed, ways of doing a job, and other new situations. Learning to adjust to changes and effectively manage stress and criticism helps you improve your self-concept. This is a reflection of good personal management skills.

◆ Motivation and Goal Setting

Just as positive self-concept and high self-esteem influence personal management skills, so do motivation and goal setting. **Motivation** is the strong desire to achieve a goal. It is the push that propels you toward an aim in life. *Goals* are specific ends toward which you direct your efforts. Motivation and goal setting are important ingredients in workplace success.

You must be motivated to work to the best of your ability. Your mental attitude must be directed toward success on the job. You must want to do a good job. The more you are committed to reaching your goals, the greater your motivation. Goal setting will help stimulate your motivation.

When people are doing what interests them and have a desire to reach a goal, their self-esteem is enhanced. There is satisfaction in meeting goals. Most people want to perform to the best of their ability. They are motivated by a need to succeed. They find satisfaction in reaching goals and take pride in their accomplishments, 7-11.

Importance of Goal Setting

Goal setting motivates an employee to perform well on the job. If each employee sets his or her own work-related goals, production often increases. Besides greater productivity, goal setting causes higher levels of performance from individuals, teams, and organizations.

7-11 Your goals are based on your personal priorities, or what you consider important in your life. Couples need to develop mutual goals.

Goals give employees a basis to judge how they are performing on the job. They have a specific direction or a clear mark of progress. By setting goals, people can make work plans and judge progress toward these plans. As an employee progresses toward his or her goals, there is more satisfaction from the job.

A clothing company asked each employee to write performance goals that would help improve his or her productivity. These would help form the basis of the employees' annual evaluation. The employees used goal setting to determine what they needed to accomplish during the year. The advertising director wanted to reach different audiences with ads about the company's new line of easy-care baby clothing. He placed advertisements with a return request card in airline travel magazines. The company received one hundred new requests for information in the first two days. An employee in the collection department set as a goal to collect at least $30,000 weekly in overdue bills. The employee decided to call ten more people each day. After six weeks, she collected over $50,000 in unpaid money each week! Goal setting motivated employees to reach higher levels of performance.

When employees have goals to reach, they learn to manage their time. They can analyze a goal and determine the steps needed to accomplish it. As employees complete each step, they receive a feeling of satisfaction. This encourages them to move ahead and complete the next step. Their personal management skills will improve.

Learning to Set Goals

An important factor in motivating yourself is to learn how to set goals. These goals serve as guides in helping you achieve desired objectives. The following suggestions can be used in setting goals.

Identify a Specific Goal

Identify a goal that is specific rather than vague. A specific goal is one that has measurable results. For example, your goal might be to increase the number of orders you write to 15 each day. This would be more specific than saying, "My goal is to increase the number of orders I write every day." The specific number results in a more definite goal toward which to work.

You should be able to close your eyes and envision what will be achieved when a specific goal is met. The goal must lead to increased performance levels and provide individual growth.

Set Subgoals

Subgoals are goals within a goal. They are stepping stones that help you reach a larger goal. It is easier to achieve a major goal if you divide it into smaller subgoals along the way. This helps you avoid discouragement before your major goal is reached. See 7-12.

Suppose you work in the leather accessories area of a department store. You know

7-12 Writing down subgoals is a way of motivating yourself to reach your goals.

the manager of the shoe department will be retiring in a year. You set a major goal to be promoted to manager of the shoe department when the present manager retires. You ask the store manager if you can work more hours in the shoe department. This becomes a subgoal. You also set a subgoal to keep shelves neat and stocked with shoes. You set a third subgoal to increase your sales in the shoe department by at least five percent each week. You can work on several subgoals at the same time to help you reach your larger goal, 7-13.

Identify Resources

Identify the human and nonhuman resources available to help you reach your major goal. Your nonhuman resources may include skills. For instance, you might be good at solving math problems. Perhaps you have strong organizational skills. Maybe you are good at deciding what needs to be done first,

Brian Kinder

7-13 Finishing a project could be a short-term goal toward reaching the main goal of getting an "A" in your English class.

last, and so forth. The people who support and help you are your human resources. Once you identify your available resources, you can reach your goals easier and faster.

Identify Potential Problems

Think through any possible problems or obstacles that might stand in the way of achieving your goals. This might include other people, items, or situations such as a lack of money or time. Plan ways to overcome or avoid these problems.

Revise Goals If Needed

Sometimes you will need to revise your goals. Perhaps you learn that the deadline for a report due next month has been moved up to next week. You may need to rethink and even revise goals to agree with the present conditions. By constantly revising your goals, you will set new boundaries within which to work.

Reaching Your Goals

Achieving your goals offers both personal and economic rewards. You experience a sense of accomplishment and pride when you complete what you set out to do.

Reaching goals can be beneficial to both the employee and employer. Goals can lead to increased performance levels. This might be measured by the number of products or service calls completed in a certain amount of time. Success can be measured by the amount of sales made by the company or the expenses saved.

Goals promote individual growth. As you achieve your goals, you feel good about yourself. This leads to increased self-esteem and a more positive attitude. You are likely to control stress and handle criticism better. Developing good habits, using sound judgment, and handling problems confidently are other ways that goals can help foster individual growth. See 7-14.

By setting and reaching goals, you will take your work more seriously. You will be motivated by your desire to meet your goals.

7-14 Working hard to do the best job possible promotes personal growth and job success.

Success in goal setting cannot be measured by one event. Rather, success is measured throughout a person's lifetime. Each person views success differently and this view changes as a person matures. However, good personal management skills will increase your success at every life stage.

Summary

Personal management skills are essential for success in the workplace. They are needed for reaching individual and work-related goals. Having high self-esteem helps you develop good personal management skills.

The development of your self-concept begins long before you are employed. Experiences with your family, your friends, and others with whom you associate help shape your self-concept. All your experiences help to form the mental picture you have of yourself.

Your self-concept has a strong effect on how well you do your job and get along with others. Employees who have a good self-concept take pride in their work and want to do a good job. People with a poor self-concept can learn to think more positively about themselves.

Motivation and goal setting enhance a person's self-esteem. Productivity and job performance are increased when employees exhibit positive self-esteem, motivation, and realistic goal setting. When goals are reached, worker satisfaction increases.

Goals help people judge the progress of their work. By learning to set goals, you will be better able to reach objectives at home and in the workplace. As you improve your self-concept and your self-esteem, your motivation increases. It is easier for you to set goals. Higher levels of performance are reached when higher goals are set. An improved self-concept, positive self-esteem, motivation, and goal setting lead to stronger personal management skills.

To Review

1. Give three examples of personal management skills.

2. How is a person's self-concept formed?

3. What are the three essential parts of self-concept?

4. List two ways in which self-esteem affects worker performance.

5. How can self-concept be improved?

6. List three positive methods of handling stress.

7. List three positive ways to handle mistakes.

8. How can criticism be handled in a positive manner?

9. Name five suggestions for setting goals.

10. List two advantages of setting goals.

11. Name three personal outcomes of motivation and goal setting.

To Do

1. Describe actions of people on the job that might illustrate low self-esteem. Contrast this with a worker who has high self-esteem.

2. Write down five strengths you possess. Describe three weaknesses you have. Try to find a corresponding strength for each of the weaknesses.

3. Write a description of yourself as you think others see you.

4. List a career goal you might have. List three ways that a positive self-concept and three ways that high self-esteem can help you work toward your goal.

5. Make a list of stressful situations you could experience on the job. Write a paragraph about how you could manage the stress in one of these situations.

6. Choose one specific long-term goal to accomplish. Write out a plan of action for reaching it. Break your goal down into subgoals. Identify resources you can use to help reach your goal. Identify potential problems in reaching your goal.

8 Group Effectiveness and Leadership Skills

After studying this chapter, you will be able to

- ◆ list and explain six interpersonal skills important for the workplace.
- ◆ describe problem-solving skills necessary to be an effective team member.
- ◆ propose five tips for solving problems with creative thinking.
- ◆ list and describe qualities of a good leader.
- ◆ summarize how you can develop leadership skills while in school.
- ◆ list student organizations that might help develop leadership skills.
- ◆ explain how competence in using systems affects employability.

Terms to Know

group effectiveness	conflict
teamwork	mediation
interpersonal skills	stalemate
empathy	leader
constructive	leadership skills
criticism	appointed leadership
destructive criticism	volunteer leadership
prejudice	parliamentary
brainstorming	procedure
networking	system
compromise	

This chapter will help you learn good group skills. It will also help you identify characteristics of a good leader. You will look at school clubs and organizations to see how they help you learn to work cooperatively as a group member. Clubs, organizations, and businesses can reach their goals when their members work together as a team.

◆ Group Effectiveness Skills

Group effectiveness is how easily several people work together to achieve a common goal. Employees need to learn skills that will help improve group effectiveness. This involves doing more than performing their assigned jobs. Employees need to get along with their coworkers by making decisions and thinking creatively.

In recent years, emphasis in the workplace has been on sharing responsibility to get a job done. **Teamwork** means individuals work together to reach a common goal. By using the talents and abilities of many people, work is done more efficiently. Also, higher productivity often results from team effort, 8-1.

In the workplace, teams help to meet the objectives of the company or organization. A large retail store depends on many teams to help reach a goal of providing goods and services for consumers. One team works together to determine the type of merchandise to buy. Different teams locate sources and purchase

8-1 The importance of teamwork in productivity is often learned in school.

merchandise. After the merchandise arrives, other teams price, advertise, display, and sell the merchandise.

Team members have a wide variety of personalities and skills. It is important to recognize the different strengths of each team member and use them to help solve problems. For a team to be successful, team members must be willing to complete individual assignments. They must also be willing to share ideas and cooperate with one another to reach group goals.

Knowing how to work cooperatively with others is the cornerstone of being an effective team member. Interpersonal skills help employees work together as teams.

Interpersonal Skills

Having good interpersonal skills will help you be a better employee. **Interpersonal skills** are skills needed to get along well with other people. How you relate and communicate with other people shows your interpersonal skills, 8-2.

8-2 Good interpersonal skills help you get along well with others at work and play.

People who get along well with others in most situations have good interpersonal skills. Good interpersonal skills can help people resolve conflicts when problems arise. They help workers function better in the workplace and help individuals become successful team members.

Building effective work relationships requires some of the same skills you need for good personal relationships. You need to respect your coworkers and recognize their unique talents. You must also be able to communicate clearly with them. Practicing the six interpersonal skills discussed next will help you get along in the workplace. When there is a breakdown in any of the following areas, problems can develop.

Use Empathy

Empathy allows you to put yourself in another person's place. **Empathy** is the ability to think and act with an understanding of how others feel. When you empathize, you can better interpret why people think or behave as they do.

A coworker may be turned down for a job promotion and feel deeply disappointed. Even though you experience no similar situation, you would be able to sense that person's sadness. You could share their feelings and express regret about the loss of promotion by listening to them and offering feedback. You are empathizing with your coworker.

Make Requests Instead of Demands

You get better cooperation from others with a request rather than a demand. A request respects other people's feelings or needs. A person making a request uses a pleasant tone of voice and has a calm manner. A person making a demand has an unpleasant tone of voice. A demand implies right or wrong and often asks for immediate action. Demands can make workers feel threatened or restricted. Requests help workers maintain their self-worth.

Saying, "Would you switch working hours with me?" is better than demanding, "Work for me next Thursday night." If you issue demands, others might become angry and uncooperative.

Be Willing to Give and Take

All relationships involve personal differences. Be willing to give and take when differences arise, 8-3. Let other people know that you will listen to and respect their ideas. When everyone has a chance to offer input to the group, communication flows unhampered. This helps you reach a joint agreement.

John and Manya's work relationship is an example of give and take. Together they oversee purchases made by the library. They know the waiting lists are long for many books on tape. Manya suggests buying two copies of each book on tape. John thinks that is too expensive and suggests shortening the checkout period for tapes. Manya checks the cost of two copies and estimates how long patrons might take to listen to each tape. After discussion, she and John decide to purchase two copies of the most popular tapes. They also shorten the checkout period for all books on tape from two weeks to one. The final agreement contains some of Manya's ideas as well as John's.

Give and Accept Constructive Criticism

People respond differently to criticism. Some people may take offense, feel hurt, and not speak to you for a long time. They may even blame you for their failures. Others will accept your criticism in the helpful manner intended and try to improve the situation. One way to achieve this last response is to use constructive criticism.

Constructive criticism is helpful and offers recommendations for improvement. It does not attack another person. Constructive criticism can improve relationships with people because you show you care about them.

8-3 Children often have a hard time with give and take. As they grow up, this becomes somewhat easier.

People still feel worthwhile when criticism is constructive.

Destructive criticism is cruel. It focuses on the person and his or her failure or shortcomings. It does not offer helpful suggestions for changes in behavior.

Tact is skill in dealing with difficult situations. For example, Joan was always late picking up Marla. Marla could have said, "Joan, you are so inconsiderate to leave me waiting every day." This destructive remark focuses on Joan and offers no suggestions to correct the problem. Instead, Marla said, "Joan, I notice you are always late picking me up. Maybe we should reschedule our meeting time for fifteen minutes later." This recommendation helped Marla get the point across without hurting Joan's feelings. See 8-4.

Avoid Stereotypes and Prejudices

A *stereotype* is a belief that all members of a certain group share common characteristics.

Constructive Versus Destructive Criticism

Constructive Criticism
- Uses reason based on facts
- Avoids personal attacks
- Focuses on issues
- Involves a calm disposition
- Includes suggestions for improvement
- Emphasizes the positive points

Destructive Criticism
- Ignores facts
- Includes insults and personal attacks
- Involves an angry disposition
- Focuses on personalities and other personal matters
- Avoids suggestions for improvement
- Emphasizes the negative points

8-4 If you must criticize, try to use constructive criticism.

Stereotypes are often negative. People may have stereotypes about certain gender, age, or ethnic groups. For instance, some people think women are too emotional to be good managers or men are too insensitive to be a good parent. Some stereotypes relate to certain careers. Believing all professional athletes are violent is an example.

Stereotypes often lead to prejudices. A **prejudice** is an opinion formed without enough knowledge. Suppose a person has a stereotype about a certain group of people. This person is likely to form a prejudice whenever meeting anyone who belongs to that group.

There is no room for stereotypes and prejudices in the workplace. They keep people from being able to work together to achieve common goals. Avoid being distracted by personal differences and stay focused on your work. The best way to avoid stereotypes and prejudice is to look for the worth in each person.

Have a Sense of Humor

As you interact with other people at home, school, or the workplace, conflict might arise. A group might get to a point where they have trouble finding a solution for a problem or need. At such times, a sense of humor can help relieve tension. It allows you to see situations in another light. Relationships with others often improve and communication flows more easily.

A good sense of humor lets you see the funny side of many situations. Laughing with others can provide a more relaxed atmosphere. Remember, though, not to laugh at or ridicule anyone. When you learn to laugh at yourself, your problems do not seem as serious.

◆ Handling Problems in the Workplace

As with all situations that involve human relations, problems will arise in the workplace.

Knowing how to face and solve problems is part of getting along with others. It is important to handle problems as soon as possible to keep them from getting out of hand. Realizing why problems occur helps you become aware of situations that can turn into problems.

When problems occur, it is important to find a solution that is agreeable to all involved. Therefore, everyone needs to help work out the solution. In this way, problems can be solved more easily and efficiently.

Use Problem-Solving Skills

Good teamwork requires problem-solving skills. Since each person often views a situation differently, this can create barriers to a group's ability to solve problems. However, listening to many different views can help the group develop creative solutions to the problem.

The same skills required to solve individual problems are needed for successful group problem solving. Problem-solving skills include the ability to recognize problems, find solutions, and evaluate results. Listed below are a number of problem-solving techniques.

Focus on the Current Problem

Once you have identified the problem, it is important to stay on the subject. Do not bring up past problems or grievances. For instance, suppose a group receives notice that a speaker scheduled for the next meeting has canceled. When discussing this problem, group members should concentrate on finding a new speaker. They should avoid bringing up the fact that a similar situation occurred nine months ago, 8-5.

Separate the Person from the Problem

Many problems are the result of something a person did or failed to do. However, it is important to focus on the problem rather than the person who created it. For example, Nathan noticed work was piling up at Chad's

8-5 Brainstorming is often used in the work setting.

end of the production line. This problem occurred because Chad was taking time to carefully inspect each product that came down the line. However, Chad was responsible for packing, not inspection.

Accusing Chad of being too picky would not have addressed the problem. Therefore, Nathan handled the situation by saying, "Chad, I'm glad you are concerned about the quality of our products. However, we need to keep the line moving. We do not have time to check every product twice. We need you to focus on packing and trust the inspectors to find defects." In this way, Nathan confronted the problem without attacking Chad.

Brainstorm and Gather Information

Brainstorming is a process used for developing and sharing ideas and information. It is a technique often used in group problem solving. When a group brainstorms, each person comes up with an idea or suggestion. One member records all the ideas regardless of whether they seem workable. Do not judge or discuss the ideas at this time. Some ideas may lead to other ideas. The group should come up with many different ideas to solve a problem.

Later, the group discusses these ideas, eliminating some and adding others. Through this process of elimination, the group makes a final choice. The more ideas generated, the more able a group is to find alternative solutions to a problem. Brainstorming works because a group has a pool of ideas and can choose those that seem best.

Use the Decision-Making Process

Another method that a group can use effectively to solve a problem is the decision-making process covered in Chapter 3. You will find it helpful to review this process to see how it can relate to problem solving. Using this process is an excellent method for solving problems at work.

The first step in the decision-making process is to identify and face the problem. List all the facts. Know who and what are involved. Consider all the alternatives and the pros and cons of each selection. Choose the one you think will best solve the problem. After the solution is implemented, evaluate and review it to be sure it is working. Revise the solution as necessary to better solve the problem.

Prioritize Issues

When more than one issue is causing a problem, a list should be formed. Then issues can be prioritized, or listed from the most important to the least important. In that way, you identify and attack the biggest problems, rather than wasting time on smaller ones. Solutions can also be prioritized. They can be listed in priority from most likely to work to least likely to work.

Utilize Charts and Graphs

Through the use of charts and graphs, statistics are more meaningful and problems can be identified more readily, 8-6. Trends and patterns are easier to spot, too. The group can visually see where the problem lies or what needs to be done to solve it.

Use Creative-Thinking Skills

Creative thinking is the ability to come up with something new—from an old way of doing things to a better way. Creative thinking involves taking a creative idea and using it to bring about change. Often the result is a more productive outcome. Good creative-thinking skills help individuals be successful team members.

Creative-thinking skills help groups or teams arrive at answers to many problems. Creative thinking allows group members the freedom to make changes when solving problems. Using creative-thinking skills can help a group figure out a problem or plan a project. Important factors that promote creative thinking include the following techniques.

Provide a Creative Climate

The climate at work should promote creativity. Employees should be able to use some of their ideas on the job. Employers should provide opportunities to solve problems in new or different ways. This motivates employees to improve their performance. An environment that values creativity helps employers solve work problems and develop new ideas.

Joe, Nazar, and Tara work in the produce section of a grocery store. The three employees would like to give food demonstrations

8-6 Charts and graphs are especially effective in presenting complex business information.

once a week to customers. They want to provide information on less common fruits and vegetables and show various ways to prepare them. Mr. Bough, the store manager, is enthusiastic about their idea. He thinks their idea might work in other departments, too.

In this example, a creative climate exists. The workers work together as a group. Employees feel free to be creative and develop new ideas. The store welcomes suggestions from employees. Management listens to workers' ideas and respects them.

Employees are given time to think about a task and recommend answers. An employer might suggest that various groups schedule time to meet and discuss ideas. For instance, store employees may start making plans for the holiday open house several months in advance.

Know Where to Find Ideas

What people, places, or things help you develop ideas? Perhaps you need to look in books and magazines. Maybe you get inspired when with other creative people or, perhaps, when working alone. Know what helps you generate your best ideas.

Whenever José needs ideas, he asks his father for suggestions. José recently spent two days trying to come up with an idea for a class woodworking project. He sat, thought, and looked at magazines. He could not think of an idea, so José talked to his father. His father suggested they browse through a furniture store. That was just the inspiration José needed. At the furniture store he saw a set of bookends that he really liked. He decided he could make a similar design for his project.

Network

Networking means exchanging ideas and information with others who share your interests. You can network with many people, not only family and friends. Networking is useful for sharing ideas within a company or organization. As you talk with people, they will pass

the word to others. Information travels from person to person. Sometimes you network with people from outside your company or organization who share your concerns and interests. This is a way to get ideas for solving problems.

Many people have successfully used networking to find a job. After graduation, you will probably want to work in a certain field. You might call people you know and ask them for ideas of where you might find a job, 8-7. Better yet, you might call people who work in the field that interests you and ask about job openings. They might offer names of other people to contact or new places to look for work.

Remove Obstacles to Creativity

Various conditions or circumstances prevent creative ideas from being suggested. For instance, some people will not try new ideas or ways of doing things for fear of failing. They should try to view their mistakes and errors as opportunities for learning. Risk-taking is a part of many new

8-7 Networking is an excellent way to find job leads.

and innovative ideas. A certain amount of risk-taking is necessary for solving problems.

Failing to understand the strengths and weaknesses of coworkers can limit creativity. Teamwork requires each member to know the strengths and weaknesses of others. In this way, groups can take advantage of each member's strengths.

Some people have narrow vision. When people fail to see the whole picture, they see only a small part of a problem. This limits the number of possible solutions to the problem. They think they have the best and only solution. One person with narrow vision in a group can limit the creativity of the entire group.

Judy is in charge of sending reports from several departments to her company's main office each month. Judy's narrow vision limits her to focus only on her task of delivering the reports on time. Her solution to this problem is to request the reports a week before they are due. However, she does not see the big picture that includes the problem of preparing the reports in each department. She does not realize one of the department heads must wait for sales figures. He cannot have his report ready a week early. By failing to consider others, Judy has caused problems for herself.

Being creative in an organization provides new ways to solve problems. The work environment should encourage creativity. It should also promote new ideas. Creative solutions to problems help companies and organizations achieve their goals.

Communicate Constructively

When disagreements arise, it may be necessary to use constructive communication techniques. These methods bring the reasons for the disagreement into the open. By discussing the situation in an orderly manner, a solution may be worked out.

In constructive communications, the issues or the problems are calmly discussed. Facts are given to persuade others to your way of thinking. Those with opposing views are not attacked verbally—no unkind personal remarks are made. Discussion centers only on the differences concerning the issues. The various ways of solving the problem are discussed.

Communicating constructively helps to clear the air and may even help improve group relations. Regardless of the outcome, discussions should end with each person feeling good about himself or herself. See 8-8.

Give and Receive Feedback

Giving and receiving feedback is part of teamwork. As group members listen and respond to each other, they provide feedback.

Talbots

8-8 *In the workplace, each employee must recognize and practice appropriate behavior. Coworkers must be able to interact easily and successfully.*

Feedback might provide support or approval. Sometimes team members need to provide feedback to promote changes in an employee's behavior. Using feedback provides information about how well a task was completed. Feedback can provide praise and recognition for outstanding work. This type of feedback can help employees understand how their roles and activities fit into an organization's overall plan.

Learn to Compromise

The best way to handle many problems is with a compromise. A **compromise** is an agreement reached when each person gives in a little. With a compromise, there are no winners or losers. Instead, the solution satisfies everyone. You must be willing to compromise and adapt to changing situations.

Working together in a team helps groups solve problems and make decisions. As stated earlier, teammates must be willing to share ideas and cooperate with one another to reach the group's goals. New ways to solve problems evolve when people use good teamwork skills and problem-solving skills.

Resolve Conflict

Sometimes disagreements become intense enough to cause conflict. **Conflict** is a hostile situation resulting from opposing views. Resolving a conflict requires more effort than simply solving a problem. All aspects of the matter must be addressed to permanently settle the issue as well as the anger.

One method of conflict resolution is negotiation. *Negotiation* is the process of give and take between two or more sides needing a solution to a central problem. It is a type of bargaining that involves persuasion and compromise. Negotiation occurs all the time—between parents and children, husbands and wives, workers and employers, and even between nations. It can be relatively cooperative, as it is when both sides seek a solution that is mutually beneficial. This is often called a "win-win" situation, or cooperative bargaining.

On the other hand, negotiation efforts can be confrontational, as when each side tries to win at the expense of the other. This is commonly called a "win-lose" situation. It cannot be considered a resolution since it usually causes more conflict.

Another way to resolve conflicts is through mediation. In **mediation,** opposing sides are brought together by a neutral person to discuss a fair settlement to the dispute. The mediator helps both sides identify the source of the conflict and possible solutions. Through help from the mediator, the opposing parties discuss and design a solution themselves.

A **stalemate** is a standoff during which no solution satisfies the disputing parties. In this case, neither side can prevail in the conflict, no matter how hard it tries. Often parties must reach a stalemate before they are willing to end their dispute.

The most formal type of conflict resolution is arbitration. *Arbitration* is the process of settling a dispute by a neutral person whose decision is binding on all sides. Arbitration is a step taken after both negotiation and mediation have failed. It is the most official type of conflict resolution. Arbitration sometimes involves a judge's ruling or a legally binding contract.

◆ Leadership Skills

In addition to group-effectiveness skills, leadership skills are important in the workplace. Leadership skills help everyone work together more successfully to meet objectives.

A **leader** is any person who plans, directs, or guides the activities of others toward a common goal. Such a person is demonstrating **leadership skills.** By using these skills, a person encourages others to carry out responsibilities and accomplish its goals.

Types of Leaders

The workplace needs good leaders at all levels—not only in top management. A person may influence his or her work group to do a specific job well. An employee may motivate a coworker to improve his or her individual performance. Thousands of employees may be inspired by the company president to outperform the competition. These cases demonstrate the three basic types of leadership—appointed, shared, or volunteer.

Appointed Leaders

Designating a leader to be in charge is known as **appointed leadership.** This type of leader has the power and responsibility to make decisions that influence his or her group or organization. Examples of people in appointed leadership positions are company presidents, managers, and supervisors. Other appointed leaders in the workplace include project directors and engineering managers who oversee separate departments, 8-9. At school, the appointed leaders are the elected officers of organizations, such as the president or secretary of a school club.

Shared Leadership

In a shared leadership role, more than one person makes decisions. One example is various department teams or committees formed to analyze problems and find solutions. No single person makes all the decisions. Everyone works to move the company toward desired goals. When decisions are made by those most familiar with the problem, better plans often result.

Clubs and associations also have many people sharing leadership. An appointed leader may ask a committee to handle an assignment and make a decision for the group. Individuals or a group may make decisions without seeking the president's approval—such as the luncheon menu chosen by the food committee. The leader may simply want to know that the committee has the meal planned.

Within the work teams, two or more individuals may be selected to "lead" the group. At other times, various team members may rotate the role of leader, depending on the scope of the job and the expertise of the individuals.

Volunteer Leaders

In **volunteer leadership,** a group member asks to be in charge of a committee or function. For example, a member who has publicity experience may volunteer to handle the public relations committee. Another member may assume leadership for another committee. Parents often volunteer to coach Little League baseball teams. All are volunteer leaders.

What Is a Good Leader?

Many people have a natural ability to lead other people into action. Those who are not born leaders can learn leadership skills. They

8-9 Leadership responsibilities are appointed to various department managers in business settings.

can learn to organize, motivate, and provide direction. Good leaders also have the following important characteristics.

Leaders Are Good Decision Makers

Perhaps one of the most important skills of a leader is the ability to make good decisions. A leader recognizes the needs of the organization and its members and acts to meet those needs.

Good leaders can quickly analyze and define a problem. Leaders can look at various alternatives and see the pros and cons of each option. This helps leaders decide the best solution.

Leaders Have Good Communication Skills

Successful leaders are able to communicate decisions to a group through effective speaking and writing. Good leaders are also good listeners who hear the concerns of individual group members.

A leader's communication skills should encourage active two-way participation. Effective leaders must be alert and sensitive to the feelings of others. For instance, a student council president might ask Joe to serve as a classroom greeter for an open house at the school. Joe asks to change to the physics lab because his award-winning project is on display there. In addition, his teacher has asked him to demonstrate his project to parents. The student council president agrees that Joe should be a greeter in the physics lab and changes Joe's assignment.

Leaders Can Motivate and Persuade

Good leaders present convincing arguments that motivate and persuade others to take action, 8-10. They come to meetings prepared to discuss key issues. Good leaders are persuasive and do not clash with members. They know how to get the best performance from the members. They motivate even reluctant members to become involved.

Leaders Have Self-Confidence

Leaders believe in themselves and in their ability to lead. They appear "in control" by what they say and do. Their leadership can also inspire confidence among the members of the group.

Consider the case of the Spanish club's interesting guest speaker who talked for 15 minutes past the time limit. The program announcer did not know how to successfully stop the speech but Jim, the club president, did. He walked to the front of the room near the speaker, waited two minutes, and then moved to the microphone. Jim apologized for interrupting, thanked the speaker for an excellent program, and explained that cars were waiting to take students home. He invited the speaker to return for another program and club members agreed with a loud cheer. Jim realized the need for leadership to tactfully bring the program to a close.

Leaders Know How to Delegate Responsibility

Good leaders must be able to do all the work themselves, yet smart enough to know

Family, Career, and Community Leaders of America

8-10 These FCCLA leaders know how to motivate fellow members into action.

how to get others to help. They must decide which group members are suited to various types of jobs by the skills each possesses. Good leaders use this knowledge to *delegate*, or assign, responsibilities to others.

Leaders Get Along Well with Others

Good leaders work well with all types of personalities. They develop a *rapport,* or good relationship, with all the organization's members. Such leaders have the ability to guide and direct people while still retaining their respect.

Good Leaders Know the Job

In business or industry, good leaders often move up the ranks because they know their jobs well. They usually are productive, skilled workers. Others in the organization recognize their special abilities and look up to them. Often these people are appointed to leadership positions because of their in-depth understanding of work.

◆ Getting Involved in School Clubs and Organizations

Not everyone is a born leader, but there are things you can do to help develop group effectiveness and leadership skills. Joining clubs and organizations is a good way to learn these skills. It is also a good way to have fun, spend free time productively, and enjoy a feeling of belonging, 8-11.

Most schools and communities have numerous clubs and organizations. Many classes have special interest clubs that allow students to pursue their interests. For instance, computer clubs and math clubs help reinforce and expand the knowledge and information learned in the classroom. Many vocational programs in schools have student organizations that are related to future careers.

If you become involved in student clubs and organizations, you will gain valuable experience. As a club member, you will participate in

8-11 Joining a chemistry club is a smart move for students interested in pursuing a science-related career.

activities and group projects. You will work as a team member to meet the objectives of the organization. While working on group activities and using leadership skills, you will experience situations similar to what you might find on the job. The activities of student clubs and organizations generally focus on the following four areas:

◆ career development
◆ community service
◆ social activities
◆ fund-raising events

Career development activities help students expand their career-related knowledge and skills. Organizations may sponsor field trips to worksites and speakers from business and industry. Monthly meetings may focus on a career or professional development topic. Members might participate in job fairs or trade shows.

Community service activities include projects that help improve the school and community. Carrying out service projects shows club members the value of sharing time and talents. Projects that benefit the community range from delivering fruit baskets to shut-ins to picking up litter. Projects that benefit the school might include special programs with guest speakers or a clean-up project.

Social activities such as parties and picnics help club members get to know each other better and have fun. These events help teens learn to socialize in group settings.

Fund-raising activities help finance the work of organizations. Groups might raise money through car washes, candy sales, auctions, chili suppers, and other activities.

School Organizations and Future Careers

Many programs in school have organizations related to future careers. Whether you are considering a career in business, agriculture, human services, or other areas, these organizations can help you.

Through your studies and activities, you will have a better idea of what to expect in many career areas. Joining organizations can also provide you with opportunities to develop your group effectiveness and leadership skills. The student organizations listed below describe organizations related to future careers.

Family, Career, and Community Leaders of America (FCCLA)

This is a national organization for students enrolled in family and consumer sciences courses. It is the only student organization with the family as its focus. FCCLA activities focus on various youth concerns, including pregnancy, parenting, family relationships, substance abuse, peer pressure, teen violence, and career exploration. The organization focuses on the multiple roles of family member, wage earner, and community leader through activities that build character, creative thinking, and practical knowledge, 8-12.

Business Professionals of America (BPA)

Students enrolled in business and office programs might join BPA. Its purpose is to help students succeed as members of the business workforce and promote leadership abilities. BPA brings business, industry, and education together as a force for the growth of youth. Students are also encouraged to network with professionals across the nation and help their communities through good-works projects.

DECA–An Association of Marketing Students

Students preparing for entrepreneurial, marketing, or management careers can join DECA. Through program activities and competitive events, students develop career skills

Family, Career, and Community Leaders of America

8-12 FCCLA members are preparing gift bags to give to needy families during the holidays.

to use in their business and personal lives. The skills include career competence, leadership, social and business etiquette, civic responsibility and ethical behavior. (The organization began in 1946 as the Distributive Education Clubs of America.)

Future Business Leaders of America–Phi Beta Lambda (FBLA-PBL)

Students interested in business and business-related fields can join FBLA-PBL. This organization helps students explore careers in business through on-site visits to companies and guest speakers at meetings. The organization also helps students in their transition from school to work. See 8-13. Chapters are available for middle school, high school and postsecondary students.

Health Occupations Students of America (HOSA)

HOSA has a two-fold mission: to promote career opportunities in the health care industry and to enhance the delivery of quality health care to all people. Membership is open to secondary, postsecondary, collegiate, and adult students enrolled in health occupations education. Students learn the technical and people-oriented skills needed to become valuable members of the health care team.

National FFA Organization

FFA prepares members for careers and leadership in the science, business, and technology of agriculture. The organization is committed to helping youth develop their potential for leadership, personal growth, and career success through agricultural education. This organization has chapters throughout the United States and its territories. (The organization was established in 1928 as the Future Farmers of America.)

Skills USA–VICA

Preparing for leadership in the world of work is the organization's motto and chief goal. Membership is open to high school and college students, as well as professional members,

Future Business Leaders of America

8-13 Future Business Leaders of America members participate in activities related to careers in business.

enrolled in technical, skilled, and service occupations, including health occupations. The organization emphasizes leadership, occupational, and teamwork skills. (The organization's original name was the Vocational Industrial Club of America.)

Technology Student Association (TSA)

TSA is the only student organization devoted exclusively to the needs of technology education students. Membership is open to students who are taking or have taken technology education courses. TSA helps elementary, middle, and high school students in 47 states develop personal and career skills. Activities include competitive events, leadership opportunities, and individual and group projects.

School Organizations and Leadership

Working together in an organization helps club members learn skills needed in the workforce. Being a club leader helps prepare teens for future roles. Students who are leaders in organizations have some of the same responsibilities as leaders in the workforce. These include the following activities:

◆ ***Learn to direct activities.*** Leaders must be able to guide the activities of members through completion of their projects and activities. This requires skills in organization and time management. It also requires insight into recognizing potential problems and finding quick solutions.

◆ ***Learn to work toward goals.*** Organizations and clubs usually have one or more goals for the year. Leaders direct the work of the organization toward completion of these goals. An organization might choose a goal such as improving lifestyle habits. Leaders and members plan activities for the year centered on this goal. These might include a fun run, drug awareness program, and driver safety practices. Every member

needs to work with others to achieve the goals of an organization.

◆ ***Learn to involve members.*** The leaders or club officers need to involve their members. It is important that everyone has a job and responsibility within the group. Leaders can delegate jobs to others. Committees often are formed to do various jobs. The club needs enough projects and activities to involve all members.

◆ ***Learn to conduct meetings.*** Most clubs and organizations conduct meetings in a similar way—by using **parliamentary procedure.** These guidelines help them conduct orderly meetings to reach decisions and conduct business fairly. As a club member, you need to understand rules of parliamentary procedure. A few basic rules of parliamentary procedure used for business meetings are listed in 8-14.

The Business Meeting

Most organizations follow the *Robert's Rules of Order* for conducting business. This recognized book on parliamentary procedure is the basis for conducting formal meetings. The most common order of a business meeting is outlined in 8-15 on the next page.

Rules of Parliamentary Procedure
◆ Only one motion is discussed at a time.
◆ A motion must receive a "second" before it can be discussed and voted upon.
◆ Each member making a motion must stand and be recognized by the president.
◆ Members should sit quietly, listen, and participate in the proceedings.

8-14 Meetings using parliamentary procedure are orderly and accomplish a great deal of business.

Parts of a Formal Business Meeting
Call to order
Roll call
Reading and approval of the minutes
Reports of officers
Standing committee reports
Special committee reports
Unfinished business
New business
Program
Announcements
Adjournment

8-15 Most business meetings follow this order.

Prior to the meeting, members usually receive an agenda. The agenda lists a schedule for the meeting and any special business matters. Sometimes members sign an attendance sheet to keep on file. The secretary counts members in attendance to determine if a quorum is present. *Quorum* means that either a majority of members or the number required by the group rules is present. If a quorum is not present, the group cannot conduct business.

Call to Order

The president, or presiding officer, usually calls the meeting to order. He or she does this by tapping a desk or table with a gavel and saying, "The meeting will now come to order."

Reading and Approval of the Minutes

Then the president says, "The secretary will now read the minutes." The secretary stands and reads a business summary of the last meeting, which highlights any decisions that were made.

The president then asks, "Are there any additions or corrections to the minutes?" Any member may stand and add information or corrections to the minutes. If there are no corrections, the president says, "The minutes stand approved as read." If there are corrections, the president says, "The minutes stand approved as corrected." The secretary files the minutes for reference in case a question comes up later.

Reports of Officers

The president then asks for reports any officers may have. The treasurer makes a report at all meetings to provide information on the financial status of the group. The report includes the money collected by the group, the expenses, and the balance in the group's account. After the report, the president says, "The treasurer's report will be placed on file for audit." This means that the treasurer will file the financial record. At the end of the club year, an appointed committee or outside agency will *audit,* or check, all records to be sure they are accurate. After the treasurer's report, other officers give any reports they may have.

Standing Committee Reports

The next order of business is to call on the president of each standing committee for a report. *Standing committees* are permanent committees in the organization. They function to carry out the ongoing affairs of the group. A membership committee, program committee, or hospitality committee are examples.

Special Committee Reports

The president may appoint special committees to accomplish *special assignments,* 8-16. Examples of special committees are a Valentine's Day dance committee, a children's toy drive committee, or a park clean-up committee. The president asks the president of each committee to summarize their progress. These committees give a report at each meeting until they accomplish their work. After preparing a final report, they disband.

Unfinished Business

After all the committees have reported, the president asks, "Is there any unfinished business?" This might include reports requested for

8-16 Committees meet informally to conduct their special business and then report back to the larger group.

the next meeting or other topics needing further study. If a topic was introduced at the previous meeting and the group is not prepared to handle it at this meeting, they can *table* it. Tabling postpones a topic for discussion or voting until another meeting.

Juan may raise his hand and say, "At our last meeting, the program committee asked for suggestions for speakers on weight control." Judy raises her hand. The president recognizes her by calling her name. Judy rises and says, "Mrs. Green from the nutrition department told me that she could come on Wednesday, the 24th, and give the program."

The president then might say, "Do I hear a motion to invite Mrs. Green to speak?" A *motion* is a proposal for a group to take action. Melody rises and the president recognizes her by saying her name. Melody replies, "I move that we invite Mrs. Green to come and speak on weight control."

A member who agrees with the proposal *seconds* the motion. This member stays seated and says, "I second the motion." The president asks, "Is there any discussion?" At this time a motion is *on the floor,* and comments pro and con can be expressed. If you have information that the group needs to hear to make an informed vote, this is the last opportunity.

After discussion, the president says, "All those in favor, raise your right hand." Members respond and the secretary counts the vote. The president will then say, "Those opposed, raise your right hand." Members who have not voted may respond, and the secretary tallies the vote. If a *majority,* or more than half the members present, vote in favor of the motion, the president says, "The motion passes" or "the motion carries."

New Business

The president now asks, "Is there any new business?" New business includes future group events, dates for future activities, or new matters that one or more members feel need to be addressed by the group. After discussion, it may be necessary to table new business for further action at the next meeting.

Program

At this time the meeting is turned over to the program chairperson, who stands and introduces the speaker and the meeting's program. Afterwards, members are asked to voice any questions, which the speaker then answers. The program portion of the meeting concludes with the presentation of a token of appreciation to the speaker. The program chairperson then briefly announces the program for the next meeting and turns the meeting over to the president.

Announcements

The president then asks if there are any announcements to make, such as the date and time of the next meeting and any upcoming special events. Members may note other items of interest to the group, 8-17.

Adjournment

After announcements, the president usually asks for a motion to *adjourn,* or close the meeting. A member says, "I move that the meeting be adjourned." Another member seconds the motion. This motion is not debatable. The president will then say, "All those in favor, say yes. (Members respond.) All those opposed, say no. (Members respond.) The meeting is adjourned." With a rap of the gavel, the president adjourns the meeting.

Participating in extracurricular activities will give you many of the same types of experiences as you will have on the job. You will gain an insight into job responsibility and working with others. As you practice making good decisions at school and at home, you gain skill in being a good team member and a good leader.

◆ Am I Ready?

Part II of this text has been concerned with readiness skills for the workplace. Being a productive worker requires certain understandings of how to function within various systems. You are already familiar with a number of systems. For example, you have learned

8-17 Special awards may be given to members during the announcement segment of a business meeting. If you have prepared adequately, you will feel confident stepping into the world of work.

how to function within your family as well as your school. Both of these are social systems requiring certain interrelationships in order for harmony and order to exist.

You are a part of other social systems, too, such as a neighborhood and an ethnic group. Geography defines your community, while beliefs and customs define your ethnic group. You play a role in both these systems. Within school, perhaps you are a member of certain groups or clubs. These are smaller subsystems within the larger social system of the school.

A **system** is an independent group of parts or members forming a unified whole. The system has a goal or purpose to which all parts contribute. Besides social systems, there are organizational and technological systems. The Internet, television broadcasting, and the computer are examples of technological systems. Examples of organizational systems include the federal government, the human body, and the banking system. See 8-18.

Stop and think of all the systems that affect or involve you. Sometimes systems are very large, with more parts than you can see or touch—such as the solar system. Sometimes systems are very small, like a single cell. These examples help to clarify what is meant by terms such as *systems thinking* or *a systems approach*. They mean "looking at a broad picture and examining all related parts."

Your future employer will add more systems to your life. It will be an organizational system in which you have a role (a job) that contributes to the company goal or purpose. Your employer will be a social system, containing employees with whom you interact in work and nonwork settings. Finally, your

8-18 *The type of money used is just one way in which banking systems differ from country to country.*

employer will possess technological systems that are involved with the work you and your coworkers do.

Thinking about systems and their interconnections can help you analyze problems and concerns in everyday life. You can see all the related parts—more of the big picture. By seeing how all the pieces fit together, you can better manage the events that affect your daily life. In this course, you have studied how preparedness for work relates to employability. Do you see the connections between career preparation and workplace success?

Summary

Group members have many roles and responsibilities. To be effective in a group, you must have good interpersonal skills. You must know how to work well with others and know what to do when problems arise. Problem-solving and creative-thinking skills help people work as a team to meet group objectives.

Leadership skills are useful in every occupation at all job levels. Good leaders share many common qualities. Good leaders know how to make decisions and delegate responsibility. They know how to work with individuals and groups to accomplish goals.

School organizations and clubs can help you develop leadership skills. Most schools have many extracurricular activities that you can join. These activities provide opportunities to develop leadership skills and learn about various careers. Becoming involved in leadership roles while in school can make you be a better worker.

As a productive worker you need to function within many systems. Each of these connecting systems must work together for the good of all.

To Review

1. List four interpersonal skills necessary for getting along with others.

2. Discuss how having a sense of humor helps you in your work relationships.

3. What is wrong with stereotyping and having prejudices?

4. Why is the use of teams considered very important in the workplace?

5. Describe one step in the decision-making process that can help a group solve a problem.

6. Name and describe one creative-thinking skill that can help a group solve a problem.

7. Why is it necessary for some organizations and companies to share leadership responsibilities?

8. List five characteristics of good leaders.

9. List three ways that involvement in student organizations helps you learn leadership skills.

10. Name three student organizations that help develop leadership skills.

11. List the parts of a formal business meeting.

12. Name four systems that strongly affect who you are and explain their importance to your life.

To Do

1. Assume you need to improve the results of your club or organization. In a small group, brainstorm possible ideas. Select one method the group feels would work. List and discuss how you might use three interpersonal skills in reaching the group decision.

2. In small groups, identify a problem and try to solve it through the use of compromise. What was the reaction of those who compromised? Share individual reactions in a report to the class.

3. Try to identify a student who is a leader in your school. What qualities make that person a leader? What qualities does he or she lack? Summarize your findings.

4. With two or three other class members, write a script illustrating two or three good and poor leadership skills. With other group members, role-play one or more comparisons.

5. Interview a president or other officer of an organization. Find out his or her duties and the main purpose of the organization. Ask about recent group activities and plans for the future. Write a report summarizing your findings.

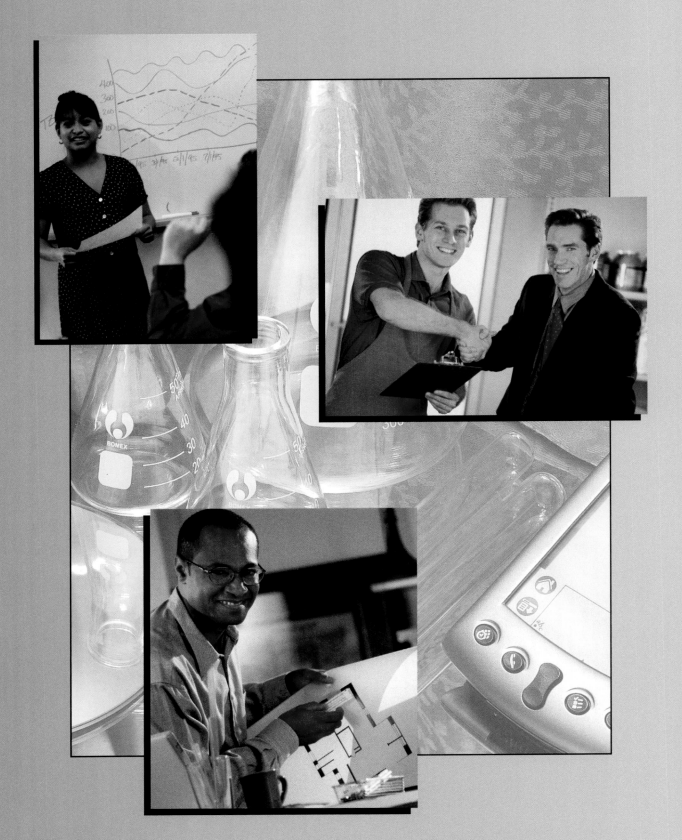

Part III
Achieving
Job
Success

9 ◆ The Job Search

After studying this chapter, you will be able to
- ◆ identify sources of job leads.
- ◆ prepare a personal data sheet.
- ◆ complete a personal resume.
- ◆ prepare a personal portfolio.
- ◆ write a letter of application.
- ◆ fill out a job application form.

Terms to Know

placement office	reference
employment agency	resume
Civil Service	portfolio
Commission	letter of application
personal data sheet	application form

One of the most important steps in your career will be the job search. Knowing where to look and how to get the job you want are important skills. Finding work that interests you and uses your skills should be your goal.

Job hunting is hard work, but it is easier if you have a plan, 9-1. The first step is to locate job openings. Next, you will need to organize your personal data for an interview. You will need to know how to prepare your resume and write a letter of application. You should also review information in your portfolio. Finally, you will need to know how to interview for a job opening. This chapter will provide you with the techniques and information to help you prepare for your job search.

◆ Sources of Job Leads

To locate job openings, you will need to find employers who need workers with your skills. Prospective employers can be found through a variety of sources. Family and friends, want ads, placement offices, employment agencies, and other sources can provide

9-1 You must plan ahead to get a satisfying career.

158

important job leads. Use as many kinds of leads as you can. The more job openings you can find, the better will be your chance of finding a job you really like.

Family and Friends

If you want a job in your own community, talk to family members, relatives, and friends. They can be some of your best sources for job leads. They may know of employers who need a person with your skills and abilities. For instance, you might ask people in your house of worship if they know of possible job openings.

If you belong to organizations, check with fellow members. Tell them you are looking for work. They may know employers who are hiring people with your skills. Checking personal contacts is one of the best ways to learn about openings. Through networking, you can often hear about employment opportunities.

Newspaper Want Ads

Want ads in newspapers are a common source of information about available jobs, 9-2. The Sunday editions of newspapers generally have more ads than daily papers. By reading ads, you can see the types of work available in the job market. Want ads often list skills and training needed to qualify for a job. They might list salaries being paid. Some want ads list jobs available in other parts of the United States. If you do not mind moving, one of these jobs may interest you. Some people need to look in a different area of the country to find the right job.

Often, you will find jobs listed under different headings. Some possible headings are *administrative, computers, education, sales,* and *technical.* Look through all the headings because jobs that interest you or use your talents might appear under a different heading. Many ads contain abbreviated words that may be unfamiliar to you. Terms often used in want ads are shown in 9-3, on the next page.

If you are looking for short-term employment, you can advertise your availability for a certain job in the newspaper. You might run an ad that says, "Will babysit in your home," or, "Student looking for lawn-mowing jobs." List your phone number or address. There is generally a cost for running an ad in the paper.

Placement Offices

Most postsecondary schools and colleges have **placement offices.** These offices receive information about job openings, or listings, from employers. When students register with the placement office, they indicate the type of job they are seeking. The placement office notifies them when there is a listing for that type of job. Students can then interview for the job. Some

9-2 Classified advertisements in newspapers give helpful information about job openings and skills needed. Sometimes the ad states the beginning salary.

Abbreviations Used in Want Ads			
admin	administration	ind	industrial
appt	appointment	med	medical
avail	available	mfr	manufacture
BA	Bachelor of Arts degree	mo	month
BS	Bachelor of Science degree	nego	negotiate
bldg	building	ofc	office
co	company	PC	personal computer abilities
const	construction	pd	paid
dept	department	ref	references
EOE	Equal Opportunity Employer	req	required
etc	and so on	sal	salary
eves	evenings	secy	secretary
exc	excellent	temp	temporary
exp	experience	w/	with
grad	graduate	wk	week
hr	hour	wpm	words per minute
HS	high school	yr	year
inc	include, including		

9-3 Becoming familiar with abbreviations used in want ads will help you understand the ads better.

placement offices maintain files of job listings. Check these files frequently for new listings.

Community organizations, such as the YMCA or the Salvation Army, may have job placement services. Workers' unions sometimes have placement services, too. Investigate and use the many sources available to you.

Employment Agencies

An **employment agency** is a place where you can find out about job opportunities. Businesses and industries often list jobs they have available with an employment agency. When you are looking for work, you can list your name with an agency. The employment agency is like a clearinghouse for available jobs and job hunters. The two types of employment agencies are public and private.

Public employment agencies are supported by the government. These offices are also

called *state employment services*. You will find these offices located in most large towns and cities. Look for *Employment Office* or *Employment Service* under the name of your state in the telephone directory. Also look under the heading *United States Government* for federal offices. If there is a Civil Service Commission in your area, it will be listed there. The **Civil Service Commission** is the federal agency that hires people who work for the U.S. government, 9-4. These government agencies do not charge a fee for their services.

Private employment agencies are in business to help people find jobs. They receive a fee from either the employer or the applicant. Fees vary with different agencies. Some agencies charge the applicant one week's pay from the new job. Others charge thousands of dollars. If you are using a private employment agency, read the contract carefully before signing any papers.

9-4 To be hired as a government employee, such as a postal clerk, you must pass an exam by the Civil Service Commission.

Other Sources

There are a number of other places where you can check for information about jobs. Sometimes a position available will be as obvious as a "help wanted" sign in a window of a business. Other job openings will not be this easy to locate. At times you may need to do more in-depth searching.

There may be a job fair or career expo in your community. These are usually held at a hotel, university, or convention center. Typically, dozens of employers set up booths or tables and have representatives available to talk to job seekers about their company and its needs. There are career possibilities from entry-level positions to high-tech specialists.

This is a good time to learn about different companies and their hiring needs. Some of the job fairs are specialized, such as fairs for health care positions only. Find out if the event covers your area of interest. Come prepared with background information and dress presentably. Don't go expecting to get an immediate interview. However, bring your resume and other information if, in fact, you do get an on-site interview.

Some communities have job service offices providing information about employers in the immediate area. Your library will have many resources about job hunting and specific careers, 9-5. Often local radio stations announce job openings. Look for "help wanted" ads on community bulletin boards. You may find help wanted ads posted in supermarkets, banks, and libraries.

Check the classified pages in your telephone directory for names of firms that might hire workers in your area of expertise or interest. Call the local chamber of commerce for any new businesses that may be moving into town. New businesses generally hire from the community even if they bring in management personnel. Call these businesses and ask what jobs will be open and when they will begin hiring.

There are many job searching and recruiting pages on the Internet, but not all of them are legitimate. A reliable source of job information is

9-5 Placement offices and libraries have resource materials about various job opportunities.

employers themselves. Go to the Web sites of companies and other employers, where many list job openings and government databases. Also look for links to newspaper help-wanted ads and job banks. It is well worth your while to check the different career-related sites and find several that are appropriate for you. Many offer interactive e-mail links so you can personalize your job search in a matter of seconds.

◆ Getting Ready to Apply for a Job

Before you contact an employer, you need to collect information about yourself. This information goes into a personal data sheet that will help you prepare your resume and fill out job applications. You will also need to have a social security number.

Your Social Security Card

Chances are, you already have a *social security number* that you received when you were young. Can you find your card and do you know your number? If you do not have a number, contact the social security office or your local post office for an application blank. You must present a social security card to your employer when you are hired.

Social security is like insurance. When you work, your employer deducts a certain percentage of your income for payment to the Social Security Administration. Your employer must also make a contribution for you. After you retire or if you become disabled, the total of your account and the number of periods that you worked determine your benefits.

Be sure to keep your social security card in a safe place and treat your social security number as private information. Your new employer will need your social security number to record your earnings and paid taxes to the Internal Revenue Service. Before giving your number out for any other reason, always ask if it is absolutely necessary to reveal it.

Personal Data Sheet

A **personal data sheet** will provide a quick reference to all the important facts about you. It is not given to others, but serves as a ready reference for preparing a resume and filling out forms. In addition to your address, list your date and place of birth. Also list your e-mail address, if you have one. See 9-6.

Your personal data should include information about your education. Where did you go to elementary, middle or junior high, and high school? When did you attend? Record names, addresses, and the years you spent at each school. List the program of study you followed. This might be general, business, tech prep, or college prep. Also include any higher education or special training you have received. Note the years for all schools and special programs you have attended. List your major area of study and any degrees received. State your letter or grade point average from your latest school year.

Brian Kinder

9-6 Complete a personal data sheet before making any employer contacts. This helps you gather and organize all your important personal information.

Your personal data sheet should include a list of your work experiences. Write down any part-time jobs, such as babysitting, lawn-mowing, or newspaper delivery. List any full-time jobs you may have had. For each job you list, write down the name of your employer, the address and phone number, and your supervisor's name.

Record special skills you have. List types of work you do well, especially those related to jobs for which you might apply. For instance, if you were applying for the job of office assistant, you would list word processing skills. Note the business machines you can operate and any other languages you speak.

List organizations and activities in which you have been involved. Perhaps you belonged to 4-H or have been active at your place of worship. Have you participated in community projects, such as bike-a-thons or other fund-raisers for charity?

List honors or awards you have received. Have you held any club offices? This indicates to an employer that you have leadership ability. Include your hobbies and interests, especially those that are job related. Keeping a record of all these facts will provide easy reference when you fill out a job application.

Last, write down the names and addresses of at least three individuals you could use as **references.** These are people who know you well and could give information regarding your character and abilities. Teachers, club advisers, and counselors are excellent people to use as references. Use their correct names, titles, addresses, and telephone numbers. It is important that you get permission from these people to serve as your references before giving their names to potential employers.

◆ Your Resume

Getting ready for your job search will also involve preparing a resume. A **resume** is a brief outline of your education, work experience, and other qualifications for work. When sending in your resume, be sure to include a letter of application. By looking over your resume, an employer can quickly see a summary of your background and experience. Much of the information you will use will come from your personal data sheet. A well-written resume can help you get a job interview.

Categories and Contents of Your Resume

When writing a resume, place your name, address, and phone number at the top of the page. Use headings to divide your resume into major categories. These usually include *Job Objective, Education, Work Experience, Honors and Activities, Special Skills and Interests,* and *References.* An example of a resume is shown in 9-7.

RYLAND WISNIESKI
125 Pearl Street
North Belt, VT 05007
(906) 536-1234

Employment Objective
A position assisting a chemist or utilizing my science skills
  in a chemistry laboratory.

Education
Graduating from West Fremont High School in May, 2004.
My courses include four years of science classes and three
  years of family and consumer sciences.

Work Experience
October, 2003 to present:
  Sales clerk, Arnold's Electric Company, Marriot, VT
September, 2002 to August, 2003:
  Customer Service, Deli Ice Cream Shop, Marriot, VT

Honors and Activities
First place winner in district science fair.
Coauthored article on nutritional balance for athletes in
  Science School News.
Member FCCLA. Chapter secretary, junior year; president,
  senior year.
President of Student Council during junior year.
Member of marching band for three years.

Interests
Soccer, reading, swimming.

References available upon request.

9-7 A resume provides a quick and easy way for an employer to learn more about the job applicant.

Job Objective

Describe the type of job you want with a brief phrase or two. It is better to say a "retail management position with XYZ Company" than to say "any job in your company." Focus on the type of position you are seeking. With the use of a computer, you can save your resume and modify the stated objective to match each job you pursue.

Education

List the schools you attended, summarizing the last school first. List dates of graduation or when you expect to graduate. You might list your grade average if you wish. List your area of study and any certificates or degrees received.

Work Experience

Describe any work experience, especially that relating to the position you are seeking. List the major responsibilities of your current and past jobs. Include community and volunteer work. If you served as a candy striper or helped organize a fund-raiser, include these experiences to show that you can handle responsibility.

Activities and Honors

List the organizations you have joined at school and in your community. This will help the employer get a clearer picture of your abilities and interests. Include any offices held or honors received.

Special Skills and Interests

Always mention your special skills. For instance, list any skills you have in operating computer software programs. List your hobbies, especially those relating to the job that you desire. For instance, list your hobby of saving postcards from hotels you have visited if you seek a job in the travel and tourism industry. A brief list of your special talents makes you appear to be a well-rounded individual.

References

Write "Available upon request" or similar words. By obtaining prior permission to use three or more people as references, you are ready to furnish their names to prospective employers. To respect the privacy of your references, provide information about them only when the employers request it.

Preparing Your Resume

A resume is not written in paragraph form and does not usually contain full sentences. For someone just entering the career world, a finished resume is generally only one page long. As you gain work experience, you may wish to add a second page.

After you have drafted your resume, have a friend, a teacher, or your parents check it for errors and readability. Make sure it is 100 percent correct in grammar, punctuation, and spelling. Before you submit it for a possible job, review it again.

Keep your resume current. It is easier to revise a resume as information changes than try to remember and add it later. An accurate, well-written resume is a valuable record that can be updated as you progress along your career path.

The same resume will not be appropriate for all the jobs you may seek at a given time. Use a computer to create your master resume and then tailor it for each position. Resume readers like to see action words. Use words such as *achieved, managed, supervised, accomplished, designed,* and *created* instead of less descriptive words such as *did* or *used.* If you are sending it by mail, print the resume on good quality white or ivory paper.

Electronic Resumes

When pursuing a new position, it is best to find out whether the employer prefers e-mail resumes or those sent by mail. The growing preference is for the e-mailed version. That resume can be easily copied to an employer's database of applicants.

To prepare an e-mail resume, you do not need to write a new one. You will simply alter your prepared resume's format so that it is compatible for e-mail. First, make a copy of your resume in plain text, or "text only." This removes all design features such as bold face and indents. Name this version *resume.txt* and have the computer save it as text only.

Adjust the *resume.txt* file for easier readability as e-mail. Use all capital letters for the section headings. Make the lines shorter, no more than 65 characters long. After the last word that fits on a line, hit the *enter* key to force words to the next line. You can indent lines by using the space bar.

When finished, e-mail a copy to yourself and a friend. This exercise will let you see how your e-mailed resume looks to recipients. If formatting problems still exist, correct them before sending your resume out to employers.

When responding to a job ad or posting, use the specified job title or reference number on the *subject* line. Include a cover letter with the resume in a single e-mail message. You still need to explain why you are the perfect candidate for the job. Ask if a printed copy of your resume is needed for the record. If so, you can send the formatted version that was designed originally. Make sure you follow all the instructions given in each case for applying via e-mail. Not doing so will guarantee your resume goes to the reject pile.

To take full advantage of the Internet, you may want to consider posting your resume in a databank. Employers looking for your qualifications may see it. Before using an online database service, recognize that your resume will become a public document. Also, find out how the service operates by asking the following questions: Who has access to the database? Can you update your resume at no cost? Will resumes that are not updated be automatically deleted within a certain period? As a general rule, resumes are deleted after three months if they are not updated.

The Internet has permanently changed the way in which job seekers can find new positions. Using the Internet to respond to a specific employer or help-wanted ad is fast, inexpensive, convenient, and often effective for both sides. However, posting your resume on Internet databases may bring no job offers at all. Making personal contacts with employers and following other sources of job leads are still the best ways to find work.

◆ Your Portfolio

A professional portfolio can help you find a job. If you want to go into business or have your own business, a portfolio can help you get new clients. A **portfolio** is a collection of information that highlights your special expertise and achievements. It emphasizes your skills, talents, and knowledge.

Start building your portfolio by collecting items that you create. This can include work samples and other materials that emphasize your accomplishments. Organize your material logically and place it in an attractive binder.

Your portfolio should include your personal resume. Include samples of your work. Examples of successfully completed work show your talents. An example of your work might be fashion designs you drew for a class. If you have a lawn care service, you might include photos of a well-groomed yard with attractive, blooming flowers and shrubs. Newspaper articles and photos highlighting your achievements make important additions to your portfolio.

Keep your portfolio looking attractive and professional. It should not include more material than potential employers and clients are willing to review. Add items as you accomplish new goals or reach new achievements, and eliminate less significant items.

The following checklist includes items you might want in your portfolio:

◆ samples of your work
◆ letters of commendation
◆ news articles about you, with your name highlighted
◆ reports of special projects you completed

◆ Letter of Application

To apply for some jobs, you will need to write a **letter of application** or cover letter. You might write this letter to the president or owner, if it is a small organization. In larger companies, the letter is usually written to the personnel manager or department manager. This letter helps you introduce yourself and get the employer interested in your qualifications. Ultimately, your goal is to encourage the employer to invite you for an interview.

Preparing Your Letter of Application

The letter of application should be a short business letter with three or four strong paragraphs. Keep it brief and to the point. Letters of application are often used in the following cases:
◆ to answer a newspaper advertisement
◆ to accompany a resume mailed to a prospective employer
◆ to respond to an employer's request for a letter of application

Use a computer to write the letter of application. Research the name, spelling, and title of the most appropriate person to receive your application. Print your letter of application on quality, standard-size white or ivory paper.

When writing a letter of application, follow the standard business style discussed in Chapter 5. Be sure to spell the employer's name correctly in the inside address and salutation.

The body of the letter will tell why you are writing. Be sure to include
◆ the title of the job you are seeking
◆ where you heard about the job opening
◆ your strengths, skills, and abilities that are suited to this job
◆ why you think you should be considered for the position
◆ when you are available to begin work
◆ a request for an interview

List your major accomplishments and provide enough information so the employer will want to interview you. If you are including a resume, be sure to mention this in your letter.

In the signature area, sign your name in ink above your printed name. An example of a letter of application is shown in 9-8. After you are finished, read your letter of application very carefully. Correct any errors and redo it if there are smudges. This letter must be as nearly perfect as possible.

When you begin your job hunt, write out a sample letter of application to use as a basic guide. You will want to reword it slightly to fit different circumstances. Always send it to a specific person. Your letter of application is your first contact with the employer. It should make a favorable impression.

Mailing the Letter of Application and Resume

If you are mailing your letter of application and resume, fold both neatly into thirds. Place both in a business-size envelope that matches the stationery used. Put the employer's name and address and your return address on the envelope. Seal, stamp, and mail it to the employer. Hopefully, you will soon receive a reply inviting you for an interview.

◆ Job Application Form

After you have sent your letter of application and resume, the employer may ask you to complete a job application form. If you apply in person at a job site, you may be asked to complete a job application form before you do anything else. Sometimes the form is the first contact you make with a prospective employer.

Job **application forms** ask for information about you, your education, and any work experience. They are useful to the employer in screening applicants for skills needed on the job. An example of a job application form is shown in 9-9.

123 Oakdale Drive
Boone, TX 70963
May 12, 2004

Mr. Robert Moore
Personnel Director
Mayer Sports Shop
7654 Frederick Drive
Mason, TX 70895

Dear Mr. Moore:

I am writing in response to your ad for a sales clerk in your sports shop. I learned of the available position through an ad in the *Herald Tribune*. I would like to be considered for the summer sales position.

During this past year, my junior year, I played on the girls' basketball team and was an active spectator in all other sports. I feel I can relate easily to athletes, as well as to other people looking for sports equipment.

I have taken a merchandising class and basic business courses in high school. Last year at Cleveland North High School, I participated in a work-study program in which I spent approximately 40 hours in the field as a tennis coach. I feel I could perform well in this sales position.

I would like to discuss this position and my qualifications with you in greater detail. I will be available to work after June 6. My resume is enclosed for your consideration. I look forward to hearing from you so we can arrange an interview. You can reach me at 906/382-4905 weekdays after noon.

Sincerely,

Sheri Moen

Sheri Moen

9-8 A letter of application will let potential employers know your interest and qualifications.

What foreign languages do you speak fluently? _____   Read fluently? _____   Write fluently? _____

U.S. Military or
Naval service _____   Rank _____

Present membership in
National Guard or Reserves _____

Activities other than religious–(civic, athletic, fraternal, etc.)

OFFICE EDUCATION ASSOCIATION, STUDENT COUNCIL,

WASHINGTON MARCHING BAND, 4-H CLUB

(Exclude organizations whose name or character indicates the race, creed, color, or national origin of its members)

FORMER EMPLOYERS List below last three employers starting with last one first

Date Month and Year	Name and Address of Employer	Salary	Position	Reason for leaving
From *8/03* To *PRESENT*	*WALLACE ADVERTISING AGENCY 1110 MILLER STREET CHICAGO, IL 60605*	*$7.50/HOUR*	*OFFICE ASSISTANT*	*DESIRE MORE RESPONSIBILITY*
From *5/03* To *8/03*	*BEST MAIL SERVICES 215 RIVER ROAD CHICAGO, IL 60611*	*$6.50/HOUR*	*OFFICE ASSISTANT*	*SUMMER JOB*
From To				

REFERENCES Give below the names of two pers

Name

1   *REV. BILL CALDWELL*

2   *MRS. EVELYN WELLS*

PHYSICAL RECORD

Have you any disabilities that might affect your job

NO

In case of
emergency notify   *MRS. JEAN JOH*
                              Name

I authorize investigation of all statements containe
called for is cause for dismissal.

Date   *JUNE 12, 2004*   Signa

APPLICATION FOR EMPLOYMENT

PERSONAL INFORMATION

Date *JUNE 12, 2004*   Social Security Number   *012 - 34 - 5678*

Name	*JOHNSON*	*BEVERLY*	*MARIE*
	Last	First	Middle

Present Address   *687 SPRING STREET*   *CHICAGO*   *IL*   *60638*
                              Street   City   State   Zip

Permanent Address   *687 SPRING STREET*   *CHICAGO*   *IL*   *60638*
                                 Street   City   State   Zip

Phone No.   *773 / 555 - 1234*

If related to anyone in our employ, state name and department   Referred by   *BILL MATSON COMMUNICATIONS DEPARTMENT*

EMPLOYMENT DESIRED

Position   *WORD PROCESSING*   Date you can start   *JULY 1, 2004*   Salary desired   *OPEN*

Are you employed now?   *YES*   May we inquire of your present employer?   *YES*

Ever applied to this company before?   *NO*   Where _____   When _____

EDUCATION

	Name and Location of School	Years Completed	Subjects Studied
Elementary School	*OAK PARK SCHOOL* *OAK PARK, IL*	*8*	*GENERAL EDUCATION*
High School	*WASHINGTON HIGH SCHOOL* *CHICAGO, IL*	*4*	*TYPING, SHORTHAND* *BOOKKEEPING, ENGLISH*
College	_____		
Trade, Business or Correspondence School	_____		

Subject of special study or research work   _____

9-9 Job applicants should always completely and neatly fill out the job application form.

The appearance of your completed application form will give the employer his or her first opinion about you. You will want to make a good first impression. Bring a pen and your personal data sheet for reference. You will want to complete the form accurately and neatly.

You might complete a job application in the personnel department or an employment office. Sometimes you might receive the job application form, if requested, by mail. Fill out the form completely and carefully using your personal data sheet for correct information. Being called for an interview may depend on the information you list and how carefully you complete your job application form.

If you are asked what wage or salary you expect, write "open" or "negotiable." This means you are willing to consider offers. See chart 9-10 for tips to remember when completing your job application form.

When you finish filling out the form, give it to the correct person. The next step is for the employer to review all the application forms and choose the top candidates for an interview. If you have done a good job of completing the application form, you will likely be considered for the desired position.

Tips for Completing a Job Application
◆ Read through the form first before you answer any of the questions. Determine on which line you should begin writing.
◆ If some of the statements do not apply, such as years in military service, write "N/A" for "not applicable." You can also draw a dash through the space so that the interviewer knows you did not overlook the question.
◆ Follow the directions. If the form asks you to print or type, be sure to do so neatly.
◆ Think before answering. After "position desired," write the specific job you want rather than "any job available."
◆ Plan ahead. Notice how much space you have for answers and use it accordingly. If you must erase, do it completely and neatly or ask for another form. Do not risk being rejected because of a messy application form.

9-10 By first looking over the job application form, you can plan your responses.

Summary

There are many sources of job leads. Check with parents and friends about possible job openings. Read the job want ads in newspapers and on bulletin boards. Contact your community, state, and federal placement offices and agencies. Check out the Internet. The more job leads you have, the more likely you are to get a job.

Organize your information for job hunting. Complete a personal data sheet and have it ready to use. Obtain a social security card if you do not already have one. Start preparing your portfolio when you are still in high school. Add to it as you make major accomplishments or receive honors and awards. The Internet has changed the way many job searches are conducted. This can be helpful for both the company seeking workers as well as for the job hunter.

A letter of application introduces you to the company. A resume often accompanies the letter of application. It describes your education, work experience, and other qualifications. A well-written letter of application and resume will help you make a good impression.

You may complete the job application form at the time you apply for a job. Know what you need to include so you can fill it out completely and correctly. Use your personal data sheet to answer the questions precisely.

Knowing what to expect when you job hunt and being prepared for the search will help you reach your goal. A successful job search will end with an interview and hopefully a job offer.

To Review

1. Name five sources of job leads.

2. Where would you look in the telephone directory to find a government-supported employment agency?

3. What is the name of the agency that hires people to work for the federal government?

4. Why is it helpful to compile a personal data sheet before you begin applying for jobs?

5. What should be included on your personal data sheet?

6. What should a resume include?

7. When might you change your resume?

8. List five types of materials that a portfolio might include.

9. What is the purpose of a letter of application?

10. What major points should be included in a letter of application?

11. What is the importance of having a neat, well-organized letter of application and resume?

12. List three guidelines for filling out a job application form.

13. What is a recommended way to respond to a question about the wage or salary you expect on the job?

To Do

1. From a collection of newspaper job ads, choose a job you would like to have someday. List the skills needed for that job. Share this information with the class.

2. From newspaper job ads, find five abbreviations and circle them. Attach the ads to notebook paper and write out the meanings of the circled words.

3. From the classified pages of the telephone book, find your state employment agencies. Under what listing did you have to look?

4. Select a job from newspaper job ads. Write a letter of application that includes major points discussed in the chapter.

10 Job Interviews

After studying this chapter, you will be able to
◆ explain how to prepare for a job interview.
◆ describe proper clothing and grooming for a job interview.
◆ demonstrate good job interview techniques.
◆ list fringe benefits that a company might provide.
◆ list factors to consider when evaluating a job offer.
◆ describe the procedures for accepting or rejecting job offers.

Terms to Know

preemployment test
performance test
sabbatical

Cindy was on her way to her first job interview. She was becoming nervous because she wanted the job very much. "Do I look all right?" she wondered. "Will I know what to say?"

These are typical preinterview fears. Cindy felt confident in the fact that she had done her homework. She had learned as much as she could about the company. She had even practiced interviewing with her older sister. Cindy felt well prepared and believed she could do a good job in the interview. She knew she was dressed appropriately for this interview. Being prepared helped to calm her fears.

There are many steps involved in getting a job. It requires a great deal of preliminary work, as you learned in the last chapter. Assembling and organizing your personal data is important. Maybe you sent a letter of application and your resume to call attention to

your abilities. You might have completed an application form or made a phone call. However, it is the interview that will determine whether you receive a job offer. The interview is the most important step in a job search.

In this chapter, you will learn tips and suggestions to help you prepare for an interview. You will also learn about the interview process itself and what to do following the interview.

When that important job offer comes to you, how will you know whether to accept it? This chapter will also help you learn how to make decisions about job offers.

◆ The Job Interview

The job interview serves many purposes. If you are seeking a job, your purpose is to convince the employer that you are the right person for the job, 10-1. The employer or interviewer wants to find out whether you have the skills to do the job. He or she will be evaluating you on how well you would work within the company. An interview also gives you a chance to find out more about the job and company.

An employer's first impression of you is through your correspondence. The appearance, content, and style of your letter and resume can help you obtain a job interview. Your skills must match those desired by the employer. During the job interview, you can explain your qualifications for the job. The interview will also allow you to assess whether the job is right for you.

10-1 Feeling good about your appearance helps to calm your interview fears. Wear clothing that fits well with the company image.

Preparing for the Job Interview

Once you receive an offer for an interview, it is time to prepare for your appointment. You can do this by finding out more about the company. You can practice for the interview. Your appearance during the interview will also be important.

Find Out About the Company or Organization

Prepare for your interview by finding out as much as you can about your potential employer. See 10-2 for topics to explore before your interview.

You can find information about companies at your local public or school library. Ask the reference librarian for directories, such as *Dun & Bradstreet's Employment Opportunities Directory, Standard & Poor's Register of Corporations,* or *Thomas Register of American Manufacturers.* By using these resources, you can learn more about companies. These resources list the location of the company or business, their products or services, telephone and fax numbers, and the names of company officers. For information about associations or

Employer Topics to Consider
◆ Major services offered or products produced
◆ Size of the company or organization
◆ Company's history and origin
◆ Major competitors and their locations
◆ Number of employees
◆ Types of jobs available
◆ How the organization operates
◆ Company expectations of employees
◆ Advancement possibilities
◆ Company's reputation

10-2 It is important to learn as much as possible about the company.

organizations, you might use the *Encyclopedia of Associations*. See 10-3.

Another way to find out more about a company or organization is through its newsletter or magazine, if there is one. You can also ask to receive a copy of their annual report. Check back issues of newspapers for articles about a particular business. Also, search the Internet for information about the company. If it has a Web site, read every page of it to get a good overview of the company.

Contact the chamber of commerce in the city where the organization is located. Request any printed material about the company. Read it over to become more familiar with the firm that will interview you.

You might also try to locate people who know about the organization. Maybe you can even find someone who works there. Perhaps they know the person interviewing you. An informal visit with someone like this often gives you an idea of how it would be to work for that particular organization.

Review Your Skills, Abilities, and Talents

Review your personal data sheet and portfolio. It is a good review of the skills and abilities you will want to emphasize. Make a list of some of your important accomplishments, including dates and results. It is very important to provide accurate, honest answers at the time of your interview. A complete review will prepare you for answering the interviewer's questions.

The interviewer will probably start by saying, "Tell me about yourself." You should have an answer planned. You will not need to have a set answer, but an answer that you feel highlights your strengths and skills. You can adapt and relate your answer to the job to which you are applying.

Listen carefully during the interview. Some questions might directly relate to your skills or abilities. Think of how you would apply your skills to the job for which you are interviewing. The interviewer might ask you

Apple Computer

10-3 Prepare for your interview by finding out as much as you can about the employer. Libraries, the chamber of commerce, and the Internet are good sources.

how you would handle a special situation. Your answers will help the interviewer relate how your abilities might fill their needs.

It will be easier to concentrate and answer the interviewer's questions if you have prepared ahead. This will help you convince the interviewer that you are the person for the job.

Practice for the Interview

Practice going over interviewing techniques so you will be more comfortable during the interview. Many people have trouble communicating. They have poor eye contact and use improper English when they speak. Use of slang may be acceptable around friends, but it is not proper for a job interview. Before your interview, practice the following aspects of an interview:

- *Introducing yourself.* Go through some typical interview situations. Practice your opening remarks. You might say to the receptionist, "Good afternoon. My name is Sam Adams. I have an appointment with Mr. Banks at three o'clock." Speak clearly and confidently. Then practice the meeting. Take the lead in introducing yourself. At other times practice responding to his greeting.
- *Your handshake.* A firm handshake shows you feel confident in yourself. Practice with a friend. Always use your right hand and grasp the other person's hand firmly. Know when to end your handshake. Generally, this is in two to three seconds.
- *Responding to questions.* Interviewers typically ask job candidates a number of questions. Questions often asked by interviewers appear in 10-4. Practice answering them so you can handle questions easily. Never say anything negative about yourself, another person, or a company. Stress the positives and avoid the negatives. Always maintain eye contact. If a group is interviewing you, respond to the person asking the question, but do not overlook eye contact with other group members.

Interviewer Questions
1. How would you describe yourself?
2. What are your greatest strengths and weaknesses?
3. What do you hope to be doing five years from now?
4. What is your long-term career goal?
5. How do you think you can make a contribution to our company?
6. What qualifications do you have to work for this company?
7. Do you think your grades are a good indication of your work ability?
8. Why did you decide to seek a position with our company?
9. Why did you leave your last job?
10. Why should I hire you?

10-4 It is a good idea to practice responses to these questions so you can answer them easily during an interview.

- *Asking questions.* Usually, an interviewer will ask you if you have any questions. Have two or three in mind that you can ask. Some examples might be the following: Have I answered all your questions satisfactorily? To whom would I be reporting? What training would I receive for this job? What are some prospects for advancement within this company?

Think About Your Appearance

You should take great care to dress in a manner that is appropriate clothing for the setting. Plan what you will wear to the interview. Choose clothing that is neat and conservative in style. Dark colors are always safe. Jeans, T-shirts, and athletic shoes are not appropriate for interviews.

Generally, men should wear a shirt, tie, sports jacket and slacks, or a suit to a job interview. Wear dark shoes and socks. Take time to clean and polish your shoes. Good choices for women are a suit or dress, or a skirt, blouse, and jacket. These should be businesslike in appearance. Always wear hosiery. Avoid gaudy jewelry and shoes that have very high heels or extreme styles. Leave your cell phone or pager at home. This goes for large briefcases or purses, too. Shuffling through reams of paper searching for material doesn't present a very organized picture. There may be exceptions to these guidelines, but these are fairly standard for job interviews.

Good grooming is essential. Clothing must be clean and well pressed. Hair should be clean with a becoming style. Avoid any extreme or unusual hairstyles. Heavy makeup or strong perfume or aftershave lotions are not acceptable. Most employers prefer young men to be cleanshaven. Fingernails must be clean and at an appropriate length. Well-groomed hands and nails are important assets to your appearance. Make sure you have taken a bath or shower and applied deodorant. You do not want to allow poor grooming to spoil your chances of getting a job, 10-5.

10-5 Be sure you are fresh and clean for the interview. Avoid using anything that is strongly perfumed or scented.

The Day of the Interview

You are almost ready to meet the interviewer face-to-face. Before you do this, there are a few details you should consider. For instance, how early should you arrive? How should you greet the interviewer? When will you know that the interview has concluded? Knowing what to do in these situations will help you overcome any last minute concerns.

Know where you are to go for the interview. Double check to make sure you have correct directions. Know how long it will take you to get to your destination. You may want to make a practice run if you will be taking a bus or public transportation. Then you will know exactly how much time to allow.

Be early for your appointment. Plan the timing so you will not need to rush, but can arrive about five to ten minutes early. You may want to allow time to find a restroom for a final check on your appearance before the interview. If you must rush, this will only add to your nervousness.

Take paper and pen with you for taking notes and filling out any forms. Also, take along your personal data sheet.

Go to the interview alone. Never take along a friend or a parent. Do not chew gum or bring anything to eat or drink to an interview. If you wear sunglasses, remove them before you enter the interviewer's office.

One person often interviews a job applicant at first, 10-6. This might be a human resources person or a person from the

MT Crave

10-6 In a job interview, pay close attention to information the interviewer gives you about your job.

department that has the job opening. Later during that meeting or in a follow-up meeting, other employees of the organization meet the interviewee, either one by one or in a small group. Since most new employees work with several coworkers, everyone's input on who to hire is important.

Meet your interviewer with a warm greeting and a firm handshake. If you are carrying a briefcase or papers, keep them in your left hand so your right hand is free for the handshake. Remember the name of the person interviewing you and use it in your greeting. For example say, "It is a pleasure to meet you, Mrs. Klinger." Do not sit until you are asked. Then sit up straight in a comfortable, relaxed position.

Look alert and try not to fidget or act nervous. You have prepared well and now you want to present a positive image. A friendly smile and enthusiastic manner will make others want to know you better. Act self-assured and you will feel more confident.

Do not do anything that would be distracting or disturbing, such as cracking your knuckles. Never interrupt while the interviewer is speaking. Avoid looking out the window or reading items around the room or on the interviewer's desk, 10-7.

The interviewer will tell you about the job and what your responsibilities will be. He or she may also ask you about your qualifications or about responses on your application form or resume. Answer these questions as completely as you can. If possible, use the interviewer's name when you answer questions. Look interested, relaxed, and happy to be there.

Allied Van Lines

10-7 Make good eye contact when you are interviewing. Listen carefully to each question.

Salary Questions

It is best to avoid asking questions about salary or benefits early in an interview or during a first interview. Wait until the interviewer brings up the subject. If you ask about salary too soon in the interview, the interviewer may think all you care about is the money.

Each company determines salary schedules. People with more education and experience often receive more pay. Sometimes, you can negotiate your starting salary. This means, through discussion, you reach an agreement with an employer.

Andrea chose to negotiate with her prospective employer. When he asked her how much she would like to earn, Andrea said she would like between $8.00 and $9.00 an hour. She had retail experience and was already making $7.00 an hour at her job in a hardware store. She was not shy about stating an amount. In addition, she was pursuing a degree in the retail field. She would earn college credits for her work in this job. The interview had gone well, and she felt qualified for the job. This was a good approach for Andrea, as the company hired her for $8.50 an hour.

If an interviewer asks you what salary you will need, you may state, "What is the salary range for this position?" Another response is, "I think my salary should reflect my work in the company. I know you will be fair."

Preemployment Tests

Some employers may ask you to take **preemployment tests.** These tests help an employer assess your skills, abilities, and health. This information often helps employers decide which job applicant to hire.

There are several different types of tests, depending on the job opening. **Performance tests** require you to perform a certain skill. For instance, if you are applying for a newspaper reporter's job, it will be necessary to demonstrate your writing skills. Some employers may test you on your math skills if it is important to know math well for the job you will perform. Some tests indicate how quickly you can perform certain tasks, 10-8.

In order to provide a drug-free work environment, drug screening is now required by most companies. These preemployment drug tests identify drug users. It is best to be receptive to these tests, as they often are a requirement for employment.

If you will be applying for a job that involves preemployment tests, talk to someone who has taken a similar test. Find out what the test might involve so you will know what to expect.

Ending the Interview

When the interviewer asks you if you have any more questions, this is usually a sign that the interview is ending. The interviewer feels he or she has all the information needed. If you want the job, tell the interviewer that you are very interested in the position and that you are confident you could do the work.

10-8 Some performance tests may check your ability to recognize correct grammar and punctuation.

Often the interviewer will stand and offer his or her hand to shake, indicating an end to the interview. Thank the interviewer by name. While shaking hands, you might say, "Thank you, Mr. White, for your time today." If you did not receive a job offer, you can ask if you may call back in a few days to find out any decision. You might say, "I'm sure I'll have some questions. When is a good time to get back to you?" After you have agreed on a time, you may say, "Thank you, Mr. White. I'll call you Wednesday between two and three o'clock."

Seldom will an interviewer offer you the job at the end of the first interview. He or she must have time to consider your qualifications. Perhaps there is the need to check your references and credentials. The employer will also weigh your qualifications against others who have applied for the job.

After the Interview

Within 24 hours, write a follow-up letter to the interviewer. A follow-up letter is a brief business letter thanking the interviewer for the interview. An example of a follow-up letter is shown in 10-9. If the position still interests you, mention it in your letter. Indicate that you want to know the interviewers decision. Your follow-up letter could be what influences the employer to hire you for the job or ask you to return for a second interview.

◆ Evaluating Job Offers

Let's say that your job search is successful. You have one or more job offers. How will you decide which, if any, to accept? You are looking for a job that is right for you. A successful job brings you satisfaction, but how will you know what job will accomplish this? It is not always the job that pays the most. You must consider other factors as well. You might ask yourself the following questions on the next page.

802 South Morris
Tabor, NC 24711
August 30, 2004

Mr. Richard Carter
Personnel Manager
Carters Department Store
607 Main Street
Thayer, NC 25841

Dear Mr. Carter:

I appreciated the opportunity to talk with you on August 29. The information you shared with me about Carters Department Store was excellent. I am very excited about the possibility of applying my education and experience to the position we discussed.

Please let me know if I can provide you with any additional information. I look forward to hearing from you soon.

Sincerely,

Chelsey Birch

Chelsey Birch

10-9 After the interview, write a follow-up letter thanking the interviewer for his or her time and interest.

◆ Will this job help me to achieve my career goals?
◆ Are there opportunities for advancement?
◆ What additional costs will this job require, such as the use of a car or special clothing?

◆ What are the working conditions?
◆ During what hours would I be working?
◆ What fringe benefits does this company offer?

Looking at Fringe Benefits

Fringe benefits are the monetary extras that come with a job. They are employment benefits provided by the company but they do not affect your basic wages. Benefits offered vary by companies. The fringe benefits provided often play an important part in a total financial package. Often they represent many dollars that you would need to pay out of your own pocket for emergencies or special needs. You might consider whether a job offers any of the fringe benefits described here.

Insurance

Many companies offer group health, dental, and life insurance. Find out whether the company offers any of these. How much coverage do the policies provide? How much will you pay versus the employer? Does the plan include your present dentist and doctors, or must you switch to something unfamiliar? See 10-10.

Retirement or Pension Plan

Many companies provide some form of pension, or provisions after retirement. Does the company set aside a certain amount of money to contribute to a retirement or pension plan for you? Will the company also set aside some of your money for this purpose? If so, how much will be paid into the plan?

Must you work a certain number of years for the company before you can participate in the plan? How easy is it to keep or transfer your plan if you should become employed elsewhere?

Investment Opportunities

Does the company have a profit-sharing plan. It is a plan sponsored by the company that distributes a portion of the profits to employees. Sometimes this is an incentive for employees to work harder. When would you be eligible to become a part of this plan?

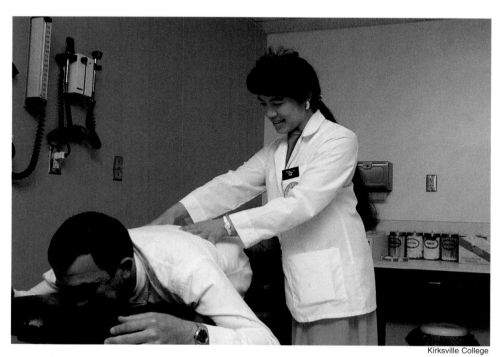

Kirksville College

10-10 Most companies offer some type of health insurance plans for their employees.

Vacation, Sick Leave, and Personal Leave

Will you receive paid vacation time with this company? If so, find out how many days per year, 10-11. Most companies give a certain number of vacation days based on the length of time the employee has worked for them. Are you limited to a certain time of the year when vacation days must be taken? Does the company pay for any days you are sick and unable to work? If so, how many? Does the company pay for any other time off, such as for attending funerals or handling emergency matters?

Parental Leave

Does the company have a plan for maternity or paternity leave? Is time allowed for staying home with children when they are sick? Companies often find that employee absenteeism is mainly due to parents staying home with sick children.

Child Care Provisions

A number of companies offer child care services on the work premises or near the work site. Workers' children attend the supervised child care center while parents work. Some companies allow parents to eat lunch with their children and spend work breaks with them. A few companies even provide care if the children are sick. Child care provisions at the workplace are an important feature for many working parents. They find this a valuable fringe benefit.

Educational Opportunities

Will you be paid to continue your education? Does the company provide time off to attend classes? For instance, if you want to take a special class that starts one hour before work ends, can you leave early on the class days? Are you offered tuition assistance or any other incentives to further your education?

Virginia Division of Tourism

10-11 One or two weeks of paid vacation time per year is a common fringe benefit.

Other Fringe Benefits

Some companies give yearly or holiday bonuses. Others might provide a company car. If you need to move to take a job, some companies pay moving expenses. Exercise and recreation facilities are sometimes provided for employees. Other companies provide sabbaticals, if you have worked for the company for a number of years. A **sabbatical** is a leave of absence used for more schooling or training. The purpose of a sabbatical is usually to improve your job skills.

Part-time employees generally do not receive any of these fringe benefits. Benefits offered to full-time workers vary widely from company to company. When making a final decision about a job, you will need to consider fringe benefits as well as the pay. You will need to consider other factors too. These might include job location or work hours.

Getting a Job Offer

When you receive a job offer, you may want to take a day to think about it. Find out when the company needs an answer. Try to get back to the company with your decision as soon as possible.

If you decide to accept the job offer, phone the company employee that offered you the job. Thank him or her and express your pleasure in joining the company. Find out when, where, and to whom you should report for work. Ask if you will need to bring anything special with you on the first day.

If you decide not to accept a job offer, phone your decision to the appropriate person as soon as possible. Be polite. Thank him or her for the job offer and the company's interest and confidence in you.

Sometimes job hunters send a letter of rejection after their call. This is done when the job seeker wants to be remembered by the employer. Perhaps during the interview, you learned that a more interesting job will be available in six months. Depending on what you write, your letter of regret today may make you a leading candidate for the future position.

What to Do If You Do Not Get the Job

Finding the right job can be a long, slow, and often disappointing process. During an economic slowdown, companies avoid hiring workers. Perhaps you may even need to take a temporary job before you find a more desirable one. You may send out many letters and resumes and go on numerous interviews. Do not become discouraged by these rejections.

There is always something to learn from each job interview. In your mind, review your interview. Ask yourself if you were able to answer the interviewer's questions. If you had been the interviewer, would you have hired yourself for the job? What would you do or say differently in another interview? If you did poorly on one interview, you will know better how to handle the situation next time.

If you are turned down repeatedly, you may want to ask why you did not get the job. You may also want to consider improving your work or personal management skills. Perhaps you might take classes in areas that need improvement. You may need to prepare yourself better for each interview. Maybe you need to look at different types of jobs. All of this may take more time and effort, but you will eventually find the job that is right for you.

Summary

Before going on a job interview, plan and prepare your presentation. Find out as much as you can about the company and type of work you will be doing. By going over job interview techniques, you will feel more comfortable and confident. Double check directions to the interview site. Review and prepare materials that you need to take along to the interview.

Dress appropriately for the appointment. Arrive early to allow time to relax and refresh yourself. Greet the interviewer with a warm, friendly manner and a firm handshake. During the interview, concentrate on the questions asked. Answer each question as completely as you can.

Some employers require certain preemployment tests. Check with those who have taken similar tests to know what to expect.

After the interview, write a letter to the interviewer thanking him or her for the interview. Express your interest in the job. When you receive one or more job offers, evaluate them in terms of job satisfaction as well as salary and benefits. Respond quickly and courteously with your acceptance or rejection of a job offer. If you do not get a job after several interviews, take time to review and evaluate your interviews. Then, work toward improving the weak areas of your interviewing process.

To Review

1. How does a job interview benefit both the employer and the interviewee?

2. List five kinds of information you should try to find out about a company before you go on a job interview.

3. Where can you find information about a company?

4. What is the first question an employer often asks an interviewee?

5. Describe what a person properly dressed for an interview wears.

6. List five good interviewing tips or techniques.

7. Why do employers sometimes give preemployment tests?

8. List five fringe benefits that a company might offer.

9. Name four factors you should consider when evaluating a job offer.

10. Describe how to accept a job offer.

To Do

1. In a group of four students, role-play a person well prepared for a job interview. Then role-play someone poorly prepared. Evaluate each role-playing situation. Rotate positions within the group.

2. Make a list, contrasting good interview techniques with poor techniques.

3. Role-play job interviews. Critique each interview, giving suggestions for improvement.

4. Look through job listings in a newspaper. Cut out a listing for a job that interests you. Research the company

and list sources used. Indicate company location, number of employees, product produced, or service provided. List title and name of two company officers.

5. In a circular response, state what you would look for in a job applicant during an interview if you were an employer. Explain why.

6. From magazines and other sources, find pictures of people appropriately dressed for job interviews. Describe orally or in writing why you consider them well dressed for an interview.

11 Job Orientation

After studying this chapter, you will be able to
◆ predict what to expect during the first few days of a new job.
◆ list job expectations of employees.
◆ list job expectations of employers.
◆ explain typical employee policies.
◆ describe types of payroll deductions.
◆ summarize provisions of the Fair Labor Standards Act.

Terms to Know

discrimination	net pay
equal opportunity	payroll deduction
sexual harassment	Internal Revenue
personnel policies	Service (IRS)
wages	dependent
overtime	premium
salary	Fair Labor Standards
commission	Act (FLSA)
tip	minimum wage
gross pay	seniority

You have completed the interview process and landed a job. Now, your role as a worker begins. You will probably have many questions concerning your job.

Adjusting to a new job can be difficult if you do not know what to expect. In this chapter, you will look at those first days on the job and learn how you can prepare yourself. This will reduce your anxiety and give you more confidence.

Getting Ready for Your New Job

Getting ready for your first day on the job is similar to preparing for the first day of school. You want to make a good first impression, 11-1. You will want to choose appropriate clothing and be well groomed. Be ready with a smile, look friendly, and act self-assured. This will help others accept you more quickly.

Make any necessary arrangements for the first day. If you need to complete employee and tax forms, do so as soon as possible. You may need to get a physical examination or take a drug-screening test. If you need uniforms or special equipment for the job, take care of these tasks. Purchase any new clothes you need. If you will be moving to a new apartment or house, try to complete the move before you start your job. Know how you will get to work and plan to arrive a few minutes early. If you need child care, arrange it early so you can plan for any schedule changes.

Have a positive attitude about your job. Realize there will be many new experiences and problems. Prepare yourself mentally by thinking of what you will be able to contribute. Then you will indeed be ready to begin your new job.

11-1 It is important to look your best for your new job.

First Week on the Job

When there are several new employees starting at once, group-training sessions may be planned. You will be given general information about the company and the part you play in the organization. During this time, company policies, rules, and regulations will be explained.

You might receive training specific to your job. Listen carefully to the instructions. Bring a notebook and pen to write down information you need to remember. The length of training usually depends on the difficulty of the job. Training policies vary from company to company.

As you begin your actual work, you may feel confused and frustrated about your job

responsibilities. Until you get a better grasp of your job, these feelings are quite normal. If you do not understand something, ask your trainer or supervisor. Other workers are usually willing to help a new person. Watch what others are doing and learn from them.

Getting Acquainted

Some people are better at meeting new people than others. It is best to just be yourself and act natural. Be friendly and polite. Others will be impressed with your good manners.

Introductions

Your supervisor or someone else in the company may begin your first day by introducing you to other employees. As the supervisor introduces you, say "How do you do, Mr. Brown?" or "Hello, Janice." You will remember names better if you repeat them each time.

Some people may ask you to call them by their first name. It is best to address others, especially supervisors and older persons, by Mr., Mrs., or Miss. If you do not know if a woman is married, the title Ms. is appropriate.

If no one introduces you, introduce yourself. It can be awkward working beside someone you do not know. You can smile and say, "Hi, my name is Chanci Dorrell." The other person will usually say his or her name, or you can ask, "What is your name?" After introductions, you could make some comment about this being your first day. Then you might add that you are excited about your new job. Show an interest in your new coworkers by asking them questions.

Establishing Friendships

Be friendly to everyone you meet, but proceed slowly in forming close friendships. You will want to associate with people who do a good job at work and lead well-rounded lives. When friendships are formed, you will have opportunities to participate in new social, athletic, or entertainment events outside of work.

Avoid coworkers who are members of the "wrong crowd." They are usually not productive in their work. Some care little about their work habits. They may be the office "gossips" and you would then be considered one of them. Take your time when getting to know others.

Making a Good Impression

When your new coworkers first meet you, they are forming an impression of you. You want to present yourself as someone others want to know and with whom they want to work. Your dress and grooming make the first impression. What you wear and how you look will create your job image, 11-2.

Your Clothing

Dress properly for your job. Find out the type of clothing appropriate for your place of work. Your supervisor will instruct you on proper attire. Note what other people wear on the job and wear similar clothing.

Many jobs have a dress code that outlines what workers should and should not wear. For example, a grocery store may require young men to be neat, clean, and have long pants and shirts with collars. Requirements would be similar for women. Dangling jewelry of any type would probably be forbidden.

Restaurants and many other industries require you to wear a uniform. Since the uniform represents the company's image, you will be required to keep it clean and neat.

Some careers require business-type attire. Obviously, someone in banking will dress differently from someone working in a manufacturing plant. Each job indicates a certain type of clothing. The type of clothing chosen will depend on job requirements. Jobs that involve direct customer contact have some of the strictest dress codes.

Your clothes for work may form the major portion of your wardrobe. These clothes will not be the only items in your wardrobe, but they may be the most expensive items. The amount of money you will need to spend on clothing may be an important consideration in the choice of a career.

J.C. Penney Co., Inc.

11-2 Notice what others are wearing to work in your company. If other workers wear suits, that is what you should wear.

Good Grooming

Do not overlook the importance of personal grooming. Clean hair, fingernails, and clothes create a positive image. In contrast, unkempt hair, poorly manicured fingernails, and bad breath present quite a different impression. See 11-3 for a checklist of good grooming practices.

Your clothes and grooming say something important about you. Always being neat and well groomed indicates to others that you care about yourself. Looking your best also helps you feel more confident and self-assured. The result—you feel good about yourself.

Good Grooming Practices
Bathe or shower daily.
Use deodorant or antiperspirant every day.
Keep your hair clean and at an appropriate length.
Clean fingernails and keep at an appropriate length.
Brush and floss teeth daily.
Clean and press clothing.
Keep shoes clean and well polished.
Use perfume and aftershave lotions sparingly.
For women, tone down or moderately apply makeup.
For men, be clean shaven.

11-3 To look your best, check these good grooming points every day.

Your Actions

Be friendly and courteous to others. In addition to your appearance, people judge you by your actions. By treating others fairly and doing your job well, you will gain the respect of others. By showing your willingness to work, you will get off to a good start.

It is best to leave any personal problems at home and solve them outside work. Use appropriate language at work. Slang and swear words are not appropriate in the workplace. Listen to what your supervisors are saying and how they say it.

Try to get along with everyone. By being cooperative and carrying out your job professionally, you will be a valued employee. People like to associate with this kind of person.

◆ What Your Employer Expects of You

You received your job because someone in the company thought you could help the company meet its goals. Now you need to be ready and willing to do your part. Your employer will be investing time and money into your training. He or she expects you to perform according to company standards. In addition, your employer expects you to do the following:

◆ Give a full day's work for a day's wage.
◆ Take directions well.
◆ Follow through on assigned tasks.
◆ Work productively and effectively.
◆ Cooperate with supervisors and coworkers.
◆ Observe rules of the workplace.
◆ Show loyalty to the company.

Give a Full Day's Work

Your employer expects you to put in the full amount of work time. This means you are to arrive on time and stay until the end of the workday. Extra-long breaks cost the company money in lost productivity. If you were the employer, you would not want your workers to take off more time than is allowed.

Many workers waste time by visiting with other people, constantly going to the water fountain, and finding other ways of avoiding work. Remember, you are being paid to do a job. Employers do not like you to waste the company's time, 11-4.

If you work with a computer and have access to the Internet, visiting nonwork Web sites compromises productivity and possibly your job. Many companies monitor employees' online use of inappropriate Web sites and e-mail. Workers do not have the same rights to privacy in the office as they do at home. It is important to follow the company policy regarding Internet and e-mail use.

Take Directions Well

When a person in charge gives you oral or written directions concerning your work, you should follow them. Ask questions if you want to know why you are to perform a job in a particular way.

11-4 Your employer expects you to put in a full day's work for a full day's pay.

Some companies have suggestion boxes for ideas. Employees can place suggestions for increasing job performance in the box. Some employees might offer ways of improving workplace facilities. If a company adopts an employee's idea, it may reward the employee with a check or other means of approval. However, when starting a new job, accept the approved method of doing a job. After you have been with a company for a while and have a valid suggestion, you may present your ideas.

Follow Through on Assigned Tasks

Once you have received directions, you must follow through with them. This means carrying the directions out fully, completely, and exactly as given to you.

For the worker, there is a feeling of self-satisfaction in seeing a project through to its completion. However, some people have a habit of starting many projects but not seeing them through to the end. This is especially difficult on other coworkers if they must take over where you left off, or if they cannot begin until you finish. Once you start a project, you should finish that project, unless your supervisor says otherwise.

Be Productive and Effective in Your Job

Try to learn the skills and functions of the job as quickly as you can. Do your fair share of the work. Do not be afraid to do more than your share. Be responsible for your own work as well as your own mistakes. As a new worker, you will make mistakes, but try to learn from them. Show that you have productive work habits and attitudes.

Having a job is a serious responsibility. Your employer is paying you to help the company make a profit. If you do not carry out your end of the agreement, there is no reason to keep you as an employee. When workers do not produce, the company does not make money. If a company does not make money, it cannot pay its employees, and workers can lose their jobs. Bankruptcy or other financial problems might arise for the company. By staying productive, you can help the company make money and grow.

Cooperate with Supervisors and Coworkers

Many problems arise in a workplace because employees cannot cooperate with their supervisors and coworkers. Working on a job requires team effort. Each member must work with and help others. If one or more team members are unwilling to work with the group, friction and conflict can develop.

Even if you work alone, your project may fit into a larger project within the company. If you do not complete your part, the whole workforce may suffer.

Conflict with supervisors may be particularly difficult. If you do not cooperate, you may lose your job, 11-5. Supervisors are in charge of the operation of a company or business. They expect their workers to follow their leadership.

Observe Rules of the Workplace

Each workplace develops its own rules and standards for the smooth operation of its business or service. Many companies have an employee handbook or policy manual that states company rules. It is best to learn about

these and adhere to them. Company rules and policies exist to answer a need.

Many rules protect the health and safety of employees. Other rules may relate to employees' appearance and behavior. Breaking the rules may be embarrassing or could cost you your job.

Be Loyal to the Company

Being loyal means you speak well of the company. When you talk about your job, give positive comments concerning your employer and the company. Perhaps you do not always like what the company is doing, but do not complain to others about it. Employers expect you to keep company business confidential.

If you cannot be loyal to the company, maybe you should look for another job. Resist speaking negatively about your former employer

11-5 Cooperation is one of the finest traits you, as a worker, can possess.

to new job prospects. This may hurt your chances of being hired by another company.

◆ What You Can Expect from Your Employer

You are obligated in many ways to your employer. On the other hand, your employer has certain responsibilities to you, the worker. In general, these responsibilities are to train you, to pay you, to provide a safe environment, and to treat you fairly.

Job Training

It is the employer's responsibility to provide you with proper training for your job. Job training will be better and more complete in some companies than in others. Some companies or businesses provide extensive and thorough training sessions. In other companies, you will need to learn your job by observing other people. Some companies may train you on the job, 11-6. Still others may send you to a training school or classes for additional training.

Pay

Before you were hired, you reached an agreement on your pay or salary. Most companies pay their employees once or twice a month. Your employer will inform you of the company policy regarding pay periods. Some companies can deposit your pay directly into your bank account. You receive a statement indicating the amount of money deposited. It is the employer's responsibility to pay you the agreed amount at the specified times.

A Safe Environment

Your employer must provide a safe working environment. It must be free from hazards

Long John Silvers

11-6 As you learn more your job duties from your employer or trainer, your chances for success will increase.

that could cause serious physical harm or death. All equipment should have the necessary safety features. The company should immediately repair unsafe equipment. One of the reasons for proper job training is to ensure a secure and safe environment. Before you begin a new job, be aware of any potential dangers associated with the job.

Fair Treatment Without Discrimination

You have a right to fair treatment by your employer. By law, no one can discriminate against you because of race, religion, age, sex, or national origin. Treating a person differently because of one of these factors is known as **discrimination.** In the workplace, you have a right to fair and equal treatment. That right is known as **equal opportunity.**

Another form of employment discrimination on the job is **sexual harassment.** Sexual harassment includes any unwelcome sexual advances, requests for sexual favors, or other sexual conduct. Such acts are illegal if they threaten your job or interfere with your work. Sexual harassment is a deliberate attempt to take advantage of your rights. There are two basic types of sexual harassment.

Quid pro quo harassment. The term *quid pro quo* means "something given to receive something else." In this case, one person makes unwelcome advances toward another while promising certain benefits if that person complies. The promised benefit may be a pay raise or promotion.

Hostile environment harassment. In this case, a person makes an environment unpleasant enough to interfere with the other worker's performance. For example, the worker may be unable to do a job as expected because of another person's unwanted staring, touching, signs, pictures, music, or other forms of sexual messages.

Sexual harassment is illegal under many state and federal laws. Everyone has the right to be treated with respect. As an employee, you should receive just and fair treatment from others.

◆ Employee Policies

As stated earlier, each company or industry has certain work policies, rules, and standards regarding their employees. These also include policies regarding your pay. Your supervisor may go over these with you or you might receive an employee handbook. Sometimes you may need to ask your supervisor to clarify a policy.

Personnel Policies

Personnel policies outline the behavior expected of all employees as well as their dress. For example, there may be policies concerning the length of the working day, breaks, and mealtimes. Personnel policies are usually explained in a booklet called the employee handbook. The handbook will list the work hours. It may outline policies concerning smoking on work premises, if it is allowed at all.

What happens if you arrive late or stay home sick? Work policies will indicate the procedure for taking sick leaves and the number of days allowed. The policy will also indicate whom you should contact if you are sick or will be late for work.

The policies also define excused and unexcused absences. For instance, if you need to attend a funeral of a close relative, this would probably be an excused absence. If you decide to go to a ball game instead of going to work, this would be an unexcused absence. An unexcused absence occurs when a worker is absent from work but doesn't call in sick and hasn't requested time off in advance.

Personnel policies define length of vacation time allowed for employees and the holidays observed. Other personnel policies affecting employees' behavior are also explained in the employee handbook. Each company draws up its own set of policies. Your ability to conform to the policies established by your employer will influence your success within the company.

◆ Pay Policies and Forms of Income

Your compensation might be in the form of wages, a salary, a commission, and/or tips. **Wages** refer to pay received for hourly work. Paycheck amounts will vary depending on the number of hours you work each day or week. If you work more than forty hours per week, you might work **overtime.** Overtime pay is usually one and one-half times your regular hourly pay.

If your employer is paying you a **salary,** your pay is a fixed amount for a period of time. This is usually for a year. If you work more or less than forty hours per week, your pay is the same amount. Salaried workers do not receive overtime pay.

Sometimes an employee receives pay based on the number of units he or she sells. This is called a **commission.** The amount of the commission is usually a percentage of the cost of the items sold, 11-7. Some companies pay their salespeople a salary or wages plus commission. This guarantees the salesperson at least a certain income each pay period. A commission provides salespeople with an incentive to sell as much as possible. In so doing, salespeople can increase their incomes.

Some workers earn tips in addition to their wages. A **tip** is a certain percentage of money that customers leave for the person who served them. Waiters, hairdressers, barbers, taxi drivers, and hotel employees generally receive tips. The customer decides how much to leave as a tip, depending on the level of service provided. For good service, customers generally give a tip equaling 15 to 20 percent of the bill.

Sometimes a person who receives a tip shares them with other employees, according to company policy. For example, servers in a restaurant may share their tips with employees who clear and set the tables. These people are not in a position to receive direct customer tips. However, their prompt service helps the waiters and waitresses, so they share the tips. In some businesses, especially restaurants, employees who customarily receive tips place them in a common pool or fund. At the end of each pay period, all of these employees receive an equal share of the fund.

◆ Understanding Your Paycheck

Generally employees are paid by check. A typical paycheck has a stub attached to it that provides information about your pay. See 11-8. It will state your **gross pay,** or the total amount of money earned during the pay period. Gross pay is the number of hours you worked multiplied by your hourly wage. For instance, suppose you worked 12 hours at a wage of $6.50

J.C. Penney Co., Inc.

11-7 People who work on commission get paid according to how much they sell.

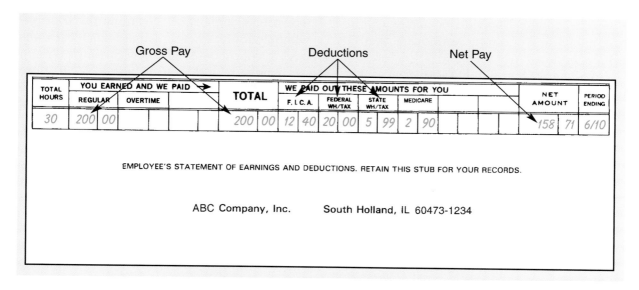

TOTAL HOURS	YOU EARNED AND WE PAID			TOTAL		WE PAID OUT THESE AMOUNTS FOR YOU						NET AMOUNT		PERIOD ENDING
	REGULAR	OVERTIME				F. I. C. A.	FEDERAL WH/TAX	STATE WH/TAX	MEDICARE					
30	200 00			200	00	12 40	20 00	5 99	2 90			158	71	6/10

Gross Pay Deductions Net Pay

EMPLOYEE'S STATEMENT OF EARNINGS AND DEDUCTIONS. RETAIN THIS STUB FOR YOUR RECORDS.

ABC Company, Inc. South Holland, IL 60473-1234

11-8 From your gross pay, deductions are made for social security (FICA) and federal and state withholding taxes. The net pay is your take-home pay.

an hour. Your gross pay would be $78.00 (12 x $6.50 = $78.00). However, the amount you will actually receive is your net pay. **Net pay** is the amount of money you have left after all deductions are taken from your gross pay. This is also called your take-home pay.

Payroll Deductions

You may be disappointed when you receive your first paycheck. Your net pay may be considerably less than your gross pay. Your employer takes out a certain amount of money from your paycheck for **payroll deductions.** Examples of payroll deductions include the following:
♦ federal and state income taxes
♦ social security taxes
♦ health insurance payments
♦ savings plans
♦ labor union dues
♦ retirement savings plans
♦ charitable contributions

Federal Income Tax

Possibly the largest deduction from your paycheck is for *federal income tax*. This tax is also called federal withholding tax. You might find it listed on your check stub as *Federal W.H. Tax*. Income tax is money paid to the federal government to provide various public services. These services include the maintenance of federal highways, parks, and museums. Federal taxes also provide money for public education and for operation of government services.

A branch of the Treasury Department called the **Internal Revenue Service (IRS)** collects these taxes. The IRS also enforces tax laws.

W-4 Form. When you first become employed, you will need to complete a W-4 tax form. The W-4 form is also called the Employee's Withholding Allowance Certificate. The information you provide on this form will determine the amount of money your employer will withhold for income taxes. The total amount withheld from your pay should come close to your total income tax bill for the year.

The government allows you to claim certain allowances on the W-4 form. Each of these allowances reduces the amount of tax withheld from your paycheck. You may claim an allowance for yourself only if no one else claims you as a dependent. A **dependent** is any person who relies on another person for financial support. Dependents include children and adults not presently employed. See 11-9 for a completed W-4 form.

W-2 Form. You should receive a W-2 form early in the year from every employer that paid you wages in the previous year. The W-2 form is a Wage and Tax Statement. The form lists your total pay and the amount of your pay withheld for taxes. You will use this form when paying your federal and state income taxes.

Compare the total on your W-2 form to your paycheck stubs. The information on the W-2 form should agree with your pay and the amount withheld. See 11-10.

Form W-4 (2004)

Want More Money In Your Paycheck?
If you expect to be able to take the earned income credit for 19XX and a child lives with you, you may be able to have part of the credit added to your take-home pay. For details, get Form W-5 from your employer.

Purpose. Complete Form W-4 so that your employer can withhold the correct amount of Federal income tax from your pay.

Exemption From Withholding. Read line 7 of the certificate below to see if you can claim exempt status. *If exempt, complete line 7; but do not complete lines 5 and 6.* No Federal income tax will be withheld from your pay. Your exemption is good for 1 year only. It expires February 15, 19**XX**.

Note: *You cannot claim exemption from withholding if (1) your income exceeds $650 and includes unearned income (e.g., interest*

and dividends) and (2) another person can claim you as a dependent on their tax return.

Basic Instructions. Employees who are not exempt should complete the Personal Allowances Worksheet. Additional worksheets are provided on page 2 for employees to adjust their withholding allowances based on itemized deductions, adjustments to income, or two-earner/two-job situations. Complete all worksheets that apply to your situation. The worksheets will help you figure the number of withholding allowances you are entitled to claim. However, you may claim fewer allowances than this.

Head of Household. Generally, you may claim head of household filing status on your tax return only if you are unmarried and pay more than 50% of the costs of keeping up a home for yourself and your dependent(s) or other qualifying individuals.

Nonwage Income. If you have a large amount of nonwage income, such as interest or dividends, you should consider making

estimated tax payments using Form 1040-ES. Otherwise, you may find that you owe additional tax at the end of the year.

Two Earners/Two Jobs. If you have a working spouse or more than one job, figure the total number of allowances you are entitled to claim on all jobs using worksheets from only one Form W-4. This total should be divided among all jobs. Your withholding will usually be most accurate when all allowances are claimed on the W-4 filed for the highest paying job and zero allowances are claimed for the others.

Check Your Withholding. After your W-4 takes effect, you can use **Pub. 919,** Is My Withholding Correct for 1995?, to see how the dollar amount you are having withheld compares to your estimated total annual tax. We recommend you get Pub. 919 especially if you used the Two Earner/Two Job Worksheet and your earnings exceed $150,000 (Single) or $200,000 (Married). Call 1-800-829-3676 to order Pub. 919. Check your telephone directory for the IRS assistance number for further help.

Personal Allowances Worksheet

A   Enter "1" for **yourself** if no one else can claim you as a dependent . . . . **A** _____

B   Enter "1" if: {
 • You are single and have only one job; or
 • You are married, have only one job, and your spouse does not work; or
 • Your wages from a second job or your spouse's wages (or the total of both) are $1,000 or less. } . . **B** _____

C   Enter "1" for your **spouse.** But, you may choose to enter -0- if you are married and have either a working spouse or more than one job (this may help you avoid having too little tax withheld) . . . . **C** _____

D   Enter number of **dependents** (other than your spouse or yourself) you will claim on your tax return . . . . . **D** _____

E   Enter "1" if you will file as **head of household** on your tax return (see conditions under **Head of Household** above) . **E** _____

F   Enter "1" if you have at least $1,500 of **child or dependent care expenses** for which you plan to claim a credit . **F** _____

G   Add lines A through F and enter total here. **Note:** This amount may be different from the number of exemptions you claim on your return ▶ **G** _____

For accuracy, do all worksheets that apply.
 • If you plan to **itemize or claim adjustments to income** and want to reduce your withholding, see the Deductions and Adjustments Worksheet on page 2.
 • If you are **single** and have **more than one job** and your combined earnings from all jobs exceed $30,000 **OR** if you are **married** and have a **working spouse or more than one job,** and the combined earnings from all jobs exceed $50,000, see the Two-Earner/Two-Job Worksheet on page 2 if you want to avoid having too little tax withheld.
 • If **neither** of the above situations applies, **stop here** and enter the number from line G on line 5 of Form W-4 below.

- - - - - - - - - - - - - **Cut here and give the certificate to your employer. Keep the top portion for your records.** - - - - - - - - - - - -

Form **W-4** Department of the Treasury Internal Revenue Service	**Employee's Withholding Allowance Certificate** ▶ **For Privacy Act and Paperwork Reduction Act Notice, see reverse.**	OMB No. 1545-0010 **2004**

1 Type or print your first name and middle initial *KRISTY A. JAMES*	Last name	2 Your social security number *987 65 4321*

Home address (number and street or rural route)   *1027 CEDAR STREET*

3 ☐ Single ☐ Married ☐ Married, but withhold at higher Single rate.
Note: If married, but legally separated, or spouse is a nonresident alien, check the Single box.

City or town, state, and ZIP code   *FRANKLIN, IL 65432*

4 If your last name differs from that on your social security card, check here and call 1-800-772-1213 for a new card . . ▶ ☐

5   Total number of allowances you are claiming (from line G above or from the worksheets on page 2 if they apply) . **5** _____
6   Additional amount, if any, you want withheld from each paycheck . . . . **6** $ _____
7   I claim exemption from withholding for 1995 and I certify that I meet **BOTH** of the following conditions for exemption:
 • Last year I had a right to a refund of **ALL** Federal income tax withheld because I had **NO** tax liability; **AND**
 • This year I expect a refund of **ALL** Federal income tax withheld because I expect to have **NO** tax liability.
 If you meet both conditions, enter "EXEMPT" here . . . . ▶ **7** _____

Under penalties of perjury, I certify that I am entitled to the number of withholding allowances claimed on this certificate or entitled to claim exempt status.

Employee's signature ▶ *Kristy A. James*   **Date ▶** *January 2* .**2004**

8 Employer's name and address (Employer: Complete 8 and 10 only if sending to the IRS) | 9 Office code (optional) | 10 Employer identification number

Cat. No. 10220Q

11-9 By filling out a W-4 form when you begin work, your employer will know how much income tax to deduct from your base pay.

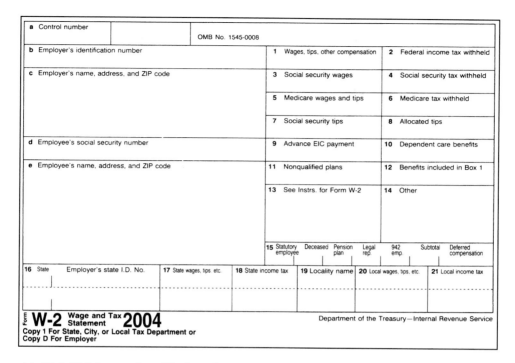

a Control number		OMB No. 1545-0008		
b Employer's identification number			**1** Wages, tips, other compensation	**2** Federal income tax withheld
c Employer's name, address, and ZIP code			**3** Social security wages	**4** Social security tax withheld
			5 Medicare wages and tips	**6** Medicare tax withheld
			7 Social security tips	**8** Allocated tips
d Employee's social security number			**9** Advance EIC payment	**10** Dependent care benefits
e Employee's name, address, and ZIP code			**11** Nonqualified plans	**12** Benefits included in Box 1
			13 See Instrs. for Form W-2	**14** Other
			15 Statutory employee Deceased Pension plan Legal rep. 942 emp. Subtotal Deferred compensation	
16 State Employer's state I.D. No.	**17** State wages, tips, etc.	**18** State income tax	**19** Locality name **20** Local wages, tips, etc.	**21** Local income tax

Form **W-2** Wage and Tax Statement **2004**
Copy 1 For State, City, or Local Tax Department or
Copy D For Employer

Department of the Treasury—Internal Revenue Service

11-10 A W-2 form, when filled out by your employer, shows how much you earned during the year and how much money was withheld for taxes.

State and Local Tax

Your paycheck may have state or local taxes deducted. State income taxes pay for various state projects. They help pay for public education. They also might pay for state highways, prisons, and other agencies and services. Only a few communities have a local income tax. Most local taxes are based on property owned rather than on income.

Social Security Taxes

Almost all workers in the United States pay social security taxes. This federal tax is based on income. People pay taxes while they work. When they stop working or retire, they collect monthly social security benefits.

Your employer deducts social security taxes from your paycheck. This deduction appears on your check stub as "FICA." It stands for Federal Insurance Contributions Act.

Your employer matches the social security taxes that you pay. In other words, your employer pays the same amount of money that you pay toward your social security taxes. If $15.30 is deducted from your paycheck for FICA, your employer will also pay $15.30. Your employer sends the total amount of $30.60 to the IRS under your name and social security number.

Social security is a federal government program. The program provides benefits to workers or their survivors. Income is provided when there is a reduction in family earnings. Earnings might be reduced or stopped because of retirement, disability, or death. A worker must pay social security taxes and work the minimum time required to be eligible to receive any benefits. Medicare is another social security benefit. Medicare provides hospital and medical insurance to the elderly and disabled.

Other Deductions

Your paycheck may show other deductions. These might include some fringe benefits of working for the company. If your company has a health or life insurance plan, you may need to pay a portion of the premiums. **Premiums** are the amount of money due for the policy or plan. You would have this amount deducted from your paycheck.

You may choose to have other deductions withheld from your paycheck. For instance, you may want the company to automatically deposit a certain amount into your savings account in a bank or credit union. If you belong to a company labor union you might want dues deducted from your paycheck. Some companies have retirement plans that require payroll deductions.

If you need to wear a uniform to work, the company may supply the uniforms. A certain amount of money might be taken from your paycheck to pay for your uniform. As you can see, it does not take long for your paycheck to shrink in size.

◆ Labor Laws and Regulations

Federal and state laws help protect the safety and rights of individuals. These laws regulate business activities, protect consumers, and dictate fair employment practices. For example, employees doing the same job with the same experience should expect equal pay. The law that has the most influence on work standards is the Fair Labor Standards Act (FLSA).

Fair Labor Standards Act

The **Fair Labor Standards Act (FLSA)** is a federal law that protects workers from unfair treatment by employers. Since its passage in 1938, there have been amendments to the law. These amendments have established the minimum wage, the rights to overtime pay and equal pay, and child labor standards.

The FLSA covers the majority of workers. It applies equally to male and female workers.

If an employee feels any FLSA rules have been violated, he or she may file a complaint. The employee files the complaint with the Wage and Hour Division of the Employment Standards Administration. You can find this division listed under *U.S. Government, Department of Labor* in the white pages of most telephone directories. Labor department officers investigate each complaint to see if the complaint is valid. If the company is in violation of the law, it is notified to pay specified fines and penalties. Nonpayment results in more serious action.

Minimum Wage

Minimum wage refers to the lowest amount per hour that employers can pay workers. Federal law sets the minimum hourly wage for most workers. The state employment office in your area can tell you what the minimum wage is at the present time.

The minimum wage law does not cover everyone. For example, babysitters and paid companions for the aged and bedridden are exempt from the law. Seasonal workers may not receive minimum wages. Sometimes apprentices and interns receive lower pay rates.

Overtime Pay

Overtime means hours worked beyond forty hours a week. For this you will normally receive time-and-a-half pay. For instance, if you make $6.50 an hour, your overtime rate is your regular pay of $6.50 plus one-half of $6.50, or $3.25, for a total of $9.75 an hour. See 11-11. All employers are not required to pay overtime. You can ask your employer how the company handles overtime.

Equal Pay

Under the FLSA ruling, both men and women must receive equal pay for work that requires equal skills and responsibilities. Work done by men and women does not need to be identical. Minor differences in duties cannot

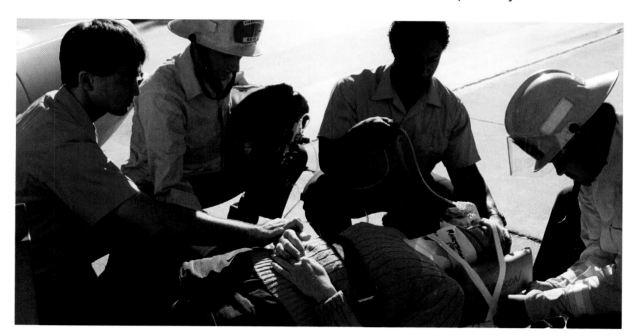

11-11 Sometimes it is necessary to work overtime. A 40-hour workweek is the norm for most full-time employees.

justify paying different wages or salaries. Sometimes there is a difference in pay because of seniority or amount of work produced. **Seniority** means those who have worked longer at a job. In addition, the quality of work produced may affect pay. The law applies to all payments, including overtime, uniforms, travel, and other fringe benefits.

Child Labor Regulations

The FLSA child labor laws accomplish two purposes. First, they prevent interference with children's schooling. Second, they prohibit children from working in jobs that could be dangerous to their health and safety. Before child labor laws existed, children could miss school if their families needed them to work. Children

sometimes worked in "sweat shops" or factories doing hard manual labor for long hours.

For those under 18 years of age, certain work restrictions apply. They may not work in any hazardous job. There are limits on when they can begin and end their workday. At ages 14 or 15, teens may not work more than three hours on a school day or 15 hours during a school week. Regulations permit 16- and 17-year-olds to work only 20 weeks during the school year.

Work regulations for various age groups appear in 11-12. These child labor standards protect the safety and well-being of young workers. It is important for you to be familiar with labor laws so you can protect yourself and your employer.

Age, Work Rules, and Regulations	
The following provisions apply to minors employed in nonagricultural occupations, as determined by the Fair Labor Standards Act. Provisions vary if a student is enrolled in work experience and career exploration programs.	
Age	**Type of Work Regulation**
Age 14	This is the minimum age for employment in specified occupations outside school hours for limited periods.
Ages 14-15	Those working in industries may not be employed ◆ during school hours ◆ before 7 a.m. or after 7 p.m. ◆ for more than three hours per day on school days, or more than 18 hours during a school week This age group cannot be employed in ◆ any manufacturing or mining occupation ◆ construction, transportation, public utilities, and communication occupations (with certain exceptions) ◆ a number of occupations in retail, warehousing, and foodservice This age group can ◆ be employed by parents in any occupation other than manufacturing or mining or those declared hazardous ◆ be employed in motion pictures, the theater, radio or television ◆ deliver newspapers Work is limited to certain occupations that do not interfere with schooling, health, or well-being. This age group may not work more than 8 hours a day or 40 hours per week on nonschool days and weeks.
Ages 16-17	This age group can be employed in any nonhazardous job for unlimited hours.
Age 18	There are no limits on the type of job or number of hours worked per week.

11-12 If you are less than eighteen years of age, the government restricts your choice of jobs.

Summary

Before you begin your job, make certain preparations. Complete any employee forms or examinations. Order uniforms or other supplies, if needed. Be sure to know how you will get to work. Being prepared and having a positive attitude about your job will help you adjust to your new responsibilities.

There will be new experiences during your first days on the job. Your supervisor will inform you of company rules, regulations, and policies. You will learn steps in fulfilling your job. You will also meet many new people.

Your employer expects you to be productive and effective on the job. He or she will expect you to perform the work for which you are being paid. Learn to take and follow directions carefully and observe the rules of the workplace. Cooperation and loyalty are important attributes.

Your employer also has certain responsibilities to his or her employees. These are to train you and to pay you a just wage. A company or business must provide a safe environment for employees. Everyone should be treated fairly and without discrimination.

Your supervisor will inform you of various personnel policies. During your job orientation, you will receive information on the method of your pay. A number of payroll deductions will reduce your gross pay.

The U.S. government has enacted labor laws and regulations. These are designed to protect workers' rights. The Fair Labor Standards Act regulates minimum wage, overtime pay, equal pay, and child labor standards.

To Review

1. List four ways you might prepare for the first day of a new job.

2. Should you address people at work by their first name? Why or why not?

3. List at least three helpful hints for making a good impression on the job.

4. Name five expectations an employer has of an employee.

5. List four responsibilities the employer has to his or her employees.

6. Name four employee work policies that might be established by employers.

7. Which amount is higher—gross pay or net pay?

8. List three amendments to the Fair Labor Standards Act and explain how they protect workers.

To Do

1. In groups of four or five students, role-play introducing a new employee to coworkers. One student should play an employer; one, the new employee; and the rest, coworkers. Practice, then switch roles.

2. With four other students, role-play a situation in which the new person on the job makes a good impression. Try to think of as many good practices as possible. Then switch and role-play a situation where the new person on the job makes a poor first impression.

3. In the library locate an article about dressing for the job. Prepare an oral report for the class.

4. Make a chart outlining job expectations of employers and employees. Find illustrations appropriate for the chart.

5. Interview an employer to find out what fringe benefits are offered to employees in his or her company or business. Report this to the class.

12 Job Performance

After studying this chapter, you will be able to
- describe work habits that influence job success.
- describe work attitudes that influence job success.
- list unsafe work practices and attitudes.
- explain the role of OSHA in the workplace.
- analyze health and fitness practices that influence job performance.

Terms to Know

punctual
dependable
responsible
initiative
attitude
self-motivation

Occupational Safety
    and Health
    Administration (OSHA)
Dietary Guidelines
    for Americans
Food Guide Pyramid
drug abuse

A remark such as "I want to see you in my office" can bring on fear and alarm. If you have ever been sent to the principal's office, you know the feeling. You can have the same feeling if your employer asks you to come to his or her office. However, a meeting with your supervisor can be about your good work, too.

This chapter will focus on work habits and job performance. You want to hear good reports concerning your job performance from your supervisor. Suggestions given in this chapter will help you learn work habits and attitudes that can help you be a better employee. You will learn safe work habits to practice. Your health and fitness practices can also influence your job performance.

Work Habits That Influence Job Success

There are certain work habits that employers look for in their employees. Employers want punctual, dependable, and responsible employees. They want employees who show initiative and will start a new task on their own. Employers need employees who are accurate, organized, and efficient. It is important to practice good work habits. Your success on the job depends on how well you follow positive work habits. The following discussion of positive work habits will help you achieve a good employer-employee relationship.

Being Punctual

Being **punctual** means that you are on time. Have you ever had to wait for someone after arranging a specific meeting time? It is a frustrating waste of time. Being punctual on the job means that you are ready to begin work at the designated time. See 12-1.

Consider this example of an employee's lack of punctuality and the boss' reaction. Jerry had a habit of coming to work five minutes late every morning. He felt justified by saying, "It's only five minutes. Nobody will miss just five minutes of my work." His employer, on the

Karen Jenkins

12-1 Punctual employees plan their schedules so they can be at work on time.

other hand, pointed out that the five-minute tardiness every day for 50 weeks equaled nearly 21 hours of work lost annually. Translated into labor costs at $10.00 an hour, Jerry's tardiness cost the company nearly $210 annually in unproductive time. If 10 employees felt that way, the company would lose over $167 a month. After talking with his boss, Jerry made it a point to report to work on time.

It is especially important to be on time if you work on a production line. Others on the line cannot do their job if you hold up the line. For example, your responsibility might be to add a certain part to a product. If you are not there, work will pile up at your station. The supervisor may need to slow or stop the production line until a replacement employee is found to handle your work. Your actions affect the output of the entire line. In this case, it would cause losses. The company loses money for time employees are not working.

If you take more than your allotted time for breaks and meals, others may not be able to leave until you return. By stretching your breaks beyond the time allowed, you might inconvenience others. They are likely to resent

your disregard for their time. Coming to work late or stretching break periods is unfair to your coworkers and the company.

Being Dependable

To be **dependable** means people can rely on you. You do what you say you will do. If you tell your parents you are going to be home at a certain time, you are certain to fulfill your promise.

Being dependable on the job means people can count on you to follow through with your assignment. You can prove that you are reliable and dependable by carrying a project through to completion. This means doing your work well and on time. See 12-2.

As a dependable worker, you need to report to work every day. When you are absent, someone else might need to do your work, which is hard on other workers. Often they do not know exactly how to do your work. If your work is not complete, others might not be able to pick up where you left off. This makes it difficult for everyone. An employer is not happy if productivity decreases.

There may be circumstances when you cannot go to work. You may wake up one morning and realize you are too sick to go to work. If you cannot report for work because you are ill, call your supervisor immediately. Explain why you cannot come to work. Employees can be fired for failing to call their supervisors due to absence from work.

There may be other times when you cannot be at work. You may need to take care of some personal business. Talk with your supervisor or consult your company policy manual concerning this type of absence. You might be able to use a day of your vacation time for personal business. The policy for personal time off from work varies with different companies.

Being truthful and honest with your employer is important. He or she expects you at work every day. Too much absenteeism can cost you your job.

Jack Klasey

12-2 You show you are a dependable and reliable employee if you complete your work on time.

Being Responsible

Being **responsible** means others can trust you to carry out your duty. How well you perform your assigned tasks determines the amount of responsibility an employer gives you. If your work is completed as requested, this shows you are responsible. Acting responsibly is a trait employers appreciate in their employees.

You might wait tables in a restaurant, for instance. Your employer expects you to restock your workstation at the end of your shift. By doing this, you show you are a responsible employee. Other staff members can count on their supplies being in place when they begin their shifts.

Being Efficient and Organized

How does your desk or locker look right now? Do you know where everything is in your room? Would you say you were quite orderly, or do you need to work on organization?

Your job might require you to keep a certain area neat and organized, such as your desk, a counter, or an office. Your employer expects you to be efficient and neat. You accomplish more work if you know where everything is, rather than having to search to find what you need.

Showing Initiative

Having **initiative** is the ability to do things on your own. When you have finished your job, you look to see what else needs to be done, 12-3. You do not wait until someone tells you what to do or directs your activities. A person with initiative will require less supervision than someone who needs constant direction.

Employers usually want their workers to take initiative. This does not mean doing work you are not qualified to do or cannot handle. Use good judgment when attempting new or different work. Notice how the work fits into the entire work structure. Employers want employees who have new ideas and a desire to contribute.

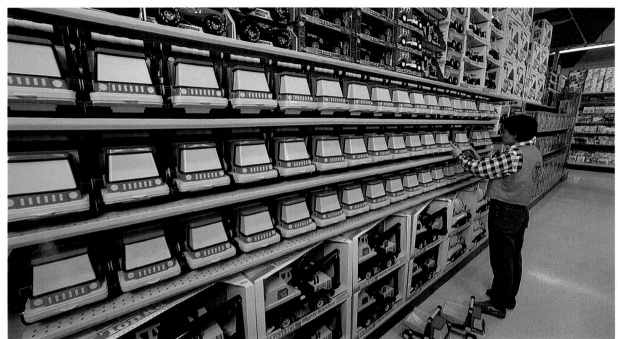

12-3 Employees who take initiative often see additional work that needs to be accomplished.

Being Accurate

Employers expect work to be accurate and free from error. Be willing to put the effort into being accurate and doing good work on the job. This is the reason your employer hired you. With your knowledge and skills, your employer expects you to be able to complete assigned tasks correctly. Fulfilling these responsibilities requires concentration. It also means full use of your abilities to do the work.

Establish productive work habits. Your employer expects high-quality work from you, not work someone else needs to redo. Strive to be accurate and productive.

◆ Work Attitudes That Influence Job Success

One of the biggest factors that determines job success is your own attitude. Your **attitude** is the way you look at what happens in your life and how you respond.

People with positive attitudes tend to see the good side of situations and other people. They are optimistic, pleasant, and cheerful. They see their life and work as worthwhile and enjoyable. Workers with positive attitudes are more productive on the job. They get along better with other people.

People with negative attitudes tend to see the bad side of everything. They may complain a great deal and believe things will not work out well. They often have a difficult time getting along with others.

Employers appreciate workers with positive attitudes. It is more difficult for an employer to change an employee's attitude than it is to change his or her job skills.

The attitude of each worker influences the atmosphere in the workplace. Employees can help improve their workplace by practicing the following positive work attitudes. These attitudes can also help you achieve personal success.

Being Friendly and Courteous

Isn't it much more fun to shop where salespeople are friendly and courteous? How do you feel when they are rude and uncaring? "A friendly smile in every aisle" attitude welcomes customers. It builds good customer relations for the employer. If you have a positive attitude, you will find it easy to be friendly and courteous.

How much business do companies lose due to rude and unfriendly employees? Customers might not want to do business with employees who treat them poorly. Other people might hesitate to approach you if they are not sure how you will treat them. If you work in a business that deals with the public, you must be especially aware of how you treat others.

Being friendly may take some effort on your part, especially on days when you may not feel well. Try to develop a positive attitude. Show interest in others by talking to them. Smiling and being concerned about other people shows you care, 12-4. People respond better to a warm smile than to a grouchy disposition. See if you can get a customer to smile by smiling yourself. Friendliness is an important attitude to develop and practice.

Even if you do not work with the public, it is important to be friendly to your coworkers. When you pass someone in the hall, doesn't it make you feel better if you receive a smile and a warm hello than to have someone ignore you? If you show an interest in other employees, they will know you care about them. Working with people who are friendly and interested in each other is easier than with people who hardly speak to you!

Being Enthusiastic and Sharing Your Enthusiasm

Enthusiastic people have a lively interest in what they are doing. They are eager to do their work. You will find an enthusiastic person

Jack Klasey

12-4 Let other employees know you are interested in what they have to say.

saying something like, "Let's get started" or, "Come on, let's go!" Enthusiasm is contagious. Cheerleaders at sports events spark enthusiasm. They get the crowd cheering for their team. Likewise at work, an enthusiastic employee can get an entire crew moving. Let the enthusiasm begin with you!

You can express enthusiasm in many ways. Facial expression, a nonverbal gesture, or a tone of voice can all communicate enthusiasm. An employee who arrives at work smiling and greeting others with a cheerful, "good morning!" is showing enthusiasm. Some employees always show enthusiasm about their work. Their enthusiasm can be contagious and spread to other employees. Good leaders often show enthusiasm. They can spark their team toward a goal by their enthusiastic attitude.

In a retail workplace, enthusiasm can affect sales. Would you feel motivated to buy a product if a salesperson showed no enthusiasm for the product? If you asked how a product worked and the response was, "I have no idea!" would you want to buy the product? A customer who comes into a store eager to buy will soon lose interest with such a negative attitude.

Practicing Self-Motivation

Self-motivation is that inner urge to get going and accomplish what you set out to do. Self-motivation prompts you to achieve and succeed. When you are self-motivated, you do not wait for others to encourage and guide you into action. You set your own goals and work toward achieving them. See 12-5.

Charles was a company sales representative. He spent a great deal of time traveling and talking to potential customers. He had initiative and energy to start each day and meet his sales goals. He worked independently, so he did not have someone pressuring him to reach a sales quota. He had to be self-motivated to go out and sell his product every day. Employees need self-motivation to get their work done. This brings job satisfaction. Your job performance is affected by your self-motivating attitude.

12-5 Self-motivated employees have an inner desire to get their work accomplished. They do not wait for someone to tell them what to do.

Being Cooperative

Cooperation is important when a team needs to complete a job. Lack of cooperation by team members might result in an unfinished job. Members of the team need to work together to accomplish their common goals. They must be flexible and willing to listen to other viewpoints. They must be willing to try different approaches or methods to complete the job.

If someone is uncooperative, the job becomes more difficult. A job often takes longer to accomplish. When people do not get along, strained relationships can occur. This will hinder work progress and productivity. In any group effort, cooperation is a vital ingredient.

The best way to show cooperation is to try to get along with your coworkers. Sometimes this requires great effort on your part. Not being able to work well with others is one of the key reasons why people lose their jobs. How you get along with your coworkers, customers, and supervisors might determine whether you remain in your job. In the workplace, employees need to have a cooperative attitude, 12-6.

12-6 Jobs take less time to accomplish when people are cooperative. Cooperation is especially important when a team effort is needed.

Being Honest and Trustworthy

Being honest with others should begin at an early age. It means being honest and truthful with friends and family members. Keeping promises and dealing fairly with people are important attributes. These are needed in your personal life and on the job.

Every employer expects honest and trustworthy employees. A company trusts employees with company money and materials. Employees who handle company money should be accurate. They should count and deposit all money according to company rules. Employees should not take company property and use it for personal reasons. Most businesses have strict rules covering these policies. For example, if you work in a restaurant there might be rules regarding the amount of restaurant food that employees can eat. A business might state what supplies employees can and cannot use. Look at the actions of the following employees and decide how you would react if you were the employer.

◆ Alison worked at a restaurant. She thought it was okay to take water glasses with the restaurant's name on them. After all, the restaurant had a large supply.

◆ Celia worked at a fast-food restaurant. When friends pulled up at the drive-through window, she gave them free hamburgers and fries.

◆ Ronald worked for a construction company where odd pieces of boards and old nails were always leftover. He did not ask his boss if he could have them because he thought nobody would need them.

All of these employees are taking items that do not belong to them. They are stealing from their employers just as surely as if they had taken money from the cash register. Most employers would promptly dismiss employees like these three.

In-house stealing is the reason consumers pay an increased price for many products and services. Often, the company has to buy new items to replace those stolen. The extra cost is passed on to the consumer in the form of higher prices.

Whether you give a friend a hamburger or take money, supplies, or merchandise, you are stealing from your employer. Each company has its own policy regarding in-house theft. Punishment depends on the seriousness of the behavior. The employee might be required to reimburse the employer. In-house stealing might cause immediate dismissal. In some cases, an employee might be charged with theft. A report of this behavior will stay on your company record. Being convicted of theft stays on a police record. Finding another job with this on your record is often difficult.

◆ Safety on the Job

Everyone in a company needs to help prevent accidents. Your employer has the responsibility to provide a safe working environment. It is up to you to practice safety on your job.

Safety rules protect the health and well-being of employees. Some companies post safety rules throughout the building, while other companies only post safety rules in certain areas. Certain pieces of equipment might be required to have safety rules attached or printed directly on them. Some equipment is very dangerous if not used correctly.

Safety rules vary according to the type of work. Some jobs are more dangerous than others. Pilots, construction workers, miners, loggers, roofers, and farmers have a higher risk level than office workers or real estate agents.

Neither working carelessly nor ignoring rules is acceptable in the workplace. Workers need to think about safety at all times. Knowing your company's safety rules is important. Following safety rules will help you avoid injuries and accidents on the job. See 12-7.

Cathy, as an example, worked in a large bakery. She was in charge of baking the cinnamon rolls. One day she was busy with customers when a pan of rolls needed to come out

US Navy

12-7 Protective clothing is always needed when fighting fires. All employees should be aware of correct safety practices at their place of work.

of the oven. She was in a hurry and grabbed a dishtowel to remove the hot pan. The towel quickly caught fire and burst into flames as Cathy dropped the pan to the floor.

She was badly burned and missed several weeks of work. She knew it was a rule to use hot pads when removing pans from the oven. Cathy did not lose her job, but she learned a painful lesson. Some companies will fire employees for not observing safety rules. They cannot afford to keep an employee who does not take safety seriously.

Accident Costs

In addition to the human suffering, accidents cost individuals and businesses millions of dollars each year. Workers face loss of income or a job, and sometimes loss of life. When a worker is hurt in an accident, everyone suffers in some way.

Injured employees suffer physical pain and other anguish. The injured employee may be hospitalized or bedridden at home. This leads to lost wages. When ready to return to work, the employee may not be able to physically carry out the former job. It may be necessary to find a new job, which can affect lifetime career plans. A permanent injury or *disability* could make it difficult for the employee to find suitable work.

Employers lose money from on-the-job accidents. A company may need to hire temporary workers and train them to do an injured person's job. As a result, production might drop. All states have laws requiring employers to carry *workers' compensation* insurance on their employees. When employees are injured, this insurance pays a percentage of the worker's wages and medical bills. More accident claims can increase the cost of these premiums. If the employee is severely injured, he or she may sue the company. There may be other lawsuits and fines. These cause hardships on the employee and employer.

Causes of Accidents

There are a number of reasons for accidents on the job. Often, accidents occur because of unsafe working conditions. Accidents also occur because workers do not follow safe work practices. Other causes are unsafe attitudes and actions as well as environmental factors. See 12-8.

Unsafe Conditions

Unsafe conditions cause accidents. Workers can correct many of these conditions. For instance, if something spills, an alert employee can immediately wipe it up so no one slips and falls. If an exit door has cases stacked by it, a worker can move them elsewhere.

You cannot correct all unsafe conditions. You can, however, bring them to the attention of your supervisor. Some unsafe conditions to stay alert to are the following:
- overloaded extension cords or outlets
- piles of oily rags
- poor lighting
- objects left lying on the floor

12-8 Taking your time and paying careful attention to your work helps prevent accidents.

- blocked stairways or exits
- poor ventilation
- lack of safety guards on equipment
- sharp equipment improperly stored
- items stacked too high

Unsafe objects or conditions can occur at any time. It is important to remove such hazards right away.

Unsafe Practices

Unsafe practices lead to many accidents that could be avoided. Workers must follow safe practices. For instance, some people fail to turn off moving machinery when it jams or malfunctions. Workers have lost limbs or even died when they tried to remove a jam from a plugged-in machine. Other unsafe practices that cause accidents on the job include the following:
- having inadequate skill and knowledge for the job
- attempting to make equipment repairs

- taking unnecessary risks
- not wearing protective gear
- not using protective shields with dangerous equipment
- using a chair instead of a ladder to reach high places
- failing to close doors or drawers

Using proper safety practices is everyone's responsibility. Being careless and reckless are threats to everyone's safety. See 12-9.

Unsafe Attitudes and Actions

Try to develop a safety-conscious attitude. Think about keeping yourself and others safe on the job. Certain attitudes and actions can lead to accidents. The following should be avoided.

- ***Being careless.*** Be aware of what you are doing and avoid daydreaming. Try to keep your mind on your work. Many costly accidents have occurred due to carelessness, such as forgetting to turn off a piece of equipment.
- ***Being a show-off.*** Show-offs often endanger other people by their actions. They take unnecessary chances to boost their own egos. For example, Ian always tried to carry too many books when restocking shelves at the bookstore where he worked. He wanted to impress Kelly, a girl who also worked there. One day he lost his balance and fell against a glass shelf. The shelf broke, Ian was cut severely, and his manager had to rush him to a hospital. Being a show-off can cause you and others serious injury.
- ***Losing self-control.*** Not being able to control your temper can cause you to react in an unsafe manner. In the heat of anger, people might forget normal safety precautions. Working at a job requires clear and focused thinking at all times.

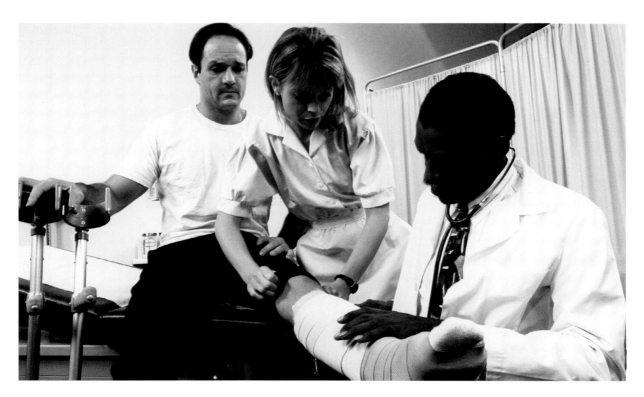

12-9 This accident occurred after someone spilled water and didn't bother to wipe it up.

◆ ***Being tired.*** Being tired increases the potential for accidents because you are not alert. You cannot do your best work when you are tired. Adequate sleep and rest are important for a clear mind on the job. Fewer accidents will result.

Environmental Causes

Accidents can result from environmental causes. For instance, employees working in an industrial or chemical operation might become sick from breathing dangerous fumes. For people who must work outdoors, hazardous weather conditions can cause more accidents. This can range from the ice and snow of winter to the high heat of summer. Some occupations are more hazardous than others. Highway construction workers are exposed to more environmental hazards than office workers.

Workers exposed to environmental hazards need to follow the special safety precautions required by their employers. Employees might need to wear breathing masks and protective clothing. They might need to take other precautions crucial to their safety.

Accident Prevention

It is everyone's job to keep the workplace safe. By practicing safety, you protect the employer's most important assets—yourself and your coworkers.

Many businesses set goals to achieve accident-free environments. They post signs stressing safety on the job. They have special safety-awareness and motivational programs to promote employee safety and accident prevention. Some companies recognize employees and departments that have accident-free records. These activities keep workers thinking about safety and practicing safety habits. See 12-10.

Some businesses hire people with special training to study the reasons accidents occur. Safety inspectors work in industries and factories. They identify conditions that might cause accidents. Employers then correct the dangerous conditions to prevent accidents.

In your workplace, learn how to correctly operate machines and equipment. This is why job training is important. Good training programs emphasize safety rules and regulations. Know and follow the safety rules pertaining to your work area.

Marcia Nelson

12-10 This company posts safety goals and accomplishments to encourage good safety habits.

Government's Role in Safety

The number of federal, state, and local regulations has increased because of employee, community, and consumer demands. Employees demand safe workplaces, communities want a clean environment, and consumers expect nonhazardous products. Many agencies work to protect the safety of all. These include the Environmental Protection Agency (EPA) and the Department of Transportation (DOT), among others.

By far, the most important government agency involved in workplace safety is the **Occupational Safety and Health Administration (OSHA).** U.S. law sets and enforces job safety and health standards in the workplace. It is the Occupational Safety and Health Act of 1970, which established the agency called OSHA.

Based on the standards set by OSHA, employers must provide a safe environment and control hazards in the workplace. If companies do not meet OSHA's safety and health standards, they can receive fines. OSHA can shut down a company until it removes hazards.

It is sometimes costly for companies to meet OSHA's safety standards. Companies might need to remove equipment that is old and install new equipment. They might need to clean up dangerous areas. OSHA receives credit for removing many dangers from the workplace. It has helped save many lives.

◆ Health and Fitness for Job Performance

Your employer expects you to be healthy and alert. You must be physically able to meet the requirements of your job every workday. If you are not healthy and fit, you cannot function well on the job. There is a greater likelihood that you could have an accident. You cannot think clearly and make good decisions if you are not well. In addition, workers who are not healthy are more susceptible to illness. This causes missed work. Absent employees create a greater hardship for coworkers as well as supervisors. It may leave more work for others to handle or it may reduce the productivity of the entire department. To maintain proper health and fitness, strive to maintain these goals daily.

◆ Follow the *Dietary Guidelines for Americans*.
◆ Get adequate rest and sleep.
◆ Avoid health risks such as tobacco, drugs, and alcohol.
◆ Maintain good mental health.

Follow the *Dietary Guidelines for Americans*

The **Dietary Guidelines for Americans** is a 10-point plan for good health that applies to people of all ages, 12-11. By following them, children grow and develop well. They perform competently in school. Adults are productive at work, enjoy life, and feel fit. The *Guidelines* provide advice around three basic messages: Aim for fitness. Build a healthy base. Choose sensibly.

Aim for Fitness

Regular exercise helps children and adults feel and look better. Physical body movements make the muscles stronger and more flexible. Exercise improves blood circulation as it makes the heart and lungs work harder and become stronger. Regular exercise prevents children from adding excess weight, which tends to stay with them through adulthood. A healthy weight is key to a long, healthy life.

Physical activity helps reduce work-related stress in older children and adults. You may feel much better after a run or a walk in the park. Even shoveling snow or a hard workout on an exercise machine can help relieve built-up stress.

The *Guidelines* recommend moderate physical activity at least four days a week, preferably more often, lasting 30 minutes for adults and 60 minutes for children. *Moderate*

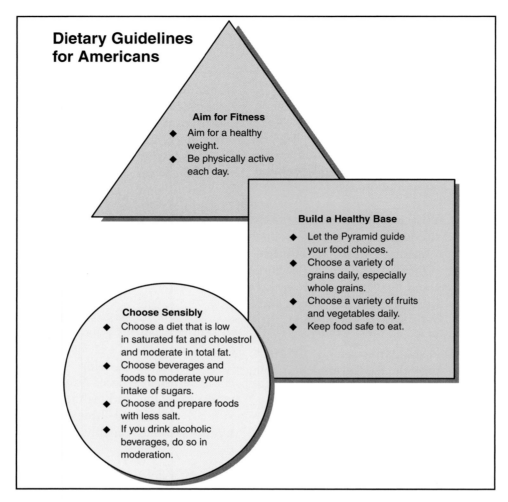

Dietary Guidelines for Americans

Aim for Fitness
◆ Aim for a healthy weight.
◆ Be physically active each day.

Build a Healthy Base
◆ Let the Pyramid guide your food choices.
◆ Choose a variety of grains daily, especially whole grains.
◆ Choose a variety of fruits and vegetables daily.
◆ Keep food safe to eat.

Choose Sensibly
◆ Choose a diet that is low in saturated fat and cholestrol and moderate in total fat.
◆ Choose beverages and foods to moderate your intake of sugars.
◆ Choose and prepare foods with less salt.
◆ If you drink alcoholic beverages, do so in moderation.

12-11 The Dietary Guidelines for Americans *lists a total of 10 guidelines under three categories.*

physical activity is defined as any activity that uses as much energy as walking two miles in 30 minutes.

Try to be more active throughout the day. For example, walk up stairs instead of taking an elevator. A minimum of 30 minutes of exercise will get you started toward fitness. Following a regular exercise program is a good way to stay physically fit. Running, walking, bike riding, and swimming are all excellent forms of exercise, 12-12. Jobs done at home such as mowing the lawn, raking leaves, vacuuming, and washing windows also provide good exercise.

Many people find exercise more enjoyable when they do it with others. Perhaps there are programs at the YMCA or YWCA that you could join. Team sports such as volleyball, softball, and basketball are also good forms of exercise.

The type of exercise you choose is not as important as doing something active on a regular basis. Start any exercise program slowly. Overdoing it at first will cause sore muscles. For those overweight, it is always wise to first consult a doctor before beginning an active exercise program.

12-12 Exercise promotes good physical and mental health.

Build a Healthy Base

The easiest way to make sure you eat a balanced diet is to select foods from each of the food groups in the **Food Guide Pyramid.** This guide helps you choose a well-balanced diet. The Food Guide Pyramid is shown in 12-13. A well-balanced diet includes foods from the following five food groups:

- breads, cereals, rice, and pasta
- vegetables
- fruit
- meat, poultry, fish, dry beans, eggs, and nuts
- milk, yogurt, and cheese

In the smallest part of the pyramid, the top, are fats, oils, and sweets. These include butter, margarine, jellies, jams, syrup, candies, salad dressings, and many snack foods. Eat them sparingly. They mainly contain calories and few nutrients.

Eat plant foods as the foundation of your meals. Choose plenty of grain products, vegetables, and fruits. These foods provide fiber and bulk in the diet. They also provide carbohydrates that give you energy. In addition, they are excellent sources of vitamins and minerals, yet are low in sugar, salt, fats, and cholesterol. Watch portion size to avoid overeating.

Keep foods safe to eat to prevent foodborne illness. Use extra precaution with perishable foods, quickly chilling them after shopping. As a general rule, keep work surfaces, hands, and food clean. Prevent disease organisms from cross-contaminating food by keeping raw, cooked, and ready-to-eat foods separate during shopping, preparation, and storage. Cook foods to safe temperatures, and promptly refrigerate leftovers. Above all, when in doubt, throw it out. Never take a chance with food that does not look or smell right.

Choose Sensibly

There are many kinds of food and many ways to build a healthy diet. A healthy lifestyle is all about making wise choices. To accom-

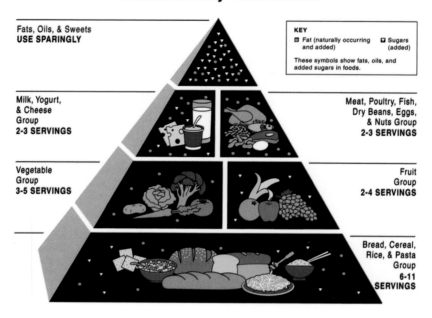

12-13 The Food Guide Pyramid helps you choose a well-balanced diet.

plish that goal, the *Dietary Guidelines for Americans* recommends the following four recommendations:

Choose a diet low in saturated fat and cholesterol and moderate in total fat. Some health problems associated with too much fat and cholesterol are obesity, heart disease, high blood pressure, and some forms of cancer.

There are several ways to adjust your fat intake to a more healthful course. Choose vegetable oils instead of solid fats. Limit your intake of high-fat meats, sausages, deli meats, and organ meats. Consider meat substitutes, such as dry beans, lentils, nuts and peanut butter, tofu, and soy products. Select low-fat or fat-free milk, cheese, cream sauces, and other dairy products. Include two servings each week of tuna, salmon, mackerel, or other fish containing omega-3 fatty acids.

Choose beverages and foods to moderate your intake of sugars. For most people, this means lowering their sugar intake. Sugars include white sugar, brown sugar, honey, and breakfast syrups. Sugars provide mainly calories and few nutrients. They contribute to tooth decay and obesity. The major sources of sugars are soft drinks, fruit drinks, cakes, cookies, pies, ice cream, and candy. As a general rule, you should get most of your calories from grains, fruits, vegetables, lowfat or fat-free dairy products, and lean meats.

Choose a diet moderate in salt and sodium. Salt contains sodium. Many processed foods contain more sodium than you might expect. Read food labels to see the amount of sodium in various foods. Limit the amount of these in your diet. Sodium is linked to high blood pressure.

Adults who drink alcoholic beverages should do so in moderation. Alcohol can cause a wide variety of problems on the job as well as at home. Young people and pregnant women should avoid alcohol completely. Adults should use it only in moderation, if at all.

Get Adequate Rest and Sleep

Getting adequate rest and sleep is an important health habit. Sound sleep is the best type of rest. Most young people need eight to ten hours of sleep each night. This varies with age and amount of physical activity, 12-14

Having a regular sleep schedule will help you feel rested and refreshed. You will have more energy and ambition. Safety experts report that fewer accidents occur on the job when people are well rested.

Avoid Tobacco

Tobacco smoking and the use of smokeless tobacco create serious health hazards. The Surgeon General warns that smoking can cause cancer, heart disease, and emphysema. Smoking may complicate pregnancy. The use of smokeless tobacco is linked to serious problems such as mouth and throat cancer. There are other reasons to never start smoking, but if you have, consider quitting.

◆ Nicotine is an addictive chemical, one that requires a great deal of work, effort, and motivation to overcome.
◆ The senses of taste and smell become dull.
◆ Smoking can discolor teeth.
◆ Smoking makes clothing and rooms smell of smoke odor.
◆ Smoking is a fire hazard, and many fires are started by careless smokers.
◆ Smoking is a very expensive habit.
◆ Smoking is prohibited in many places.

Businesses in general are moving toward making their facilities smoke-free. Many factories and offices ban all smoking on their premises. Schools also ban smoking. "Quit smoking" programs are underway throughout the country. These activities are an attempt to create a cleaner, safer, and healthier environment. See 12-15.

Avoid Drug and Alcohol Abuse

There are many drugs on the market today, both legal and illegal. Drugs are chemical

12-14 Falling asleep at your desk or on the job is a sure sign you are not getting enough rest.

12-15 *Smoking is a dangerous habit that is associated with many health hazards. For that reason, smoking is banned in practically all public buildings.*

substances that cause physical, emotional, or mental changes in people. Legal drugs are those sold over the counter as well as prescription drugs. It is important to take all drugs only as prescribed. Drug abuse can occur with any legal drug. **Drug abuse** is deliberately taking a substance for other than its intended purpose. Tranquilizers and diet pills are legal drugs that are often abused.

Illegal drugs are numerous, including cocaine, crack, ecstasy, heroin, and marijuana. These are powerful drugs. They can alter behavior, impede judgment, become addictive, and in some cases, cause death. Possessing, selling, or using any of these drugs is a serious criminal offense, punishable by fines and imprisonment.

Alcohol is the most widely used and abused drug today. It acts as a depressant. This means it hinders mental processes, slows down reflexes, and causes a lack of muscle control. It greatly increases the risk of being involved in

accidents. A person who drives or operates machinery while intoxicated can cause deadly consequences. Thousands of people die annually because of alcohol and its effects.

Not only can alcohol be damaging to the body, but it can also ruin personal relationships. Alcohol addiction by one or more family members causes the entire family to suffer. In addition, alcohol can cause work interruptions. The loss of a job due to alcohol abuse creates more family and personal anguish.

Drugs can cause a wide variety of problems on the job. They cause increased safety risks, increased absenteeism, and tardiness. Poor relationships with coworkers often occur. Workers impaired by drugs often produce products that are substandard. Most drugs also hamper work efficiency.

Policies concerning alcohol and drug use in the workplace are standard. The consequences of workers drinking or using drugs on the job can be immediate dismissal. Because of drugs, many people have lost everything important to them—their jobs, savings, health, self-esteem, friends, family, and even their lives.

Maintain Good Mental Health

Good mental health is as important as good physical health. Mentally healthy people have feelings of general well-being and a positive self-image. Mental health is not a physical characteristic. It is the ability of individuals to relate to other people and the world around them in a healthy way. See 12-16.

Good physical health is closely related to good mental health. If you are physically healthy, your mental health is likely to be good, too.

Good Mental Health

People with good mental health
- accept themselves as they are and make the best of their abilities
- are able to balance dependence with interdependence
- are able to adjust to change
- can control their emotions
- can handle difficult situations
- are able to have close and lasting relationships with others
- take responsibility for their own actions

12-16 Good mental health affects every area of a person's life.

Summary

Your employer hired you on the basis of certain qualities he or she felt you possessed. When you start your job, your employer wants a productive worker who is a credit to the company or business.

Employers expect employees to practice good work habits. They expect you to be punctual, dependable, and responsible. They also want you to be efficient and organized. Employers will look for accuracy and initiative on the job. Your work habits influence the success of your job.

Your work attitudes influence your job success. Workers need positive work attitudes. Positive attitudes include being honest, trustworthy, friendly, and courteous. People who are enthusiastic, self-motivated, and cooperative have good work attitudes.

Employers and their employees must practice accident prevention in the workplace. A hazard-free environment is important to the health and safety of workers. Accidents cost loss of work time and company productivity. Accidents can also cause much pain and suffering. Sometimes even death results from a work accident. Everyone must work to maintain a safe environment.

In order to meet the demands of the job, employees need good health habits. They need to eat a balanced diet and get adequate amounts of sleep and exercise. The use of drugs and tobacco can adversely affect the health of an individual. Good health habits are important for good job performance. A person's mental health also influences his or her job performance.

To Review

1. Name and describe two positive employee work habits.

2. Describe a person with a positive work attitude.

3. Describe a person who is self-motivated.

4. Describe what might happen when someone at work is uncooperative.

5. How can employees show they are honest and trustworthy?

6. Describe an unsafe attitude that could lead to an accident on the job.

7. List ways employers and employees can try to prevent accidents.

8. What is the purpose of OSHA?

9. Name four ways you can maintain proper health and fitness.

10. What are the dangers of using drugs while on the job?

To Do

1. Interview an employer about the kind of work habits and attitudes he or she looks for in an employee. Make a list and share responses with the class.

2. With a partner, role-play buying a product from an enthusiastic sales person versus a bored sales person. Which one motivated you more to buy the product? Give several reasons why. Which sales associate probably made the sale?

3. Ask your school principal about the kinds of work habits and attitudes he or she likes to see in a teacher. Write a one-page report.

4. With a teacher, review the safety rules for the family and consumer sciences department. Write out any suggestions for additions to these rules. Share your responses with the class.

5. Invite an employer to talk to the class about what he or she wants in an employee. Ask the employer reasons why employees are fired.

Job Evaluation and Change 13

After studying this chapter, you will be able to
- ◆ explain the purpose of a probationary period.
- ◆ describe how a supervisor might perform a formal and an informal job evaluation.
- ◆ analyze pay raises, promotions, and lateral career moves.
- ◆ list reasons for losing a job.
- ◆ list reasons for changing jobs.
- ◆ describe steps that an employee might take to change jobs.

Terms to Know
probationary period
formal evaluations
informal evaluations
cost-of-living raise
merit pay raise
promotion
lateral career move
merger
seasonal
severance pay
unemployment
   compensation
letter of resignation

In the previous chapter, you learned about work habits and attitudes that influence job performance. Employers consider these qualities when they hire people. As you begin work, a supervisor will carefully evaluate these qualities in you. Supervisors or trainers check your progress. They look at how well you have learned the job, do your work, and get along with others.

In this chapter you will look at different ways that employers evaluate the work of their employees. Job performance usually influences pay raises and promotions. This chapter will also help you understand why people lose their jobs.

◆ Probationary Period

Many companies consider the first few weeks or months of a new job as a **probationary period.** An employer often hires a new worker for a trial period to see how well he or she performs. During this time, a supervisor oversees

and monitors the employee's work. If the new employee performs according to certain standards, he or she will receive regular employee status. The employer may change the employee's assignment if his or her abilities fit better elsewhere. However, if an employee does not satisfactorily pass this probationary period, the employer may dismiss the employee, 13-1.

The Tram Restaurant hired James on a probationary basis. James started as a cook, but he was always leaving the kitchen to talk to the customers. Mr. Tram transferred James to the front counter service where he could welcome people to the restaurant and take the customers' orders. This worked out better for James and the restaurant.

Ernie's probationary period did not turn out as well. He was hired as a janitor in the elementary school. He knew many of the teachers already. He liked to visit with them as he cleaned their rooms, even though the teachers were often busy grading papers or preparing lessons.

Boatmens Bancshares, Inc.

13-1 By the end of a probationary period of employment, a new employee should be able to satisfactorily perform tasks expected in his or her job.

His supervisor told Ernie about the problem, but reminders didn't help. He continued to visit with the teachers. Ernie took twice as long to clean up the classrooms as the previous janitor. Some wastebaskets were not emptied, and he often forgot to clean the chalkboards. Ernie ignored his supervisor's directions and did not do his job well. The school asked Ernie to leave at the end of his probationary period.

◆ Employee Evaluations

By the end of your probationary period, you should have an idea of how well you are doing your job. Some supervisors will give you information about your progress as you go along. Others will wait until it is time to make out an evaluation of your work. The purpose of employee evaluations or reviews is to help you identify your strengths and weaknesses on the job.

Formal Evaluations

Many companies use written evaluation, or **formal evaluations,** to review employee's work. You may hear these called *performance reviews.* Employers may rate an individual's accomplishments as excellent, satisfactory, or unsatisfactory. Your supervisor may also evaluate you on the following aspects of your job:

◆ Do you fulfill your job responsibilities?
◆ Are you willing to accept new duties?
◆ Do you reliably accomplish your tasks on time?
◆ Do you cooperate and get along with others at work?
◆ Do you arrive at work on time?
◆ Do you have a good attendance record?

The supervisor may point out specific weaknesses and suggest ways to improve. Consider seriously any suggestions given and incorporate these into your work habits. A supervisor might use this time to praise your performance. If you are doing a good job, your employer will want you to continue. This is also a good time for you to ask questions concerning your work.

Informal Evaluations

Some employers use **informal evaluations** to let you know your progress on the job. During informal meetings your supervisor may talk to you about how your job is going. Your supervisor may offer suggestions to improve your work or may praise you for doing a good job. See 13-2.

Supervisors have different styles or methods of handling your job progress. Some supervisors are quick to criticize and slow to praise. Others offer frequent encouragement and praise.

Sometimes supervisors will not give you any indication of your progress. You may think their silence means they approve of your work. Their silence may leave you wondering. If you are unsure of how you are doing, you can ask your supervisor. You might say, "Miss Ashley,

13-2 Supervisors might praise or offer suggestions to employees while on the job. This is a type of informal evaluation.

I've been working in this job for about two months now. I'm wondering how I am doing. Can you tell me how I'm progressing?" Comments and questions similar to this will let your supervisors know you are interested in meeting their expectations.

◆ Pay Raises, Promotions, and Moves

Most employees receive performance reviews every six months or once a year. Employees with good reviews often receive pay raises. A good job review may lead to a job promotion for some employees. Lateral moves may also be discussed.

Types of Pay Raises

There are two types of pay raises: cost-of-living raises and merit raises. A **cost-of-living raise** allows you to keep pace with routine living expenses. All workers usually get the same cost-of-living raise regardless of work performance. This type of raise keeps pace with the annual rate of inflation. The *annual rate of inflation* is the percent increase in the cost of goods and services for the year.

Another type of pay raise is the **merit pay raise**. If you have done an excellent job, your pay raise may be greater than someone doing just a good job. This type of raise lets you know your employer is very happy with your work. See 13-3.

13-3 Yolanda just received a merit pay raise. She is happy to do a good job at work because someday she wants to own her own business.

Job Promotions

Being offered a promotion to a more responsible position at work is another sign of good work performance. A **promotion** is a move to a higher position with greater responsibilities. A promotion is a step upward as you advance your career. Many people have reached upper management levels by starting at the bottom and working their way to the top in a company. Each promotion means more responsibility and often a higher income.

Some employees may remain at one job for a long time, while others may move up faster. Sometimes an employee starts moving upward fast and then stops at one level, remaining there the rest of the time they are with their employer.

Some careers and employers offer more chances for advancement than others. A company may add a new upper management position and promote an employee into it. Another top-level employee may move away from the company, leaving a position open. Someone from within the company might fill that position.

If you are offered a promotion, decide if you can handle the new work responsibilities. Can you use your current skills, or will you need additional training and education to enhance your skills? How does the promotion fit your career plans? Are you satisfied with what you are doing or are you ready for new challenges? Can you use your skills to a higher degree in this new position? If advancement means relocation to another area of the country, how would you feel about this? Make a list of the pros and cons of the job offer. This will help you decide if you want to accept the promotion. Figure 13-4 shows how someone might progress in a career.

Lateral Career Moves

Moving from one job to a different but related job at the same level, rank, or status in the company is a **lateral career move.** In a lateral move, the same skills will transfer from

Advancing in Your Career

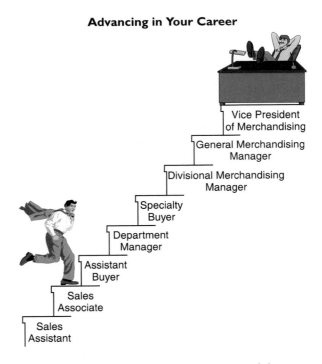

13-4 As you advance in your career, your job responsibilities and salary usually increase.

one job to the new job. Another name for this type of move is a *job shift.*

An example of a lateral career move in restaurant management is moving from food and beverage manager to bakery manager. In a retail store, a lateral move might involve changing from menswear buyer to sportswear buyer. In both cases the employee still oversees an area, but has different concerns and stock. The employee's career level remains the same. The job responsibilities and pay may be similar. The employee might need to learn some new skills.

Lateral moves help employees develop their careers. They require some work adjustment. For instance, the employee might need to learn a new set of work patterns. Employees often need to adjust to new coworkers, environment, and work expectations.

◆ Losing a Job

Sometimes the best employees lose their jobs through no fault of their own. Some workers are laid off for a few weeks; some for months at a time; others, indefinitely. Some employers call back their workers when the demand for their product or service increases. Job layoffs are often temporary, but they can be permanent.

The loss of a job can cause emotional and financial problems. The person without a paycheck can have low self-esteem. This causes discouragement and a sense of helplessness. Unemployed people may be unable to support their families. These can be difficult times for families.

Causes of Job Loss

There are many causes of job loss. Some may be due to conditions that cannot be controlled. The health of the country's economy can affect businesses, resulting in job layoffs. Companies may reorganize or merge with others. In the process, some employees may lose their jobs.

The Health of the Economy

The economy has a great deal to do with the level of employment. Economic conditions may cause a company to struggle to stay in business. If money is in short supply, there is less demand for goods and services. People do not buy as much; therefore, a manufacturing company will need fewer workers to supply products. Companies that provide services also are affected by a short supply of money. Services may not be in as much demand by consumers, resulting in company layoffs.

Bankruptcy

If a company goes into bankruptcy, it usually has to lay off employees. *Bankruptcy* means the company cannot pay its bills. The courts supervise the payment of debts to creditors. Employees may need to wait many months before they receive their back wages. In some cases, they do not receive the total amount owed them. Bankruptcy is a very serious situation. With good management, most companies do not experience bankruptcy.

Company Reorganization

Some companies may reorganize in order to operate more efficiently or serve a different need. Sometimes the company or business elects or appoints a new president. New managers may have different goals and new ways to operate the business. For instance, a business might change its emphasis of service. Elimination of some jobs might occur.

Mergers

Employees in high-level management positions may lose their jobs due to company mergers. A **merger** is the absorption of a company or business by another company, or the combination of two or more companies.

Mergers might cause employees to lose their jobs. The bigger company might keep their own managers in place. As a result, there is no need for more managers from the smaller company, who then lose their jobs.

Seasonal Work

Sometimes a job is **seasonal.** That is, after a particular season is over, the job ends, 13-5. For instance, lawn care companies hire many summer workers in the northern states. Farmers may hire more workers during the summer months to harvest crops. At the end of the growing season, these seasonal employees do not have a job. Stores often hire more salespeople during holiday buying seasons.

Payments Given to Laid-Off Workers

When you lose a job through no fault of your own, you may be entitled to some compensation. This pay generally depends on the nature of your work and the length of your employment.

Severance Pay

Severance pay is pay to an employee who is permanently laid-off due to reasons that are not the fault of the employee. The term comes from the word "severed," which means "cut." Employers are not required to give severance pay. The amount of severance pay depends on the length of employment.

Unemployment Compensation

If you are unemployed through no fault of your own, you may be eligible for **unemployment compensation.** This means you might receive unemployment checks from the state government for a limited time. Employers are taxed by the state to help fund the program. How long you receive payments depends on the length of your employment. Not everyone is eligible to receive these payments. If you apply for unemployment compensation, you

Jackson and Perkins

13-5 Migrant workers face seasonal layoffs. They constantly move to different parts of the country to plant and harvest crops.

must be actively looking for another job. You must also be willing to take a job similar to the one you lost.

Getting Fired from a Job

Some employees may be asked to leave. Employers fire workers for various reasons. Some employees are not able to do the required work. Others may have poor work habits. They waste time when they should be working. They may visit with other employees or take care of personal tasks while on the job. Usually employees are fired for a combination of reasons.

Reasons for Employee Firing

Poor job performance is a chief reason for being fired. Some people do not have the needed skills to do the job, 13-6. Even with training, their skills may not be a match for the job. For instance, Gene is hired as a salesperson for an automobile dealer. For the first two weeks he must attend new employee training sessions. By the end of a three-month probationary period, he must reach a weekly sales quota. Gene is a fast learner but hesitant to approach customers. As a result, he has trouble selling and meeting his weekly sales quota. The company asks him to leave.

Another main cause for dismissal is not getting along with coworkers and supervisors. He or she does not work well with the rest of the team. Other workers may complain if they must work with someone who has a poor attitude.

Many workers are fired because they continually arrive late to work or do not show up at all. Some employees waste time by talking and visiting with other employees. Others do personal work on the job. These are often serious violations of work policy. Jerri thought it was okay to write a quick letter to her friend during a slack period. She could have started another company project but wrote the letter instead. She was not using company time

13-6 The ability to be accurate with money is an important attribute in employees that many employers need.

adequately, and this could have been grounds for her dismissal. Other reasons employers fire employees are listed in 13-7.

Actions such as these upset other employees and employers. These wasteful actions diminish chances for pay raises and promotions. They may be a reason for dismissal. You have a responsibility to your company to produce work according to certain standards. You are being paid to work for the company, not for yourself.

What to Do If You Are Fired

If you ever lose your job, find out the reasons for your dismissal. Try to analyze how you could have prevented this from happening. Look at your performance from your employer's point of view. Learn from your mistakes.

◆ Changing Jobs

Quitting a job or changing jobs on your own takes courage. It requires considerable job hunting, searching, and questioning before finding a better job. Often the rewards of a different job are worthwhile, but sometimes they are not. There are many reasons why people change jobs. Some of these reasons include the following:

◆ higher pay
◆ better work hours or conditions
◆ change in family structure due to marriage, divorce, death, or children leaving
◆ more opportunity for advancement
◆ better use of personal skills
◆ new challenges
◆ relocation
◆ conflict with coworkers at current job

Job changes have become more common today. Reports indicate that individuals will change jobs an average of 10 times in their lifetime. They will change careers at least three times. Employee turnover rate is high for all age groups.

People often see more career opportunity and advancement when they leave their old jobs for new jobs. They also see a greater fulfillment of their dreams ahead.

Reexamine Your Career Goals

Your first job in the workforce may not be what you planned for your career. Your needs and wants may change. Your goals may change as you progress through your career. The type of jobs available may change, too. Many of tomorrow's jobs do not exist today. All of these possibilities highlight the importance of learning new job skills. Be prepared to change work several times in your lifetime.

Some people find satisfaction in climbing a career ladder, and others choose lateral careers. Yet others change to totally new careers. Each of these directions can help careers grow.

Many people do not plan ahead for career changes. They do their same job until something brings them to a halt. This might be a new job offer, job termination, or job change. Then they again sort out their priorities. Are

---

Reasons for Firing an Employee

◆ Does not get along well with the supervisor or coworkers
◆ Fails to follow rules and regulations
◆ Is frequently absent or arrives late
◆ Fails to follow instructions
◆ Abuses alcohol or drugs
◆ Is unreliable
◆ Is dishonest
◆ Does not complete assignments
◆ Causes trouble at work and problems among workers
◆ Is careless
◆ Ignores safety rules

13-7 Getting fired from a job is a serious matter. Employees must always be aware of their responsibilities to the job.

13-8 Sometimes it makes sense to work in the local area before moving to a job out of town.

they still on course for meeting their career goals? This needs to be answered before the next career decision is made. See 13-8.

When you come to a turning point in your career or job, it is a good idea to redefine your goals. Is this still the type of work you want to do? Would you feel happier or more productive if you got an advanced degree or did some further study in your field? Is this the time to try a different course of action? You may need to go back to Chapter 4 and do more research on careers. You might find it necessary and important to identify other kinds of jobs related to your skills and interests. See 13-9.

Leaving Your Job

Carefully weigh the pros and cons of leaving your current job for another job. Then decide if it is in your best interest to change jobs. If you decide a change is necessary, start looking for a new job right away.

If at all possible, keep your old job while searching for a different one. Knowing you are earning money gives you a more secure feeling. You avoid the panic factor of not having a

McCormick Spices

13-9 Sometimes you are very happy with your job but need to leave because you have other career goals. One reason for leaving a job might be to return to school.

job or money. Potential employers also tend to think that unemployed people are more desperate for work. They may believe you would take a lower salary. They are more likely to question why you are without work.

Be careful about taking too much time off your current job to look for a different one. If possible, schedule your appointments and job interviews after work or on weekends.

Tell your employer of your plans before you tell your coworkers. Most businesses require at least a two-week notice. If you are on good terms with your employer or if you will be very difficult to replace, it is good to give a month's notice. This gives the employer time to find a replacement for you.

Write a brief **letter of resignation** and carry it to your employer. You may or may not need an appointment for this, depending on how available your supervisor is. If you need an appointment, set a time in advance. Say the reason is to discuss your work.

Your letter should state when you plan to leave. Keep your tone positive and thank your employer for the opportunity to work there. See 13-10. Notice, the letter gives no details about your future plans. This does not need to be in your employee file.

Letter of Resignation

118 N. Terrace
New Downsville, AR 30928
April 12, 2004

George Fredrickson
Northwest Office Supplies
709 W. Third St.
Ada, AR 30729

Dear Mr. Fredrickson:

I plan to leave Northwest Office Supplies, effective May 1. I have enjoyed my work here and appreciate the training I have received while employed at Northwest Office Supplies. I have also appreciated the opportunity to work to my full potential as an assistant sales manager. Thank you in advance for helping me make a smooth transition in the coming weeks.

Sincerely,

Darrell Myers

Darrell Myers

13-10 This letter of resignation indicates the employee's reason for leaving the job and when he will be leaving.

When you bring your letter to your employer, start the meeting respectfully: "I wanted you to be the first to know I'm planning to leave (name the company)." If this would fit your circumstances, you may say: "I'm able to stay a month and help train a new person" or "I'd consider coming back for overload periods on (name the specific days and time)." It is good to state, "I've enjoyed working here, and I'd appreciate a short letter of recommendation to show to future employers."

Try to leave your old job under the best possible conditions. Two weeks or even one day can be a long time if you feel friction with your coworkers or boss. It is to your advantage to leave with good feelings. You may work with some of these same people again in different jobs. Continue to do your job to the best of your ability. Get your workstation in order and return any company supplies. Before you leave, thank your coworkers and supervisor for their help and friendship.

As you receive opportunities to move up in your career, it is important to be ready. This means you need to continue learning. In this way, you can more easily adapt to changes in your job. Learn to use new technology. Keep abreast of new information in your field. This encourages your employer to consider you for new positions in your area of work. See 13-11. Every employee should experience the excitement and fulfillment of lifelong career growth.

13-11 People who can use computers to do work faster and more accurately are valuable to their companies and highly sought in the job market.

Summary

Job evaluations help you know if you are working up to the expectations of your employer. These job reviews may be formal or informal. Employers rate their employees on many different points. Evaluations sometimes lead to changes in job assignments. Employees receive pay raises and promotions on the recommendation of their supervisors or trainers. Employees also make lateral career moves.

Sometimes employees lose their jobs. People are laid off because of the economy, bankruptcy, company reorganizations, mergers, or because they work a seasonal job. When employees lose their jobs, their employer or the government may provide some type of additional pay.

Employees who fail to satisfactorily perform their jobs may be fired. Causes for employee firing are often unsatisfactory job performance, poor work habits, or not getting along with coworkers or supervisors.

People of all ages make job changes many times in their lifetime. Life and career goals need to be reexamined from time to time.

If you decide to leave your present job, try to leave on friendly terms. Give your employer at least two weeks notice. Extend your appreciation to your coworkers and supervisors for their help and friendship.

To Review

1. What is the purpose of a probationary period?

2. List three work habits that might be evaluated during a formal employee evaluation.

3. Explain the difference between a cost-of-living raise and a merit pay raise.

4. Explain the difference between a promotion and a lateral career move. Give examples of each type of career change.

5. Give three reasons workers might be laid off.

6. Name three criteria to be eligible for unemployment compensation.

7. What are three reasons workers get fired from their jobs?

8. List four reasons for people changing jobs.

9. Why is it important to maintain good relationships with coworkers and supervisors when quitting a job?

To Do

1. Select another student as your partner. Role-play how you might ask for a new job assignment. How might the employer respond?

2. Interview someone from a local business who received a promotion to a current job. Discuss reasons why he or she received the job promotion. Write a report including differences in the responsibilities of the former job and this job.

3. Invite someone to speak to the class who has experienced a lateral career move. Prepare a list of questions for the class to ask the speaker. Give the speaker an idea of some questions he or she should be prepared to answer.

4. Suppose one spouse loses his or her job. The other spouse works fifteen hours a week at $7.00 per hour. Write a story about this family and how they might cope with the situation. Provide helpful suggestions for them.

5. Write a sample letter of resignation from your job as a food store clerk.

Part IV
Family and Consumer Sciences Careers

Introduction to Family and Consumer Sciences Career Clusters

There are many different careers in family and consumer sciences. This section focuses on a variety of career options and job opportunities for you in this field.

To help learn about the many opportunities available in family and consumer sciences, this text examines jobs according to six separate career clusters. A *career cluster* is a group of jobs that are similar to each other. After reading these six chapters, you may find that one career cluster interests you more than the others. This will help as you begin to make important career decisions.

As you think about your future career, try to picture yourself in a work setting. Where would you want to be? Do you see yourself traveling on business for a company? If so, careers discussed in the business cluster (Chapter 14) might interest you. Are you always helping others? Jobs in education (Chapter 15) or the human services (Chapter 16) will probably interest you. Maybe you see yourself in a science laboratory. The careers discussed in the science and technology career cluster (Chapter 17) will likely appeal to you. Do you see yourself using your creative or artistic skills? If so, you might enjoy careers in the arts (Chapter 18). Possibly you see yourself running your own business. In this case, the information on entrepreneurship (Chapter 19) may give you some ideas.

Here are brief descriptions of the career clusters that will be covered in the next six chapters. You will probably find many exciting and challenging career choices that interest you.

Careers in Business and Marketing

Jobs for those interested in business or marketing careers are generally found in companies and other profit-making operations. This area offers the widest array of job opportunities. Many business and marketing-related careers deal with foods, clothing, or housing. Jobs in food marketing, fashion merchandising, interior design, or financial planning are typical. You may desire to work in restaurant, hotel, or motel management. You might even want to gain some business experience so you can own your own business someday!

Careers in Education and Communications

Family and consumer sciences professionals working in education often teach in classroom settings. There is great demand for child care teachers, but many other jobs exist in the education sector. These include adult continuing education, cooperative extension, and educational writing.

People interested in careers in communications provide information to the public utilizing various media. Many of these professionals work in public relations. Other jobs exist with book, magazine, or newspaper publishers. Radio, television, or advertising firms also provide opportunities for work. Typical jobs are food or fashion writers, magazine editors, and television hosts.

Careers in Human Services

People working in human services help individuals and families improve their quality of life. A wide variety of career opportunities are available, include working with seniors, the homeless, and others with special needs. Also included in this career cluster are professionals who work as consumer protection specialists or as social workers in rehabilitation centers. People who enjoy helping others might enjoy preparing for a career in this area.

Careers in Science and Technology

Many scientific and technological changes affect society. People working in this area investigate problems and conduct research on topics related to the family and society. Jobs involve research in foods, nutrition, textiles, or even family relationships. Many professionals work with environmental concerns to help maintain safety. Others might provide advice in the use of water, land, or other resources.

Careers in the Arts

People working in this area find new and interesting uses and treatments for materials. Creativity is needed to design, coordinate, and attractively display fabrics, clothing, home interiors, exteriors, and furnishings. Typical jobs in this cluster are found in fashion and textile design, interior design, and food presentations. Those interested in foods might excel as chefs, cake decorators, of food stylists. People who are creative and interested in art and design may want to consider a career in this field.

A Career as an Entrepreneur

Entrepreneurs operate their own businesses, which often evolve from hobbies or jobs they already hold. Many entrepreneurs operate catering, tailoring, interior design, or child care services. Some of the most successful entrepreneurs provide a unique service, such as restoring furniture or operating an ethnic bakery. Entrepreneurs can satisfy the special needs of a community.

As you read the following chapters, you will see that many careers areas overlap. For instance, you will learn about food-related careers in many of these chapters—just the setting and focus will be different. You may find the type of work you enjoy relates to two or even three career clusters.

Each chapter ends with a discussion of skills and abilities needed for a job in that career cluster. You will also get an idea of additional training and education needed for various jobs in each area of work. Charts throughout the chapters include listings of typical jobs available. Jobs are categorized as *Entry Level,* needing *Advanced Training,* or requiring a *College Degree.* The minimum amount of training is identified for each level, but additional training is often desirable. The three career levels are described as follows:

Entry level — Jobs that require no previous training are listed as entry level. Training may be provided on the job. A high school diploma is usually assumed.

Advanced training — These jobs require additional training. This may be a vocational or technical degree, an apprenticeship, or a two-year associate's degree. Sometimes workers with training and experience from an entry-level job are eligible for these positions.

College degree — These jobs generally require a college degree as basic requirements. Occasionally workers with extensive training and experience are considered for these positions.

Featured throughout each chapter are short sketches of professionals who work in various careers within the featured job clusters. These sketches give you a glimpse into the life and work of family and consumer sciences professionals on the job.

14 Careers in Business and Marketing

After studying this chapter, you will be able to
◆ list family and consumer sciences career opportunities in business and marketing.
◆ describe personal skills and abilities needed for a business or marketing career.
◆ specify the education and training needed for various business and marketing careers.
◆ outline future trends in family and consumer sciences careers in business and marketing.

Terms to Know

food systems management
hospitality industry
cater
textiles
haute couture
fashion merchandising
marketing research analyst
real estate broker
consultant
freelance
entrepreneur

As you think about your future career, where would you like to work someday? Can you picture the setting? Do you see yourself working in a business office? Are you a buyer for a major department store? Maybe you can see yourself managing a hotel or a restaurant. Are you an interior designer or a fashion designer working in a big city? Do you have your own firm helping consumers manage their money? Are you a successful entrepreneur? If you see yourself working in any of these settings, jobs in the business cluster may interest you.

Where you find work will depend on your interests and type of work desired. It also depends on your educational preparation. You may work for a food manufacturer or a utility company. Restaurants and hotels need people trained in foodservice and management. Retail stores offer many possibilities for work. The nature of your skills and education may lead

you to work in one of the business or marketing areas.

Most jobs in the business cluster are in urban areas, but many jobs are available in smaller towns or rural areas, too. There are many job opportunities in business in foreign countries.

This chapter will give you an insight into family and consumer sciences jobs in business and marketing. You will read about such careers in nutrition and wellness, hospitality and tourism, textiles and apparel production and services, environmental design, family studies and human services, consumer and resource management, and child development and early childhood education.

Charts throughout the chapter give examples of various jobs in the business cluster. Some entry-level jobs require only a high school diploma. Others require more training or a college degree. The charts show jobs requiring different levels of training or education. In this way you see the amount of education that you might need for different types of work.

◆ Business and Marketing Careers in Food, Nutrition, and Wellness

Do you like to cook or bake? Have you ever thought that managing a dining room or a restaurant would be interesting? Do you have a flair for creating interesting and appetizing food? If you enjoy preparing food and serving it to family and friends, you may want to consider a career in foodservice. See 14-1.

Preparing food and serving it to the public is often one of the first jobs held by young people. Many fast-food and family-style restaurants hire high school students on a part-time basis. This can help you decide whether work in a certain career cluster will appeal to you. The following descriptions give more detailed information about selected jobs in the food industry.

Commercial Foodservice

Commercial foodservice is any type of business in which a customer pays for food and service. This includes work in fast-food restaurants, snack bars, family restaurants, cafeterias, and exclusive dining rooms. Some foodservice operations are part of larger businesses, such as airports and hotels.

Work in restaurant foodservice might involve preparing or serving food, or even managing the restaurant. You might work in the dining room as a *host/hostess, foodservice supervisor,* or *dining room manager. Waiters* and *cashiers* would work under your supervision.

You might work in the kitchen preparing food. You might be a *head chef,* or a specialized cook, such as a *baker* or *pastry chef.* Other positions include cook's helpers, dishwashers, and maintenance personnel.

The amount of education required for work in this area varies depending on your job. You may work in an entry-level position right out of high school. Trade and vocational schools as well as community colleges offer specialized training. Work as a head chef might require extensive training. A college degree would help you achieve a more responsible position.

Institutional Foodservice

Institutional foodservice is also known as **food systems management.** Institutional foodservice workers prepare food for hospitals, nursing homes, retirement centers, or other institutions. They prepare and serve food for residents or patrons. People who prepare food

Family, Career and Community Leaders of America

14-1 Food and hospitality careers involve working with the public. Job choices in hotel foodservice include restaurant manager, food manager, chef, cook, host, and waiter.

for your school cafeteria are institutional food-service workers.

Darla Enders, for example, is the *foodservice director* for a large school district. She plans menus for all elementary, middle, and high school students. In addition, she purchases all supplies needed for one central kitchen, supervises the staff, and oversees meal delivery to cafeterias within the district. She must be a careful planner and manager. She knows that students in all the schools are always eager to know what is planned for lunch.

Professionals who plan school breakfast and lunch menus must keep the food likes and dislikes of students in mind. They need to adjust the menus for younger elementary children in addition to older secondary school students. The food needs and likes of these different age groups vary.

People working in institutional foodservice need training in quantity cooking. They must know how to prepare food for large groups of people. They must be able to use the information provided by nutritionists and dietitians when preparing food for people with different dietary needs. For example, hospitals prepare foods for regular diets but also serve diets with low sodium, low fat, or other restrictions.

Nutrition Counselor

A nutrition counselor's main responsibility is knowing the nutritional contributions of different foods. These professionals are employed by weight-loss organizations and health clubs to help clients choose nutritious foods for more healthful meals. Some nutrition counselors work with government food programs or health care institutions. These professionals help individuals implement meal plans designed by dietitians, 14-2. (More education and training is required for dietitians and nutrition educators. See Chapter 17, "Careers in Science and Technology.")

Product Development and Marketing

New food products arrive on the market all the time. How do companies decide which items to develop? How do they inform consumers about them? This is the work of food and consumer sciences professionals working in the company's consumer affairs and marketing departments. These professionals are often called *consumer affairs specialists* or *product specialists*.

Their primary job is to help the company develop products that consumers want. This is more difficult than it sounds. First it requires an understanding of food preferences and lifestyle trends. Then it requires an ability to translate this information into successful products and recipes.

U.S. Department of Agriculture

14-2 Many nutrition and wellness counselors are needed to ensure the success of U.S. Department of Agriculture food programs.

Karen Johnson
Marketing and Consulting

In high school, Karen Johnson loved to create recipes. She won five dollars in a recipe contest and dreamed of directing a test kitchen one day. Later she reached that goal and went on to positions she never imagined.

After college and additional training at a well-known cooking school, Karen took a test kitchen position. While working on the company's annual recipe contest, she recognized a changing trend in the recipes that consumers submitted. They were shorter, used fewer ingredients, and were easier to prepare. Karen then applied those guidelines to new recipes and product concepts. "Successful recipes and convenient products translate into repeat sales, and that's good business," explains Karen. "It's very important to see the connection between consumer wants and needs and changing lifestyles."

She also styled food for advertising photos and television commercials. Working with a creative team, Karen helped develop one of the most recognized and successful advertising concepts in the food industry. Ultimately she reached her goal of directing the division's test kitchen. Of that experience, Karen says, "I learned the value of supervising young professionals and took pride in watching them develop."

When another major food company asked her to create a consumer affairs department for them, Karen was both excited and apprehensive. "The company president challenged me with a charge that I will never forget," Karen reports. "He said, 'Bring me new ideas that I can't say no to.'"

Karen proceeded to do just that—designing and staffing a foodservice kitchen and expanding the role of the consumer kitchens. She also focused product publicity in new areas and developed a system that responded to consumer questions about the company's products. Under her direction, the consumer affairs department became a key part of the marketing process.

Her excellent management of the department resulted in promotions. Ultimately, she rose to the highest level in the company and became a corporate officer. New assignments followed, including solving a quality issue that affected consumer sales in Germany. She was also asked to manage a major corporate project that resulted in improved safety, quality, and productivity for the company. "Being a risk taker and accepting unfamiliar roles are essential in the business world," Karen explains.

For those pursuing a similar career, she recommends looking at challenges as opportunities to explore, not problems to avoid. "Today's business needs are very demanding, so young professionals must be creative problem solvers and team players," Karen emphasizes. Besides having good basic skills in their discipline, she recommends a positive attitude, a sense of humor, curiosity, and a keen desire to learn. Good oral and written communication techniques are also important.

Many of today's successful products are much different from those of 20, 15, or even 10 years ago for several reasons. One reason is the increased use of the microwave oven. Another reason is the desire to reduce fat and calories in the diet. The growing interest in foods of different cultures has also influenced product development. Product specialists keep management informed of the influences affecting today and tomorrow's food buying decisions.

Companies obtain key information in many ways. One way is by monitoring consumer reaction to company products through mail and phone calls from consumers. In this way, companies learn how consumers use their products and feel about them. Companies also review consumer entries to recipe contests for information on cooking trends and ingredient preferences. Frequently, industry surveys and statistics on consumer shopping, cooking, and eating patterns are analyzed. Taken together, this information provides direction for product and recipe development.

Many product specialists in the food industry work in test kitchens, where knowledge of food chemistry is essential. They know how ingredients interact and how to achieve desired results. The recipes they develop must be appealing, make the best use of the product's features, and always work reliably. There are many trials and errors before a prize-winning recipe is developed for a package label, cookbook, ad, or commercial.

When new products are developed, these professionals are involved at the initial planning stage. They prepare competing products to acquaint the product development team with similar items on the market. They also develop a *benchmark* recipe that guides the development of the new product's flavor, texture, and color.

Product specialists also prepare food for photography and recommend the best way to display the food. They develop educational materials and review all written communications about the product before they are released to the public. In fact, few company decisions are made

without their input of the product specialists who are familiar with every aspect of how their product looks, tastes, and performs.

To obtain a position with a food company, you would need a B.S. degree with a food science or nutrition emphasis. Exposure to different cultural and ethnic food tastes and practices is a definite plus.

Other Food-Related Careers in Business and Marketing

Some professionals in family and consumer sciences work for the federal government. They may work for the U.S. Department of Agriculture (USDA), Food and Drug Administration (FDA), or Health and Human Services (HHS). Professionals employed by the USDA, FDA, and HHS are responsible for developing food programs as well as nutrition and food safety policies. Many specialists also develop educational materials and present consumer programs for state leaders to follow.

Although the employees work for the government instead of a business organization, they use business and marketing principles to do their jobs. All the government positions described here require a college degree. For more business and marketing-related job opportunities in food, nutrition, and wellness, see 14-3. The list includes entry-level jobs as well as those requiring more training.

◆ Business and Marketing Careers in Hospitality, Tourism, and Recreation

Professionals in family and consumer sciences will find many job opportunities in the hospitality industry. **Hospitality industry** careers involve jobs associated with eating, sleeping, or travel away from home, 14-4. The industry also includes sites of recreation, which range from going to the movies for two hours

Business and Marketing Careers in Foods, Wellness, and Nutrition		
Entry Level	Chef	Diet center director
Baker	Cooking teacher	Dietitian
Busperson	Dietary assistant	Executive chef
Cannery worker	Food and beverage manager	Extension food specialist
Cleanup assistant	Food demonstrator	Fitness club manager
Cook	Food grader	Food chemist
Counter attendant	Food photographer	Food editor
Dietary aide	Foodservice manager	Food marketer
Dishwasher	Gourmet food store operator	Food packaging specialist
Fast-food delivery person	Host/hostess	Food product specialist
Fish cleaner	Kitchen supervisor	Food purchasing agent
Food and beverage checker	Meat cutter	Food scientist
Food laboratory aide	Menu planner	Food stylist
Food order expeditor	Nutrition counselor	Food technologist
Food server	Party planner	Health and fitness adviser
Food tray assembler	Party service operator	Institutional dietary manager
Kitchen helper	Product sales representative	Market development specialist
Personal grocery shopper	Restaurant manager/owner	Nutritionist
Short-order cook	School foodservice director	Personal fitness trainer
Stock clerk	**College Degree**	Purchasing agent
Waitress/waiter	Athletic director	Quality control assistant
Advanced Training	Club manager	Recipe development specialist
Banquet manager	Cookbook editor	Sports nutritionist
Cake decorator	Corporate fitness director	Test kitchen manager
Caterer	Customer relations director	

14-3 Career opportunities in business and marketing areas of foods and nutrition continue to grow.

to spending a week's vacation at a theme park. You might prepare for a career in a variety of different occupations.

Hotel or Motel Management

Jobs are available in hotel foodservice, customer relations, or reservations. Since hotels and motels run 24 hours every day, various jobs are needed for keeping these operations running successfully. Many jobs help you prepare for other hospitality jobs, too. This field also includes *resort owners, camp directors,* and *country club managers.* All are part of the growing hospitality industry that serves the traveling public.

You can find entry-level work in a hotel or motel without additional training. Entry-level workers often get the least favorite assignments, such as weekend or midnight shifts, until they gain experience. A managerial

14-4 Hotel managers work directly with the public to meet lodging needs.

Hilton

position requires more training and experience. A college degree will help you achieve a managerial position sooner.

Catering or Banquet Management

Caterers, vendors, and banquet contractors are other individuals or businesses that provide food for the public. To **cater** means to provide food or service. Many individuals or firms offer catering services for parties and banquets, 14-5. Vending machines and mobile trucks, such as those selling ice cream or sandwiches, all provide food for the public.

Sometimes food is prepared and served in a school, church, country club, hall, or other location. At other times the food may be prepared in a central kitchen and delivered to the location.

As a catering or banquet manager, you would have many responsibilities. First, you would meet with your clients to discuss their needs. You would help plan the menu, considering costs, location, and number of people attending. Ordering the food and overseeing the food preparation, serving, and cleanup are your responsibility. There may be special diet

requests. You need to plan ahead so everything runs smoothly.

A catering or banquet manager might gain experience working for a caterer or in a similar job. You would need to gain experience in quantity food preparation and group management. Training or additional education in these areas would be very helpful.

Travel Director or Tour Guide

A travel director is responsible for guiding visitors to various destinations and meeting their needs. Many professionals in this industry work for travel agencies devoted to planning vacations and other leisure trips. For these travelers, the goal is a trip full of fun and adventure. Tour directors handle a broad range of responsibilities, including arranging transportation, reserving lodging, and handling other trip-related details.

University of Wisconsin-Stout

14-5 Catering careers require creative food presentations and knowledge of food preparation.

Leisure and recreational events can last for a few hours, such as a tour of the White House, or several weeks, such as cruise around the world. Travel directors provide in-depth information on an area's history, culture, natural environment, architecture, and other topics of interest. Working with travel directors are tour guides, who serve as on-site escorts. Sometimes tours are organized around specific themes, such as hiking in the Grand Canyon or visiting medieval castles in Europe.

In the workplace, large organizations hire travel directors to plan business trips for busy managers. For these travel professionals, the goal is getting employees to meetings quickly and economically. Corporate travel directors who also organize conventions and other large business and social gatherings are often called *events directors*.

Professionals in the tour and travel industry must enjoy working with people and satisfying their needs above all. These professionals must also have organizational ability as well as good problem-solving and decision-making skills.

This gives you an idea of some jobs in the hospitality and tourism industry. For additional jobs, see 14-6. You may wish to look in the reference section of the library or search the Internet for a more detailed discussion of careers in this field.

◆ Business and Marketing Careers in Textiles and Apparel

Do you have a feel for what clothes look good on different people? Do you like to shop for clothes? Do you enjoy working with colors, patterns, and designs? If so, you might consider a career in the textiles and apparel field.

Business and Marketing Careers in the Hospitality and Tourism		
Entry Level	Bed and Breakfast Manager	Country club director
Activities assistant	Bell captain	Cruise director
Bellperson	Building services supervisor	Director of catering
Carpet/window cleaner	Business travel specialist	Director of sales and marketing
Cashier	Camp director	
Counter attendant	Chef/baker	Executive housekeeper
Dry cleaning attendant	Dining room manager	Front desk manager
Fileclerk	Head waitperson	General manager
Groundskeeper assistant	Housekeeping manager	Guest services manager
Housekeeper	Reservations supervisor	Hotel manager
Janitor	Tour broker	Public relations director
Laundry attendant	Tour director	Resort owner or manager
Linen room attendant	Tour guide	Sales/marketing director
Recreation assistant	Travel consultant	Tourism coordinator
Summer camp assistant	**College Degree**	Travel writer
Theme park worker	Campground manager	Visitors and convention bureau director
Advanced Training	Convention/meeting manager	
Assistant banquet manager		

4-6 Many exciting business and marketing jobs are available in the hospitality and tourism industry.

Textiles include fibers and yarn made into cloth. Some end products of textiles are clothing, draperies, upholstery, rugs, and linens.

Working with clothing goes beyond selling and wearing nice clothes. Much more is involved. For instance, you must be aware of fashion trends from around the world.

You need to know the current haute couture in Paris, New York, Dallas, and other fashion centers of the world. **Haute couture** means the top fashions being shown by trendsetters in fashion centers. These fashion trends will influence clothing worn where you live. If you become a clothing buyer, you may need to travel to these fashion centers to make your fashion purchases. You may want a career marketing or advertising clothing or analyzing fashion trends. There are many careers in the textiles and apparel area of the business cluster.

Fashion Merchandising

Fashion merchandising refers to the planning, buying, and selling of clothing and accessories. Merchandising also includes jobs in promotion, such as advertising and publicity. Retailers sell merchandise directly to the customer through various outlets. Fashion retailers include department stores, discount stores, chain stores, mail order, and outlet stores.

Fashion merchandising is a fast-paced business with lots of career possibilities. Career opportunities in this field include retail buying, management, fashion coordination, and sales.

Retail Sales Associate

Many people interested in the clothing field begin by working in retail sales. Opportunities in retail sales exist in many kinds of stores. You might work in a department store, specialty store, or large discount store. This entry-level job can open the door to other career possibilities in the fashion world.

If you work as a retail sales associate, you must learn all you can about the merchandise in your department. You must also learn selling techniques. Many stores provide from one to five days of sales training before new employees actually begin selling merchandise.

As a sales associate, you will help potential customers select merchandise and suggest additional items, 14-7. You then handle the sales transaction. You will also need to keep shelves stocked with merchandise.

Retail Fashion Buyer

A retail buyer is responsible for selecting and purchasing the merchandise for a department in one or more stores. Examples of merchandise that a retail buyer might handle include children's wear, men's apparel, women's apparel, sportswear, shoes, or accessories. The buyer is also responsible for the sales and profits of his or her department.

If you were a buyer, you might select merchandise for your department or store by visiting manufacturers' showrooms in market

J.C. Penney Co., Inc.

14-7 Sales associates help customers choose styles, fabrics, and colors that look best on them.

centers. Designers present their new lines of clothing in showrooms in apparel market centers. A line is a collection of styles and designs produced by a firm for a given season. A designer may offer more than one new line each season. The main apparel market centers are in Paris, New York, and Los Angeles. Going to market is the term used by buyers when they travel to market centers to buy merchandise. You might also buy from sales representatives who visit your store.

At market, you would choose designs, fabrics, and colors that coordinate with other styles and lines. You need to consider your market and current fashion trends as you determine what to buy. You must have a good sense of what your customers will like. Your goal is to have merchandise in your store that customers want.

You need to order ahead so that merchandise arrives in time to be priced and ready for sale. Generally, buyers need to plan several seasons ahead so they can have merchandise available for each season. See 14-8. With the help of store displays, external advertising, and good retail sales staff, the merchandise is ready to sell. Later, you may need to reduce the price of unsold merchandise and put it on sale.

Merchandise Manager

A merchandise manager coordinates the operation of several departments. He or she oversees different aspects of retail sales in various departments. The sales staff, merchandise displays, and special promotions may be his or her responsibility. The retail buyers in each department usually report to the merchandise manager. A merchandise manager may be responsible for an entire store. Examples of stores with merchandise managers are men's and women's apparel shops, bridal shops, and fabric stores. Others are shoe stores, lingerie shops, children's shops, and sporting goods stores.

Merchandising managers have a responsibility to increase sales and profits in their departments or store each year. They need to keep an eye on competing stores to be aware of merchandise, prices, promotions, and other factors that may affect their store's sales.

Fashion Coordinator

Fashion coordinators are responsible for presenting a unified fashion picture throughout a store. They need to be aware of current fashion trends. They attend trade shows and watch for the latest fashions, fabrics, styles, and new products. Then, they provide this information to managers, buyers, and others responsible for store marketing.

Fashion coordinators may plan merchandise promotions. These include in-store displays and external advertising. Promotions may involve a certain theme, season, or holiday. An example is using red, white, and blue colors in store displays for a Fourth-of-July theme. Promotions must be balanced, appropriate, and interesting to attract the attention of potential customers. See 14-9.

Talbots

14-8 Apparel buyers provide sales associates information about different styles and lines of clothing.

14-9 Fashion coordinators are responsible for setting up merchandise displays that appeal to customers throughout a store.

Fashion Model

Some young people want to be fashion models. Having your photo on the front cover of a magazine and being paid a high salary can be a dream career. However, very few models reach this level.

Models help sell clothing or other merchandise. Some model at fashion shows,
stores, restaurants, and trade shows. Models also work in designer showrooms, for retail stores, clothing companies, and apparel firms. Top models get their photos in magazines, newspapers, trade publications, advertisements, and catalogs.

Fashion modeling is a combination of fashion, advertising, and hard work. Modeling is often a very competitive and demanding job. There are usually more models than job openings. Models must be available for a job whenever they are needed. Modeling, therefore, doesn't provide regular hours or work opportunities. Only top models receive excellent pay. Other models may need to supplement their modeling income with other jobs.

Professional models often attend modeling school to learn basic modeling techniques. Attendance at a modeling school does not guarantee a modeling job. Be sure to check the modeling school's accreditation. It is also important to attend a school with a job placement service.

Most models find work through modeling agencies. These agencies match up models' qualifications with different jobs. Most models work in large cities such as New York, Chicago, or Los Angeles. Retail stores, apparel manufacturers, and advertising agencies in many other cities, however, hire models.

Marketing Research Analyst

Marketing research analysts study consumer-buying trends. By attending conferences and meetings throughout the country, they learn what is selling in different areas. Sometimes they visit stores to obtain information from buyers, store managers, and consumers. They know the type of customer that buys certain merchandise as well as what merchandise will attract new customers. They often determine what type of merchandise will be in demand in the future.

Marketing research analysts help designers and manufacturers learn what types of products

Linda Turner Griepentrog

Magazine Editor

Linda Griepentrog is the editor of a monthly sewing publication and a bimonthly machine embroidery publication. Her job makes her one of the leading authorities on trends and new products affecting the home sewing market.

Linda's primary responsibility is managing the editorial content of two magazines. She determines the story lineup, assigns stories to writers, coordinates photography, works with industry resources, and supervises the art and editorial staff. Linda and her staff write one or two columns for each issue.

"Publishing is a great profession, but it's very demanding and deadline oriented," says Linda. "If deadlines aren't met every day, the publication won't go out on time." Occasionally Linda works evenings and weekends to make sure deadlines are met. This kind of pressure requires a high energy level!

All the work gets done, even with Linda's hectic schedule. Half her time is spent traveling to trade and consumer shows, to speaking and teaching engagements, and for company-sponsored tours. Her travels keep her in contact with fashion, fabric, and sewing experts and help her determine what is important to the sewing market.

"This is a great job because we're always 'in the know,' learning about the latest trends and products before anyone else," reports Linda. She and her staff share a love for fashion sewing and for keeping readers informed of new ideas. Linda also gets inspiration for story ideas from readers' letters and from the many samples of fabric and sewing products sent to her from manufacturers.

Part of Linda's job is to manage the publications' budgets and the contents of the company Web site. Flexibility is key since most days bear no resemblance to her to-do list.

"I feel very fortunate to have found the perfect job," says Linda. "It lets me combine work with a love of sewing and fabrics." She previously taught high school and college and worked for companies in the sewing industry as an advertising coordinator, home economist, and product development manager.

customers in different parts of the country want. Retail buyers and store managers use market research to determine what to have in stock.

For a list of job opportunities in the business areas of clothing and textiles, see 14-10. Formal schooling in a vo-tech school or college will give you a stronger background and preparation for work in most positions in the clothing and textiles area. You might need to take special training for some types of work.

◆ Business and Marketing Careers in Environmental Design

Does working in a showroom and helping people choose home furnishings sound interesting to you? Perhaps you would like to help young people choose furniture for their first apartment. Maybe you would enjoy decorating homes for others.

If you worked in a business career related to housing and interior design, you might work with many different clients. You would need to be able to evaluate and recommend different ways of solving various housing and decorating problems. Being a self-starter and being creative are important traits of people working in this field.

Home Furnishings Merchandising

As in fashion merchandising, home furnishings merchandising refers to the planning, buying, and selling of home furnishings. Retailers sell merchandise directly to the

Business and Marketing Careers in Textiles and Apparel		
Entry Level	Garment maker	CAD specialist
Designer's assistant	Hat maker	Catalog inventory analyst
Retail sales associate	Jewelry designer	Fabric market reporter
Sales trainee	Laundering expert	Fashion buyer
Sewing machine operator	Leather repairer	Fashion director
Stock clerk	Pattern designer	Fashion editor/illustrator
	Pattern maker/spreader	Fashion merchandising
Advanced Training	Personal color analyst	manager
Alterations specialist	Quilt restorer	Manufacturer's representative
Bridal consultant	Retail store manager	Market development specialist
Bridal shop manager	Sample maker/cutter	Market research analyst
Customer relations	Sewing room supervisor	Merchandise manager
representative	Sewing machine repair	Product development
Display designer	person	specialist
Dry cleaner	Showroom manager	Purchasing agent
Fabric designer	Tailor/custom tailor	Quality control analyst
Fashion consultant	Theater costume designer	Retail buyer
Fashion coordinator	Wardrobe consultant	Textile buyer
Fashion designer		Textile preservationist
Fashion historian	**College Degree**	Textile sales representative
Fashion model	Apparel production manager	

14-10 There are many interesting and exciting careers in business related to clothing and textiles.

customer through various outlets. These include mail order catalog and various stores, such as furniture, department, discount, outlet, and specialized stores. Examples of specialized stores are wallpaper and carpet stores.

There are many career possibilities in this area of business. These include retail sales, buying, and management.

Home Furnishings Sales Associate

Home furnishings include items used in the home, such as carpets, draperies, furniture, textiles, and home accessories. It may include the sale of appliances. Specialty stores and large department stores sell home furnishings. Informed sales associates help customers make satisfying purchases. Good sales associates are able to work with people, answer their questions knowledgeably, and sell the store's products.

A home furnishings retail sales job is an entry-level position that may lead to other jobs. For instance, you could work your way up to home furnishings buyer or store manager.

Home Furnishings Buyer

The job of a home furnishings buyer is similar to that of a retail fashion buyer. Buyers need to be aware of furniture trends, sources, and their market area. They should also understand furniture design, quality, fabrics, and consumer behavior. The buyer needs to plan the type of furniture to buy for the store or for special clients. Some stores custom-order furniture for their clients. A *custom order* is a request by a customer for furniture in a special style, color, and fabric.

Extensive experience in furniture sales and management is needed for a position as home furnishings buyer. A college degree in interior design will be better preparation for this job.

Household Products and Furnishings Manufacturer

There are many career opportunities in the home furnishing manufacturing business.

You may be able to work for a company that produces draperies, carpeting, appliances, furniture, or the products used to care for them. You might work as a member of a production team or a sales team. You might work on developing new product ideas for the home.

From the time a new product is planned, tested, marketed, and sold, a company is working toward one goal—offering a product that consumers prefer over all others. In this way, the company makes sales that turn into profits, which pay employee salaries and help the company grow and prosper. Your responsibility is to help the company be profitable. This may involve informing consumers about the product's use and features to encourage sales.

Understanding design and drafting would be helpful for jobs in the production area, 14-11. Being able to use a computer in your work would be essential. A college degree in engineering, marketing, or a specialized field will help you succeed in the manufacturing business.

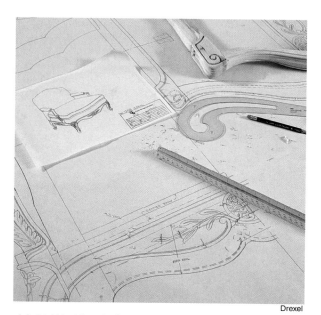

Drexel

14-11 Working in furniture design requires an understanding of basic art and design.

Gail Heeb
Consumer Affairs

Laundry aids, food storage wraps and bags, and household cleaners—items found in every home—are the heart of Gail Heeb's job. Gail (shown on the left) is involved with practically every aspect of developing and marketing her company's household products.

"I really work as an internal resource, providing technical assistance to the consumer affairs and other departments in the company," Gail explains. Her job is a unique blend of responsibilities that she helped to shape. She did this by continually assuming tasks that went beyond her scope of responsibility.

Gail recommends viewing new duties as opportunities, not annoyances. "By taking on new assignments, you can expand your position and ultimately create your dream job," Gail advises. "Develop the habit of considering new assignments as a vote of confidence in your abilities, and above all, never say, 'That's not my job.' "

Among her many tasks, Gail analyzes trends affecting the food and home care fields and helps explore new product ideas and marketing approaches. All copy developed by the advertising and promotion departments is reviewed by her for technical accuracy. She coordinates an outside advisory panel that provides the company with home-testing information and new product evaluations. She also oversees food styling assignments, handles trade show exhibits, develops consumer education materials, and works with media contacts.

For those aspiring to a position similar to Gail's, a solid technical foundation is a must. "First and foremost, employers look for strong technical skills, which a B.S. degree in family and consumer sciences provides," says Gail. She also credits her previous teaching experience and her work with an appliance manufacturer for providing many skills that she uses in her current position.

Gail encourages teens looking for the perfect job to talk with people who hold jobs that interest them. "Too often teens think they know what the job entails but really don't," Gail observes. She recommends writing the professional a sincere letter expressing an interest in knowing more about the position. "Professionals in the field will be happy to schedule time to talk with you in person or by phone," says Gail, "if you give them an opportunity to find a break in their busy schedules."

On-the-job experience gives teens a clear-cut advantage in the job market, according to Gail. She suggests looking for internships that are offered through school or membership in a professional association. She also recommends finding a part-time job directly related to the specific field of interest. "If these efforts don't lead to a full-time job with that organization, they'll definitely look great on your resume and catch some employer's attention."

Upholsterer or Drapery Maker

Draperies and upholstered furniture are an important part of any room. However, draperies fade and upholstery becomes worn and soiled. Adding new draperies gives their rooms a fresh look. Customers may still like the style of their sofa or chair with torn or worn fabric. Rather than buy a new piece of furniture, they hire upholsterers to recover their favorite furniture pieces, 14-12.

Drapery makers work in small businesses as well as for large manufacturing firms. They may make custom draperies for individual customers or mass-produce them for the general market. There is always a need for draperies in many different designs and fabrics. Decorating or redecorating homes and offices produces a steady market for these products.

Drexel

14-12 An upholsterer needs to measure carefully in order to match fabric designs when upholstering furniture.

Upholsterers repair and recover furniture. They remove the old cover, padding, and springs to get down to the frame. Then they glue, rebuild, or repair the basic piece of furniture. They may also need to repair the springs or padding. Finally, they replace the outside covering. The upholsterer needs to have a sense of color, design, and proportion in order to help the customer select a suitable new covering.

An upholsterer may work in his or her own shop or for a furniture store. They may work for a furniture manufacturer. Others may have jobs upholstering seats for cars, vans, or recreational vehicles. This type of work is interesting and varied as it involves meeting different customer needs.

Real Estate Broker

Real estate brokers or real estate agents help people buy and sell property. Residential real estate brokers sell houses, townhouses, and condominiums. They may also sell commercial properties, such as stores or office buildings.

You must pass a test and be licensed in order to sell real estate. A degree in family and consumer sciences is excellent preparation for work as a real estate agent. Course work may include classes in family life, housing, and interior design. These professionals understand the stages in the family life cycle and can relate to the housing needs of different people.

Selling property is a business that is dependent on the economy. At times, demand for houses is high and they sell quickly. At other times, when prices and interest rates are high, or there is uncertainty in the economy, houses do not sell as readily.

Real estate work may be irregular. An agent may be very busy showing and selling houses. At other times the buying market is slow.

Beverly Taki
Real Estate Marketing and Sales Consultant

Beverly Taki is a licensed real estate sales agent, specializing in single family homes, condominiums, land, and residential income properties. Her real job, however, is matching families with the homes of their dreams.

"The first step in the real estate business is learning the inventory of available properties in a specific marketing area," reports Beverly. "The next step, however, is the most important one—understanding your buyers' wants and needs." She scouts for properties that fit each family's unique lifestyle. When the right property is found, Beverly negotiates the client's offer. After the seller accepts the offer, she helps her clients obtain a home loan with terms that fit their financial situation. Then she guides them through the closing process.

"You must enjoy working with a variety of people and paying attention to detail," she reports. To completely service the client's needs, Beverly tries to solve any problems that arise from relocating, selling, or buying a home. For those aspiring to the profession, she recommends a spirit of independence and the ability to handle rejection. She also recommends a willingness to learn and an ability to work long hours. "A background in sales is not vital to success in the real estate business, but these qualities are," Beverly emphasizes.

One reason why Beverly is well known and respected in her area is her involvement in community and charity events. She also prepares flyers, press releases, and advertisements to publicize her services. She even created a cable TV show that she hosts to showcase available area homes. "Above all, you must be self-confident, a risk-taker, and a good decision maker," adds Beverly.

Many of the skills she uses now were developed in her earlier positions with an appliance manufacturer and a microwave foods company. Beverly traveled throughout the country conducting microwave cooking classes, training sales personnel, supervising trade shows, and talking

to TV and radio audiences about microwave cooking. She also coauthored a microwave cookbook and developed sales and marketing programs for food seasoning products. "People skills are the most important skills to nurture and polish to succeed in this profession," she adds.

Beverly's career is a perfect example of how family and consumer sciences skills can foster success in many different career areas. As a result of professional experience with food and appliances, she has a unique perspective on the kitchen and the features that today's consumers expect in that room. "The kitchen has always been an important room in the home, but now it's even more important than the living room," explains Beverly. "It sometimes is the room that sells a house."

Realtors often need to work evenings and on Saturdays and Sundays when prospective home-buyers are not working.

People working in any area of environmental design need to keep up with trends and advances in the field. New decorating and design trends complemented by new products make this field ever changing. See 14-13 for other business opportunities in environmental design.

Business and Marketing Careers in Family Studies and Human Services

Careers in business related to human services involve meeting the personal needs of individuals and families. Professionals in this area often work with children, with families in need, and seniors. People working in these careers often become very involved with the people they serve. Training in family and consumer sciences provides a strong background for many careers in this area.

Home Management Consultant

Home management consultants help individuals and families plan and organize their work in the home, their space, their time, and/or their finances. Time and money are two very important commodities in working families. Any service that helps to organize these is increasingly in demand. Work as a home management consultant may include meal planning,

Business and Marketing Careers in Environmental Design		
Entry Level	Furniture historian	Equipment specialist
Carpet cleaner	Furniture refinisher	Furniture designer
Carpet flooring/installer	Home builder	Historic preservationist
Designer's aide	Home security consultant	Home furnishings author
Furniture salesperson	House remodeler	Home furnishings buyer
Home furnishings sales associate	Housing rehabilitation specialist	Home furnishings editor
House cleaner	Interior decorator	Hotel designer
Picture framer	Kitchen planner	Housing analyst
Roofer	Moving consultant	Housing finance specialist
Upholsterer's assistant	Property manager	Interior designer
Wallpaper remover	Real estate broker	Kitchen designer
Advanced Training	Upholsterer	Lighting designer
Apartment manager	**College Degree**	Manufacturer's representative
Closet planner	Appliance design engineer	Public housing administrator
Draftperson	Appliance manufacturing engineer	Residential planner
Drapery maker	Architect	Space planner
Drapery/upholster estimator	Corporate designer	Utility consultant

14-13 A variety of jobs in business and marketing exist in the environmental design area. This chart lists some of the different kinds of work available.

kitchen rearrangement, closet design, financial services, or other help that will save time, organize space, and manage money.

Retirement Care Administrator

With the aging of the population, there is a need for more facilities to care for seniors. More of the elderly are moving to retirement centers where specialized services are provided. Nursing homes and retirement centers are businesses that employ managerial personnel.

If you were a manager of a retirement home, you would need to provide safe, comfortable, and dependable living conditions. You would need to hire a competent medical, nursing, and dietary staff. This staff might include doctors, nurses, physical therapists, dietitians, and cooks. These people will oversee the health of the residents. You would also hire people to plan social and recreational activities. See 14-14.

As a property manager, you would be responsible for the general upkeep of the facility. You would promptly handle requests for services or repairs and resolve any complaints. You would also be responsible for proper financial management of the business. The home should operate smoothly and profitably. Managers must be able to communicate effectively with the residents.

◆ Business and Marketing Careers in Consumer and Resource Management

Many types of businesses employ people in consumer management positions. For instance, banks, credit unions, and investment firms have financial consultants. Gas and electric companies have energy consultants. These businesses help families solve some of their everyday problems.

Donelda Novy

14-14 A retirement home manager makes sure that entertainment is regularly scheduled for the residents.

Specialists in Family Economics

Helping families use their resources to reach goals is the role of specialists in family economics. They help families make choices based on their resources of time, money, energy, education, and abilities. Job titles in this area include financial planner, consumer credit counselor, utility company consultant, and personal shopper.

Financial Planner

Helping families plan for financial security is the task of a financial planner. The financial planner helps the family identify its long- and short-term financial goals. Then the planner works with the family to set up a financial plan. The family decides how to manage its money so it will be able to achieve its goals.

For instance, a family may have two children who hope to go to college. The family might use a financial planner to help them work out a plan to make this possible. The planner might suggest investing in stocks, bonds, real estate, retirement plans, or special savings programs.

Financial planners must have proper training to advise clients on financial matters. This training may be available through vocational schools, colleges, or financial management training programs. Many companies provide their own training.

Some financial planners work independently in their own business. Most financial planners work for insurance companies, investment companies, or other financial institutions. See 14-15.

Today there is an increase in demand for well-qualified financial planners. Families often find it hard to know how to make their savings grow. Numerous investment options are available. Many families need the assistance of financial planners to help them choose among the many options.

Consumer Credit Counselor

Families and individuals with debt problems can use the skills of consumer credit counselors. These trained professionals work with families to help them solve their financial problems.

14-15 Financial planners help individuals and families manage their money. They help develop savings plans.

The counselor begins by gathering data on all aspects of a family's finances. Knowing the family's expenses and the amount of money owed to others helps a counselor understand the family's money problems. The counselor works out a debt repayment plan with the family. Then he or she helps plan a program to better manage the money. The counselor suggests ways for controlling spending.

Many professionals in family and consumer sciences serve as financial advisors. They help families get out of debt and learn to live within their means. Individuals are advised to work only with those counselors with the proper credentials of *certified financial planner.*

Utility Company Consultant

People employed as utility company consultants have various job titles. For example, utility company consultants may be called *energy advisors.* They are experts in the areas of energy-efficient appliances and housing systems as well as energy conservation methods. They may consult with home and office builders on the most efficient methods of energy usage for a particular design. During times of energy shortages, their services are particularly in demand.

Personal Shopper

Personal shoppers work for themselves or for clothing and department stores. For people with too little personal time, personal shoppers do the "leg work" of finding personal and household items their clients desire. Perhaps the client needs new curtains and bedspread to update a bedroom. The shopper first determines the client's wants and preferences, and then collects a number of possible choices from which the client can choose. Personal shoppers generally work around timetables and meeting places convenient to the client, whether at work or home.

Personal shoppers need to work well with people and be aware of classic designs and current trends. Above all, they must have a good sense of style and know how to translate that knowledge into satisfying customer needs. Besides the business and marketing careers in consumer and resource management described here, see 14-16 for more choices.

◆ Business and Marketing Careers in Child Development and Early Childhood Education

If you are concerned about the care and protection of children, you may be interested in a business career related to child development and early childhood education. Some businesses provide on-site child development centers as an employee benefit and need such

Business and Marketing Careers in Consumer and Resource Management		
Entry Level	**Advanced Training**	**College Degree**
Personal shopper	Commercial energy auditor	Certified financial planner
Product demonstrator	Credit counselor	Consumer affairs director
Residential energy officer	Household manager	Consumer education director
	Product representative	Energy efficiency specialist

14-16 Many interesting job opportunities focusing on business and marketing in the consumer and resource management area.

experts to run these facilities. Designers of educational toys for children and playground equipment present other opportunities for business careers focused on children. For more information on career opportunities focused on children, see Chapter 15, "Careers in Education and Communications," and Chapter 16, "Careers in Human Services."

Other Careers in Business and Marketing

Some professionals in family and consumer sciences work as consultants. **Consultants** give advice or ideas to businesses, organizations, or individuals. A consultant is very knowledgeable in a specialized area. Often businesses hire consultants for a specific project. After completing it, the consultant works with other companies on new projects. Food consultants may help with recipe analysis, recipe development, or food styling. Clothing professionals find work as image or wardrobe consultants. Other professional consultants specialize in consumer affairs, financial planning, or housing. Most consultants gain knowledge by first working in the field. Consultants often set their own fees.

Freelance professionals pursue their profession without a long-term commitment to any employer. They may work on a variety of different assignments or jobs. For example, one assignment may require a freelance professional to apply knowledge and skills in nutrition. The next assignment might involve planning the layout of a kitchen for an architect. Some may freelance as writers or editors. Others may produce resource materials in various areas of family and consumer sciences.

Many professionals in family and consumer sciences are **entrepreneurs.** This is another term for *self-employed*. Entrepreneurs own their own businesses. They may work out of their own homes or another location, providing a product, service, or both. Chapter 19, "A Career as an Entrepreneur," provides more information

about being in charge of your own business.

Personal Skills and Abilities Needed for a Career in Business or Marketing

Good personal skills and abilities are needed for success in a business or marketing career in family and consumer sciences. The necessary skills include the following:
◆ decision-making skills
◆ communication skills
◆ interpersonal skills

Decision-Making Skills

You will need to make many decisions when you work in business. Supervisors, coworkers, clients, and other people rely on decisions made by each other. It is important to make decisions that will not delay a process or hold up other people. Good planning and organizational skills help managers make decisions. A company president may need to make long-range plans for the growth of his or her business. The president may meet with key managers to decide ways to proceed. Then committees might meet to accomplish their assignments.

If you were an interior designer, you might be asked to design draperies for a client's home. You would need to decide what drapery styles and fabrics to recommend and what fee to charge. Many smaller decisions affect the final decision. Suppose it will take a full week to sew the draperies but your work schedule is full for two weeks. The delivery date would hinge on that information. A successful business is often the result of good decision making from beginning to end.

Communication Skills

Strong communication skills are very important in the business world. You must be able to express yourself clearly both in speech and in writing. You need to understand customers' needs and desires. You must be able to communicate with them about their concerns. Many jobs, such as an appliance demonstrator or a retail sales associate, require that you clearly explain how to use a product.

Not only will you be communicating with customers, but you will also have many contacts with supervisors, coworkers, and others in your field. Strong skills in using the computer and telephone, as well as writing, are very important.

Interpersonal Skills

A career in business requires good interpersonal skills. Good relations with clients and business contacts is important. For instance, buyers must be able to relate to managers, manufacturers, and sales associates. Sales associates need to be friendly, outgoing, and helpful. If a sales associate is rude, customers will probably not return to that business.

Careers in business involve a lot of interaction with coworkers. For example, working as a restaurant chef means working closely with cooks, servers, and managers. For the kitchen to operate smoothly and efficiently, everyone needs to work together. A career in business requires excellent interpersonal skills. See 14-17.

◆ Education and Training Needed for a Career in Business or Marketing

There are a number of entry-level positions available in the business cluster. Many do not require education past the high school level. For instance, foodservice jobs such as waiters and waitresses are entry-level positions. You can also work in some retail sales jobs with no training beyond a high school diploma.

There is usually ample opportunity to get first-hand experience while you are in school. In this way you can test your aptitude and ability in various career interests. You might get a job in hospital foodservice, helping prepare trays for patients. Your high school cafeteria may need students for part-time work. Many businesses hire high school students for summer or holiday work. Teens often start retail careers by working in summer or part-time jobs.

National Cotton Council

14-17 Business and marketing careers in family and consumer sciences require good communication and interpersonal skills.

Some employees receive on-the-job training at work. They start working in jobs that require easily learned tasks. The job of a fast-food cook is one example. Some restaurant chains offer training programs for employees to improve their skills or advance to managerial positions.

High school courses that may be helpful for careers in business or marketing include foods, clothing, and interior design, depending on your career interests. Courses in family living and personal relationships will help you understand families. They will also help you get along with your business associates and customers. Psychology and sociology courses help you understand people's behavior. Accounting and other business courses are very important, too.

Vocational schools offer special programs such as foodservice, hospitality, and clothing alterations. By completing these programs and gaining experience and new skills, you will probably find a job sooner. You also have a better chance of being hired for a good job after completing these programs.

If you enjoy fashion and want a career in this area, you should explore two- or four-year college programs. You will probably take courses in textiles, clothing construction, marketing, retailing, advertising, economics, psychology, and consumer behavior.

Four-year college graduates hold most better-paying positions. People with more education and experience tend to climb the career ladder faster than those with less schooling. Some business courses are needed to obtain the better careers. It also helps to specialize in a particular area of interest within family and consumer sciences. Also, you may need to complete an internship as one requirement for your college degree.

Future Trends

Changes in family living are creating an increased need for businesses that provide services, both at home and away from home. The demand for people trained in the areas of foodservice and hospitality continues to grow. With more people eating out, jobs in foodservice are among the fastest-growing occupations. The outlook for jobs in tourism also appears very good. Spending on travel and lodging will probably increase for many years to come, 14-18.

Nutrition and food information continues to be important to consumers. They want to know what to eat and what to avoid in order to have optimum health. There is a close correlation among health, wellness, and the kind and

14-18 Some lodging facilities provide activities for children as part of their basic services.

amount of food eaten. Those who provide this information are much in demand.

The fast paced retail sales areas continue to provide employment for a varied segment of employees. This may be one of the first jobs young people have. With more training and experience, employees can work up the career ladder to more responsible jobs in this sector.

Home improvement will be a big part of the picture in the next decade. Because of longer life spans, people will be able to enjoy fuller lives while living on their own. They will rely on others, however, for special services. People want their homes to be convenient, comfortable, and safe, but don't have time to do the work themselves. People with knowledge and skill in providing services for the homeowner or renter should see a continued need for their services.

Managing money is more important now than ever. With limited time to research investment options, people will continue to seek financial planners. There will be more demand for people trained in helping others manage their finances.

Those desiring a business or marketing career in family and consumer sciences can prepare for the future by keeping up with new developments in their area. It is also important to stay aware of changes occurring in society that impact the business world. By staying abreast of these changes, newcomers to the profession will be prepared to meet new challenges in their careers.

Summary

Business and marketing jobs in family and consumer sciences include the following areas: food, nutrition, and wellness; hospitality, tourism, and recreation; textiles and apparel; environmental design; family studies and human services; consumer and resource management; and child development and early childhood education. Many different career paths can be followed in each area.

Professionals in family and consumer sciences will find a wide variety of opportunities in the business cluster. Some jobs require only a high school diploma. Other jobs require post-secondary training while many require a college degree. Special training is needed to obtain many jobs or advance to higher-level jobs.

Good decision-making skills are essential for work in the business field. People working in business need excellent communication skills, too. It is also very important to be able to work well with others.

Changes in family living have created an increased need for businesses that provide services. People will need help with managing their finances. An aging population will mean an increased demand for facilities and services that cater to their needs. With limited time at home, dual-career families will be looking for services to help make their homes convenient, comfortable, and safe.

More services will be needed to help people who are on the go. Foodservice and hospitality career opportunities will expand. People will eat out more often or purchase food already prepared to take home. There will continue to be a need for jobs in the travel industry.

Changes in technology and communication will affect the family, society, and jobs. It will be very important for family and consumer sciences business professionals to keep up with changes and new developments in the field.

To Review

1. Name and describe one entry-level job in institutional foodservice and one that requires a four-year degree.

2. Why is the demand high for jobs in hospitality?

3. Name and describe two different jobs in fashion merchandising.

4. What is the primary focus of a marketing research analyst?

5. Identify five different items that are manufactured and merchandised by home furnishings professionals.

6. Explain what an individual must do to be able to sell real estate.

7. List three duties of a retirement home manager.

8. Name three types of employers that hire financial planners.

9. Name and describe three personal skills needed for a family and consumer sciences career in business or marketing.

10. What single trend will cause an increase in jobs for money managers and home improvement specialists?

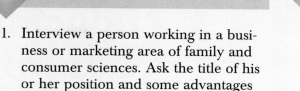 ## To Do

1. Interview a person working in a business or marketing area of family and consumer sciences. Ask the title of his or her position and some advantages and disadvantages of working in this job. Prepare an oral report for your class.

2. Have students prepare a bulletin board illustrating several different jobs described in this chapter.

3. Brainstorm types of jobs with potential growth that might be available in the career fields discussed in this chapter. Which might be found in your community?

15 Careers in Education and Communications

After studying this chapter, you will be able to
- ◆ list family and consumer sciences career opportunities in education.
- ◆ list family and consumer sciences career opportunities in communications.
- ◆ describe personal skills and abilities needed for a career in education or communications.
- ◆ specify the education and training needed for various careers in education and communications.
- ◆ outline future trends in family and consumer sciences careers in education and communications.

Terms to Know

stewardship	journalist
trade association	syndicated
webmaster	editor
reporter	copy editor
correspondent	demonstrator
writer	advocate

Many professionals working in the field of family and consumer sciences are teachers. Years ago, teaching was the main career option for those who had an interest in the home and family.

Today, teaching continues to be the chosen field for a large number of students, but there are many other career options. New careers in education and communications have developed in response to changes in society.

Many educators enjoy working as classroom teachers at elementary, secondary, or college levels. See 15-1. Others may work in company training programs or other nonschool settings. In the communications field, people are employed in newspaper, television, or other media jobs for schools, community agencies, companies, or public relations firms.

You will find a wide scope of job opportunities in this career cluster. From working as a preschool teacher to writing television scripts, the education and communications area offers a diverse range of jobs. People with knowledge in family and consumer sciences and skill in communications are in great demand. Talent and training in this area can lead to many stimulating and rewarding careers.

In this chapter, you will explore family and consumer sciences job opportunities in education and communications. A majority of these jobs require two or four years of college. A few jobs require less education. If you like to work with people to help them learn, you should explore jobs in this career cluster. Since information is vital in today's economy, careers in these areas have a bright future.

15-1 The traditional classroom is the most common setting in which educators work.

◆ Career Opportunities in Education

Family and consumer sciences educators teach various age groups in many settings. Some people prefer to teach younger children and become involved in preschool and nursery school education. Working with school-age children appeals to many. Some educators work in programs that help troubled youth, while others work with adults in continuing education programs. Some family and consumer sciences educators teach skills in foreign countries.

If you have an interest in the field of family and consumer sciences and would like to teach, there will be many job opportunities open to you.

Teaching Preschoolers

Nursery schools, preschools, and kindergartens all employ teachers. Child care centers primarily provide care for infants, toddlers, and preschoolers. Though teaching may take place in these centers, this is not their primary function. In Chapter 16 you will learn more about child care centers.

Preschool teachers help young children make the change from home to group learning. Preschoolers enjoy group activities. By planning group activities, teachers help children learn to interact socially with other children. Preschool children are enthusiastic learners, eager to absorb information and try new things. See 15-2.

Preschool teachers are very influential in the lives of small children. They must provide the guidance and experiences that will have a

15-2 If you enjoy teaching children, you may want to work as a preschool teacher.

positive effect on children's growth and development. Preschool teachers must be innovative and flexible in planning activities. They must be generous with their love and their ideas, and responsive to children's needs. Preschool teachers enjoy watching children think and act. If you enjoy young children, you may want to consider a career in this area.

Teaching School-Age Students

If you think you might enjoy teaching school-age students, you might consider being a family and consumer sciences teacher. In many schools, family and consumer sciences classes begin in the fifth grade and continue through high school.

Family and consumer sciences courses in middle schools are often exploratory courses. In these courses, many subject areas are examined. Courses apply to students' roles in the home, workforce, and at school. These courses often include the study of nutrition and wellness, textiles and apparel, consumer education, and child development. They also cover

personal development, decision-making skills, and family relationships. At the secondary or high school level you might teach introductory or advanced courses. Some may be a semester in length in a specialized subject.

Secondary teachers must be aware of problems and concerns facing teens. Many courses taught in family and consumer sciences focus on the following key interests of teens:

◆ making decisions
◆ managing resources
◆ choosing a career
◆ choosing a mate
◆ dealing with family relationships
◆ avoiding unplanned pregnancies
◆ understanding nutrition and wellness
◆ avoiding drugs, alcohol, and tobacco
◆ avoiding AIDS
◆ solving environmental problems

Courses in family and consumer sciences are very popular with teens because they cover issues that directly relate to them. The courses discuss ways to make better decisions about health, money, family needs, and future goals.

Cheryl Murray
High School Family and Consumer Sciences Teacher

Cheryl Murray teaches in the family and consumer sciences department of a Kansas City high school. The five classes that she currently teaches prepare students for fashion careers.

Students in Cheryl's classes organize and present a fashion show each year. The students begin by developing a theme for the show. They are responsible for contacting retailers and choosing fashions, backdrops, and music. They write scripts for the clothing modeled and also prepare publicity.

During their senior year, students can receive on-the-job experience in local fashion businesses. Cheryl helps students obtain employment in fashion-related jobs. Employers evaluate students on their work performance. Class work includes a study of the fashion industry, designers, and fashion merchandising.

If Cheryl were teaching in a smaller school, she might teach classes in several areas of family and consumer sciences, such as child development, family living, and foods and nutrition. In larger high schools, teachers can specialize as Cheryl does.

"I really like what I do," Cheryl says. "One reason is our students choose to be in our classes. They especially enjoy the hands-on activities. Courses in family and consumer sciences are not required subjects in most schools. Therefore, we keep students informed of our course offerings so they know what we have to offer."

According to Cheryl, teachers spend several hours each day preparing for the classes they teach. "Lessons have to be prepared and papers graded," Cheryl explains. "In addition, we contact guest speakers and arrange for field trips. There is also a lot of paperwork involved in programs that receive federal funds, as ours do."

Cheryl feels that programs in family and consumer sciences remain strong because they benefit students in two ways. Students not only learn information that will help them in their personal lives, but they also learn important career skills. Classes in family and consumer sciences often introduce young people to new career options.

"Though I teach about fashion careers, we also encourage our students to become teachers of family and consumer sciences. It is predicted there will be a shortage of teachers in this field in the near future," Cheryl relates. Another advantage of a degree in education is that you learn many skills that can be used in other jobs as well.

Teachers of family and consumer sciences prepare students to handle the dual responsibilities of family and job plus the many life roles they will acquire.

Family and consumer sciences teachers must be able to relate the skills they teach to the needs of their students. They help students use information to solve everyday problems, 15-3. By encouraging their students to apply knowledge, teachers help students work toward a better life.

Family and consumer sciences teachers have frequent personal contact with their students because of the courses they teach. If you go into this field, you must enjoy working with young people and helping them learn about home and family living.

15-3 Students use what they learn in family and consumer sciences classes to help solve everyday problems, such as making wise wardrobe choices.

Teaching at the Postsecondary Level

There are many family and consumer sciences teaching positions at the postsecondary level. These positions are in vo-tech schools, two-year community colleges, four-year colleges, and universities. Educators at this level help students prepare for various careers in the field.

If you teach in a vo-tech school, you will teach occupational family and consumer sciences courses. You might teach courses in foodservice, CAD, tailoring, or child care services. Students may work part-time while attending a vo-tech school. The teacher may help students find work and meet with employers to discuss student progress.

Community and junior colleges hire family and consumer sciences teachers for their occupational programs. These teachers may help students upgrade their skills to meet employment needs. They also provide employee job training or retraining. Sometimes they help students plan two-year programs of study. (These programs are discussed in Chapter 4.)

Other postsecondary educators work in colleges and universities. College professors concentrate their teaching to one area of family and consumer sciences. For instance, a college professor might teach only child development courses. Another professor might teach courses in environmental design or some other department.

Teaching at the college level generally requires at least a master's degree. Some professors divide their schedule between teaching and conducting research. Professors in higher education not only teach classes, but also advise students. They may supervise graduate research projects.

Most institutions expect faculty members to also conduct research. Educational journals and magazines publish faculty research papers.

Peter D'Souza
Associate Professor

Peter D'Souza, an international award-winning chef, shares his knowledge of the culinary arts with university students in the hospitality and tourism program. He teaches classes on restaurant management, banquet catering, wines and spirits management, as well as dining etiquette and professional dress. A full-service restaurant is operated by the students in the program. In this very real setting, students learn on-the-job skills.

"I love teaching because it gives me the opportunity to show young people the right way to prepare foods and perform management tasks," explains Peter. "I can make more of a difference in an industry that needs well-trained professionals. If I worked in the field, I could only teach the people who worked for me. In an educational setting, I can have an impact industry-wide."

As a teacher, he also receives great satisfaction in seeing former students achieve good positions in the foodservice industry. "You feel you had a hand in helping them become successful. This motivates me to continue to educate others," says Peter.

There are some disadvantages to his job. His workdays are long since the student-operated restaurant requires his supervision until late at night. He cannot delegate this work to others as he would in the industry. In addition, professional chefs often receive much higher salaries than he and other university professors do.

Peter received his training in India and began his career as a chef at the Bombay Taj Mahal InterContinental Hotel in Bombay, India. Though he enjoyed his years as a hotel chef, he also likes to help students prepare for foodservice careers. He received international recognition for his role as a teacher by being chosen for the International Foodservice Educator of the Year award by CHRIE, the Council of Hotel, Restaurant, and Institutional Educators.

A university setting gives Peter a forum for sharing his professional skills with others. "Teaching forces me to stay current with what is happening in the field, and helps my students to feel confident in their preparation for their future careers," Peter reports.

Dr. Esther Glover Fahm
Professor

Dr. Esther Fahm is Professor of Food and Nutrition with the University of Wisconsin-Stout. She teaches dietetics, community nutrition, and nutrition for young children besides handling many other responsibilities.

"My activities range from teaching to planning educational programs," Esther explains, "to working with high schools, businesses, government agencies, community groups, and others. It also involves managing budgets and writing reports. Often I work with teachers and administrators at other universities, always finding time to help students. All of my activities require people skills, communication skills, and decision-making skills."

Esther directs a multicultural scholars program funded by the U.S. Department of Agriculture for recruitment and retention of minority students at the university. She assists with grant development, community nutrition activities, curriculum development, and special projects. She also serves as guest speaker for professional and community conferences.

"The many different responsibilities of my job keep my work interesting," Esther says. "Helping others succeed is the greatest reward of my work. By so doing, I also succeed and develop personally and professionally."

Earlier she served as Vice Chancellor for Academic Affairs, working with students, faculty, and staff to accomplish the goals of the university as well as individuals' career goals. Before that, Esther served as Dean of the School of Human Environmental Sciences, providing overall leadership for its four departments. The school's central focus is to give students a family and consumer sciences education that meets current and future workforce needs.

Esther is very happy to again teach dietetics, the job that launched her university career. "As a teacher, I enjoy seeing students learn and develop skills for their future careers," explains Esther. "Seeing their curiosity and joy of achievement and working with students to overcome learning challenges makes teaching a stimulating experience. Teaching requires that you keep up-to-date in your field. In addition, a teacher must continually develop new materials and methods, including technologies for different learning styles and needs. A college teacher fills many roles—an advisor, mentor, researcher, author, and team member for community projects."

Teaching Adults

Adult and continuing education teachers organize and teach programs for groups of adults. Community colleges, libraries, park districts, and other agencies conduct adult and continuing education programs. Adult educators may work in schools, hospitals, or within some companies. Teaching at junior or community colleges may be a full- or part-time job.

Adult educators may teach one or more family and consumer sciences subjects. A person might have a full-time job and teach an adult course at night. The subjects taught could range from healthy eating for aging adults to a course helping parents increase their children's self-esteem. You might enjoy teaching adults quilting or gourmet cooking in an adult education class.

Most adult education classes center on the interests and needs of the local area. Consequently, if you teach in this field, you should have a genuine interest in the community, its people, and its future. You also need to be able to work closely with your students.

Many adults go back to school for retraining or to learn new skills for a job. Sometimes adults take noncredit evening classes to expand their knowledge in a given field. For instance, some adults may want to improve their computer skills, while others might need courses in nutrition and wellness. Adult educators help these students reach their goals. See 15-4.

Adult and continuing education coordinators organize the adult programs by determining areas of need and developing new courses. It is also their responsibility to locate teachers. For instance, a financial planning course would be a very useful addition in a community that suffers the shutdown of a major employer. Good leadership and communication skills are important for this role of adult and continuing education coordinator.

15-4 Some educators enjoy teaching and working with adults.

University of Wisconsin-Stout

Avie Barmann
Parent Educator

Students are not always children or teens. Parents as First Teachers is a program designed to educate parents. Avie Barmann has been involved with this program since it began in Missouri in 1985. "I work with parents of children five years old and younger, teaching them how to become better 'teachers' of their children," explains Avie.

Avie's role as a parent educator begins with a family when the child is about six weeks of age. She first identifies any physical problems, such as hearing or sight problems, and refers families to area agencies for help if needed. Information on what to look for in their child's development is given to the parents. "I visit each family's home four times a year," reports Avie. "I often take educational materials and toys that would enhance the child's learning."

Group sessions are held for parents on such subjects as children's illnesses, discipline, and eating problems. Group meetings give young parents an opportunity to discuss common concerns they have in rearing children. "I often learn as much from these sessions as the parents do! Parents have good ideas that they share with each other. Since I have children of my own, I'm always looking for better ways to handle difficult situations," states Avie.

"You meet so many different people in this job—people of various educational levels and lifestyles," explains Avie. "You have to be flexible in order to meet their needs." Since every day is different, Avie feels you must be open-minded, patient, and organized.

This program works because parents are their children's first teachers. Avie, as a parent educator, serves as a resource person, helping parents with this important job. "It's nice to be able to help parents at this very important time in their lives, especially if theirs is a first child. As new parents, they often need encouragement and reassurance. I can assure them they are doing a fine job."

Education Careers in Nonschool Settings

Interesting job possibilities exist in the education field for someone wanting to combine a family and consumer sciences background with a nonschool setting. You could work for the Cooperative Extension Service or become an author of educational materials. These are just two of the many career possibilities for educators who work in nontraditional areas.

Cooperative Extension Educator

The Cooperative Extension Service represents a large network of educators who teach in nonschool settings. These educators, called *cooperative extension agents* or *specialists,* are staff members of land-grant colleges.

The land-grant system began in 1914 when a federal act gave land to each state for research, experimentation, teaching, and learning. State universities sprang up under this system. The goal of the land-grant system has been to develop research and apply the findings—through education and other "extension" efforts—to benefit people, communities, and the nation. The Cooperative Extension Service focuses on agricultural, environmental, and human sciences under the direction of the U.S. Department of Agriculture.

Cooperative extension educators work in all counties in the United States. They usually report to county offices, but travel throughout their counties, working in rural, suburban, and urban areas.

Agents who focus on family and consumer sciences provide programs on related educational topics. These include food safety, child development, youth and families, health and wellness, and environmental stewardship. **Stewardship** is the careful and responsible management of something entrusted in one's care.

The primary job of an extension agent is developing programs for the specific needs of people in his or her county. The programs provide up-to-date information from the university.

For instance, a family and consumer sciences educator may conduct sessions on new food safety facts that affect seniors. Another educator may show new energy-saving techniques for the home. Agricultural educators may present workshops on pest and insect control or soil management.

Extension educators also provide leadership training for both youth and adults. They work with young people in 4-H clubs and other youth groups.

Extension educators often work with other community agencies to provide programs. They also rely on research from land-grant universities in other states, the U.S. Department of Agriculture, and other government agencies. Extension specialists on campus provide educational support and information from new research to county staff members. They also conduct in-service training for county extension educators.

People working as extension educators need good oral and written communication skills. Many write weekly news columns for local newspapers or present educational radio or television programs. Cooperative extension educators must enjoy working with a wide variety of people.

Author of Educational Materials

Some educators enjoy writing textbooks and other educational materials. This is an example of how the education and communications segments of this career cluster tie together.

Many educators write articles for journals, magazines, or newspapers. Some authors publish their own materials. See the next section of this chapter for more information on writers and editors.

Family and consumer sciences professionals write about many subjects. Some authors write about human relations issues, such as divorce, marriage, aging, and personal relationships. Others choose to write about food preparation and nutrition. The field of family and consumer sciences lends itself to a wide variety of interesting and timely topics.

Not until you become well known in your field and have written many books and articles can you afford to make a living as a full-time writer. You usually need to have another job, which is often teaching. Many high school and college professors write textbooks.

There are other opportunities for those who enjoy writing. You could write scripts for educational television. You could write educational materials for the classroom. You might produce a television program for consumers. For example, you might write a program on teen involvement in preserving the environment. The need for educational materials utilizing computer and Internet technology continues to grow, too.

◆ Career Opportunities in Communications

What do reading, writing, listening, speaking, and watching have in common? They are all ways that people send and receive information. Since this is the information age, communications is a popular choice for a career.

Information bombards you every day. There is a vast amount of material available through print, radio, television, movies, and the Internet. See 15-5. Look at how much mail your family receives! This will give you an idea of how much information is constantly being relayed. You may listen to the radio and watch videos or television several hours a day. Perhaps you spend considerable time on the Internet. Many people are involved in bringing all of this information and entertainment to you.

Apple Computer

15-5 The increasing use of the Internet is creating interesting job opportunities for those who can use it to communicate family and consumer sciences information.

Professionals in family and consumer sciences use various means of communication to reach consumers with information. They write newspaper columns and appear on television programs. They work as reporters, writers, editors, and product demonstrators. Some even have their own radio or television shows or Internet sites. They all use their skills to inform, persuade, entertain, or enlighten audiences.

Communications is a challenging field, full of rapidly changing technologies. What will happen in ten or twenty years? Communicators who know how to use the technology of the day will be in demand.

Public Relations Specialist

Public relations specialists build and maintain good relations with all the audiences important to an employer. The primary audience is the company's employees. Other key audiences may include the local community, government regulators, the press, and the general public.

The goal of public relations specialists is to maintain communications between the company and its audiences. These specialists provide information about the company's policies, activities, and accomplishments. By doing so, they present a positive image of the company. They also inform the company of any issues they uncover that require attention. This helps companies recognize and handle difficulties before they become widespread problems that attract negative publicity.

Many family and consumer sciences professionals work in public relations departments. They work in universities, hospitals, hotels, large retail stores, and restaurants. Many professionals work for public relations agencies, manufacturers, or trade associations. **Trade associations** are groups of business people or manufacturers involved in a particular trade or industry. They join together for the protection and advancement of common interests. These associations may also be called bureaus or councils.

The United States government is one of the largest single employers of public relations specialists. These specialists keep the public informed about the activities of government agencies. For example, the U. S. Department of Agriculture provides food guides and other nutrition information for the public.

Public relations professionals develop and write informational material such as annual reports, sales brochures, and press releases. See 15-6. Newspapers, television, and other advertising media use press releases. If you work in public relations, you must always have current information available about your organization's products or services. Public relations professionals also organize promotional events and direct the production of photos, films, videotapes, and Internet sites.

The Internet presents additional career opportunities for those whose responsibilities extend to the company's Web site. **Webmaster** is the new title of specialists who create the appearance and of these sites and/or write the information they contain.

Hormel

15-6 Public relations specialists write and develop press kits, brochures, and other advertising or marketing materials.

Often public issues involve a company. Issues might arise regarding health, nutrition, energy, or environmental concerns. For example, the public might have a concern that a food manufacturer is adding an ingredient to its product that might be harmful. If you worked in the company's public relations department, you would compile information to address this concern. Then, you would use various means to educate the public about your company's side of the issue.

In addition to top-notch communication and business skills, professionals in public relations must be able to build relationships with many types of people. This is often a high-pressure, deadline-oriented career area where a nine-to-five schedule is not the norm.

Radio or Television Broadcasting

You might want a job working in radio or television. *Announcers* and *newscasters* are the more obvious jobs in broadcasting, but behind the scenes there are many more *writers* and *program planners* developing themes and scripts for future programs.

Many radio and television programs feature topics relating to family and consumer sciences. Programs on cooking, fashion, or design always have large audiences, 15-7. With training in environmental design, you might host a program on home repair or decorating. As a radio or television program host, you would need to be thoroughly familiar with your subject matter.

Reporter or Correspondent

Reporters gather information and prepare stories that inform their audiences about current events and issues. In covering a story, they may conduct research on the subject and interview experts. Generally, they take notes while interviewing. They need to know what questions to ask to get needed information so attention to detail is critical. Many reporters

and correspondents use laptop computers to compile information and write stories in the field. Then they send their material electronically to the newsroom or office.

Reporters assigned to other cities and countries are known as **correspondents.** Correspondents prepare stories on major news events occurring throughout the world. They must do the same careful investigative work as reporters. Reporters and correspondents may work for newspapers, magazines, radio, television, or other media.

Reporters and correspondents with a background in a specialized field, such as family and consumer sciences, may analyze and interpret news from that field. For instance, some may write about fashion, consumer affairs, travel, or finance. They may acquire

Johnson and Wales University

15-7 Shows featuring top chefs are popular with television audiences.

Nancy L. Zieman
Television Show Producer and Host

Tune in to *Sewing with Nancy* to get the latest instruction on sewing. Nancy Zieman is the producer and host of this very successful public television program. Sometimes a popular fashion feature can be traced to one of Nancy's programs.

Nancy began her television career in 1982 when cable television was in its infancy. "I was doing freelance work, putting on sewing seminars around the country, when I was invited to be a guest on a cable TV show," explains Nancy. "Following my appearance, I was asked if I would like my own show. In the beginning, I did most of the work myself. We even taped the pilot shows in a living room!"

Nancy now hosts 26 half-hour shows a year. She and three assistants decide on the techniques or projects to be presented on each show. They may plan three programs on each topic. The script is written in a step-by-step format, and then samples are made that show the progression. According to Nancy, the key skill in hosting a how-to show is being able to divide a project into understandable parts.

The shows are taped year-round, and it takes about five hours to tape one show. "You have to be super-organized. You can't go to the studio unprepared," says Nancy. "Being a TV host is not glamorous! It's hard work. You have to learn to talk to a camera like it is a person and not be afraid."

According to Nancy, sewing has gone through an evolution. "We used to focus more on sewing as a way to save money," she explains. "Now more people sew as a hobby. It's an art that allows people creative expression." Many of Nancy's viewers are looking for ideas of items they can make to give to others. Examples include wall quilts, christening gowns, home decorating projects, and gifts for men.

"Doing this show allows me to teach a large audience a skill that I love. I also enjoy the creative challenge of coming up with new projects and techniques to show my audience," Nancy adds. She is famous for developing easy sewing steps that create a fashion look.

Nancy believes that broadcasting has tremendous potential for growth. With up to 200 cable TV channels available, there will be many opportunities to reach creative individuals. There will also be more school-to-school teaching via camera in the years ahead.

some of their information from press releases, manufacturers, and public relations firms. Good reporters, however, go directly to the sources for first-hand information.

If you think you might like to work in this field, you will need good writing and public speaking skills. You must be able to work under tight deadlines to meet a broadcasting or printing deadline. Frequently you will be under great pressure to meet these deadlines.

Writer or Editor

Good communication skills and creative ideas are central to the work of a writer, author, or editor. To work in this area, you need to be able to communicate through the written word. You can be a writer or editor for many different types of publishing companies with a family and consumer sciences background.

Writers develop materials for magazines, trade or technical journals, and newspapers. They also write books, reports, advertisements,

company newsletters, and radio and television scripts. Some writers work from their homes. **Journalists** are people writing for newspapers and magazines. They may need to do some traveling to collect information for their writing.

Writers begin their work by selecting a topic, sometimes assigned by an editor. Then they research and gather information about the subject. They may observe activities and conduct interviews. From the information gathered, they select the material they want to use. They write it so the reader can easily understand the information. Writers often must revise and reorganize their work many times, 15-8.

Ann Paige, a former teacher, now writes a news column called "Ask the Teacher." Parents write in with their questions about education. Other journalists in family and consumer sciences write columns about staying physically fit, spending money wisely, or updating a home's interior. Some of these columns are **syndicated**, or published in newspapers throughout the country.

15-8 Writers must be able to express ideas clearly and logically. Usually they have others read their material to point out ways to improve it.

Sara Barkley has a career as a food writer and radio host. When her food news and recipe newspaper column became popular, the newspaper asked her to do a morning call-in radio show. Callers ask questions pertaining to topics in her column. She provides suggestions and ideas on food and nutrition subjects. She answers questions about foods that are in season, labeling, nutrition, or other food concerns.

Technical writers specialize in putting scientific and technical information into words that most people can understand. They prepare manuals, parts lists, and instructional materials for the industry to use in their sales or service department. See 15-9.

Copywriters write advertising copy for use by magazines, newspapers, or other media. They often work for advertising agencies and trade associations. Some are self-employed. These freelance professionals contract with businesses to prepare advertising for special projects. Copywriters provide clear, accurate information that will help promote their clients' products. Computers have helped make this a good freelance job. Copywriters have various software programs that make layout and writing much easier.

Copywriters might be hired by food manufacturers to prepare advertising copy for new products. They may write catalog copy for products being promoted. Copywriters also prepare material for radio or television advertisements.

Editors review manuscripts written by writers or authors. They *edit,* or review, reorganize, and rewrite authors' manuscripts as needed, preparing the material for publication or broadcast. *Managing editors* help form the policies for their department, magazine, newspaper, or trade journal. They plan the contents of the publication and supervise its preparation.

IBM

15-9 Technical writers translate specialized information so consumers and others easily understand it.

Copy editors check for accuracy and clarity in the written copy. They make sure the copy fits and adheres to the publication's correct style. Copy editors may design and edit news pages as well as feature pages in magazines and newspapers. See 15-10 for other writing possibilities.

Product Demonstrator

A **demonstrator** is someone who shows others how to perform a process. Product demonstrators might work for businesses such as food companies or appliance stores.

You may see professionals in family and consumer sciences demonstrating a new appliance on the market. New food products are often introduced this way. Others might demonstrate sewing methods or clothing tips. Product demonstrators work on TV and at sewing centers, supermarkets, department stores, conventions, and fairs.

Writing Opportunities
Advertising campaigns
Audiovisual scripts
Books and magazines
Consumer information materials
Corporate programs
Fund-raising events
Government information
Grant proposals
Internet sites
Legislative reports
Newspaper feature articles and reports
Public relations programs
Radio and television scripts
Sales materials
Resumes
Speeches
Teaching materials

15-10 If you like to write, the wide variety of writing opportunities is almost endless.

Angie Moore and Sue Williams are product demonstrators who work for a craft company. They attend conventions and craft shows across the country. There they set up a booth where people can come and see how to use the company's products to make various crafts, such as wreaths and stuffed animals. This is good publicity for the company. The young women travel throughout the country and meet many people.

Some showmanship is needed for demonstration work. If you choose a job such as this, you must be comfortable speaking to the public. You also must be able to think quickly and answer questions about your product.

Can you motivate others to buy your goods? Do you like to talk in front of a group? Are you persuasive and direct? Can you smoothly handle negative comments from an audience? These are skills needed for this job.

Software Developer

With increased use of computers in the home and classroom, there is a need for more software programs, especially in the areas of family and consumer sciences. Most software developers work for software companies, rather than create software items to sell on their own.

You might find a job developing software for computer use. For this position, you would need to know the subject matter well and how to best present it.

Developing educational software requires special knowledge about methods to present information that promote learning. These professionals must also know how to structure tests and other evaluation tools.

Developers of entertainment software, on the other hand, do not have similar requirements. All software developers, however, must know how to present their topics in interesting, creative ways because of intense competition in the market.

Gail Brown
Writer

With eleven books and hundreds of articles to her credit, Gail Brown is one of the most widely read authors on sewing and home decorating. She has written books on such subjects as sewing with sergers, sewing wedding gowns, and creative sewing for the home. She gives advice on making quick-to-sew fashions, slipcovers, window treatments, bed covers, and table accessories. Her articles have appeared in many magazines and newsletters, and she appears frequently on craft and sewing shows. She considers sewing "an incredible gift because it takes you on wonderful, creative journeys."

Gail first became interested in sewing through 4-H and her school family and consumer sciences classes. She helped fund her college education by sewing special-occasion clothes for others. Gail was always an avid reader and seemed to have a natural gift for writing. One of Gail's early jobs was writing educational materials for a knit fabric company in New York. Because knits were new on the home-sewing market, she and a friend decided to write a book on the subject. At the age of 22, she felt she didn't have anything to lose and was willing to accept possible failure. An interested publisher was found, and her writing career began.

Gail offers this advice to would-be authors: "Take advantage of every opportunity to write. Write for your school paper or local newspaper. Take writing classes. The more you write, the better writer you become. Use your best writing samples to get a job in the field. A person who can write will always find job opportunities." According to Gail, it's also important to read as much as you can. From reading you learn better and different ways to communicate.

Writers enjoy many freedoms. "As a writer, you have the freedom to be creative—to express yourself however you want," says Gail. "There are many ways to say the same thing, and working with the possibilities is exhilarating."

"Writers are also free to schedule their time as they wish. Also, by using modern technology, they can live anywhere they want, even in small towns."

"There are, however, some disadvantages to being a writer," Gail continues. "You have deadlines that must be met. Sometimes you have to make personal sacrifices in order to meet those deadlines. You must have a great deal of self-discipline to stay on task. You also spend much of your time alone."

As a freelance writer, her fax, modem, and on-line services provide instant communication with publishers, editors, and readers. Gail is thankful to her readers who have, in their support of her writing, "granted me the wonderful and rare freedom to work and live as I choose."

◆ Other Careers in Education and Communications

Accurate information is always needed outside classrooms, where much of the population's learning occurs. Other career opportunities in family and consumer sciences for those with education or communication backgrounds are discussed here.

Family Studies and Human Services. Some professionals work as advocates for families and individuals who need help. An **advocate** is one who works vigorously to promote or support a cause. By writing, speaking, and meeting with leaders and lawmakers, advocates spread the word about needed policy changes. Advocacy issues include affordable housing, reliable health-care, quality child care, and effective community schools. Senior citizens and members of ethnic groups are examples of people who are the focus of advocacy efforts. Advocates work for social service agencies, nonprofit organizations, and charitable groups.

Consumer and Resource Management. Now more than ever, busy consumers need help with balancing their time, money, energy, and other resources. Utility companies, for example, employ specialists to show consumers how to conserve gas and electricity in their homes. Financial institutions hire counselors to help customers budget for a new home, a quality education, an affordable retirement, and other goals. Family and consumer sciences professionals with useful tips for balancing limited resources will have an eager audience. See 15-11.

Hospitality, Tourism, and Recreation. In this highly competitive field, businesses thrive by promoting their facilities and services well. Creative communicators who can develop messages that attract the traveling public are keenly sought.

Educators in this specialty field are needed, too, as explosive industry growth fuels a growing need for qualified graduates. Companies in the industry also seek educators to custom-

design employee workshops and seminars that address specific company issues. Examples include programs for improving customer service, managing employee conflict, and preventing discrimination.

Textiles and Apparel. The very nature of the fashion world—with its ever-changing styles, colors, and fabrics—provide continuing opportunities for communicators and educators. The fashion aspect of this field is widely communicated through magazines, Web sites, TV programs, and other media outlets. There is the obvious need for teachers and extension agents to continue providing information about new textiles and their use and care. In the business world, product manufacturers employ specialists to educate sales and customer service staffs about product features. Such specialists work in

15-11 Most people struggle daily with money, time, and energy limitations. They are eager for helpful tips on balancing resources wisely.

companies that make or sell fabrics, apparel, and anything that uses textiles.

Environmental Design. The education and communication careers in this field resemble those in the area of textiles and apparel. Communication and teaching opportunities are increasing as new discoveries translate into technologies that benefit consumer lifestyles and the environment.

Food, Nutrition, and Wellness. Educators at all levels are needed to teach the lifelong habits of good nutrition and physical fitness. See 15-12. Career opportunities are available with health clubs, exercise centers, and other health-focused employers. In publishing and communication industries, writers and reporters with scientific backgrounds who present facts clearly to the general public are eagerly sought. Consumers want accurate nutrition and wellness information at a time when confusion and inaccuracies predominate.

15-12 Communicating the message of how to stay physically fit is one that must be emphasized to audiences of all ages.

Personal Skills and Abilities Needed for a Career in Education or Communications

Educators are often role models for their students and should set a good example for them. Teachers inspire and guide students in their career decisions and, consequently, impact their lives forever. Teachers and other educators need to help students realize the importance of higher education. As an educator, you would play a vital role in helping students develop the skills and knowledge needed for achieving success.

If you choose a career in communications, it is your responsibility to search for facts and report them accurately. You must be eager to take the necessary steps to ensure accurate reporting and news gathering. Also, you should be able to talk one-on-one with people in order to obtain information.

Education and Training Needed for a Career in Education or Communications

Most careers in education require a four-year college degree. In most states, a license to teach can only be obtained after receiving a bachelor's degree in education. Teachers at the postsecondary level usually have a master's degree or higher. Some adult education teachers may not need a college degree if the primary requirement to teach is knowledge and expertise in a field, such as scriptwriting or film directing. Extension educators, on the other hand, often need a master's degree.

Most careers in communications require a four-year college degree. See 15-13 for educational requirements concerning different jobs in

Education and Communications Careers		
Entry Level	Writer	Journalist
Craft demonstrator		Legislation lobbyist
Library assistant	**College Degree**	Magazine editor
Messenger	Advertising director	Marketing specialist
Preschool aide	Career counselor	News correspondent
Recreation assistant	Child life specialist	News director
Teacher's aide	College instructor	Newspaper columnist
	Computer software developer	Personnel director
Advanced Training	Consumer education specialist	Preschool teacher/director
Adult education teacher		Public relations specialist
After-school program supervisor	Cooperative extension specialist	Radio newscaster
Associate teacher	Curator	Reporter
Bookmobile attendant	Curriculum developer/specialist	Special education teacher
Computer programmer		Teacher trainer
Head start teacher	Editor	Technical writer/editor
Personal assistant	Elementary or secondary school teacher	Teenage parenting educator
Product demonstrator		Television newscaster
Special education aide	Food or fashion editor	Textbook editor
Tutor	Government affairs specialist	Vocational counselor

15-13 *Education and communication skills can translate into many exciting career opportunities.*

this career cluster. Some jobs may require technical writing experience, but not necessarily a college education. For instance, writing about crafts, hobbies, or travel are some examples.

You can take high school writing, photography, or public speaking courses to gain experience for a career in communications. Working on the yearbook, writing for the school newspaper, or preparing community or preschool bulletins will give you additional experience, 15-14.

If you are interested in a career in education, you might get some related experience while still in school. The following are some suggestions to pursue:

◆ ***Work as an aide in a preschool, elementary school, or community recreation department.*** In this position, you could see if you liked working with children. You would be able to see the problems a teacher might encounter and also experience the fun of being with children.

◆ ***Give lessons or tutor.*** If you have a particular talent or skill, you might give lessons to younger children. You could teach cooking, crafts, computer skills, sports for kids, or bike repair. You might tutor a specific subject if you have good grades in it. Giving lessons or tutoring will help you experience the process of helping others learn.

Brian Kinder

15-14 Working on school yearbooks and newspapers is a good way to decide whether you might like a career in communications.

Education careers in family and consumer sciences help students develop and improve decision-making skills. Courses focus on the home, the family, and the impact of changing family values and structures. These courses are especially important in helping teens adjust to their future roles in life. Jobs for family and consumer sciences teachers are available in middle schools, secondary schools, and vo-tech centers.

Communication technology will continue to impact the job market. With computers being used for more management functions in the home, the need for well-written software programs will increase. Consumers want to incorporate the latest technology into their everyday lives.

An increasing number of seniors means that more students will be adult learners. Educators are developing more courses that interest this audience while communicators are finding new ways to reach this population group. Being able to communicate and work with people of various ethnic groups is also necessary.

As you can see, the ability to convey ideas and thoughts to others is vital for most jobs. The education and communications job cluster can serve as a springboard to many careers. This area can provide an exciting future for those with the skills and abilities to provide creativity and responsiveness to their jobs. This is, indeed, a very versatile combination.

Future Trends

The employment outlook is good for those desiring a career in education or communications. Accurate, up-to-date information is needed on every aspect of life.

Summary

There are many job possibilities in family and consumer sciences in this career cluster. Traditional classroom teaching is a very desirable career option, but there are many other options as well. You might like to teach children in preschool or older adults continuing their education in the workplace. Other educators, such as cooperative extension specialists or authors of educational materials, prefer a nonschool setting.

There are numerous career choices in communications. If you enjoy writing and promotion, you might like to work as a public relations specialist. If you enjoy being in the public eye, you might like to be a radio or television host, announcer, newscaster, or demonstrator. Work as a writer, author, editor, reporter, or correspondent may interest you. Accurate reporting is necessary in the communications field as the public expects correct information.

Almost all family and consumer sciences jobs in education and communications require a bachelor's degree. There are, however, a number of interesting jobs that do not require a college education. You may find these jobs if you have special abilities in a particular area. You might be able to get a job demonstrating a particular skill.

The outlook appears bright for work in this job cluster. Information is a way of life in our current society. Keeping up with new trends and changes will be important to future employment in this field. Both education and communications are springboards to many other career opportunities. This is a combination with great potential.

To Review

1. What is the difference between the role of a preschool teacher and that of a child care worker?

2. High school family and consumer sciences classes focus on key concerns of students. Name five key teen concerns.

3. Name two jobs in the education field other than traditional classroom teaching.

4. Explain the primary job of a cooperative extension agent.

5. Name two main functions of public relations personnel.

6. Identify the steps that a writer uses to write an article.

7. Name four places product demonstrators might work.

8. List two personal skills or abilities teachers need when working with students.

9. What level of education is needed for most family and consumer sciences jobs in education and communications?

To Do

1. Interview a family and consumer sciences teacher about his or her career choice. Write a report and share it with the class.

2. Prepare publicity posters for family and consumer sciences classes or careers in education and communications. Obtain permission to display them in the school halls and family and consumer sciences classrooms. Post them during open house for new students and enrollment periods.

3. Write a paper discussing how changes in society are influencing family and consumer sciences jobs in education and communications. Identify the prospects for future jobs in this field.

Careers in Human Services 16

After studying this chapter, you will be able to
◆ list career opportunities in human services.
◆ assess the personal skills and abilities that would help you succeed in a human services career.
◆ describe the education and training that might be required for a career in human services.
◆ outline future trends in human service careers.

Terms to Know

human services	paraprofessional
child care	fraud
family child care	counselors
nanny	displaced
children in self-care	homemakers
disadvantaged	demographics

Working to improve the lives of individuals and families by helping and understanding others is a field called **human services.** Nearly one-half of all family and consumer sciences professionals are employed in this field. They work with millions of people throughout the world. Their varied talents adapt to a wide variety of helping occupations that benefit individuals, families, and communities.

Professionals in family and consumer sciences are needed to plan and supervise programs and to research better methods of serving people. Their training enables them to communicate their skills and knowledge to others. At the same time, they must be sensitive to the needs of individuals.

These professionals help people with a wide range of problems. They help families manage their finances, meet their nutritional needs, and resolve family conflicts. They work with all age groups. Sometimes they work with people who are poor or underprivileged, or

have physical or mental disabilities. At times they serve as consultants to other professionals, such as doctors, nurses, and social workers. Professionals in family and consumer sciences can become Peace Corps volunteers, child welfare professionals, or consumer protection specialists. This field offers a wide range of entry-level as well as professional positions dealing with the home and family, 16-1.

Human services professionals are employed by schools, churches, hospitals, clinics, and community and rehabilitation centers. Many work in local, state, or federal government agencies, such as Head Start and welfare agencies. Public housing authorities, associations for the disabled, and offices that serve the aging employ professionals in family and consumer sciences. Nonprofit organizations as well as private businesses seek their skills.

In this chapter you will look at the wide range of human services occupations that help meet individual and family needs. You will

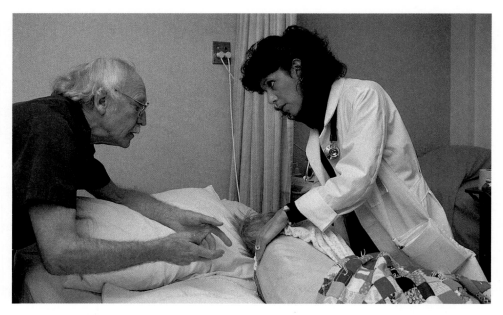

16-1 People who select a career in human services must have a special desire to help other people.

examine the type of training and background needed. There are many job opportunities in this field for young people who care to make a difference in people's lives.

Career opportunities in this wide field range from working with children to working with the elderly. Improving the lives of individuals and families is the chief purpose of various careers in many specialized areas. Counseling and rehabilitation job opportunities are also covered in this section.

◆ Human Services Careers in Child Development and Child Care

People working in child development and care services look after the interests of youth. If you think you would enjoy working in this area, you will find a variety of jobs available.

Careers helping children are found in many different settings. Depending on your education and experience, you might work in a children's

hospital or a center for children with physical or mental disabilities. With advanced training, you could be a child care worker or a nanny. With a college education, you could be a children's program director. This section will describe several ways you can work with children and young people in a helping environment.

Child Care Workers

Child care workers and *directors* work in group day care programs. Their primary responsibility is the care of children while parents work. Child care workers attend to the well-being and safety of children in their care.

Child care refers to programs that operate for extended hours. For instance, some centers operate from 6 a.m. to 6 p.m. or similar periods. Their operating hours are usually determined by their customers, the parents who need care for their children on workdays. These programs offer services for children from infancy to preschool age. Many, too, offer supervised care of children after school and on school holidays.

Lynette Auffert
Child Care Center Director

Lynette Auffert's love of children determined her career path. From her early babysitting days to her present position as director of a child care center, children have always come first in her life. The center she now directs enrolls over 80 children, ranging in age from six weeks to 14 years.

"When the age spread is this great, you have to be prepared with a wide variety of activities and degrees of care," reports Lynette. One minute she is calming a crying baby in the nursery, while the next minute she is supervising activities with teenagers. The older children spend time at the center before and after school and during the summer. Separate areas of the building are used for the different age groups.

"This is always a busy place," Lynette says about the center, which opens its doors at 6:30 a.m. and stays open for 12 hours on weekdays. As director, Lynette is responsible for hiring and training the staff, managing the budget, handling enrollment, and creating publicity. She also prepares staff schedules, attends meetings with parents and staff, and arranges special events, such as field trips and guest speakers. With her supervision, supplies are maintained, clothing is laundered, and meals and snacks are ordered and served. She also makes sure that age-appropriate activities are planned for the children.

"At one time I wanted to major in business, so this position gives me the best of both worlds," says Lynette. The downside of the job, however, is the long workday. Child care directors usually work beyond the normal eight hours, and emergencies or special events often stretch the days even longer. The job outlook for quality care providers, however, is very positive.

The best part of Lynette's job is seeing children learn about the world around them and achieve new milestones. "It's always a joy to watch them show their parents what they've learned," she explains, "and to see the parents react with surprise and excitement."

Lynette believes that people who enjoy working with children will find a child care career very rewarding. "You have to be a real 'people' person and you need unlimited energy to keep up with the children," Lynette advises. "It's also important to have a sincere concern and love for children, lots of patience, and a good sense of humor."

Programs offering child care differ somewhat from the early childhood education programs discussed in Chapter 15. The goal of early childhood education programs is to provide an organized, preschool experience. While many child care programs may provide similar daily activities, education is not their main concern. Their primary function is to provide children with safe, reliable care, 16-2.

Child care workers may work in a center or someone's home. This is called *in-home care.* The home may be the child's, the caregiver's, or someone else's. In **family child care,** several children are cared for in a caregiver's home.

It is very important for child care workers to know all they can about the care and guidance of children. Education and training requirements vary from state to state. Even entry-level workers are encouraged to continue their education and improve their skills.

Child care directors manage the operation of child care centers by hiring and supervising staff members. They manage the business affairs of the center, too. This includes enrolling children and collecting fees, purchasing food and supplies, and supervising the activities planned for the children. The director must be a good business manager, able to work well with parents and others in the community.

Nanny

Nannies have been part of British life since the late 1700s. Jobs for nannies now exist in many areas of the world. The term **nanny** means a person living with a family who cares for their children. Nannies take care of children while their parents are away or at work. Parents will discuss discipline and other personal child care preferences with their nanny. Nannies need to provide social activities for the children.

A nanny's job varies according to the needs and wishes of the parents. Some nannies only care for children. Others may do light housecleaning and prepare some meals. Nannies may also take the children to the doctor or dentist. Nannies may go on vacation with their family, perhaps having the chance to travel to different countries.

Nannies usually have their own apartment or room in the family's home. In this way, they

16-2 Child care workers focus on children's care and safety.

are available during the night or whenever needed. This also gives them a private place to rest or relax when they are not caring for the children.

Children's Program Directors

Child development specialists are often hired as children's program directors for activities involving youth. Their work varies from that of organizing, coordinating, and directing activities in one or more centers to sponsoring youth programs for special needs.

Some program directors work with organizations or youth clubs. These include YMCA, YWCA, Camp Fire Girls, Boy Scouts, and Girl Scouts. Others work as directors of FCCLA on the state and national level in program development. Some work with the Big Brother and Big Sister organizations to help direct their activities, 16-3.

Operating the Head Start program across the country requires many professionals trained in human services. Other government-sponsored programs may work with migrant children to help them adapt to the surrounding culture. Learning English as a second language is another type of program these professionals often direct.

Self-Care and After-School Program Directors

Directors in some communities work with *latchkey programs* for **children in self-care.** These are children who have no adult care before or after school. Program directors present information and train children on ways to stay safe when home alone. They may write public service messages on after-school safety for radio and TV. By working with the media, these program directors educate government

16-3 A director of community youth programs may sponsor cheerleading camps during the summer for children of related age groups.

officials, employers, and the public about self-care issues.

An example of this type of children's program is Project Home Safe. The program promotes safe and appropriate after-school arrangements for school-age children. Its purpose is to keep children safe and help them become more self-reliant while parents or caregivers are away.

◆ Human Services Careers in Family Studies and Human Assistance

This vast field focuses on the care of the elderly, the disabled, the poor, and others regarded as disadvantaged. A person who is **disadvantaged** lacks basic resources or conditions regarded as necessary for an equal position in society. Human services careers in this area of family and consumer sciences involve many different jobs that help families cope with a wide variety of circumstances.

Geriatrics

People working in geriatrics work with the elderly. A *gerontologist* is one who is trained to address the special needs of this age group. Professionals in family and consumer sciences are uniquely suited for one-on-one helping relationships that serve members of this age group.

Places of employment include adult day-care centers and senior nutrition programs. Other employers are retirement homes, nursing homes, YMCA or YWCA, and park and recreation departments, 16-4.

Geriatric aides generally work in nursing homes under the supervision of registered and licensed practical nurses. They provide most of the routine care for the residents. This care includes taking and recording vital signs such as temperature and pulse. Helping residents in and out of bed and assisting with bathing, dressing, and feeding are additional duties. Geriatric aides should have an upbeat personality with a desire to develop caring relationships with the residents.

16-4 Community centers provide a variety of craft programs and activities for local seniors.

Many changes are occurring in families that affect the elderly. These include smaller families and more single-parent families. Also, families are moving more, which separates adult children from their aging parents. As a result, seniors are often left with no close support system. Many young families have their own pressures and problems to handle. They may not be able to care for aging family members. Often the emotional, financial, and health support needed by the elderly is handled by local community resources.

Companion for the Elderly

Many people enjoy the company of older adults and find personal satisfaction in being companions to the elderly. For the most part, elderly people who live alone can take care of themselves, but they may need extra help with a few tasks. Companions for the elderly may drive them to doctors' offices, stores, a house of worship, or wherever they need to go. In addition to serving as chauffeurs, they may be housekeepers and cooks as well. Other activities may include reading to the elderly, writing checks or letters for them, playing cards, and taking short walks with them. Sometimes the companions just need to be good listeners!

Rehabilitation Services

If people have disabilities, they may need help in learning to meet their personal needs. Professionals in rehabilitation help these individuals recover from or learn to live with their disabilities. Helping people with disabilities live independently is the goal of rehabilitation professionals. They work with individuals who need special help with everyday living, such as those with physical, mental, or emotional disabilities.

Rehabilitation specialists work in many different settings. These include various residential and group institutions, such as mental institutions, prisons, hospitals, and community centers. Schools for the sight- and hearing-impaired

need workers who can help them in their day-to-day living. Some rehabilitation workers live in group homes and supervise the household chores as well as implement self-help programs. Others work with individuals in the client's home.

Professionals in family and consumer sciences are in a position to teach a wide variety of homemaking skills to people with disabilities. They can advise them on preparing their food, dressing themselves, and arranging their living areas for safety and convenience. People who have physical disabilities may have a hard time finding clothing to wear. Rehabilitation specialists can help them adapt clothing to fit their needs. Perhaps they have limited use of their arms and hands and need special kitchen tools. The rehabilitation worker can help them find or adapt tools to prepare their meals more easily. Learning homemaking skills is important in helping the disabled to live independently.

Working with individuals as they overcome drug addictions is another form of rehabilitation services. Often these professionals work with the client's family. A background in family studies helps professionals in family and consumer sciences form helping relationships with these patients and their families.

Rehabilitation workers are often part of a health care team. They work with doctors, nurses, and therapists in helping people with disabilities function more successfully. See 16-5.

Homemaker and Home Health Services

Services of homemaker/home health aides go by a number of different names. In some communities these workers are called homemakers, the title that will be used here. You may find them listed in the phone directory's yellow pages as *home care services* or *home chore services*.

Homemakers provide light housekeeping duties and other types of task for clients. Families may call upon homemakers during

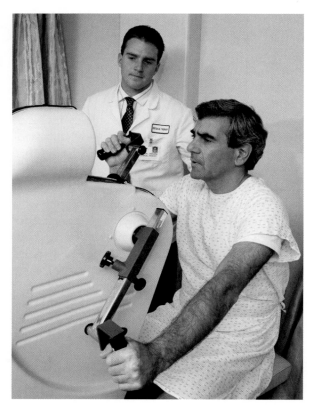

16-5 Rehabilitation experts help patients return the functioning of their bodies to as near normal as possible.

periods when a member is recovering from an injury. *Home health aides* provide health-related services, such as making sure that medicines are taken on time and in correct quantities. *Housekeepers* are workers who are hired to clean houses, hotels, or offices. They may even live and work in their employer's home.

Homemakers

Families may call upon homemakers during periods of crisis when family members are temporarily unable to provide for themselves. This might occur when a head of the household dies or a member of the family is hospitalized. Services provided might include food preparation, light housekeeping, laundry, marketing, and child care.

Sometimes families need a homemaker if the parents are traveling for an extended period. If parents are away from the children during long workdays, a few hours of a homemaker's help may need to be arranged. This may involve a worker staying with the children after school. Perhaps they also make the evening meal so it is ready when parents come home. These services help families cope better with stressful situations.

Having the services of a homemaker often means a person is able to stay in his or her own home rather than having to go to an extended care facility. This is what happened to Mrs. Housener, an elderly widow who lived alone. She had meals-on-wheels deliver food five days a week. Once a week a visiting nurse stopped to check her blood pressure and answer her health questions. A homemaker did light housekeeping and laundry on Thursday mornings. These visits helped Mrs. Housener live comfortably in her own home. Many other older adults are able to care for themselves and their homes with a little help from services such as these.

Adult Care Assistant

An adult care assistant works with adults who need help in individual families or in group homes for people with mental or physical disabilities. Those who work in this capacity must have a good understanding of the special care each patient needs. The assistant must be able to follow directions and make on-the-spot decisions. Being observant and tolerant of others' shortcomings are important traits for those in this field.

Home Health Aide

Home health aides help those needing assistance with their health care in their own homes. The aides carry out the assignments given by social workers or registered nurses. These assignments may include helping patients with their medicines, taking their vital signs, and checking on their general health.

The people working in this career are considered paraprofessionals. A **paraprofessional** is a trained aide who assists or works under the supervision of a professional.

Home health aides work with many different clients. They work with the elderly, the young, or those recovering from illnesses. Their work might include giving a bath to an elderly person, or changing linens and making the bed for a homebound patient after an operation. Other duties include helping at-home patients with physical therapy.

These paraprofessionals can make a real difference in the lives of their clients by helping them handle health problems in their own homes.

Home health aides visit homes where family life is disrupted by sickness or physical disability. Many people need a little assistance after returning from the hospital or recovering from illness.

Housekeeper

Housekeeping jobs vary from workplace to workplace. Sometimes housekeepers work in private homes. They may be hired to clean homes on a weekly or biweekly schedule. Other housekeepers care for only one home and may even live in that home. The responsibilities of a housekeeper change with each household. In one home, housekeepers may be asked to do periodic cleaning. In another, they may do cleaning, washing, ironing, grocery shopping, and more. See 16-6.

Housekeepers also clean offices and businesses, usually during nonbusiness hours at night and on weekends. Working as a housekeeper in a motel, hotel, or hospital usually involves performing a regular cleaning routine during daylight hours.

U.S. Department of Agriculture

16-6 Some housekeepers are responsible for doing the grocery shopping for their employer.

Pat Foster
Homemaker's Aide

For people who find even the simplest homemaking chores difficult because of age or physical disability, Pat Foster is ready to help. Pat (shown here on the right) handles the household tasks that disabled residents can't, thereby making it possible for them to continue living at home. Without her help, many of Pat's clients would need the full-time assistance of a nursing home or long-term care facility. "I feel that I am making a valuable difference in their lives," Pat says proudly.

She visits several homes each day, doing whatever needs to be done. Tasks include housecleaning, vacuuming, dusting, washing dishes, doing the laundry, shopping, and making beds. "I like being around people and attending to their needs," says Pat. "Not everyone would find this work rewarding, but I do."

Sometimes she reads to her clients, writes letters, helps with their correspondence, or just updates them on the latest news. "I am the only contact some of my clients have with the outside world," she admits. "I try to be supportive and listen to what they have to say, but I always remain professional and keep their comments confidential."

Pat helps her clients with their personal care needs, too. She shampoos their hair, assists with dental care, and helps them dress, undress, and bathe. Workdays vary according to the needs of her clients. After a few visits, a routine is established and followed with each succeeding visit. Her clients include an interesting mix of new faces and familiar faces, some of which have been with her for over 15 years. "It's a joy to help because my clients are always so friendly and grateful for my work," says Pat.

For Pat, the most difficult aspect of becoming a homemaker's aide was feeling comfortable in someone else's house. Though she knew the job well, she felt awkward taking charge of a stranger's home. She soon realized that the homeowner felt the same. "I found that people first need to take a little time to get acquainted, then a good working relationship always follows," Pat reports.

One of the constant concerns affecting her job is the weather. About traveling to clients' homes during bad weather, Pat says, "They are so happy to see me show up. That inspires me to make a special effort in bad weather to get through to them."

Pat believes that opportunities for homemaker aides will continue to increase as greater numbers of people enter their retirement years. She explains, "It's natural for people to want to live in their own homes as long as possible."

Consumer Protection Services

Protecting consumers against unfair and deceptive practices is another career option in the family studies and human services area. *Consumer protection specialists* and *directors* work in local, state, and federal levels of the government. They are also found in independent organizations such as credit bureaus and the Better Business Bureau.

The focus of consumer protection work is identifying and stopping companies or individuals from using fraudulent practices on the public. A **fraud** is the intentional twisting of the truth in order to get someone to give up a right or something valuable.

Another goal of consumer protection services is educating the public to prevent individuals from becoming victims of fraud.

Checking questionable claims about the nutritional or health benefits of food and drug products is a big focus of their work. Checking the truthfulness of environmental claims is another important area. Other current consumer-protection topics include high-tech and Internet fraud, telephone scams, and phony investment schemes.

◆ Human Services Careers in Consumer and Resource Management

The knowledge and skills related to decision making, problem solving, and goal setting are a key focus of the consumer and resource management area. Human services occupations in consumer and resource management help individuals use management techniques to improve their well-being.

Professionals in this area also utilize the wide range of personal, community, and environmental resources to improve the human condition.

Social Work

Many professionals in family and consumer sciences are employed as *social workers*. These professionals help improve the quality of life for individuals and families in need. City, county, state, or federal government agencies employ many social workers. Others are employed by voluntary social service agencies, community and religious organizations, hospitals, nursing homes, and home health agencies.

No matter what their position, social workers must first assess the needs of their clients. For example, when working with a particular family, the social worker must first determine its needs. Are any members of the family unemployed? Do they have adequate housing? What kind of government services could help them? Are they able to obtain services to which they are entitled? These services may include Medicaid, Medicare, housing assistance, disability compensation, food stamps, and legal advice.

Once the social worker has assessed the needs of the family, plans are made to meet those needs. Some social workers counsel clients on budgeting, home management, and consumer practices. Sources of public assistance are identified, and information on credit rights and responsibilities is given.

Sometimes social workers advise families on ways of keeping a clean and organized household. Some families may need help in planning nutritious meals, buying wholesome food, and preparing meals.

In some families, members have problems getting along with each other. Help in the area of communication may need to be provided. Social workers may advise parents on child care practices and parenting skills, if needed. If children are having serious problems adjusting to school or society, social workers can help. Many social workers specialize in child protective services, such as investigating reported cases of child abuse and neglect.

Social workers assist others in the community to help relieve social problems and pressures on families. As stated by one caseworker, "You have to learn to understand different people and then look for ways to help people use their own resources to solve their problems."

Counseling

Counselors help people deal with personal, family, and social problems. Their duties depend on the people they serve and the settings in which they work.

Counselors must have a genuine interest in helping people and the ability to create a feeling of security and comfort. There are many specializations within the counseling professions. Some may be trained as family counselors or marriage counselors. These professionals are trained to understand, explain, and help resolve personal or family problems. They may work with couples that have marital problems. Several family members may seek a family counselor to help them resolve difficulties, 16-7.

Mental health counselors work with people who have emotional problems. They counsel rape victims and victims of violence and abuse. Others provide counseling services for the elderly or for drug and alcohol abusers. Still other counselors work as employment counselors, school counselors, or vocational counselors.

Employment or Career Counselor

About 10 percent of the nation's workers switch occupations each year. Many of these displaced or disillusioned workers seek the help of employment or career counselors. Employment counselors serve veterans, teenage mothers, people who have lost their jobs, and displaced homemakers.

Displaced homemakers are those who have stayed at home most of their adult lives and now want to earn an income. Some displaced homemakers want to work because their children have grown and they want a job to fill their time. Others may be widows or divorced homemakers who now need to find a way to make money. Many have no marketable skills.

16-7 Family counselors work with husbands and wives or parents and children to help them establish normal family relationships.

Shirley Twombly
Career Counselor and Gender Equity Coordinator

What would you do if, after spending a lifetime raising a family, you suddenly needed to find a job? Would you know what to do or where to go? Many displaced homemakers do not. Displaced homemakers make up one of the target groups for New Perspectives, a resource that Shirley Twombly directs in northwest Missouri.

This statewide network of centers helps members of special populations enroll, enter, and complete vocational programs. Services are provided for displaced homemakers, single parents, single pregnant women, men and women interested in nontraditional careers, and individuals with physical, economic, or other barriers.

Shirley says, "The program's goal is to help people become more employable and self-sufficient by improving personal and vocational skills." The centers also help people find and keep gainful employment. They do this by providing vocational assessment and career counseling.

Shirley (shown here on the left) helps jobseekers identify their strengths and interests. "I help them see what the possibilities are," she explains. Shirley then identifies the training needed for specific entry-level jobs, and a career plan is formed.

According to Shirley, most of her clients have very low self-esteem. "I like to help them see their possibilities—they can become self-sufficient and independent. I try to teach them to be assertive." She believes that people considering a job such as hers should have patience and a desire to help people who are very unsure of themselves and their abilities.

It is sometimes difficult for Shirley to accept the fact that she can't help everybody. "Adults are different from children," she explains. "You can't take them by the hand. You want to do everything for your clients, but sometimes they're not ready."

New Perspectives helps people feel better about themselves, learn new skills, and become gainfully employed. "This job requires patience, determination, and a commitment to people and their abilities," Shirley says. Her work is similar to that of a school counselor, except her students are spread over a large geographic area and range in age from middle school to adulthood.

Shirley also assists area schools with career days, career counseling, vocational assessments, and nontraditional workshops. "Careers Have No Gender" is a popular program she presents to raise student awareness of nontraditional careers and the need for career planning. In addition, she offers workshops and technical assistance to educators on such issues as sexual harassment, gender equity, multiculturalism, and diversity.

They may have worked in the home all the years their children were growing up, but they never held or trained for any specific job.

Employment or career counselors are trained to help others make important career decisions. They help prepare people for entry or reentry into the job market in a number of ways. Typically, they administer aptitude and interest surveys to help identify the prospective worker's interests. These surveys also indicate the kinds of jobs for which the individual might be suited. Counselors cannot make decisions for their clients. They can provide information and tools to help them make more informed decisions, but the individual must take the next step.

Counselors may recommend courses needed in order to find and get a job. By following the job market closely, counselors are able to direct clients to areas where the need for workers is greatest.

School Counselors

School counselors help children and teens understand themselves better. Counselors may also help them with any social, behavioral, or personal problems. These might relate to a student's conflicts with others, school discipline problems, or conflicts in family relationships.

Sometimes child guidance counselors work with youth at risk. *At-risk youths* are those whose environments, behaviors, and individual characteristics may prevent them from reaching their full potential. They may have difficulty adjusting to society. Their environment may be characterized by poverty, homelessness, abuse, and neglect. Family relationships may be extremely difficult for them, putting them at risk of chemical abuse, sexual activity, pregnancy, dropping out of school, and other behavioral problems. Individual characteristics, such as mental illness, physical disabilities, depression, or school-related problems, may also put them at risk.

Counselors often work very closely with parents, teachers, school nurses, psychologists, and social workers. By observing children at play or during school activities, counselors can better evaluate children's strengths as well as their problems. They can then help them with their special needs.

It is important that counselors gain the confidence and respect of the children or youth with whom they work. Counselors must be able to keep students' comments confidential and help them in nonthreatening ways. The children must feel comfortable in sharing their thoughts and concerns with the counselor. Work in this area is often challenging. On the other hand, it can be very rewarding, 16-8.

Vocational Counselor

Schools often employ vocational counselors. They help students select courses needed to prepare for a career. Through various tests, they can help students determine career-related strengths and weaknesses, likes and dislikes. They help students identify possible career areas of interest and plan the training needed. By providing this as well as other job-related information, counselors help prepare students for the world of work.

16-8 Many pressures in today's society cause children and adolescents to seek the advice of their school's counselor.

Some vocational counselors are employed by state employment agencies, guidance centers, and in private, nonprofit, or commercial agencies. They work with people of all ages who are looking for work or changing career paths.

Sometimes vocational counselors work with groups of individuals, such as employees of a failing business. Vocational counselors can assist displaced workers find comparable jobs. Issues such as job retraining, resume writing, and interview procedures are addressed. Sometimes a motivational speaker is brought in to encourage the group to stay upbeat and optimistic during the job search.

Human Services Administration

Most of the human services jobs described in this chapter involve direct work with people on a one-to-one basis. However, administrators are needed to do the behind-the-scenes work. Administrators manage the programs that help those who need assistance. Administrators carry out the duties needed to operate an agency, organization, program, or business. This may be a nursing home, retirement home, community service agency, or other facility.

Job titles for administrative positions vary. *Human services administrators* may be called *program directors, program coordinators, directors of development,* or *operations managers.*

Many of the duties of a human services administrator are the same as those of any administrator. They are responsible for making sure the objectives of the organization are met. Typically, most organizations have a board of directors that develops policies and procedures. The administrator, then, carries out the board's decisions.

Administrators oversee the day-to-day operations of the program or facility. They supervise employees, assign responsibilities, and get feedback from their clients, 16-9. Managing finances

16-9 Human services administrators make sure the goals of their organization are met.

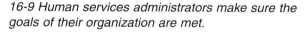

is an important activity of administrators. They are responsible for how funds are used and sometimes for fundraising, too.

Administrators may become involved in public relations work in the community by presenting their organization to the public. This is done through news and information that is given to local radio, newspaper, and TV reporters.

Many laws and regulations govern human services. Some of these regulations concern clients' rights to privacy, safety, health, and information. Administrators must constantly stay knowledgeable about the laws and policies affecting the field.

Marilyn Lee Thayer
Program Administrator

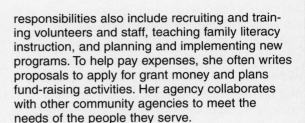

Marilyn Thayer is the project coordinator of the Fort Collins Even Start project in Colorado. This program encourages parents and children to work together and learn from each other. It was established in the belief that early parental involvement significantly influences how well children develop and learn.

The program provides educational and support services to families with children who, without the extra assistance, would probably drop out of school. Marilyn and her staff work with parents in homes as well as at learning center sites. Toddler, preschool, and after-school programs are available for children as well as educational programs for teens and adults. "We help parents raise their children with the skills required for success in school and in their personal lives," explains Marilyn.

Besides supervising educational programs, Marilyn handles informal case management. "One refreshing aspect of my position is that no day is typical," reports Marilyn. "Each day is unique and involves different challenges." For example, she may spend the day helping a family obtain legal assistance, a housing referral, or a community service that offers food or clothing. She may receive a phone call from a school counselor, inquiring about a truant student, or she may meet with a staff member to discuss alternatives for a participating family. Sometimes her work involves crisis intervention.

"This position requires passion, high energy, and a commitment to serve others," Marilyn reports. "The families have many needs and there is so much to do. You sometimes feel you are moving in many different directions!" When that happens, Marilyn reminds herself that she can't do everything. "You learn to walk away from situations that are not for you to solve and, occasionally, take time out for yourself." Marilyn's

responsibilities also include recruiting and training volunteers and staff, teaching family literacy instruction, and planning and implementing new programs. To help pay expenses, she often writes proposals to apply for grant money and plans fund-raising activities. Her agency collaborates with other community agencies to meet the needs of the people they serve.

Marilyn loves the continual challenge of her job and recommends it to others. "When making a career choice, remember to follow your passion in life, whatever that may be," she advises. "It is important to believe in and be committed to what you do."

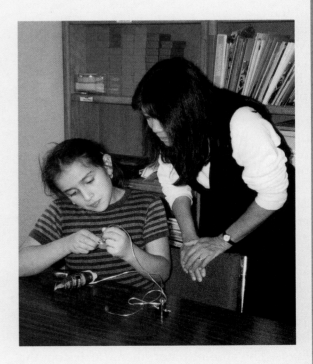

Peace Corps Volunteer

Professionals in family and consumer sciences help people throughout the world live better lives by serving in the Peace Corps. Some volunteers teach nutrition and food preparation classes, particularly to mothers of small children. Topics range from preparing balanced diets for family members to recognizing nutritional disorders. Other subjects include home care, sanitation, gardening, food preservation, and child care. Peace Corps volunteers often train local people to work with individual families.

Assignments consist of a two-year tour of duty in a country that has asked for Peace Corps assistance. Volunteers work with local people on projects ranging from health care to farming to road building, 16-10. At centers in this country, volunteers study the language and background of their assigned country. Technical knowledge and skills required overseas are also studied. Volunteers must understand their assignment and the role it plays in the total development of the country. Emphasis is placed not only on physical conditioning, but also on helping

Peace Corps

16-10 Many interesting opportunities await those who become Peace Corps volunteers.

trainees gain confidence in their ability to live and work in another culture.

Peace Corps workers are given allowances for food, clothing, housing, and incidental expenses. They receive no salary while abroad. Nevertheless, this is an excellent opportunity to live and work with people of a different culture. No special degree is required to work as a volunteer; however, many are teachers.

◆ Human Services Careers in Hospitality, Tourism, and Recreation

There are many career options for those who cater to guests on business or pleasure. For example, large hotels and resorts have trained personnel who work to improve the comfort of their guests. They may offer restaurant suggestions and point out attractions in the area. Workers in the recreation field also organize and direct activities that help people enjoy their leisure time. A wide range of career opportunities are available in this field beyond those mentioned here.

Activity Coordinators

Fun and exciting activities are the heart of the hospitality, tourism, and recreation field. To make sure people take advantage of these activities, businesses hire employers to handle their questions and concerns. Many different job titles exist in this field.

Theme parks, tourist attractions, and firms that offer vacation excursions employ *greeters*. *Hosts, hostesses,* and *guest services agents* work in sports and entertainment centers, hotels, resorts, and athletic clubs. *Program leaders* work in community park and recreation departments. They oversee evening, weekend, and summer programs that involve games, sports, crafts, and many other activities.

The hospitality, tourism, and recreation field has an unusually large number of part-time, seasonal, and volunteer jobs. However, summertime employment and part-time work during school may lead to a full-time job. Most of these workers are *camp counselors, lifeguards,* and *craft specialists.* College students fill many of these positions.

Activity Director

Activity directors plan the programs and manage the coordinators who carry them out. When recreational programs are extensive, as with cruise lines and theme parks, the job of the director is really a business or marketing occupation. Advertising, purchasing equipment, training staff, and balancing budgets are their primary responsibilities.

Activity directors of smaller programs have more contact with actual program participants. Often they plan the programs and carry them out, sometimes with part-time or volunteer helpers. Their involvement with program participants has equal or higher importance than their planning and managing roles. Community centers, nursing homes, retirement centers, and adult day care programs are common worksites for human services occupations in hospitality, tourism, and recreation. See 16-11.

Individuals with creativity, unlimited patience, and ingenuity are needed to serve as *activities directors for seniors.* The wishes of the group and the abilities of the members must always be kept in mind. Each month special events are planned, such as summer fairs, birthday parties, and holiday celebrations. The director develops and posts an activities calendar and promotes coming events. Cooperation of the dietitian and kitchen staff in planning special meals and parties is necessary. Occasionally directors may schedule groups to learn a new game or craft.

One activity director for a nursing home invited a high school class to model old-fashioned clothing for the residents. The residents really enjoyed seeing clothes that they remembered from long ago. You could hear a number of them remark, "I remember when I wore something like that!" The students thought it was a lot of fun, too. Organizing these and other fun activities makes this job interesting, rewarding, and challenging.

16-11 A recreation director of a retirement home may schedule a dance group to entertain residents.

Donelda Novy
Activity Director

Providing activities and entertainment for nursing home residents is a demanding job, but Donelda Novy enjoys every minute of it. Donelda is the activity director of a 160-resident nursing home that offers a wide variety of events and entertainment for its mostly senior residents. "We believe that keeping our residents involved in everyday activities and community events is important to their morale," says Donelda.

Some of the most popular outings are to museums and nearby scenic areas. With her four assistants, Donelda even takes the residents shopping, to restaurants, and to picnics in the park. Everyone especially enjoys local fairs and festivals, so the activity calendar includes them whenever possible. "Sometimes circumstances call for impromptu activities, so you have to think quick and work with what you have," she adds.

Before embarking on any outing, Donelda plans the event carefully. "We need to take wheelchairs into consideration and the physical disabilities of the residents, such as limited walking ability," she explains. She makes sure that residents are transported back and forth to the site safely and plenty of helpers are available to provide whatever care and attention is needed.

The residents love parties, too, so birthdays and holidays are usually celebrated with local bands, dance groups, or both. She also arranges for visiting choral groups to sing to the residents. "Seeing them smile and tap their feet to the music is very satisfying to all of us." Donelda says. "Good music and good food means good attendance by the residents."

Between festive events Donelda plans quieter activities, such as movies, bingo matches, and card games. "I must constantly keep in mind the interests and abilities of all our residents when planning the activity calendar," she explains. It also is her job to schedule the religious services that are regularly offered to the residents. Intergenerational programs, too, are held to encourage residents to interact with different age groups. "Having babies visit the residents is always a big hit," comments Donelda.

Good organizational skills, creativity, and flexibility are the qualities needed in activity directors, according to Donelda. When the job involves seniors, she believes that a special appreciation for the age group and a desire to help them enjoy life are the most important qualities.

Head Housekeeper

A position often found in hotels, motels, and resorts is that of head housekeeper. This person is responsible for hiring, supervising, and coordinating the housekeeping staff. This may involve making time sheets and work schedules for general housekeeping duties. The job also involves ordering and stocking cleaning supplies, and managing laundry facilities, 16-12.

Facilities that cater to the public need to be clean and orderly. High standards of cleanliness and sanitation must be maintained. It may take a large staff to do this effectively. The head housekeeper is responsible for making sure the work is thoroughly done in a timely manner.

◆ Human Services Careers in Food, Nutrition, and Wellness

Many professionals in family and consumer sciences work for the government in food-related careers that focus on human services. Many

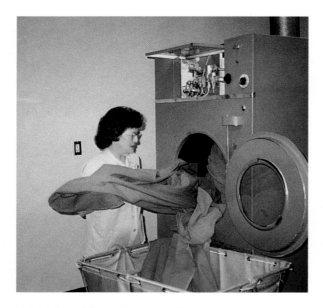

16-12 Head housekeepers often oversee a large staff that includes laundry workers.

of these professionals work with U.S. Department of Agriculture (USDA) feeding programs. They are active in the National School Lunch program, the WIC (Women, Infants, and Children) program, and others.

Nutrition and wellness professionals working in local operations give help directly to people in need. They also oversee staff workers and volunteers to make sure the local programs meet national guidelines.

◆ Other Careers in Human Services

Careers in human services can be found in other areas of family and consumer sciences. One such career is related to the textiles and apparel area. Some *apparel specialists* go beyond satisfying basic clothing needs to provide apparel that helps people feel better about themselves. They make clothing for people with disabilities so they can manage easily on their own.

Accessibility specialists in the environmental design area also address special human needs. They focus on making internal environments usable for people with physical limitations. They design and modify living, sleeping, and work areas in homes so all family members can use them. Accessibility professionals also design tools for people who have difficulty reaching and grasping objects.

Environmentalists represent another career area that focuses on human services. Sometimes these professionals are known as *environmental activists*.

Often environmentalists work for independent research groups that advocate safer air and water, more responsible land use, and greater energy conservation. Often, but not always, environmentalists work to better living conditions for the general public and future generations. This is achieved when the interests of all affected parties are considered.

Personal Skills and Abilities Needed for a Career in Human Services

Having good interpersonal skills is most important for a career in human services. You must be able to interact well with many people. You must not get discouraged too easily or become annoyed at small things, as progress is often slow. There are many satisfactions, however, such as seeing others learn new skills and gain self-confidence. Helping others recognize that it is possible to overcome difficulties and experience a brighter day is very rewarding.

Good decision-making skills are required for all these careers. Decisions must be carefully considered as they affect people's lives.

Workers in human services must have good communication skills. Being good listeners is vital to their success. They must be able to talk to their clients and identify their needs and concerns.

Above all, they must be caring individuals, sensitive to the needs of others. Being "people oriented" is important in this work. Those working in human services must like to help others and have a sincere interest in their welfare.

Job satisfaction comes primarily from helping other people. Assisting others in trying to better themselves gives a person a sense of accomplishment.

Education and Training Needed for a Career in Human Services

Human services workers must be trained to meet the special needs of the people with whom they work. Their educational preparation will depend on the type of service they will provide and the ages of the people they will serve. Their clients may be the very young, very old, or somewhere between these extremes. Their services may range from recreation to rehabilitation.

There are many entry-level positions available in human services that do not require advanced training. A list of jobs is shown in 16-13. It includes entry-level jobs as well as those requiring advanced training or a college degree.

Most professional positions require at least a bachelor's degree in the field you prefer. This degree may be in child development, gerontology, or recreation. Supportive courses in the behavioral sciences, such as psychology and sociology, are helpful. Specialized courses such as human relations, counseling, rehabilitation, recreation management, and nutrition are also important.

Administrative or supervisory positions require advanced degrees as well as experience. A background in management and accounting is also helpful for these positions. For some counseling professions, such as family and marriage counseling, a master's degree is usually necessary.

Preparation for employment in some fields may also require an internship. For instance, a master's degree in social work, an M.S.W., requires supervised field instruction. The combination of classroom work with practical experience enhances a resume and can prove beneficial on the job. Part-time work or volunteer experience in service-related occupations is also helpful.

Future Trends

In years past, families provided for themselves, one way or another. Today, more responsibility is being placed on society for care of the elderly, the poor, and those with physical or mental disabilities. With more people turning to various agencies for help, the future of jobs in human services appears very favorable.

Human Services Careers		
Entry Level Activity specialist Adult care assistant Adult day care aide Babysitter Camp counselor Child care attendant Community service worker Companion for the homebound Elder care aide Homemaker Host/hostess/greeter Housekeeper Lifeguard Nursery school aide Personal/home care aide Playground assistant Playroom attendant **Advanced Training** Activity director Adult day care director Camp director Community aide Concierge	Eligibility aide Family service worker Geriatric aide Guest services agent Head housekeeper Home health aide Hospice case manager Housing coordinator Nanny Peace Corps volunteer Recreation director Recreational therapist Social director Volunteer coordinator **College Degree** Child advocate Child guidance counselor Children's program director Community center director Community organization director Consumer protection specialist Credit counselor Drug and alcohol counselor Employment counselor	Environmentalist Family counselor Family life educator Fraud investigator Gerontologist Group home administrator Head Start director Human development consultant Human services administrator Long-term care facility administrator Marriage and family therapist Mediator/arbitrator Product safety advocate Recreation director Rehabilitation services director Residential care administrator Retirement facility director Social caseworker Social service coordinator Youth counselor Youth services director

16-13 Many jobs are available in the field of human services at all educational levels.

Professionals in family and consumer sciences can help families adjust to new and different ways of living. They can make a difference in the lives of others by helping them reduce the stress and anxiety associated with altering living patterns. They are in a unique position to use their knowledge to help solve the complex problems of families.

In the future, there will be a great need for *professional life-organizers*. That means people will be needed who can help families manage their resources and structure their daily lives. Professionals in family and consumer sciences can help families regain control over their personal, social, and economic environments.

Demographics provide clues to future employment opportunities related to human services. **Demographics** are population statistics such as the annual number of births, deaths, and marriages. By analyzing demographics, professionals in human services can identify trends that will affect the need for certain services. One big trend is the growing number of retiring senior citizens. Future careers needed to serve this large audience include preretirement financial advisors as well as tour operators and recreation providers who specialize in activities for seniors, 16-14. Also, more geriatric aides, senior housing administrators, homemakers, and home health aides will be needed.

The majority of new entrants into the labor market in this decade will be women, minorities, and immigrants. With more women in the workforce, there will be an increased need for family services. Families of immigrants may seek others who can speak their language and understand their needs.

Other areas that should see continued job growth include counseling, health, and recreation. A need for employment counseling will continue for those seeking new careers, either due to job loss or a job change. More programs will be aimed at staying healthy and physically fit. The demand for recreation programs, especially for adults, will continue to grow. Also, the need for credit advisors, fraud counselors, and product safety advocates is expected to increase with current economic trends.

Careers in the human services can also serve as springboards to other occupations. The skills and abilities people in these occupations possess are similar to those needed in education as well as business. These many factors point to increased job opportunities.

16-14 More tour operators will sponsor vacation packages as well as one-day trips that cater to seniors.

Summary

Helping people help themselves is the aim or goal of most human services jobs. Professionals in family and consumer sciences work in a wide variety of human services careers. Schools, hospitals, clinics, government agencies, nonprofit organizations, and private businesses employ them.

Good human relations skills are required of people in order to succeed in this field. Good decision-making and communication skills are also important.

Jobs in human services are available for the unskilled, semiskilled, and professionals. People who want a professional career in human services should take courses in family and child studies leading to a four-year family and consumer sciences degree. These courses can be supplemented with behavioral science courses. Preparation for employment may also include internships in a related field. Volunteer experiences are also helpful.

Future job opportunities in human service appear very favorable. Professionals in family and consumer sciences are in a unique position to use their knowledge and expertise in helping families solve complex problems.

More nontraditional jobs will become available. With the changing roles of women in society, there will be an increased need in the area of child and elderly care. As the interest in health and fitness grows, more programs will be directed toward these areas.

During the last two decades, many social, political, economic, and technological changes have occurred that directly affect the family. Thus, there is a continued need to help individuals and families improve the quality of their lives. People involved in the helping professions will find many rewarding and satisfying careers.

To Review

1. Name three types of jobs in human services that involve working with children or adolescents.

2. Name two organizations that may employ camp directors.

3. Identify three reasons families are having a difficult time caring for the elderly.

4. What types of people may need the services provided by rehabilitation programs?

5. What is meant by the term "displaced homemaker"?

6. What kinds of services are available to help the elderly live in their own homes?

7. Name two counseling specialties.

8. What is the most important personal skill needed for human services professionals?

9. Which occupational area has the greatest numbers of part-time, seasonal, and volunteer jobs?

10. Why does the future for jobs in human services appear promising?

To Do

1. Interview a Peace Corps recruiter or past Peace Corps volunteer. Find out types of available work related to family and consumer sciences. Prepare an oral report.

2. Ask a counselor from your school to describe the training he or she received and summarize the advantages and disadvantages of counseling as a career.

3. Volunteer to work in a nursing home for a few hours. Observe the activities available for the residents.

Careers in Science and Technology

After studying this chapter, you will be able to
◆ list career opportunities in science and technology.
◆ describe personal skills and abilities needed for a career in science and technology.
◆ specify the education and training needed for various careers in science and technology.
◆ identify future trends for careers in science and technology.

Terms to Know

technology
dietetics
nutrition
dietitian
nutritionist

food science
prototype
automated teller machine (ATM)

Have you ever wanted to know what makes something work? Do you like to conduct experiments? Do you enjoy finding solutions to practical problems? If you are interested in discovery, perhaps working in an area of science and technology might interest you. You may hold a career that explores the unknown and uncovers new knowledge. Would you like to be a part of this action? The science and technology cluster offers many challenging career possibilities for family and consumer sciences professionals, 17-1.

University of Wisconsin-Stout

17-1 Many different careers are available for people interested in science and technology.

Science provides the knowledge base for improving people's lives. **Technology** is the application of knowledge to solve problems and improve and extend human capabilities. (You learned one definition of *technology* in Chapter 3, and this new definition is related.) Technology affects the health and well-being of all family members.

Scientists conduct research to add to our store of knowledge.

◆ *Physical scientists* conduct research on matter and apply their findings to practical problems. Chemists, mathematicians, and physicists are physical scientists.

◆ *Life scientists* study plants and animals. Biologists, botanists, food scientists, and dietitians are life scientists. By conducting research, they learn about living things and the environment.

◆ *Social scientists* study human behavior. Sociologists and psychologists are social scientists.

Some family and consumer sciences professionals may work as technologists. Their jobs involve the practical application of scientific knowledge. Technology continues to create new products and services—many of which were unheard of only a few years ago! New machines have taken over tasks formerly performed by family members. Future technological advances will continue to affect our lives, creating new career options, 17-2.

This chapter will help you explore family and consumer sciences careers in science and technology. Careers options are discussed for food, nutrition, and wellness; textiles and apparel; environmental design; family studies and human services; child development and early childhood education; hospitality, tourism, and recreation; and consumer and resource management.

Innovative Cooking Enterprises

17-2 These professionals in family and consumer sciences are testing recipes using bread machines from many different manufacturers.

◆ Science and Technology Careers in Food, Nutrition, and Wellness

Do you enjoy experimenting when cooking or baking to see what will happen if you change some ingredients? Do you like to compare the nutrient content of different foods? If you have an interest in science and technology and are concerned with the welfare of families, you will find many interesting jobs in this career cluster.

Today's food markets offer consumers an overwhelming variety of choices. Think of all the new products you see on supermarket shelves every time you shop. Many of these were mere concepts in the minds of food technologists only a few years ago. Thanks to the work of dietitians and nutritionists, people are also more aware of the role nutrition plays in overall health.

Dietitians and Nutritionists

Decades ago, there was less concern about diet or the effect of food on health. People ate food because it tasted good and satisfied hunger. People also ate certain foods as rewards. Today, there is a growing interest in nutrition and wellness and related careers.

Dietetics is one of the most popular choices in the nutrition and wellness career area. Dietetics is the science of applying the principles of nutrition to food selection and food preparation. **Nutrition** is the study of how your body uses the food you eat. Food provides nutrients needed by the body for proper growth and development.

Nutritionists and dietitians are professionals who offer nutritional services for people. The chief difference between nutritionists and dietitians is in the type of work they do. A **dietitian** is a member of a health care team. Dietitians evaluate patients' nutritional needs and plan diets or eating plans. They may teach food preparation. A **nutritionist** is a nutrition expert who usually works as an educator or researcher. Nutritionists teach people how food affects the body and how to eat well for good health. They help people form good eating habits.

Dietitians work in many different settings. *Clinical dietitians* work in hospitals, health clinics, nursing homes, and other health care facilities. They may form part of a medical team as they work with doctors and nurses to determine patients' medical needs, 17-3. Based on these needs, the dietitian plans the patients' diets and informs them of what they can and cannot eat.

Community dietitians work for government and public health agencies in rural and urban areas. They may develop nutrition programs for children or the elderly, or work with school lunch programs. Some community dietitians coordinate nutrition awareness and disease

U.S. Department of Agriculture

17-3 Dietitians are experts on food and how it affects health. They plan menus for patients based on medical recommendations.

prevention programs in child care centers or health and recreation clubs. These dietitians may work with government programs, such as Head Start, to help teachers provide nutrition training for children and parents.

Research dietitians work in research laboratories in colleges, universities, or food companies. Research dietitians may examine how food affects the body, how food plays a part in disease and recovery, and how the body uses food. They may research the nutritional value of new or existing food products. Many work in colleges, instructing students on the science of nutrition.

Administrative or *management dietitians* work in restaurants, hospitals, nursing homes, schools, prisons, and other institutions. They are concerned with the nutritional value of the food served. Tasks associated with this role include planning menus, purchasing food, and directing food preparation. They are responsible for seeing that nourishing, attractive meals are served.

Dietitians employed by food corporations may work in product development or menu development, 17-4. Some dietitians work for companies that sell food and nutrition products. Some assist with media relations.

Consultant dietitians work independently. They help promote good eating habits by giving seminars to groups, or through their writing, TV appearances, or radio programs. They might design nutrition and fitness programs for athletes, dancers, and other clients. Some consultant dietitians work with health clubs, medical centers, food manufacturers, or pharmaceutical firms.

Dietetic technicians work under the supervision of dietitians. Typically, they work as members of the food service or health care team. They analyze patients' diets to see whether patients are eating nutritionally balanced meals. They might take diet histories and screen patients' nutritional status. Dietetic technicians may provide diet counseling to people who are not at risk nutritionally. In some settings, they may supervise dietetic assistants, diet clerks, or food service personnel.

Nutritionists study the way the body digests and uses food. They determine the nutritional

Hormel

17-4 These dietitians work in product development for a major food company.

value of various foods. Nutritionists often focus on the role food plays in the prevention or cause of certain diseases. They conduct research and study the relationship of food to such diseases and conditions as bone density, heart disease, and cancer. They share this information with other professionals, such as doctors, nurses, scientists, and other researchers.

Nutritionists often work with people who have special diet concerns. These include pregnant teens, the elderly, and those recovering from illness. They analyze special diets for weight control, physical endurance, and muscle development. The emerging field of sports medicine utilizes the expertise of nutritionists. Many nutritionists offer individual consulting services for athletes and others interested in good physical health. Other nutritionists might provide nutrition education in hospital settings, medical schools, or health clinics. They may work for community health organizations or public health agencies. Some nutritionists work with drug and alcohol rehabilitation centers.

LuAnn Soliah
Professor and Research Dietitian

As a university professor and director of nutrition sciences, LuAnn Soliah teaches classes and conducts research in nutrition, food science, and therapeutic nutrition. "I have a genuine interest in nutrition and health care careers," says LuAnn. "I wanted a profession that emphasized disease prevention and wellness."

LuAnn believes dietetics is a very important course for students to take "since nutrition and health go hand in hand. Students learn that decisions they make have long-term effects on their health."

Besides teaching several classes and conducting research, LuAnn advises students on course choices, scheduling, and career planning. As part of their training, dietetic students serve as interns in various hospitals. LuAnn helps students make their dietetic internship selections. "I especially enjoy helping seniors launch their careers," she says. "After they're done with their internship, I stay in touch and help them find their first job."

Another part of LuAnn's job is reviewing scientific literature each week for several hours. "You must stay current in the field," she explains, "and you can only do that through reading." This is a very time-consuming aspect of her job.

LuAnn is proud to receive letters from former students who develop successful careers. Many conduct research that is published in journals. "Dietetics is a good career for the future," LuAnn says. "The connection between nutrition and health will only get stronger. The need for dietitians is growing."

Besides traditional fields like hospital work, LuAnne recommends exploring job opportunities in nontraditional areas, such as community or consulting work. "People entering this profession must be accurate, enjoy writing, and have an aptitude for science. Also, they should enjoy exploring the ever-changing fields of nutrition and health care."

Food Scientists and Technologists

Food science is the study of the production, processing, storage, preservation, utilization, evaluation, and safety of food. The professionals in this field are called food scientists and food technologists. They oversee the quality and healthfulness of food and are employed in both industry and government. Depending on the roles they play in their organizations, food scientists may have many titles.

They may conduct research in food safety or in the effects of different temperatures and air exposure on food. They may test foods to check quality or nutrient retention under certain physical conditions. Food scientists need to know scientific testing and analysis procedures. Based on their research, food scientists may find ways of improving the quality of food from the producer to the consumer, 17-5.

Many food scientists are employed in the food industry primarily to develop new foods or improve existing products. They work closely with specialists in the company's packaging, engineering, marketing, sales, and consumer affairs departments, transforming ideas into consumer products.

Food scientists who work in the research and development (R&D) labs are called R&D technicians or *product development specialists*. They perform various tests and develop samples of possible new products.

Helping product development specialists refine their lab samples are *sensory analysts*. These scientists analyze and evaluate the taste, aroma, color, consistency, and other sensory qualities of the samples, 17-6.

Is the sample too sweet or too salty compared to its leading competitors? Does it have the right color and aroma? With sensory evaluations, the lab sample is refined into a prototype. A **prototype** is a working recipe for a potential food product.

McCormick

17-5 Food technologists continually conduct tests to improve the quality of their food products.

McCormick

17-6 Quality control inspectors check the quality of products at all stages to meet precise standards and specifications.

Product specialists conduct consumer-use tests by examining the new product in every possible way that a consumer might use it. They also compare its results to those of its competitors. If the new product needs more work, it goes back to the lab.

On the other hand, if it performs well, a trial run takes place. This step involves converting the prototype's formula into a recipe large enough to supply a normal production run.

Often, enlarging a recipe to commercial size results in some changes to the desired flavor, consistency, or appearance of the original recipe. Food scientists adjust the commercial recipe until the desired result is achieved.

Still in the test phase, selected consumers examine the potential product in their homes. Depending on consumer reaction, food scientists may be asked to make further refinements before the product is ready for market introduction.

Product specialists in the test kitchen then write package instructions and recipes for cookbooks and ads. Their preparation directions must be so precise that consumers get nearly identical results, no matter when or where the product and its recipes are made.

In the manufacturing plants, food technologists examine samples of the new product continuously, 17-7. These scientists are called *quality control technicians* because they check and recheck products around the clock directly from the production line. They also check the quality of the ingredients coming into the plant.

These steps, and all others discussed here, are continually repeated as new products are developed and existing items are updated.

University of Wisconsin-Stout

17-7 Taste testing is an important part of the development of new and better food products.

Nancy Rodriguez
Product Development

Did you ever wonder how companies decide what new food products to offer? The company Nancy Rodriguez owns conducts research and development that addresses the issue. Food companies, advertising firms, supermarkets, and restaurants work with her company to conduct research on various food products.

"Our mission is to develop and market retail and foodservice products that win awards, make money, and delight customers," Nancy explains. "We can take a food product from the idea stage to the supermarket shelf."

How does the company create new products? "After the client comes up with a concept," Nancy says, "we monitor consumer trends and design products that fit specific marketing strategies." All aspects of product development are considered in the process, including the following:

◆   specific sensory targets
◆   availability of ingredients
◆   handling issues
◆   processing requirements
◆   packaging requirements
◆   sales and distribution needs
◆   cost targets

Before Nancy started her own business, she worked for a food research and development laboratory. She gained experience as a taste tester and continues in this role today. Her company employs a panel of taste experts, trained in the art and science of tasting. Tasters are trained for one year, then apprentice for six months. Using a technique called descriptive sensory analysis, taste experts describe flavors and textures of the new products. Then, they assign an intensity level to each flavor and texture. Data from the taste panels directs new food product design.

"Chemical tests can distinguish ingredients, but not taste. We understand taste," she says proudly.

In her previous jobs, Nancy managed employees and budgets, planned projects, gave oral presentations, and prepared detailed data reports. She now uses these skills in the operation of her own company. Nancy markets services to clients, writes proposals, and reports scientific findings. "Most of my workday is spent writing," she reports.

Nancy loves her job and recommends it to anyone desiring challenges, responsibilities, and opportunities. "People who are curious, are willing to try new things, and have a keen eye for what's new and different will enjoy the innovative, artistic challenges of food product development."

Chefs and Bakers

Many food preparation careers relate to science. Combining food ingredients in the proper proportions and in the appropriate manner to yield a healthful and tasty product is indeed a science. The best chefs and bakers receive special training in food preparation techniques. The following descriptions of these food professionals will give you an insight into these careers.

Reaching the level of a successful chef needs special food preparation skills and considerable experience. Some may start in the foodservice business as *kitchen assistants* and advance through the ranks to *chef* or *cook*. This route is becoming less common for chefs and head cooks as the field requires more occupational training. Most chefs study at professional culinary schools, vocational schools, or two-year colleges. Then, they apprentice to become chefs, 17-8.

The work of a chef includes more than just preparing food. It often involves developing recipes, planning menus, ordering food, and overseeing the entire foodservice staff. Chefs and cooks work in hotels, restaurants, and corporate dining rooms. Some chefs work in people's homes. After they build a reputation for high-quality food preparation, some chefs start their own catering services.

Who can resist stopping at a bakery counter? Bakers are responsible for all the wonderful aromas you smell as you walk past. Some bakeries have particular specialties such as French bread, doughnuts, or unique pastries. Making and decorating wedding and other special-occasion cakes are services offered by many bakers. Bakers work in supermarkets, restaurants, bakeries, and baking companies. Some are managers of their own bakeries.

Bakers work with large quantities of ingredients. They need to know the cause and effect of each ingredient used in a product. They also need to know the amount and kind of mechanical action needed to yield the appropriate structure for each baked product. For instance, too much flour or too much mixing will cause a heavy, tough product.

In addition to baking skills, bakers must know their market. Each community has its own special tastes, and certain products are unique to a locale. For instance, some bakeries specialize in ethnic baked goods, such as poteca, kolache, strudel, and baklava. Bakers need to know what will sell in their area.

Johnson and Wales University

17-8 Culinary programs provide training in all aspects of food preparation.

Becoming a baker requires training and experience. Many baking skills and techniques can be learned by preparing baked goods at home. Working in a bakery provides experience in large-quantity baking methods and bakery operation. Today, more professional bakers attend special trade schools or two-year colleges to learn skills in baking and operating a bakery business.

These are some of the many careers in food, nutrition, and wellness that involve science and technology. Lists of various careers in this career cluster are shown in 17-9.

◆ Science and Technology Careers in Textiles and Apparel

When you go shopping or look in fashion magazines, you see many new clothing styles and designs featured. Fabrics, colors, and textures are different from last season. How were these colors and textures created? How are new fibers and fabrics developed?

Science and technology plays a very important role in the clothing industry. The result is a wide selection of styles, fibers, and fabrics. Fiber and fabric research produces a wide variety of fabric finishes to meet consumers' needs. By skillfully blending dyes, the industry produces a vast array of color combinations for the market.

Most apparel and textile manufacturing in the United States takes place in plants and textile mills located in the eastern and southern parts of the country. These plants are often located in small towns with main offices in New York City. Today, a great deal of apparel production takes place in Asia and other Far Eastern countries because labor costs are lower.

Producing clothing from fiber to the finished product involves people working in many different areas of science and technology.

Science and Technology Careers in Food, Nutrition, and Wellness		
Entry Level	**College Degree**	Health and fitness advisor
Baker	Administrative dietitian	Health education coordinator
Candy maker	Clinical dietitian	Microwave food specialist
Cook	Community dietitian	Nutritionist
Dietary aide	Corporate fitness manager	Product development specialist
Food laboratory aide	Dietetic technician	Public health nutritionist
Advanced Training	Dietitian	Quality assurance technician
Chef	Diet center director	Quality control director
Dietetic technician	Evaluation scientist	Quality control technician
Executive chef	Exercise testing technician	Research assistant
Food grader	Food chemist	Research dietitian
Food laboratory aide	Food development specialist	Research nutritionist
Food tester	Food inspector	Research technician
Laboratory assistant	Food production chemist	Sanitation supervisor
Pastry baker	Food product specialist	Sensory analyst
Pastry chef	Food scientist	Sensory technician
Quality control aide	Food technologist	Sports nutritionist
Sous-chef	Health inspector	

17-9 Numerous career opportunities exist in science and technology related to food, nutrition, and wellness.

Textile research and apparel production are two areas of work in this field. The field of clothing and textile care and preservation offers other career opportunities.

Textile Research and Development

People working in research and development careers use the latest information to develop new products or improve products already on the market. *Textile research and development scientists* work with fibers, fabrics, dyes, and textile finishes. They are involved in product development and testing and in giving technical advice to clients. They may have job titles such as *product development specialist, textile chemist, textile physicist,* or *manager of textile testing.*

Many textile scientists research new types of fibers, dyes, and finishes. For instance, some scientists might help develop new or improved dye colors. They may develop processes that improve the colorfast quality of fabrics. *Colorfast* means the color in garments will not bleed or fade when washed. Other scientists might develop finishes that improve the feel, performance, and appearance of textiles, 17-10.

Textile research and development scientists work for many kinds of firms. These include research and development laboratories, fiber or fabric manufacturers, textile mills, and private testing agencies. Textile scientists may work in manufacturing companies, making sure the fibers, fabrics, or clothing produced meet certain specifications. Some textile scientists may help develop easy-care fibers for carpeting, upholstery, drapery fabrics, and other home interior products. Other textile scientists work as chemists or lab technicians with the government. They test whether certain textile products meet government standards.

Textile scientists conduct research on the care of different textile fibers and garments. They then translate technical information into words that consumers can understand. Product

Sulzer Ruti, Inc.

17-10 Textile scientists are familiar with the processes and machinery that develop new and better fibers and fabrics.

labels and hangtags carry this information. Commercial dry cleaners also need information on the proper care of different fabrics and fibers.

Textile laboratory technicians often work with textile scientists to help conduct research. They help set up equipment and record data. Sometimes they help categorize or analyze experiments.

Some lab technicians are involved with quality control. *Quality control technicians* check fibers, yarns, fabrics, or garments to see that certain production standards and specifications are met. For example, they may check the fabric color, making sure it's the correct shade and the colors used for coordinating garments match.

Lab technicians must be exact in their work. They must be able to follow directions precisely and conduct tests accurately. Good analytical skills will be necessary to write laboratory reports. Lab technicians generally need technical or trade school certification.

Karen Mueser
Textile Engineer

Karen Mueser may not be in direct contact with her company's customers, but what she does affects them nonetheless. Karen works for one of the largest department store chains in the country. Her job as group engineering manager is to assure the quality of the textile items sold in their stores.

"My department provides support to the buying, product development, and specifications departments for apparel and home fashions," explains Karen. "We test the products being considered for sale to determine if they meet our standards. We test for shrinkage, colorfastness, effects of bleach, and damage by light. In addition, specific textile products may be tested for flammability, breaking and tearing strength, bursting strength, seam strength, yarn slippage, abrasion resistance, stretch properties, water resistance, and other factors."

After the tests are completed, the department analyzes the results and writes reports to inform store buyers of the quality of the items being considered. "If a problem is found, we work with the manufacturers and mills to improve the products," Karen says.

She also provides correct terminology for the permanent care labels. "I'm responsible for verifying that products and labeling comply with all the law," Karen continues. "This means I must have a working knowledge of the federal laws pertaining to textile products and keep informed of any changes made to them."

She and her staff also analyze any customer complaints related to their textile products. "We try to be the customers' advocate. We know that for every complaint we receive, there are a certain number of customers who won't bother to complain at all. They will respond by not returning to our stores," explains Karen. "We would like to prevent a complaint from happening in the first place."

Karen's job includes many other tasks. She prepares performance standards manuals that are used by the specifications staff and buyers. She

visits independent testing laboratories, which are sometimes used for additional tests, to evaluate their facilities and staff. She also provides training for the textile lab technicians or the buying staff.

Karen's job requires that she work with many different kinds of people. "The buyers are creative people who are not too interested in the technical details. They don't want to be told that a popular item is not of acceptable quality. I welcome the chance to go to technical meetings to talk to my counterparts at other companies. We have a good support system," Karen says.

Karen is a member of the industry associations that give her a voice in shaping textile testing methods and standards. In addition, she is in contact with others in the textiles industry who help keep her informed of new developments.

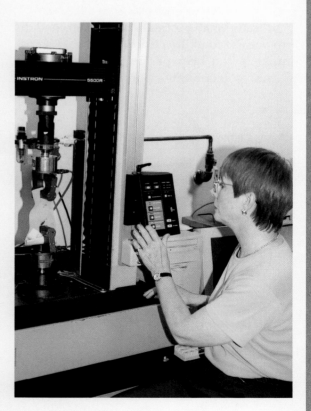

Apparel Production Careers

The clothing for the ready-to-wear market is produced in large quantities on factory assembly lines. There are many different types of jobs involved in getting garments from fiber to finished product. Production workers hold a variety of jobs, but management positions are also available.

Production Workers

Production workers begin their work when clothing designers complete theirs. In apparel production, the first step is to make a sample garment. *Sample makers* follow the designer's pattern and make a sample garment. Then, they check the designer's specifications against the sample to be sure everything is correct. For example, they may check the garment's fit on the model form. Perhaps changes need to be made to ensure a better fit.

In traditional garment production, people with specialized skills perform the next steps. Computers can help perform the steps faster and more accurately. Some computerized processes make it possible to prepare and cut out the garment pieces with little human labor.

Pattern makers transfer each piece of the sample garment to heavy paper or fiberboard. They work closely with the designer to copy each garment piece exactly to produce a master pattern. Some pattern makers use the computer to accomplish this process.

Then *pattern graders* reduce or enlarge patterns for the different sizes desired by a manufacturer. For most manufacturers, this process is now computer-assisted. Using a computer helps perform these processes quickly and easily, 17-11.

Spreaders are the workers who prepare the fabric for cutting. They carefully layer many pieces of fabric. Again, computerized equipment helps accomplish this process accurately and precisely.

When the fabric is ready, workers called *markers* arrange the pattern pieces on the fabric in the most efficient manner. They determine the best placement in order to waste the least amount of fabric. Computers can efficiently create these layouts and organize pattern pieces in the tightest possible layout.

Gerber Garment Technology, Inc.

17-11 Computers allow pattern graders to create different sizes of the same design quickly and easily.

Next, *cutters* use special cutting devices to cut around the patterns arranged on the stacks of fabric. This process might be computerized, using lasers to automatically cut through the fabric. Lasers are much faster than workers and very precise.

Sewing machine operators use commercial sewing machines to construct garments. Operators who sew clothing usually focus on one step and therefore do their small job quickly. By specializing on one task, machine operators build up speed and accuracy.

For example, one section of factory workers may only sew straight seams, 17-12. Inserting sleeves or doing buttonholes would fall to other sewing machine operators.

Sewers working on higher-priced garments, on the other hand, may construct the entire garment.

Finishers do the hand sewing necessary to complete a garment. They may attach buttons, hooks, and eyes. Some hand sewers may specialize in one technique, such as adding trims or securing linings. They need to be fast, accurate workers.

Drexel

17-12 Sewing machine operators must be accurate and efficient in their work.

Plant Operations

For a textile or clothing manufacturing plant to run efficiently, various managers are needed. The highest person in the company involved with plant operations is usually a product manager. *Product managers* coordinate and oversee all aspects of manufacturing a line of products. In addition, product managers are responsible for successfully selling and delivering the items to retail buyers.

Before the manufacturing step, product managers need to decide whether a design is practical. Is it too expensive to manufacture? Can the products be sold in current retail outlets using similar sales techniques? Can garment delivery coincide with seasonal demand? It is the responsibility of the product manager to see that every phase of the design, manufacture, and distribution of a garment is planned and carried out well.

Industrial engineers plan the production steps of the total manufacturing operation. In order to do this, they must understand all manufacturing equipment and processes needed to produce each item. They design the ideal layout for machines, materials, and workers to achieve the best pattern of workflow. Industrial engineers examine the most cost-effective methods of production without reducing quality. They recommend certain work methods to meet the company standards and specifications.

The *production manager* or *plant manager* is responsible for actual production operations in the plant. This includes estimating costs of production, scheduling the flow of work within the plant, and hiring and training new workers. Purchasing, cutting, sewing, shipping, and warehouse operations are the responsibility of the production manager. The production manager must also make sure the manufactured products meet the specified standards.

The production manager's job requires good management skills. It is important to coordinate the work of all departments so production runs smoothly. For instance, the production manager might need to interact with a product manager and quality control engineer. Usually production managers work up through the ranks. This is a complex job and is achieved only after many years of experience in the field.

Managerial positions in manufacturing plant operations are not unique to the textile and clothing field. In fact, positions similar to those discussed here exist in factories that make food products, furniture, appliances, and all other household goods. These positions generally require a college degree and many years of experience in manufacturing operations or a related area.

Dry Cleaning Workers

Dry cleaners use nonwater solvents to clean textiles. Properly cleaned garments should not smell of dry cleaning solvents. Dry cleaning can cut down on shrinkage of garments and preserve fine tailoring details. Dry cleaning establishments are located in almost every community and provide a variety of jobs, 17-13.

When garments arrive at the dry cleaners, *sorters* put identity tags on them. They inspect each garment for stains and damage. They also check pockets to be sure they are empty. Then sorters sort the garments by color, fiber content, and type.

If a spot or stain needs to be removed, a *spotter* treats it with proper spot-removal methods. The method used must not harm the fabric.

The *operator* may measure some garments to be sure they return to the same size after dry-cleaning. He or she then cleans the garments in the solvents, using specialized cleaning equipment. They are tumble dried or air dried.

After drying, *finishers* press and reshape the garments for appearance. If needed, the finishers reattach buttons and other fasteners. They then hang or fold the garments neatly and package them for the customer.

Through research and technology, manufacturers determine how to best clean certain fabrics or clothing. Dry cleaners need to follow the manufacturer's directions.

17-13 Dry cleaners employ many workers in various jobs.

Textile Conservators

Many fabrics, clothing, and other items from earlier periods have historical value. They can be saved and protected from ruin. Textile conservators work to preserve these garments and fabrics to maintain valuable pieces of history.

Some articles are made of materials not available today. Many old laces and other fine fabrics are no longer produced and can only be seen in museum collections. Textile conservators can help preserve these items as historical records for future generations to study and admire.

If you have an interest in clothing, history, and science, you might enjoy working as a textile conservator.

Various career opportunities in science and technology in the clothing and textiles field are shown in 17-14. Most of these careers require education and training beyond the secondary level. Many entry-level jobs are quickly disappearing as computerized machines are developed to do routine tasks.

Science and Technology Careers in Environmental Design

Think of how routine chores around the home have changed in recent years. Today, technology makes it much easier for families to launder clothes, prepare meals, and clean up.

People working in science and technology careers in environmental design may develop new materials for the home-building industry. They may work to improve appliances, household products, or cleaning agents for the home. Professionals in this field may test new products or advise customers of product features. The following descriptions will help you learn about a few of the scientific and technical jobs available in this field.

Design engineers and *product development scientists* work in companies that make household products or their components. They also create new finishes, coatings, processes, and materials that make household products more durable and easier to maintain. Scuff-resistant floors,

Science and Technology Careers in Apparel and Textiles		
Entry Level	Laboratory technician	Industrial engineer
Apparel production assistant	Leather cleaner/dyer	Product development
Cloth shrinking tester	Pattern cutter	specialist
Dry cleaning sorter	Pattern grader	Product manager
Fabric dyer	Production pattern maker	Production manager
Fabric spreader	Sewing machine operator	Quality control specialist
		Textile chemist/researcher
Advanced Training	**College Degree**	Textile colorist
Clothing production finisher	Apparel engineer	Textile conservator
Color paste mixer	Apparel production	Textile designer
Color tester/checker	specialist	Textile production specialist
Dry cleaner	Apparel technician	Textile scientist
Fabric marker	Design engineer	Textile stylist
Fur cleaner	Fiber analyst	Textile tester
Laboratory assistant	Industrial designer	

17-14 Science abilities combined with an interest in fabrics and clothing open the door to a wide variety of jobs in the textile and apparel industry.

nonstick skillets, and refrigerator surfaces that resist fingerprints are a few examples.

Developing soaps, detergents, laundry aids, and household cleaners and polishers represents another broad area of product development. In addition to making a dependable product, scientists in this industry also focus on the package. They devote considerable research to developing materials that can be recycled.

Product design and development scientists also work for appliance manufacturers. Before new appliances are designed, component parts must be checked by *product analysts* and *product testers*. These specialists make sure the parts meet specifications. This is a very important step because the performance of the final product depends on the quality of each component, 17-15. Components must perform according to specifications. Appliance engineers constantly work to make appliances more durable, dependable, energy efficient, and affordable.

Even after products are developed and on the market, their testing continues. Often the purpose of this testing is to rate products by price and performance to help consumers make purchasing decisions. The government also conducts tests to make sure the products pose no safety problems.

Many factors affect how well appliances operate, not the least of which is where they are installed. Location is particularly important for heating and cooling systems.

Utility advisors work for gas and electric companies to help builders select and install effective systems for new buildings. Utility advisors also teach consumers how to make their homes more energy efficient. They may present programs on insulating and caulking windows, installing storm windows, or taking other measures to conserve energy. Utility advisors can make a big difference in the overall goal to save the country's energy resources.

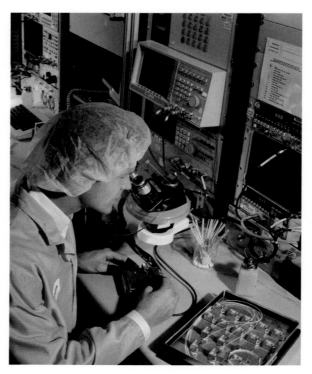

17-15 *An important step in appliance manufacturing is checking computer chips and electronic controls since these actually operate most new appliances.*

◆ Other Careers in Science and Technology

Until now, this chapter has focused on science and technology careers associated with the physical and life sciences. Besides these sciences, career opportunities also exist in the social sciences. For example, psychology, sociology, and the behavioral sciences offer other career options in family and consumer sciences. Some of those opportunities are discussed here.

Consumer and Resource Management. Those interested in the science of consumer and resource management may be involved in researching cultural differences in consumer behavior. They may measure the cost

Sandra Flinton
Utility Advisor

Sandra Flinton is a customer services coordinator for a public natural gas utility. Her job is to help people use their gas appliances correctly. She also develops programs for dealers to increase sales while promoting energy efficiency.

Sandra originally wanted to be an elementary teacher, but her studies led her in another direction. Now Sandra develops brochures and other support materials on gas appliances and gas usage. She trains company employees by giving demonstrations on natural gas equipment. Another aspect of her job is to educate teachers and community leaders in natural gas safety. She laughs, "I am a teacher, but not in a classroom."

Sandra's previous experience includes working with architects, building firms, and appliance manufacturers. How does the knowledge gained from these jobs help her today? "I can still call builders to promote the use of gas," Sandra reports. "My experience is also helpful when I work with dealers who sell appliances. I know about sales and marketing as well as how appliances are shipped and sold."

Sandra enjoys working with many people, including customers, appliance dealers, home builders, and educators. "I like the one-on-one contact," Sandra says. "I give people information so they can make wise choices."

Her work offers a wide range of opportunities and is never dull. Since jobs are rapidly changing due to technology, she encourages young people to get a broad educational background. "I advise any individual to learn about writing, accounting, sales, and advertising," Sandra asserts. "This makes it easier to promote yourself as jobs change."

Daniel Chiras
Environmental Scientist

In his lectures, books, and articles, Daniel Chiras outlines ways to make homes and lifestyles more environmentally friendly. He is a writer, consultant, teacher, lecturer, and activist.

"Human civilization is rapidly destroying the life support systems of the planet, which will ultimately affect our economy and our very existence," Daniel asserts. He shows readers and students how to change their lives and reshape policy and management decisions. Daniel is working to create a "sustainable society"—one that meets life's physical needs while ensuring future generations the ability to meet theirs.

At the University of Denver, Daniel teaches in the Environmental Policy and Management Program. "I show how people can make a difference by making changes in their lives, homes, and places of work. I offer advice on ways to cut energy demand in homes, vehicles, and businesses," Daniel reports. He describes ways to tap into renewable energy resources, such as solar energy, to heat and power homes and cars. Recycling and water conservation are other ways he advocates to protect resources. He believes these measures will help us to protect the earth.

Daniel and his family try to live what he teaches. Their Rocky Mountain home is a superinsulated, passive-solar home. Despite frequent bitterly cold nights, their annual heating bill is very low.

The Chiras family has used other strategies to create a more sustainable course. "For instance," Daniel says, "we have tempered our buying habits. We do not overconsume, but buy wisely and carefully. Recycling and composting are a way of life." In addition, they grow some of their own food in an organic greenhouse and garden. Because their home is heated by the sun, they can grow spinach, chard, and tomatoes indoors throughout the winter.

Through their conservation habits and use of water-saving devices, the Chiras family uses a tiny fraction of the water of a typical household. Environmentally-safe products are used for cleaning. Since Daniel and his wife work mainly in their home, they do not have to drive much. When they do, they travel in energy-efficient cars. By making these changes in their lives, they are working toward building a more sustainable future.

of operating different appliances under various conditions. They may examine how to best employ manufacturing resources—such as workers, raw materials, plant equipment, money, and time—to make products most efficiently.

Other professionals in consumer and resource management may design and develop new technologies to help consumers better manage their resources. Many newer technologies are due to advances in computers. One such technology is the **automated teller machine (ATM).** An ATM is a machine that allows customers to conveniently get cash from their accounts at any time.

Other example of technology that helps consumers manage resources are money management Internet sites. Many Web sites offer up-to-the minute financial data and advice. Some provide tools such as calculators to let consumers figure the results of various spending and savings options. These sites help consumers spend wisely, especially when a major expense such a home or car is involved. Professionals in consumer and resource management help design the sites and the information they provide.

Child Development and Early Childhood Education. Intelligence and learning are two subjects that, after decades of study, are still only partially understood today. Often the findings from one study inspire new questions and more studies. Research on these topics span the behavioral, physical, and life sciences.

New discoveries about human intelligence present clearer pictures of how learning occurs. From these findings, experts make recommendations for improving teaching methods, parenting practices, toy designs, and children's diets. Researchers also analyze the effectiveness of computer technologies for learning. See 17-16. These studies guide parents, teachers, and policymakers to make decisions that improve children's development and learning.

Family Studies and Human Services. Professionals are needed in various areas of behavioral science to address the modern challenges affecting the family structure. These

17-16 Scientists combine their knowledge of human intelligence and technology to develop computer programs that promote learning.

challenges include increased stress, violence, substance abuse, and child neglect, among others. Studies on stress, coping skills, and resiliency provide insight into helping individuals and families deal with change. Well-researched studies provide the data needed to promote public policy decisions consistent with the well-being of children and families.

Hospitality, Tourism, and Recreation. Researchers play a significant role in the overall success of the hospitality industry. Hotels, convention centers, and tour operators routinely examine every aspect of their business and compile many statistics. These studies analyze the needs and desires of the public and help managers determine how to best address them.

One service all customers want is fast, accurate information to help them make better plans. Web sites answer that need with up-to-the minute information and pictures of facilities and coming events. Technology specialists help create the appearance and content of company Web sites.

Systems that increase safety and automate reservations and billing are examples of other technologies important to the industry. These are developed by technology experts who understand the desires of the traveling public and the business needs of their employers.

◆ Personal Skills and Abilities Needed for a Career in Science and Technology

Science and technology as it relates to food, clothing, and housing offers many areas for investigation and research. Professionals in this type of work must have an inquisitive mind. They must enjoy experimenting and keeping track of details. Solving problems in an objective and analytical manner is necessary for interpreting data accurately. A research career demands solid scientific knowledge. It also requires qualities of preciseness, imagination, and thoroughness.

Often perfecting a process or developing new techniques takes many years. People in science and research must be patient and determined to seek solutions and stay abreast of scientific advances, 17-17. They must have the discipline to organize their own work. Much of a researcher's work is just part of a team effort, so being able to communicate ideas and findings to others is necessary.

The personal skills and abilities needed for a career in science and technology will vary depending on the specific field chosen. People who work in nutrition and dietetics should care about people, their needs, and their health. They should be able to analyze clients' eating habits and counsel them in how to help themselves. They should enjoy working with people and applying scientific knowledge to improve their lives.

Managerial positions require good interpersonal skills and supervisory skills. Managers also need to be experienced in conducting research so they can supervise employees through the steps of the scientific process.

17-17 Scientific studies need carefully controlled procedures and continuous follow-up.

Education and Training Needed for a Career in Science and Technology

Most scientific and technological careers in family and consumer sciences require at least a bachelor's degree. Professionals in very specialized jobs often need a master's degree or a doctorate.

A strong background is necessary in the basic science upon which the subject matter is built. Nutrition, wellness, and other food science fields, for example, require thorough knowledge of chemistry, physiology, and microbiology. Textile research is based on chemistry, physics, and mathematics. Family relations and child development are supported by studies in psychology, sociology, and anthropology.

Those who enter the dietetics field must have a bachelor's degree in dietetics, nutrition and wellness, or foodservice systems management. Students must complete a dietetic internship, which is usually offered as part of a degree program, 17-18. After completing an internship, they must successfully complete an examination. Only then can individuals become *registered dietitians,* entitled to use *RD* after their names.

The American Dietetic Association (ADA) is the organization for professional dietitians and dietetic technicians. It establishes standards for college programs and approves schools that meet the standards. ADA also sets standards for individual professional certification. After individuals gain professional ADA certification, they are required to maintain it by taking frequent refresher courses.

Dietetic technicians must have an associate degree in foods and nutrition. They must complete on-the-job training and pass a special test, which entitles them to use *DTR* after their names. This indicates the individual is a *Dietetic Technician, Registered.*

The titles of *dietitian* and *dietetic technician* are tightly controlled, but nutrition-related titles are not. Some people take advantage of

U.S. Department of Agriculture

17-18 Dietetic internships are available in hospitals, corporations, school cafeterias, or anywhere a dietitian can monitor the performance of the student in training.

the public's interest in nutrition by using the term *nutritionist* in their business title. These individuals claim to be well-read, but have little scientific background. According to experts, true nutritionists generally have a bachelor's degree in human nutrition, dietetics, or a related science as well as a master's degree. The advanced degree is in a specialty area such as pathology or immunology.

To hold a science and technology career in textiles, a degree in industrial engineering, operations research, or management science may be needed. A foundation in such courses as textile chemistry, chemical engineering, physics, and apparel technology is essential. Related work experience or an internship with a textile manufacturer can provide a valuable introduction to this career area.

Careers in apparel production require computer training since most manufacturing operations are computer-assisted. For management positions in manufacturing plants, individuals often need an engineering or related business degree. In addition, they need extensive work experience in their particular fields.

Those interested in science careers in environmental design should take courses in physics, chemistry, and environmental science. Some colleges offer majors in household equipment. Related areas of study such as consumer economics, engineering statistics, and cost estimating would be useful.

◆ Future Trends

The rapid growth and application of scientific knowledge touches many consumer fields. This is especially evident in the areas of foods, fibers, and housing. Advances in science and technology will continue to cause changes in the way families live and work. These trends indicate a positive future for science and technology careers in family and consumer sciences.

Scientific emphasis on nutrition and wellness will continue. Identifying the food components that promote good health and prevent disease will be a high priority, 17-19.

Modifying foods genetically to increase nutrition content and crop yields is another growing area of research. More scientific work is also needed to improve food safety, disease prevention, and health maintenance.

Concern for preserving the environment and conserving natural resources will continue to influence all product development. That concern will encourage the creation of more reusable and recyclable packages for food and household products. The environmental trend will also affect appliance design and home construction. The result of all these concerns will be more environmentally friendly homes that use less energy.

Goods and services will continue to be improved as a result of new technology. People who help families make choices concerning these goods and services based on their values and goals will be needed. How do these new products and services affect them? Do they need them? How will they help them? Will these new products and processes improve the quality of life for individuals and families? All of these are concerns for those interested in finding answers to questions and helping to create a better tomorrow.

17-19 Science and technology careers will be important to the continued health of family members.

Summary

The science and technology cluster offers many different career possibilities for family and consumer sciences professionals. Careers related to the sciences can be found in food, nutrition, and wellness; textiles and apparel; environmental design; family studies and human services; child development and early childhood education; hospitality, tourism, and recreation; and consumer and resource management.

Manufacturing firms, industries, hospitals, institutions, government agencies, and private enterprise employ workers in science and technology. They are employed in research and development, production, management, and health care positions.

Characteristics of these professionals include having a scientific mind as well as an interest in the well-being of individuals and families. Some jobs require the ability to work with individuals to help them solve their problems. Much of the work in research is done as a part of a research team. Research findings need to be communicated to others. Managerial positions require good personal relationship skills and the ability to make decisions.

In some careers, a two-year degree or a bachelor's degree will be satisfactory, but continued updating in the field will be necessary. In other cases, a master's degree or a doctorate is required, particularly for jobs in research and development.

Future projections indicate increased emphasis on wellness, nutrition, health, and conservation. Educating families concerning choices and researching critical issues involving the health and well-being of families will be essential.

To Review

1. Explain the relationship between science and technology.

2. What is the difference between a dietitian and a nutritionist?

3. What is the main reason that food scientists are employed by the food industry?

4. What is the most common type of job in this country's textile manufacturing industry?

5. How do computers assist apparel production?

6. How does a product manager's job differ from a production manager's job?

7. Describe two types of jobs possible as a design engineer.

8. Which family and consumer sciences professional would be most able to advise you on the efficient use of energy in your home?

9. What personal characteristics might be needed for most jobs in science and technology?

10. List three trends that are affecting family and consumer sciences job opportunities in science and technology.

To Do

1. Brainstorm possible technological changes that might occur in foods and nutrition, clothing and textiles, housing, furnishings, and equipment.

2. Discuss how the technological changes listed in the preceding activity might affect careers in these areas.

3. Prepare a bulletin board display of family and consumer sciences careers in science and technology.

4. Choose a specific job in the science and technology field of family and consumer sciences. Research the career using resources from the library or other sources. Prepare a written report describing the job and the qualifications needed. State what you might like and dislike about the job.

Careers in the Arts 18

Creativity is an important part of life. People who have artistic talents, good color sense, and imagination might consider a variety of family and consumer sciences careers. Someone interested in clothing might choose a career as a textile stylist, fashion designer, or color consultant. Many food-related careers require decorating and styling skills. Some professionals design and furnish private homes, public buildings, or commercial establishments.

In this chapter, you will study family and consumer sciences related to art and creative expression. You will learn what personal characteristics can help you succeed and the type of education required for each of the careers.

All these careers require an understanding of ever-changing consumer needs. Each year brings new styles, designs, and trends. Family and consumer sciences professionals in the arts interpret trends and develop designs that will fill consumer demands. They should be open to new ideas and influences.

◆ Art Careers in Textiles and Apparel

When you think of a career in fashion, do fashion centers such as Paris and New York come to mind? Does your mental picture include working with famous designers and modeling the latest clothing? This sounds glamorous and exciting. Many people who work in fashion do have stimulating and rewarding jobs. However, the work may also require many long hours spent over a drawing sketch board or computer. Jobs in design are labor intensive and consumer oriented. Many skills are needed to design merchandise consumers will buy. Success in the field often depends on how well each design sells.

Textile Designer

Think of the textiles and fabrics used in your home. This includes towels, sheets, upholstery, and drapery fabrics. The designs you choose for your clothing and home furnishings are created by textile designers.

Textile designers know a great deal about the characteristics and performance of each yarn. They are familiar with fabric properties as well as fibers, dyes, and finishes. In order for their designs to be developed easily and economically, they must understand all phases of the textile manufacturing process.

Many textile designers use computers to create designs. They can analyze a design and determine the weave or knit needed to create the desired fabric. This is much faster and more accurate than the older method of weaving ideas into samples on looms, 18-1.

Textile designers are employed by fabric manufacturers or textile mills. Most of these jobs are located in New York, Paris, or other fashion centers. Some designers work on a freelance basis and sell their designs to many different companies. The competition for jobs in this field is very intense.

University of Wisconsin-Stout

18-1 Weaving filling yarns over and under warp yarns produces a particular pattern in fabric.

Textile Colorist

Textile colorists choose the color combinations that will be used in textiles. They paint various color combinations on designs created by textile designers or create color combinations using a computer. They know from their research and records how different dyes will look on fabrics. After final approval, colorists send specific instructions to the mill for the manufacturing process to begin.

Textile colorists have an eye for appealing, interesting color combinations. They have the ability to visualize finished fabrics. Colorists cater to current fashion looks. They also use classic colors that are popular season after season. They create color combinations that make customers enthusiastic about products. Colorists often work under pressure to meet deadlines and keep fabric production on schedule.

Textile Stylist

Textile stylists coordinate the design and color departments with the production staff at the mills. They contact garment manufacturers about what fabrics they want in their merchandise. Based on assessments of the market and expectations for the clothing line, they suggest the best patterns and colors to use.

Textile stylists must maintain a wide range of business contacts and resources. They read forecasting reports of fashion editors and textile firms to help in their decision making. They are familiar with manufacturing processes and economic conditions that affect consumer buying. Stylists need experience in the textile and fashion industry to predict the direction of the buying public. Often the success of textile firms depends on the talents and abilities of their stylists.

Fashion Designer

Fashion designers use their creativity to design new clothing and accessory styles.

Bridget Haugh
Fashion Photo Technical Director

As a photo technical director, Bridget Haugh is responsible for setting up shots for photographers. Her company produces books that explain sewing procedures step-by-step.

"I was hired to construct the items to be photographed, but they needed someone to help arrange them for the shots," says Bridget. "I work with clothing samples in different stages of completion for the how-to shots and finished items for the larger beauty shots that appear in the books." Bridget is responsible for making sure each shot is technically correct from the sewing standpoint. If she thinks something should be changed, she discusses it with the writer to determine the best solution. "I check that everything in the shot fits into the allotted space and shape," adds Bridget. "Finally, I make sure the shot looks aesthetically pleasing."

Bridget isn't a photographer, but she's learned a great deal on the job. She works closely with the photographer and the art director to determine the most advantageous lighting and camera angle. Bridget says, "The beauty shots are the most fun, because we can be more creative. It isn't always as easy as it sounds, but it is interesting and challenging work.

"When doing a photo shoot, we have a lot of freedom," she says, "and we get to use our creativity and problem-solving skills." She works on a very tight schedule because each book has to be shot in about six weeks. Although she occasionally travels to outside locations for special shots, Bridget usually works in a dark studio all day.

Through her job, she has met well-known sewing professionals and learned about new products and technology as they become available. "I have always loved sewing," says Bridget, "and to have a career in sewing is absolutely ideal."

Cy Crosse, Inc.

Their jobs involve sketching designs, designing patterns, overseeing production, and promoting styles. Most designers concentrate on a certain type of apparel, such as children's wear, sportswear, or bridal wear. They may design four or five lines, or collections, each year. There are about fifty items to most collections.

Some of the most talented designers work for large fashion houses in cities such as New York, Dallas, or San Francisco. Salaries are very high for those who design exclusive lines. Designers employed by these firms may be well known in the fashion world.

Those who work for manufacturers of moderately priced apparel may be part of a staff of designers. The staff might include a head designer, one or more designers, and assistants. They spend a great deal of time sketching designs. Sometimes designers are required to produce a certain number of sketches per week. A few of these are selected for the company's line.

Most fashion designers work for manufacturers of ready-to-wear apparel in the medium-priced or low-priced categories. Companies that mass-produce low-priced clothing employ the largest number of designers. These people adapt high-priced designs to lower-priced apparel using methods that cut manufacturing costs. Entry-level jobs that offer opportunities to gain experience are often available with these companies.

Designers may work with fabric to see how it drapes on a mannequin or dressmaker's form. They choose fabrics and make models of selected styles. Some supervise the construction of samples and oversee the production of the designs. Designers must produce the designs their markets want. They are responsible for the designs from conception to marketing.

Since most companies use computers to produce designs, computer knowledge and experience is helpful. Computers allow designers to visualize their ideas through computer-aided design. Using this method, different designs can be combined from hundreds of possibilities. The designer can use the computer to add various features such as pockets or yokes to the pattern. Collar and sleeve styles can be modified easily on the computer screen. The designer can adjust fullness and change color schemes. When the design is finished, it can be saved and used to create patterns.

Some computers have special equipment to photograph the design. Others can copy parts of designs and develop images into enlarged fashion photographs.

Fashion designers must constantly come up with new ideas for their creations. They might be inspired by studying historical fashions. Some inspirations come from nature. They also receive current fashion news through magazines and newspapers. Fashion designers work far ahead of seasons and are attuned to the changing color and style preferences. They interpret market forecasts and design fashions that set trends. See 18-2.

Those interested in fashion design should have an appreciation of clothing as more than just wearing apparel. They need to be creative artists who can develop original ideas. Designers need a sense of color, line, shape, and texture. In addition, they need the ability to work with the principles of design—balance, proportion, emphasis, and rhythm. The effective use of these principles achieves **harmony,** or a sense of unity.

Fashion designers should consider practical aspects when designing apparel. Consumers look for factors other than appearance when choosing clothing. Comfort is one significant consideration. Ease of care is important to customers who don't want the hassle and expense of dry cleaning. Finally, clothing should meet certain safety standards. Some fabrics are treated with a flame-retardant finish. Clothing made from this fabric would burn slowly, and the flames would easily extinguish.

People trained in fashion design can choose from a number of related careers. Some maintain their close association with this field by becoming fashion illustrators or photographers for magazines, newspapers, or pattern companies.

Talbots

18-2 Production of new designs and clothing styles begins far ahead of the next season.

Fashion Illustrator or Photographer

Fashion illustrators draw pictures of clothing designed by others. They focus on the good points of the design to help sell the fashion. Fashion illustrators prepare sketches for retail stores, pattern companies, and advertising agencies.

Illustrations emphasize key points. For example, a pattern company's illustrations show construction detail. In fashion magazines, the garments or trends featured are illustrated. Advertising companies want drawings that entice buyers.

Most fashion illustrator opportunities are located in large cities where competition for jobs is great. Illustrators who have many contacts in the field often freelance. Freelance work can be more profitable than working on a staff, but the work is not as regular. When assignments are received, they must be completed within tight deadlines.

Fashion photographers take promotional pictures of clothing and accessories, often using live models. They create a mood with props, backgrounds, and lighting. Their photos may appear in television, magazine, or catalog ads. Some work is done in a studio. Other times, photographers may travel for location shoots. Fashion photographers may be freelance artists or salaried employees of advertising agencies, magazines, stores, and photo studios.

Careers with Commercial Pattern Companies

Commercial pattern companies that create patterns for home sewers employ many fashion-oriented people, such as designers and pattern makers. Pattern designers get ideas for new patterns from many sources, including fashion markets and couture collections, which are custom-made. They then determine style trends suitable for their customers.

Connie Schwartz
Clothing Designer/Tailor

As a designer and tailor, Connie Schwartz specializes in fine hand-tailored suits, couture sewing, and original designs. She received her training in a clothing services program at a Wisconsin technical college.

Connie makes one-of-a-kind garments for customers who contact her with designs or fabrics in mind. "Sometimes people want me to combine different styles from two photographs," says Connie. "They might want the sleeves from one dress with the neckline from another." Working together, she and her client compose a unique garment. Connie considers her work "wearable art," made to pass from one generation to the next.

"People have me design special occasion garments for specific dates, so I often have to work against a deadline," Connie reports. She once created a flower girl's gown in one day, because on the eve of the wedding her gown had not yet arrived.

Connie finds that many skills are necessary in her line of work, especially diplomacy skills. People bring in pictures of garments they want her to make. First, she has to decide if it is possible to construct the garment. Then, she considers body type. A dress that looks one way on a model may not hang the same way on the client, even though the dress is constructed the exact same way. "If the finished item won't look the same on them, I have to honestly tell them what they can expect," explains Connie. "You walk a fine line to please your customers."

Connie has found that owning a business also requires a knowledge of bookkeeping, advertising, marketing, and public relations skills. She knows these are important in order to interact positively and professionally with her customers. "I have a love for art and a love for working with people," says Connie. "This career lets me pursue both."

Designers draw original sketches of their designs. Designs are drawn for various pattern categories. They include menswear, women's wear, children's wear, sportswear, window treatments, and other areas.

Pattern makers work with the designer's sketch to make a rough draft from heavy paper. *Garment makers* then use the pattern to construct half a garment, called a *half-drape,* from muslin. This is draped on a master-size dress form and checked for fit and cut. After approval, a complete muslin garment is made that incorporates all variations shown on the pattern. The muslin pattern is then checked on a live model, or *fitting model,* for size, fit, comfort, and style. The master pattern is cut, based on the results of these tests.

Professional dressmakers make the garment using home sewing techniques. Many professional dressmakers may be employed by the pattern company. Each view of the pattern is checked again on the live model.

Artists and illustrators make the drawings that accompany the printed patterns. Technical writers produce the sewing directions found in patterns. The responsibilities of those in the pattern design industry are similar to related positions in clothing design and fashion promotion.

Custom Tailor, Dressmaker, or Alterations Specialist

Custom tailors and dressmakers do custom sewing for others. Some tailors and dressmakers may specialize in particular garments, such as wedding dresses or suits. Alterations specialists make minor changes in the size or length of clothing. Some tailors, dressmakers, and alterations specialists work out of their homes, while others conduct business from shops.

Custom tailoring is done according to customer specifications. Some people may bring in a sketch of a design they want duplicated. Tailors and dressmakers make the pattern to fit the individual, using skillful construction and fitting techniques. Sometimes they work from one pattern or a combination of several patterns. They need to visualize and then create what the customer wants.

Sometimes the customer has definite ideas about the design. At other times, they need help choosing a flattering style and fabric. Tailors and dressmakers need to be tactful when working with customers.

Standard sizes of ready-made clothes are not always suitable for all people. If a garment does not fit perfectly, it may need to be altered. An alterations specialist might shorten sleeves or hemlines. Seams might need to be adjusted. Neckline and sleeve alterations are more complex, and therefore more expensive.

Theatrical Costumer

Costume designers create the garments for movies, shows, and plays. They work for theater companies, television networks, movie studios, and costume shops. These designers know what clothes are best suited for each media, 18-3.

Costume designers must be familiar with the background of the performance and coordinate the costumes with the props. If the production recreates an earlier era, the designer researches styles from the specified time period. The wardrobe designer is the head of the costume department. Other jobs at all levels of costuming include research, pattern making, fabric selection, draping, and sewing.

Textile and Clothing Historian

Historians, conservators, and *costume curators* work with historical clothing collections, which may include uniforms and gowns worn by famous people. Textiles are studied, identified, and then exhibited in places where the public can view them. Historians are interested in antique clothing and old textiles because they give us glimpses of life in years past.

Conservators are concerned with the preservation of the garments and textiles,

18-3 Costume designers make theatrical costumes look as authentic as possible.

which sometimes need restoration. Garments are cleaned with special equipment. Since all textiles weaken with age, they should be handled and stored very carefully.

Vintage clothing and textiles are a part of most historical collections in museums and libraries. **Vintage** refers to items from a past era. Costume curators prepare garments for exhibit in these places. They make sure garments are dated accurately and accessories from the correct historical period are used. Curators use their creative ability to present the displays in a historically correct way.

Wardrobe or Image Consultant

Your image is a picture that you project to others. This image is determined by what you wear, how you act, and what you say. People want their appearance and actions to project a positive image.

Wardrobe or image consultants help people choose clothing and accessories that project their best image. Some consultants who specialize in color analysis are called *color consultants*. They analyze their clients' hair, eye, and skin coloring. The consultants then help clients select clothing in their most attractive colors.

Some wardrobe consultants called *personal shoppers* work for large department stores. Personal shoppers select clothing for busy professionals who do not have time to shop for themselves.

Knowledge of the customer's personal style and color preferences helps consultants determine the right choices. Sometimes they choose clothes that will mix and match to form many outfits.

Nancy Nix-Rice
Image Consultant

Nancy Nix-Rice is a successful image consultant who helps others project a positive appearance. "People form an opinion about your educational background, financial status, and social position within 15 seconds—based entirely on appearance," says Nancy. "Developing a successful image involves learning to project the correct messages to people."

For people who request Nancy's help, the first step is a color analysis. Nancy uses a computer-aided program to pinpoint a client's very best wardrobe and makeup shades. "Sometimes clients need time to adjust to their new colors and styles; then they usually love the effect," reports Nancy. "Color analysis is not about making people do something they hate. It's giving them the knowledge to do what they like in the most effective way."

About 60 percent of her customers also request a silhouette analysis. In this process, Nancy takes their body measurements and helps them choose the most flattering styles for their body shape. Sometimes customers need additional assistance. Nancy helps them go through their closets and appraise the clothes they already own. Then, she helps them determine which clothes to keep as well as what they need to buy.

"Diplomacy is a key skill in working with clients," explains Nancy. "People often ask for consultation when they need a boost in their confidence, and we help them call attention to their assets."

Nancy also conducts workshops that emphasize the importance of nonverbal and spoken communication. Participants learn to interpret nonverbal cues, such as eye contact, personal space, and handshakes. Other topics covered include courtesy among employees, telephone etiquette, travel and dining tips, and making introductions correctly. Nancy's workshops emphasize the importance of choosing appropriate clothing for office and casual wear.

Nancy uses not only her color theory and design knowledge, but also her personal speaking and writing skills. She enjoys her job, saying, "It is extremely flexible and always fun; it never feels like work." According to Nancy, one unfortunate aspect of image consultation is not seeing the final results. After a consultation, Nancy might not see the client again. On the other hand, seeing clients who are thrilled with their new appearance gives her a great feeling of accomplishment.

◆ Art Careers in Environmental Design

There are many careers involved in housing and interior design. Professional designers help customers plan offices and homes. They help decorate everything from hallways to entire office buildings. Some professionals, such as lighting consultants and kitchen designers, specialize in one area. Furniture designers create the styles used for household furnishings. Display artists create various merchandise displays to attract customers to stores. These and other design careers require artistic talent.

Interior Designer

Whether redecorating an entire house or planning one room, interior designers must meet the decorating needs of their clients. They help make living and working spaces more attractive and useful. They may specialize in commercial or residential interiors, or both.

Residential interior designers help families decorate and organize their living space. After studying the clients' needs, interior designers usually make a scaled floor plan of the proposed room. They choose possible colors and present illustrations, sketches, color charts, photography, and samples to the clients. They provide estimates of the costs of furnishings, materials, labor, and other charges. After the plan is finalized and accepted, designers sometimes purchase the furnishings and supervise the decorating process, 18-4. In other cases, the purchasing and installation is completed by the client after the plan has been approved.

Home lighting consultants help clients choose lighting products for new or remodeled homes. The lighting consultant might visit the client's home to give suggestions on appropriate types of lighting. For example, a client may need help combining glarefree lighting for reading with bright task lighting for working. The consultant would advise the client about different options and the effects of each.

18-4 Residential designers sometimes recommend specific furniture pieces to complete the design.

Home lighting consultants prepare estimates and write orders. Sometimes they oversee the installation of the lighting to make sure the job is completed to a client's satisfaction. Consultants may work for a company or for themselves. Self-employed consultants make contacts with several lighting companies in order to present a wide range of styles and prices to clients.

Kitchen designers and planners specialize in designing attractive, functional kitchens. They might design kitchens for new houses or redesign kitchens in older homes. Kitchen planners are employed by kitchen cabinet manufacturers, home improvement centers, and residential homebuilders. Many are self-employed, too.

Kitchen planners first make floor plans of the interior space. They prepare the plans to scale, showing the placement of all cabinets, appliances, and other furnishings. They may recommend certain cabinets, appliances, floor and wall treatments, and color schemes. Estimates are prepared for all costs of equipment and supplies.

In some cases, the kitchen planner simply creates the plans, leaving the homeowner to execute them as desired. At other times, the kitchen planner oversees the entire kitchen design project to the client's satisfaction. He or she coordinates the work of the cabinet and appliance installers, wallpaper hangers, painters, and lighting specialists.

Commercial interior designers work with public buildings such as shopping centers, restaurants, schools, offices, and government buildings. Their activities may include the design, selection, and placement of furnishings and accessories. Their work is similar to residential interior designers, but their clients' needs are much different from those of families. The preferences of a larger group of people must be considered. Furnishings should accommodate the many people using the facilities, 18-5.

Commercial interior designers work within the budget limitations of the organization. They draw up specifications and a **bid**, or a price estimate for a project, and present them to the clients. The clients then choose the bid that is most favorable. When a contract is accepted, the designer is responsible for fulfilling the terms of the agreement.

Designers are also employed in home furnishings departments of stores, companies, and businesses. Besides creating model room arrangements, they assist customers with various decorating needs. Some designers may work with building contractors in housing subdivisions. The decorator plans color schemes and selects furnishings for the builders' model homes. Mobile home manufacturers employ decorators to plan and coordinate their home interiors.

Some designers work with specific aspects of decorating. In the entertainment industry, designers create sets, backgrounds, and props for movies, television, or theatrical productions.

18-5 Commercial interior designers must consider the many needs of a business when creating efficient and attractive work and meeting spaces.

Jo Ann Hartman Adams
Interior Designer

As an interior designer, Jo Ann Hartman Adams works with clients who have home or office decorating needs. She may design window treatments, plan an office arrangement, or completely redecorate a house. Some clients may need help choosing new furniture or color schemes. Others may need the right decorating accent for their home.

"Work varies from client to client," reports Jo Ann (shown here on the left). "Each project creates a different challenge." For one project, she planned the decorating design for a family with twelve children. The high traffic in the family's living area created problems in choosing carpeting and furnishings. By using a thicker pad and commercial-grade carpeting for the stairway, the heavy-traffic area problem was greatly reduced.

Do people always agree with Jo Ann's choices? "Many clients have their own ideas," Jo Ann laughs. "I try to guide them. Sometimes people find a piece of artwork and want to decorate the room around it. I give them pros and cons, and tell them how they should balance the color if they use it. There is no right or wrong way to decorate." It is important for an interior designer to remember that the house must express the client's personality, not their own. That's where creativity comes in.

Most clients call to arrange a consultation for work they want done. Sometimes, though, people come into the store to browse and ask her questions. From there, they decide to work with her on a project. Jo Ann has helped restore historic homes, and one of her design projects became the setting for a scene in a movie!

"Getting along with people is more important than art," Jo Ann continues. "If clients don't trust you, they won't accept the design. You must have the clients' best interests at heart."

An exciting part of her work is seeing all the new home furnishings products that are introduced every six months—furniture styles, fabric collections, rug designs, and color schemes. This is one of the reasons why every project is different and why interior design work is never boring.

Rich Sistos Photography

Joan M. Eisenberg
Kitchen and Bath Design Consultant

Joan Eisenberg is a Certified Kitchen and Bath Designer. This prestigious certification, awarded by the National Kitchen and Bath Association, indicates that she has completed specialized courses and passed a rigorous certification examination.

Incorporating her knowledge of design and efficiency, Joan works to create a dream kitchen or bath for her clients. She says, "I like the creativity involved, and the job allows me to interact with people. The personal satisfaction gained by seeing my ideas go from paper to reality is tremendous."

Joan first meets clients at their house to talk about their needs and take room measurements. She makes preliminary, rough-scaled drawings and discusses ideas with the clients. "The primary goal is to create efficient, safe, and aesthetically pleasing spaces that reflect the clients' needs and lifestyle," Joan says.

"At this point, the client is window-shopping for products to use," Joan explains. "Then I use CAD to do most of the drawing." Once the design and products are determined, contractors can bid on the job. As an independent design consultant, Joan does not sell any products.

Since there were no CAD programs when Joan was in college, her knowledge of CAD is self-taught. "There are three or four kitchen design programs. I researched them, bought one, and taught myself to use it." She has now upgraded her program three times.

According to Joan, deadlines are usually determined by the client. "However, once the

foundation of a project is in, I have to guide the clients through each decision to make sure the project isn't held up," she explains. Joan has worked on restoring historic homes and designing the most modern structures, from small townhomes to some of the largest homes available.

Historic preservation is a relatively new area for interior designers. With the increased emphasis in many towns and cities to preserve their heritage, many decorators focus on restoring older homes. They search for antiques or reproductions of architectural features and furnishings. They may work for historical societies, architectural firms, art galleries, museums, or individuals.

Furniture Designer

Furniture designers create furniture styles for manufacturing firms. They may work on a particular specialty, such as historical period furniture or outdoor furniture. They sketch the designs and prepare the specifications of materials. They may also oversee the construction of the furniture. Those designers who have developed a popular line may become independent business owners.

Furniture designers know details about period furnishings throughout history. They have a thorough knowledge of styles, woods and other materials, and finishes. They must have an understanding of trends and use good design principles. Some well-established designers custom design furniture for specific customer needs. These designers usually have a reputation for fine craftsmanship.

Display Artist

Display artists and designers use their artistic talents in visual merchandising. **Visual merchandising** is the promotion of a store's image through its storefront, interior decor, and merchandise displays. Together, these create presentations that encourage consumers to pause, admire, and buy the items displayed.

Display artists work in all areas of a store. Window displays should be striking to attract attention and bring people into the store. The interior decoration might be an indication of the merchandise price range. For example, stores offering superior goods might have an elegant look, while a discount store's decorating would be minimal. Display artists might change store decorations seasonally. Merchandise displays focus on particular items, including those on sale. Display artists and store managers determine the theme. Then, the designers use their talent to make attractive displays, 18-6.

Floral Designer

Floral designers need a keen sense of color and design whether they work with fresh flowers or artificial arrangements. Floral designers work for florists in greenhouses or other business

University of Wisconsin-Stout

18-6 Display artists use clothing that will attract customers' attention.

establishments. They often provide floral arrangements for weddings, funerals, birthdays, and other occasions. They may plan floral and plant arrangements for showrooms and often help prepare them. Florists work under tight time constraints to provide fresh flowers at their peak.

Floral designers know the characteristics of each plant so they can use it to its best advantage. For this reason, they may also study botany and horticulture in addition to design.

◆ Art Careers in Food, Nutrition, and Wellness

Many careers that blend family and consumer sciences with the arts exist in the foods area. Food is most appealing when it looks appetizing. Chefs, bakers, food stylists, and photographers all know the importance of an attractive presentation. These careers all require creative abilities and the desire to want to make food dishes look their best.

Food Stylist

Food stylists arrange the food for the mouth-watering pictures you see in magazines and cookbooks. They produce a visual effect to emphasize a particular selling point. With the help of a photographer, stylists can create images that make food look steaming hot or icy cold and refreshing. They know the characteristics of various foods and how to display them to their best advantage.

Food stylists need a good sense of design to present the food in the most appealing way. They must consider color, shape, and form. Stylists also must know the effects of lighting. Food that looks juicy on a plate may appear dry in the photograph. Some food stylists work on staffs of food companies and magazines while others work independently.

Cake Decorator

Cake decorators are employed by bakeries and caterers. Some specialize in special-occasion cakes, such as wedding or birthday cakes. The art of cake decorating requires creativity, skill, and practice. Cakes prepared for special occasions are usually displayed as centerpieces before being served to guests, 18-7.

The decorator's main tool is a pastry bag filled with icing. Special shaped tubes are attached to the bag to create different designs as the icing is squeezed out. Cake decorating techniques require design ability and careful control.

Pastry Chef

Pastry chefs make baked goods such as cakes, pastries, and pies for restaurants and bakery shops. Some of their desserts, such as cream

18-7 Beautifully decorated cakes can sometimes be works of art.

Stevie Bass
Food Stylist

Stevie Bass is a food consultant who works as a food stylist. Stevie says, "I love cooking and art. Preparing food to look its best for a photograph is a type of art." Food photos may be used in a variety of ways, including brochures, cookbooks, advertising, packaging, and newspaper food pages.

There are several steps to Stevie's job. First she designs a layout of how the food and props will be arranged. "I meet with the clients to determine if the arrangement will satisfy their needs and whether they like the look," she explains. Then she selects props and buys groceries that will be needed for the photo. She prepares any food or recipes that may be made ahead.

On the day of the photo shoot, Stevie prepares the food and sets up the arrangement in front of the camera. Each setting may have a different theme. All the food products and props are arranged; then a final "grooming" makes the food in the picture appear fresh and appetizing.

"I work fast to keep the food looking fresh," Stevie explains. Exposure to hot lights for long periods of time makes food look dry. She brushes on a little water or corn syrup to keep food looking as natural as possible, but avoids using other chemicals. Then, those at the shoot can eat the food later.

"Time is a constant consideration in food photography," Stevie reports. "We always have deadlines to meet. We schedule the shoots for certain days, and sometimes people have to fly in from different parts of the country. We have to be ready for them so the project goes smoothly."

The workday doesn't end until everyone is happy with the shots. Some subjects are harder than others, so food stylists must be flexible and willing to work long hours. Stevie especially likes having many different clients. "You have to feel comfortable working with people and different personalities, be a good listener, and give 100 percent effort."

puffs, strudels, or tortes, are more elaborate. Pastry dough is folded or rolled into complex shapes. Some pastries are then filled with custard, cream, or jam. Chefs painstakingly decorate the pastries with intricate designs. These delicate desserts are delicious and elegant works of art. Pastry chefs must possess artistic talent as well as a great deal of patience.

◆ Other Careers in the Arts

Art abilities and creativity are important in the other family and consumer sciences areas beyond food, fashion, and interior design. There is a need to incorporate color, form, texture, balance, and unity in many aspects of the environment.

Professionals in human services, for example, sometimes use the arts to stir patients' imagination and sense of accomplishment. Those in child development are especially attuned to the importance of color and other art principles in their work and play with children. Hotels, restaurants, theaters, and other establishments in the hospitality industry make strong use of art and design in every aspect of their businesses. Even consumer and resource managers employ the arts to enhance the appearance of management tools. Attention to colors and pattern arrangement make tools more understandable and easier to use, too.

Whether your interests are in clothing, foods, interior design, or other areas of family and consumer sciences, you will find exciting job opportunities in the art and design field. The world of art has many careers for those with the talent and determination to succeed.

◆ Personal Skills and Abilities Needed for a Career in the Arts

People who are successful in the arts generally have some artistic talent. They must have an ability to apply art principles to materials, fashions, furnishings, or foods. Creativity and good taste are necessary in meeting most job requirements. They need an appreciation of art history as well as knowledge of social and economic conditions that influence current art design. The ability to follow and apply current trends is valuable.

For those careers such as interior designer and custom tailoring that involve work with clients, you need good interpersonal skills. Good organizational skills are also needed since these professionals work closely with others on projects. They need good communication skills to relate to customers, suppliers, dealers, and coworkers. Salesmanship helps them sell their work.

Computer skills are important, especially since many bookkeeping and organizational tasks are done on computers. Designers in all fields are using CAD to work more quickly and efficiently. Some computer skills can be learned on the job, but basic knowledge is necessary in any career.

Finishing the work within the specified time and budget restraints is important to the professional's reputation. They must be able to operate in a competitive environment and work well under pressure. Working hours can be long, especially when urgent tasks are being completed to meet a project deadline, 18-8.

One of the most important characteristics of designers is the ability to work well with clients. Designers must be sensitive to each client's individual needs and financial limitations. Above all, designers cannot impose their taste on clients, but should present good design alternatives to address different needs.

◆ Education and Training Needed for a Career in the Arts

The education needed for a career in the arts will vary depending on the specific job. A

Pendleton Woolen Mills

18-8 Designers often spend many hours creating designs.

bachelor of science degree is a basic requirement for entry to most of the design fields. Many design firms and department stores hire only graduates of four-year design programs.

A number of art and design schools award an associate degree for two years of study. Many employers accept this degree for employment. Specialized training or short courses are important for certain kinds of work, such as furniture design, dressmaking, and alterations. Vocational schools offer specialized courses in baking and cake decorating.

Some occupations, such as display artists, only require on-the-job training. Often these individuals obtain their jobs because of their superior design talent.

For art careers that are business oriented, courses in marketing, accounting, management, and business relations are recommended. Knowledge of mathematics is necessary for jobs that involve estimating costs, preparing bids, determining measurements, and writing specifications, 18-9. Other required courses may include art, science, drafting, color analysis,

architecture, landscape design, and art history. Computer courses in CAD are necessary for today's designers since most firms do work with computers.

Most interior designers are graduates of four-year college programs approved by the American Society of Interior Design (ASID). To have *ASID* accreditation after their name, individuals must obtain a bachelor's degree and pass a written and practical examination.

Kitchen designers need to pass special tests to practice as Certified Kitchen Designers and display *CKD* after their names. Many have B.S. degrees and some also have ASID certification. The kitchen and bathroom are the most challenging rooms to plan and design. This requires certified professionals to develop their specialized knowledge through extensive experience and on-the-job training. These professionals must take continuing courses to maintain their certification. A list of family and consumer sciences careers in the art and design field is shown in 18-10.

18-9 Working with measurements and estimating costs are routine tasks for interior designers.

Future Trends

Career opportunities in the art and design field should continue to expand. Homes are being redesigned to keep up with current lifestyles and make space for new appliances invented through new technology. More families have home-based businesses and redesign portions of their homes for those needs. With the current trend in fitness, families often need space for exercise equipment. More families prefer to live, socialize, and entertain in "great rooms" created by removing walls that often separate kitchens, dining rooms, and living rooms. All these changes create demand for designers and decorators.

Family needs are constantly changing, and research is required to anticipate these needs.

What will families in the next century require? How will energy be conserved in the future? What impact will these factors have on fabrics, housing, and design? Considering current environmental conditions, these questions must be addressed. New technology will offer new products and techniques to help tackle these challenges. Specialists in various fields will need to stay abreast of these advances through continuous training updates.

As you have seen, there are many career possibilities in the arts relating to family and consumer sciences. Your talents and interests, whether they are in clothing, foods, or housing, may direct you toward the art and design field. To be a good designer, you should enjoy creating a sense of satisfaction, comfort, and pleasure for others.

Careers in the Arts

Entry Level	Fashion illustrator	Wardrobe consultant
Craftsperson	Fashion photographer	**College Degree**
Lawn maintenance worker	Floral arranger	Architect
Model	Floral designer	Art conservator
Personal shopper	Food stylist	Art teacher
Advanced Training	Furniture designer	Creative director
Alterations specialist	Furniture refinisher	Fashion director
Art appraiser	Garment maker	Fashion historian
Cake decorator	Home lighting consultant	Furniture historian
Chef	Image consultant	Interior designer
Conservator	Interior decorator	Kitchen designer
Costume curator	Jewelry designer	Landscape designer
Costume designer	Pastry chef	Package designer
Display artist	Pattern maker	Textile colorist
Dressmaker	Personal color analyst	Textile designer
Fabric designer	Tailor	Visual merchandiser
Fashion designer	Theater costume designer	

18-10 Would any of these careers interest you?

Summary

Family and consumer sciences professionals in the arts develop designs that reflect current interests, needs, and trends. Many careers that deal with textiles, interiors, and food place a heavy emphasis on art and design. Technological advances are expanding opportunities in this field.

Careers in textiles and apparel include textile designers, textile colorists, textile stylists, fashion designers, fashion illustrators, and photographers. Commercial pattern companies employ pattern makers, designers, and dressmakers. Wardrobe and color consultants work with clients to help them make good decisions regarding their appearance.

Residential interior designers strive to improve living and working spaces for individual families. Some specialize in designing products that enhance living. Commercial interior designers plan interiors for buildings used by the public. Other career possibilities in the area of environmental design include lighting consultants, kitchen designers, furniture designers, and historic preservationists.

Professionals involved with presenting food to the public know the value of appetizing appearance. Food stylists prepare dishes to look their best in photos. Pastry chefs and cake decorators incorporate principles of design into their creations.

Many professionals in art-related careers graduate from approved design programs. They take classes in art, sciences, math, business, and computer graphics. Additional training may be necessary for specializations. Designers should have aptitudes and abilities in applying art principles to interior space and consumer products. Because designers work with many resource people and customers, they also need good interpersonal skills.

To Review

1. What is the difference between textile designers and fashion designers?

2. Where do fashion designers get their ideas for new styles of clothing?

3. Why is computer experience helpful in many careers in the arts?

4. What is the goal of a fashion illustrator?

5. What is the difference between residential and commercial interior designers?

6. Name the three elements of visual merchandising.

7. Describe the job of a food stylist.

8. Name four personal skills or abilities needed for a career in the arts.

9. How does new technology create a demand for professionals in the housing and interior design field?

To Do

1. Write an essay on how a background in family and consumer sciences can prepare you for careers in the arts.

2. Research the career of a famous fashion designer. Write a report on how his or her designs affected trends.

3. Suggest decorating ideas for a room in your house. Find illustrations in magazines to use as possible suggestions.

4. Go to a local store. How do the store's displays and decor affect your attitude about the merchandise? Give an oral report to the class.

5. Interview a cake decorator or baker to find out where he or she received training. Ask how he or she uses artistic abilities on the job.

6. Brainstorm changes in our environment that may influence clothing and housing in the future.

19

A Career as an Entrepreneur

After studying this chapter, you will be able to
◆ list the pros and cons of business ownership.
◆ describe the basic types of businesses.
◆ explain different business entry opportunities for entrepreneurs.
◆ describe the ways that businesses are organized legally.
◆ identify the responsibilities of entrepreneurs in operating a business.
◆ point out entrepreneurial opportunities in family and consumer sciences.

Terms to Know

entrepreneurship	unlimited liability
venture	partnership
retailer	corporation
wholesaler	shareholder
inventory	fixed expense
consignment	flexible expense
franchise	business plan
sole proprietorship	bankruptcy

Mary smiled as she recalled the day she quit her job. Her coworkers gave her a plaque that read: "Find a job you enjoy and you'll never work again." "How true," she thought. She risked a good job with a large corporation to turn her grandmother's old home into a bed-and-breakfast. Repairing the house required considerable work and money, but her careful planning made the business a success. She was right in believing that people would enjoy her home for overnight lodging and breakfast.

"I work many more hours now," she says, "but I get to set those hours, and they're a lot more fun. It doesn't even seem like work!" This is how a person feels when lifestyle and vocation go well together. You'll never hear that person say, "Oh no! I have to go back to that job again."

When your work draws on your natural talents and abilities, you enjoy it more. Also, you are more likely to do the job well. Many people fail to realize that what they enjoy doing and have a talent for doing could be combined into a source of income.

Most people find joy and fulfillment working for others, but some want more independence in their lives. They want the flexibility and the opportunity to develop their particular talents and make more money. It's this drive for financial and personal freedom that sparks the ambition of many would-be business managers. Owning and operating a successful business is often a part of the American Dream.

In this chapter, you will learn about being an entrepreneur. An entrepreneur is a person who starts a new business. Entrepreneurs invest their time, money, and energy into building a business that will become successful. See 19-1. They assume all the risk, and then reap the rewards if the business is a success. They also inherit the headaches if the business fails.

Gettysburg Travel

19-1 A person who operates a bed-and-breakfast is an example of an entrepreneur.

Skills in family and consumer sciences lend themselves well to small-business possibilities. There are a number of related jobs that individuals can start as independent businesses. In this chapter you will learn different ways of starting and operating a business. After completing the chapter, you will know better if entrepreneurship is for you. **Entrepreneurship** is taking the risk of developing and managing a new business.

◆ Entrepreneurship and Our Economy

Our economic system originated with entrepreneurs. Over the years, they contributed talents and technology to the business world and countless goods and services to everyday life. Entrepreneurs literally make something from nothing. In the process, they create new jobs and provide employment for millions of workers.

Sometimes an entrepreneur's new business is called a **venture.** This term comes from the word *adventure*. It implies risk, challenges, and even danger. This is a very fitting term for new businesses because about 80 percent of them fail. The primary causes of failure are inadequate financing and poor management, according to the Small Business Administration (SBA). The SBA is a government agency that assists individuals with developing and operating a small business.

Another cause of business failure is providing products or services that consumers no longer want. Other businesses fail because their competitors offer a better product, a lower price, or better service.

A new business that succeeds usually remains relatively small and local. Entrepreneurs of new businesses must often work hard just to survive. Some business ventures that start with just one person ultimately grow into large, well-known companies with branches around the world. The Microsoft Corporation, the Coca-Cola Company, and McDonald's Corporation are some examples. These, however, are the exceptions rather than the rule.

In spite of the high failure rate of new businesses, people with drive and determination will continue to create them. They believe that, with hard work and the right product or service, they will beat the odds. Certainly, there are plenty of successful examples to inspire them.

To a large extent, the future of our economic well-being rests on the ideas created by entrepreneurs. People are needed who are willing to take a chance with a new idea. Creative innovators and an economy that encourages them are the reasons consumers in this country enjoy a wealth of products and services today. See 19-2.

19-2 Consumers of all ages, even children, benefit from the variety of products created by entrepreneurs.

The Pros and Cons of Entrepreneurship

There are advantages (pros) and disadvantages (cons) to owning your own business. Perhaps the greatest advantage is doing what you like best and getting paid for it. There is also the freedom to work whenever and at whatever you want. You can hire whomever you want to work for you. If you work at home, your travel or commuting problems are solved.

Entrepreneurs like the challenge of developing a new company. Planning business strategies and negotiating with others is very exciting to them. Seeing a business plan become a reality can be a very rewarding experience. There also is the potential for high income.

Many home-based businesses were started because of the pressure on two-career families with children. Having one or both parents work at home while the children are young has helped parents combine work with child care responsibilities. In this way, someone can stay at home with the children and still earn a living.

There are many drawbacks or disadvantages to the seemingly ideal life of an entrepreneur. First, very little money is made during the start-up phase. Entrepreneurs take great financial risks in starting and operating a business. They must work long hours to keep their business profitable. Some say this is the most difficult period in the life of a new business.

Another disadvantage is the difficulty in getting away on vacations, holidays, or weekends. The work is nonstop and there are no paid benefits beyond what you provide for yourself. Consider, too, there are no insurance benefits, unemployment compensation, retirement benefits, or paid sick leave. You must provide all of these when you work for yourself.

Those who have children and work at home experience many distractions in their day. They often are forced to hire someone to watch the children while they do their work. If they wait until the children go to bed, they may not be working during their prime time. An at-home office may not present a very business-like atmosphere to clients if there are frequent interruptions. Having friends visit or children play nearby during work hours can hurt the business

Some believe a business takes over your life. If you own a business, you eat, drink, breathe, and sleep your work. Sometimes it is difficult to know where to draw the line between working long enough to establish the business and working too much. Entrepreneurs must constantly use creativity and new ways of approaching problems in order to cope with the many challenges they encounter.

When one entrepreneur began her decorating business, she spent most of her time at work. She believed working 80 hours a week was necessary to meet the workload. The overwhelming number of hours spent at her business meant she had to live with the guilt of staying away from her family so often. For some, spending time away from the family to work at the business may threaten their personal life.

Many business owners say the independence, freedom, and self-satisfaction they get by working for themselves is worth all the sacrifice. Potential entrepreneurs, however, should consider beforehand how much risk they are willing to take. They also should think about how much of their personal life they are willing to change or sacrifice for a business.

The Successful Entrepreneur

Although there is no single personality type required for becoming an entrepreneur, certain qualities seem to help. See 19-3. The following characteristics are typical of successful entrepreneurs:

They plan to succeed. Persons who choose self-employment do not think in terms of failure. They plan carefully and are committed to their goal of achieving success.

Personal Qualifications of Entrepreneurs
Carefully read the following list of qualifications to help you decide if entrepreneurship is for you.
◆ You believe that working hard is important and a way of life.
◆ You have a deep interest in a particular subject.
◆ You want to gain control over your own life and future.
◆ You communicate well and delegate authority to others.
◆ You are goal-oriented.
◆ You accomplish tasks quickly and efficiently.
◆ You like to solve problems.
◆ You see yourself succeeding in life.
◆ You are willing to work long after others have stopped for the day.

19-3 Did you realize that running a business would require so much personal effort?

They choose a challenge over security. Staying with the same employer and doing familiar work provides stability in life. While many people feel very comfortable with this stability, some become bored. They like the opportunity of tackling challenges. Do you like to "play it safe" or take a chance?

They are very self-confident. They believe in themselves and in what they can do. They know they can get the job done. They also are realistic and know the limits of their abilities. They are not afraid to ask for help or hire people who have the skills they need.

They have a high degree of motivation and drive. They do not sit on the sidelines and observe others. They want to get involved in the action!

They carefully organize their time and tasks. Organization is the key to any startup endeavor. They know how to approach their work and what steps are needed to complete it.

They are creative. Being creative is an important characteristic for entrepreneurs. They must constantly use creativity and imagination to find solutions to all possible problems.

Do you have these qualities? Successful entrepreneurs possess a combination of these skills and much more. They thrive on constant pressure and enjoy making decisions. As a successful entrepreneur, you must decide every detail of the business or hire talented people to help you make decisions.

◆ Types of Businesses

One of the first aspects of entrepreneurship an individual must decide is the type of business to operate. Depending on the primary activity, a business is classified as one of five basic types. It produces raw materials, processes raw materials, manufactures a product, sells goods, or provides a service.

Producing Raw Materials

Some businesses are concerned with taking raw materials from nature and selling them unchanged. These jobs are in agriculture, forestry, mining, and commercial fishing. Examples of self-employment in these areas include raising houseplants, flowers, fruits, vegetables, and Christmas trees. Other possibilities include raising livestock or poultry, mining for minerals, or fishing.

Processing Raw Materials

Processing is a step that changes a raw material grown in nature into a more useable form. These businesses work with the products harvested from agriculture, forestry, or fishing operations, or retrieved from mining, 19-4. Examples of self-employment in these areas include cutting wood for fireplaces, using wool from sheep for sweaters and other products, and grinding wheat into flour.

19-4 This logging operation is an example of a business that processes raw materials.

Manufacturing Products

This step takes a raw material that has been processed, such as flour, and transforms it into a finished product, such as bread. Goods in a department store or in the packaged-foods department of supermarkets are examples of manufactured products.

Sometimes manufactured products are component parts that go into other products. For example, a coat is a manufactured product, but so are the items used to make the coat. These include the buttons, zippers, shoulder pads, thread, trim, outer cloth, and inner lining. Usually component parts are manufactured by different businesses that specialize in their respective products.

Manufacturing businesses are perhaps the riskiest for entrepreneurs because they may require a large investment. Manufacturers must pay for all the items needed to make the products before any are sold. For example, a button manufacturer must pay for production equipment and button-making materials before selling the first button. Other initial costs might include buying a building and paying for a labor force.

To stay in business, manufacturers must know what the customer wants and have a steady, reliable market for their products. For example, the market for Nancy Croft's specialty cracker business has grown from her home state of Wisconsin to 47 other states. See 19-5. Besides baking specialty items, self-employment opportunities in manufacturing include making furniture, knitting scarves, and making all types of crafts and wearable items.

Selling Goods

This type of business brings manufactured products to buyers. Products can be sold

Croft's Crackers

19-5 Nancy's business has made cinnamon-sugar and wheat crackers for specialty shops since 1987.

through door-to-door selling, mail-order businesses, retailers, and wholesalers. Department and grocery stores are examples of retailers. A **retailer** is a business that sells products directly to consumers. A **wholesaler** is a business that sells products to retailers. Many types of consumer products are sold by mail order through catalogs or the Internet. Selling products door-to-door, however, is rarely used because people are at home less often.

In a sales business, you carry and sell the merchandise that reflects your interests. An **inventory** is a supply of goods kept in stock for a ready sale. Keeping an inventory assures that you won't be out of stock when a customer makes a major purchase!

On the other hand, buying too much inventory or the wrong kind of product may cause you to lose money. For example, consider retailers who buy an inventory of bright colored shirts when earth tones become fashionable. The goods must be sold at a much lower price than planned, and perhaps below their cost. Staying abreast of customer trends is vital to a sales business.

Losing money with unwanted inventory is avoided when the business sells goods "on consignment." **Consignment** is a selling arrangement whereby a seller displays a product, but the manufacturer maintains ownership until it is purchased. With this arrangement, the seller gives the product display and storage space and receives a percentage of the sale if it is sold. If not sold, the item is returned to the manufacturer and the retailer loses no money.

Financially, consignment is a much safer arrangement for the seller. Craft boutiques often use consignment agreements to sell goods from different crafters in the area.

Other examples of self-employment opportunities include operating an antique furniture shop or a cooking equipment or fashion accessories store. The bookkeeping is somewhat involved with sales businesses, so detailed records must be kept of inventory and sales.

Providing a Service

A service business requires the smallest financial investment and has the simplest bookkeeping. At-home service businesses are the easiest to operate. Before you start any business, however, you must be very good at what you do.

The service area provides the best opportunity for young people to gain experience as entrepreneurs. Caring for children and running errands are possibilities for at-home service businesses requiring minimum education levels.

Other possibilities include housecleaning or home delivery services. Some teens have become "house sitters" by taking care of homes while their owners are away. Tasks may include caring for houseplants, animals, or the yard, or simply visiting the homes to give them a "lived in" look. (For more ideas that teens might turn into money-making ventures, review the entry-level jobs listed in Chapters 14 through 18 of this text.)

After gaining experience, individuals can start a business involving furniture repair, estate sales, car repair, graphic arts, and web design. Desktop publishing software has made it possible for individuals to go into the business of publishing and printing high-quality materials. With a small investment in equipment and materials, they can create materials of professional quality.

For professionals with a college degree, consulting may be a good career option. Professionals who hold consulting positions include marriage counselors, public relations planners, advertising coordinators, interior design specialists, and financial advisors. Wardrobe and color consultants, hotel menu planners, recipe development experts, kitchen designers, and food stylists also work as consultants. See 19-6. Success as a consultant requires extensive work experience, proof that you have received the required training and knowledge, and references from satisfied clients.

◆ Business Entry Opportunities

After deciding the type of work that appeals most to you, you must determine how to enter the business world as an entrepreneur. There are four basic ways. You can start an entirely new business, buy an existing business, buy a franchise, or join the family business.

Starting a New Business

Many would-be entrepreneurs prefer to start a brand new business for several reasons. They are free to operate the business however they want. Often they can use their home to turn a hobby into a profit-making venture. Also, they may like the challenge of charting a new course and solving start-up problems.

One disadvantage of an at-home business is the lack of an established base of customers. A bigger disadvantage is the absence of any record of success. This makes it difficult to get a new business loan. Banks and other lenders

19-6 This consultant presents food products to selected consumers to examine their reactions and recommendations.

Kenneth Ivory
Hospitality Consulting

Kenneth Ivory is the founder and chief executive officer of a hospitality consulting firm focusing on leadership dynamics, executive coaching, team building, and keynote presentations. He is a foodservice expert with over 15 years experience in the hospitality industry, serving with well-known companies in positions from foodservice manager to vice president of operations.

Kenneth's firm is dedicated to helping clients exceed their customers' expectations. He provides assistance with menu design, food and labor cost analysis, inventory control, forecasting, and staff planning. His management development programs offer training in team dynamics, guest services, personality styles, and diversity issues, among other topics.

"Success is measured by how well we make a positive difference in the lives of the people we serve," Kenneth believes, "and our associates are the keys to success." This viewpoint, he feels, applies equally to both profit-making and non-profit operations.

Much of the reason for Kenneth's success is his habit of working as a "servant leader." During his foodservice career, he always carried his lab coat so he could "dig right into preparing food and washing dishes" whenever possible. "That's what a leader has to do to encourage his troops," he says. He now consults other businesses on the value of adopting a strategy of "servant leadership" as a management tool.

Kenneth's love for working with food began when his cousin, a member of Family, Career, and Community Leaders of America (FCCLA), introduced him to food classes in high school. His love for cooking was supported by his teachers and FCCLA advisors, who encouraged him to seriously consider a foodservice career.

With a "can do" attitude, Kenneth applied for a foodservice scholarship although it was reserved for a woman. His application caused the scholarship review committee to reconsider the .

sex requirements and offer the scholarship to both sexes. Naturally, Kenneth won the scholarship.

One of Kenneth's greatest joys was participating in his daughter's "show and tell" presentation at school. "I wore my chef's coat and hat and worked with simple fruits and vegetables that first-graders like to eat. I like to spark youngsters' interest in food," explains Kenneth proudly. Teachers and students haven't stopped talking about it.

He feels very strongly about community involvement. Kenneth makes frequent motivational presentations to young people, convincing them to pursue their dreams. Kenneth tells students to remain focused, motivated, and committed to a chosen career. "Make your dream a reality," he says. "Do not get discouraged because the road to success is always under construction."

prefer to loan money to established businesses because struggling businesses may not make enough money to pay back loans.

Buying an Existing Business

Buying an established business is easier and safer than starting a new enterprise. If the business has been successful, you will gain customers immediately. You can count on all the people who regularly buy the company's products or services to continue doing so. Consequently, you won't need to spend much money in advertising to explain who you are and what you sell. Then, too, the employees are already trained and will probably remain with the company. Loyal customers and knowledgeable employees are valuable assets.

If the owner is eager to sell the business, you may be able to negotiate a favorable price. You should, however, check to make sure you really are getting a bargain. You will want to know why the current owner is selling. Is it because of retirement, ill health, or other business interests, or is it because of declining sales? Perhaps there is too much competition in the field or decreasing demand for the product or service. Maybe the product or service appeals to customers who have moved away. The building may be too far from other shopping facilities, or parking may be a problem. Perhaps the equipment or inventory is outdated. All areas must be thoroughly explored before buying an existing business.

Owning a Franchise

A **franchise** is a binding agreement to sell a company's goods or services in a certain area. Independent business people who buy a franchise are called *franchisees*. A franchised business is a branch member of an already-existing company, called the *franchisor*. The franchisor uses franchisees to sell goods or services at the local level. Franchised businesses have a greater degree of success than independent businesses. You may be familiar with several franchises, such as McDonald's restaurants, Best Western motels, and Baskin Robbins ice cream shops. See 19-7.

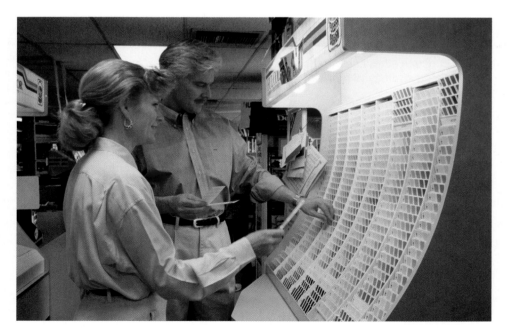

19-7 Franchises such as hardware stores are usually less risky than other types of entrepreneurial ventures.

If you buy a franchise, you have the right to use the company's name and image, its advertising, and other services. Major advantages include financial assistance and management training by the franchisor. Entrepreneurs can also take advantage of the franchisor's experience and knowledge of proven methods and successful practices. In most cases, the franchisor provides continued assistance and guidance after the franchised business is in operation.

There are a number of disadvantages, too. There is an initial fee, or down payment, that costs thousands of dollars and does not include the building, supplies, or inventory. In addition, there is a royalty fee. A *royalty fee* is a percentage of sales that must be paid to the franchisor periodically for the life of the franchise. There also are restrictions and guidelines concerning how the franchise must operate. If a business does not meet the franchisor's standards, it affects the reputation of all the other stores. As a result, some franchisees feel they have very little control over their own business.

Before buying a franchise, read the contract carefully. It should give you the option to cancel the franchise agreement. Choosing the right franchise and the right location are crucial to the success of the business.

Joining the Family Business

An increasing number of people are looking to the family business as their career choice. Many see this as a quicker way to an upper management position than would be possible in other businesses. Some combine working in the business with caring for children at home. Often the children, too, work in the business and are familiar with its operation. There is the added benefit of support and encouragement by family members.

Getting involved in a family business is not free of problems. Often it is the cause of many problems involving relationships and authority. Each member's responsibilities must be clearly understood so that friction does not arise over workload, business decisions, and money. Family members must operate as a team. For many people, continuing in a family business offers a good income and compatible lifestyle.

The commitment to keeping the business successful often is deep-rooted in family history and tradition. If an ancestor started the business, there is pride, satisfaction, and the determination to "keep it in the family."

Legal Ownership of Businesses

The legal ownership of a business can be established in three ways. The business can be organized as a sole proprietorship, partnership, or corporation. A business selects the type that best suits its interests. If it is decided later that a different type of organization would be more beneficial, the legal ownership can be changed to suit business needs. For example, a sole proprietorship can change to a corporation later.

Often the size of the business or the number of owners will determine the type of legal organization that is best for the business. There are advantages and disadvantages to each of the three types.

Sole Proprietorship

Most small businesses begin as sole proprietorships. A **sole proprietorship** is a business owned by only one person. For example, Charla Draper's business is an example of a sole proprietorship because the business is owned entirely by her.

This type of legal ownership is the most common form for U.S. businesses. Sole proprietorships are the easiest and simplest businesses to form. With this type of ownership, you have complete control over the operation and the profits, 19-8.

A major disadvantage of sole proprietorships is unlimited liability. **Unlimited liability** is a legal obligation that makes a business owner

19-8 Sole proprietors have total control over their business, but must handle all the work themselves.

responsible for all business-related debts. If the business owner has bills that go unpaid, the owner can be ordered by a court to pay the bills. In practical terms, unlimited liability means that personal property such as savings accounts, cars, and homes can be taken to pay business debts.

Partnership

A **partnership** is a business owned by two or more people. One of the biggest advantages of a partnership is the partners can pool their money to start a larger business. They can combine their individual skills and knowledge to bring more talent to the new business. For example, one partner may be skilled at keeping records, and the other, at selling. Partnership agreements should define each partner's responsibilities and the method for dividing profits.

Partnerships have the highest failure rate of the three types of business structures. With authority divided, problems can often arise. A partnership is dissolved at any time that one partner chooses to leave. The biggest disadvantage of partnerships is that each partner has unlimited liability and, therefore, responsibility for all business debts. To settle a debt, any or all of the partners may be sued.

Corporation

A **corporation** is a business that receives written authority from a state to form and operate. Establishing this type of ownership requires more time and money than other forms of legal ownership. Once established, or incorporated, the business is subject to numerous state and federal laws. A corporation has a legal "life" of its own which continues even after the founders and owners die.

One or more individuals who are called shareholders own a corporation. A **shareholder** is part owner of a corporation. Ownership occurs when an individual buys the company's stock. *Stock* is one portion, or share, of the company's total worth. A shareholder is also called a stockholder.

Company profits are split in proportion to the number of shares owned by each shareholder. Voting rights in the company are also based on the amount of stock owned. Shareholders decide important company matters, such as who serves on the board of directors. Usually, the company founders are the biggest stockholders.

Corporations can expand more easily than partnerships and sole proprietorships because they can sell stock to attract funds. The personal savings and belongings of shareholders cannot be taken to pay the debts of the corporation. The most any stockholder can lose is the amount of money he or she has invested in the corporation.

Charla L. Draper
Food Consultant

Charla Draper is president and founder of a food consulting business that provides product promotion services to major food companies. In college she decided that she wanted to work in the food field, but consulting never entered her mind. That decision came later.

She developed her wide-ranging skills while working in the test kitchens and communications departments of several well-known food companies. After a corporate restructuring, her last employer eliminated several positions including hers. Charla realized that offering her services to many companies instead of just one was the best way to continue working in the field she loved.

"I decided to draw on the abilities I already possessed to create my own business," says Charla. She already had a rapport with many in the industry who would later become her clients. Her record of accomplishments was known and her educational credentials were excellent. She made all the right moves, even establishing her business in a city regarded as a food center.

Today her food consulting service specializes in food product promotion. Capabilities include recipe development, food styling, public relations, editorial services, and nutrition communications. Charla also judges and manages national recipe contests.

"Sometimes companies simply prefer to call me instead of using their employees for special or unique assignments," Charla reports. Her business also provides special expertise on programs involving diverse ethnic and cultural groups.

"There is no such thing as an average day in this business, and that's what I like most about consulting. You have to wear many hats because every project is different." Life as a consultant swings back and forth between slow periods and hectic days of nonstop activity. Sometimes deadlines change and projects must move faster.

Anyone considering consulting should examine how well an unpredictable environment suits them. "If you like routine, 9-to-5 workdays, this definitely is not the job for you," Charla warns.

Now that Charla works for herself, she wouldn't have it any other way. "I love the freedom this job offers and the fast-paced excitement. Imagine going to work everyday and not enjoying it—that would be very frustrating. Life is much too short to spend working at something that is not fulfilling."

For those considering a similar career, Charla recommends talking to teachers, counselors, and professionals in the field to learn about the variety of opportunities. Then, get hands-on experience by working in a related business in your community.

James Hollis

◆ Business Planning

It is best to have some working knowledge of the product or service you wish to turn into a business. Your present job or surroundings are good sources of ideas. Perhaps your business will involve a new idea or an improvement of an existing product or service. See 19-9.

Redesigning a product to meet a different need is how many household products began. The Kellogg Company, for example, did not intentionally make breakfast cereal. The company's original focus was making wheat flakes for health treatments in its sanitarium. Coca Cola was a liquid cure-all sold in an Atlanta pharmacy. Levi Strauss was overstocked with tent canvas made for the California Gold Rush and used the leftover material for miners' pants.

Teenagers, too, can start a business. It may be part-time work to make extra money or the beginning of a future career. No matter how simple or complex the business idea is, the following points must be considered during the planning stage.

Choose the Right Business

Think back to the first chapters in this book when you examined your interests and abilities. You identified your key aptitudes. For example, you may have discovered that you were a math whiz, but hated doing anything creative. Based on this, you probably would not enjoy making artistic T-shirts. You would be more suited to working with floor plans and calculating the amount of materials needed in building and remodeling projects.

Choose a type of work you can enjoy and perform well. Only then will you have the enthusiasm and stamina it takes to succeed.

After examining your interests and abilities, you will have a better idea of what kind of business you would like to operate. Are you the kind of person who has the interest and energy to run a child care center or cater wedding receptions? Could you sell produce, flowers, or herbs grown at home? Are you good at art and have samples you could sell? Can you design Web pages? Based on your interests and the needs of the marketplace, select a product or service you feel you can handle.

Consider Your Time and Responsibilities

Will you be the only one to manage your business? What must you do to get it organized? What will be your day-to-day responsibilities? Work through a typical day in your mind and on paper. List all the tasks needed to open and operate your business. If you have employees, list their jobs and responsibilities. In this way, everyone will know what is expected of him or her. See 19-10.

Will this be after-school work, a summer job, or something you would like to do full

J.C. Penney Co., Inc.

19-9 Every product or service available today started as an entrepreneur's dream.

19-10 If your business requires employee help, you must train them to have a clear understanding of their responsibilities.

time after graduation? Realistically think through your time schedule. Do you plan to participate in competitive sports or school activities? You may not have the time to devote to your business and to your outside activities. Will you need to spend more time studying this year? Managing a business can take a great deal of your time.

Research Market Needs

An important step in planning a business is researching a product or service that would meet the needs of the marketplace. Your community is a good place to begin. Consider what types of jobs thrive there and why. Obviously, there is a demand for the products or services they provide. Could you handle some of the same types of work?

It is important that you examine your idea from different angles. This can help you avoid the mistake of offering a product or service that

people do not want or will not buy. There isn't much business cleaning swimming pools in a northern climate where few pools exist. Neither is there much business as a children's party planner in an area with few children. Observe critically the people in your community and what they need.

Will you be able to have enough customers to make your business profitable? If you live in a rural area and decide to make cookies in your business, who will buy them? Could you deliver them to stores and restaurants or through a mail-order business? If you live in an area with a large population of retired people, what type of service or product would best meet their needs? Is there a demand for a general errand service?

Don't forget that computers and new technologies are opening the world of job possibilities and extending your reach beyond your community. If you can do your work with a computer and link electronically with others, it doesn't matter how many miles away your customers are.

Whether you live in the country or the city, there will always be business opportunities. Staying alert to the products and services that consumers want and need is where the adventure begins. For example, Dana Selin couldn't find a ski hat to protect her face from the sun. That search led her to creating her own hat-making business.

Identify Your Competition

Identify competition in the field. Who else is doing what you want to do? Can you do it better, faster, or cheaper than the others? Many businesses often compete for the same customers, but each offers something unique in their product or service. For example, when several restaurants are in the same locale, each offers a distinct theme and menu. If your dream business is similar to others nearby, ask yourself, "What can I do to make mine better?"

Estimate Expenses

Some businesses, such as tutoring at home, may not involve any extra costs. On the other hand, extra space may be needed for a design studio or a furniture-making workshop. How much will additional rental space cost? Do you need to get permits or licenses, and are there legal fees to pay?

Materials and supplies will also be needed to operate the business on a day-to-day basis. Separate your business costs into fixed and flexible expenses. A **fixed expense** is a business cost that occurs regularly and stays the same. Examples of fixed expenses are monthly bills for rent and insurance. Other fixed expenses include start-up costs, such as office equipment and telephone installation. These items are purchased only once to get the business started. You can estimate fixed monthly expenses and reserve a set amount per month for them.

A **flexible expense** is a business cost that varies according to the amount of business that occurs. For example, if you have a cake decorating business, summer weddings may keep you busier than the months of January and February. Consequently, you will need to spend more on supplies and air conditioning during the periods of high production and sales.

Decide the Price or Fee

Pricing your product or service is not as easy as it may seem. Of course, you will need to make a profit to stay in business, so the prices you charge must cover business expenses. Ideally, the profit from the business will raise enough money for your livelihood and for business expansion. See 19-11.

19-11 A daily account of income and expenses lets you know how well your business is doing. The detailed records are also used to determine the tax bill for your business.

Dana Selin
Designer

Dana Selin worked at a community college as an administrator and taught child development classes. She never considered owning a business, but unplanned events led her down that career path.

"I loved to ski, but my skin didn't adapt well to exposure to the sun," explains Dana. "Consequently, I was always looking for hats and coverings that would shield my skin." In spite of frequent shopping trips, Dana could never find a combination ski hat and sun shield.

While skiing in Colorado, she spotted a young man wearing a floppy wide-brimmed canvas hat. She knew that she wanted one just like it except with a wider brim to protect her face. "Since I couldn't find one, I decided to see what would happen if I tried to make my own," she says.

Dana purchased fabric, sewed a hat, and the rest is history. Her neighbor saw the hat and wanted one, so she gave it away and made another. Soon there were many requests for the hats. The popularity of her hat making led to a business that now keeps her busy throughout the year. She designs and manufactures hats and other products, using natural cotton canvas. The fabric is durable, lightweight, and water-repellent.

"It didn't take long before scraps of fabric from cutting the hats began to accumulate," says Dana. "I began to experiment with ways to make use of every bit of fabric because wasted fabric is lost money."

Countless hours of trial and error led to attractive bags with many pockets, carryall totes, book covers, table runners, place mats, and table napkins. Many of her creations include attractive designs of birds, leaves, flowers, or sailboats, which she creates with her computerized sewing machine. Dana markets her products through exhibits at art and craft fairs around the country and through wholesale accounts. "I especially enjoy the craft shows," says Dana, "because I can talk with customers and see their reaction to my products firsthand." Dana recalls an occasion when a customer bought hats for everyone attending a family reunion. The customer sent a picture of the smiling reunion group with everyone wearing the wide-brimmed canvas hats. "It's so satisfying to be in a business that makes you happy as well as others," Dana says proudly.

It is important to always know what your competitors are charging. You may want your prices to be lower than theirs to appeal to price-conscious customers. You may even decide to set prices below costs and lose some profit in the short term to attract customers. On the other hand, your product may have a special feature or added service that merits a price higher than the competition's.

Sometimes the prices you set can affect a product's image, or the way customers think about it. For example, consider the case of the young manufacturer who designed and made toy soldiers. He found that he could manufacture them very inexpensively. He priced them at $1.98 apiece, but sold very few. Later, he targeted his advertising to a different market and advertised them as "originals," which they were. He raised the price considerably and stores could not keep a supply on hand! You'll need to set a price that makes a profit, is competitive, and conveys the appropriate image.

Develop the Marketing Plan

Your marketing plan refers to the methods and activities you use to attract customers. Your first step in developing a marketing plan is to define your customers. Who will buy your product or service? Is your product geared more toward younger people or older people, the general population or certain population segments?

Recall the case of the toy soldier manufacturer. The toys stayed on the shelves collecting dust before the manufacturer took the time to identify the most likely buyers. Identifying those customers and targeting your advertising messages to them is the primary goal of marketing. You may have the best product in the world, but people won't buy it if they don't know it exists.

Creating a compatible package for the product and an appropriate sales setting are other marketing activities. Your plan may also include free samples, in-store demonstrations, contests, coupons, and other promotions to attract customers.

Develop a Business Plan

All planning considerations are tied together into a master plan called the business plan. A **business plan** is a written description of all the elements of a new business. For a list of items usually included in a business plan, see 19-12.

Some refer to a business plan as a road map, because it is detailed enough for a stranger to follow. A good business plan captures all of the entrepreneur's decisions on paper and clarifies operating details. Timetables are included to explain what will be accomplished and when.

A business plan can be as simple or as complex as the business. For example, the business plan for a part-time tailoring business will be shorter and simpler than next year's plan for the Coca-Cola Company.

Elements of a Business Plan
A thorough business plan includes the following nine elements:
◆ Description of the business idea
◆ Set of objectives for the company
◆ Description of the market and potential customers
◆ Report on competitors and competing products
◆ Strategy for selling the product or service
◆ Analysis of costs, pricing policy, and anticipated sales and profits
◆ Production plan (if the business provides a product)
◆ Marketing plan and timetable
◆ Financial plan

19-12 A business plan is a road map for establishing and operating a business.

Pati Palmer
Sewing Instructor, Author, and Publisher

For Pati Palmer, home sewing is a hobby, a career, a business, and a way of life. She takes great pride in knowing that her sewing ideas are considered fun, fast, easy, and fashionable.

Pati's first major accomplishment was taking the mystery out of sewing and fitting pants for all types of body proportions. "I wrote a how-to book on the subject," Pati recalls, "which became more popular than anyone could have imagined." She published the book herself and used the proceeds to create a diversified business, which she now heads.

Today the business is the largest publishing company in North America devoted solely to the field of home sewing. It produces sewing videos and instruction books, many of which Pati

coauthored. Topics range from garment tailoring and fitting to home decorating. The company also provides unusual or hard-to-find notions to fabric stores and consumers. Its products are marketed throughout the United States, Canada, England, Australia, and New Zealand.

One of the company's best-known ventures was designing patterns for major pattern companies. Working with a partner, Pati designed and wrote instructions for nearly 100 patterns. "Our eight-hour blazer pattern became the best-selling pattern in the history of the pattern industry shortly after it was introduced," Pati says proudly.

For 15 years, Pati and her associates presented sewing seminars for major department stores and sewing enthusiasts in the United States, Canada, and Australia. Pati estimates that over 10,000 home sewers were reached through 500 seminars yearly. Today Pati and her staff conduct sewing workshops and teacher training programs at the company's headquarters.

"Hands-on teaching keeps us in touch with the best and newest sewing ideas," says Pati. "Constant contact with home sewers and stores across the country help us write clear instructions and see trends before they happen." In addition, Pati and her staff keep abreast of fashion and consumer needs by researching the market, shopping, traveling, and just watching people.

Her high school debating experience taught her early lessons about working independently and planning to succeed. "I became Montana's state champion, and that motivated me to work hard and unrelentingly on fact-finding projects," she says proudly.

For teens aspiring to a similar career, Pati recommends making to-do lists, being daring, allowing yourself calculated risks, and always wearing a smile. "It's contagious and people will want to be around you."

Some businesses fail because the owner believes the business is too small for a business plan. Consequently, the business runs into problems, some of which could have been resolved early in the planning process. Every business should have a well-thought plan.

If borrowing funds is necessary for the business, moneylenders will want to see alternative plans of action in some cases. These would describe what emergency action would be taken at key steps when problems occur. For example, consider a bridal-bouquet business that obtains all of its flowers at a good price from one grower. The business plan should include a backup plan in case an emergency forces you to buy higher-priced flowers elsewhere. It should also explain the effect of higher flower costs on the expected profits. A backup plan is especially important for businesses that are totally dependent on one supplier.

Moneylenders will want proof that your business can withstand the challenges of the marketplace. For example, suppose you plan to operate an errand service and calculate future fuel expenses with today's prices. Moneylenders would consider your plan flawed if it did not anticipate higher gas prices. Gasoline prices tend to rise, so your plan should reflect real-world conditions.

You will, no doubt, refine your business plan many times before the document is thorough enough to use for obtaining financial assistance. It should cover the startup period plus one full year of operation. If you apply for a bank loan, the business plan should also include a profit forecast for each of the first three years. After the business is established, the business plan usually is updated annually to keep the business on course.

Obtain Financial Assistance

Many businesses were started on a kitchen table, without the typical desk and the usual office equipment. New entrepreneurs hold down their expenses by using what is available. They take advantage of free resources, such as information from the SBA and the U.S. Department of Agriculture Cooperative Extension Service. Used supplies and equipment can often serve the purpose very well, and rented items may offer a tax advantage.

Bankers and other financial institutions are the usual sources for borrowing money. Other possible sources for loans include family and friends. Sometimes suppliers and distributors of the product you plan to carry will offer a loan. If you carefully analyze your plan, you may discover other sources of funding. To avoid friction over financial matters, the terms of a loan agreement should always be clearly stated.

Present your business plan when applying for a loan. Outline how much money you need to borrow, how it will be used, and when you will pay it back.

Moneylenders pay particular attention to how much of your own money you plan to invest in the business. This gives them an indication of how committed you are to making the business a success. For example, Pati Palmer published her first book with her own money. The profits helped her finance a company that she started with a partner.

If you cannot locate funding, you will need to modify your plan so that your business requires fewer start-up funds. Many entrepreneurs work for years at building a savings large enough to start their own business. Establishing a business can be very expensive, so it is a good idea to start small and enlarge the business gradually.

Know the Legal Requirements

Small-business people say that learning and complying with business rules and regulations takes more time than actually running the business. In addition to the tax-reporting requirements, there may be state and local zoning, building, and health requirements to follow.

Rules and regulations tend to vary from business to business and region to region. You can contact your state and local government agencies to learn the current requirements. Also, the SBA is a free source of help and the first place that most entrepreneurs look.

Before a would-be entrepreneur signs any contracts or spends any money for the business, it is necessary to check all the laws, regulations, and codes that apply. Experienced lawyers who specialize in the type of business you are considering may need to be consulted.

Expert advice may reveal a flaw in your plan and a need to reconsider the business idea further. More importantly, this step will spare you from expensive penalties or lawsuits that could push your business into bankruptcy. A **bankruptcy** is a business failure that results in selling all possessions to pay debts. In a bankruptcy, a business that is unable to pay its debts is forced to sell its possessions.

◆ Responsibilities of an Entrepreneur

With a detailed business plan serving as a road map, the entrepreneur knows exactly what to do, when, and how. The first step in running the business is putting the business plan into action. Another important responsibility of an entrepreneur is keeping detailed, organized records and preserving all business-related documents.

It takes a lot more than enthusiasm to run a business, but it is a necessary ingredient. Entrepreneurs should talk about the business and show enthusiasm even after the initial excitement has worn off, 19-13. After all, if the business owner is not happy with the product or service, why should anyone else be? Also, entrepreneurs should listen carefully to what customers say about the product or service.

19-13 Entrepreneurs who believe in their business tend to show great pride and excitement.

True entrepreneurs are never satisfied with simply creating a business and having it run well. They constantly stay alert to factors that may affect their business. Having the business continually gain greater success, possibly creating additional businesses, is the entrepreneur's ultimate dream.

Refining the Business Plan

After operating a business for a while, the owner may recognize that part of the plan should be changed. Business owners adjust their plan as needed during the course of the year.

On the other hand, the plan may work perfectly day after day. In this case, the plan is followed, and then reviewed carefully before developing next year's plan.

Keeping Books and Records

Good records give you an instant, business scorecard. You can see immediately how your business is doing. Detailed records also make tax time much easier because paperwork is properly organized. A record of all earnings, purchases, and receipts should be kept.

You can handle the bookkeeping if the business is not large or complex. Prepared bookkeeping systems are available in office supply stores and may be tailored for your type of business. Bookkeeping and accounting courses are available for those not familiar with bookkeeping procedures. The Internal Revenue Service (IRS) has free publications that explain the tax-reporting requirements of every type of business. Computer programs are also available to help manage business records.

Financial records are particularly easy to handle if your business has

◆ no employees
◆ expenses paid by check
◆ customers who pay at the time of the transaction

Some types of businesses require more complicated bookkeeping. For them, the SBA offers help. Some may find it necessary, however, to consult an accountant or tax specialist. This is the most expensive alternative, but specialists may be able to lessen the firm's tax obligations. Besides financial records, there are many other documents that businesses should keep for possible future needs. See 19-14.

Telling Others About the Business

Talk about your business to friends, neighbors, relatives, and business people. Not only will you get their interest and attention, but you will also hear their reactions to your product or service. They may give you important advice and tell you how to attract more customers.

Remember, you are your own best advertisement. Enthusiasm in your product or service, or a lack of it, will be obvious to others.

Important Documents and Records
Keep these items as long as the business exists: ◆ Partnership agreements, by-laws, and other documents pertaining to the organization of the business ◆ Information on the owners' contributions and withdrawals from the business ◆ All profit-and-loss statements and other financial records ◆ All tax records for the business, employees, and shareholders
Keep these items for at least three years: ◆ Permits, licenses, insurance policies, and leases ◆ Day-to-day business records, such as sales receipts, invoices, purchases, and business expenses
Keep these items for the length of their contracts: ◆ Loan and lease agreements and mortgage papers

19-14 Business owners need to keep important papers for future reference.

Cynthia Skari
Color and Image Consultant

Some people can wear anything and always look great. Most people, however, look flattering in some colors and styles, but not in others. For those wanting professional advice on selecting the colors and styles that most flatter them, Cynthia Skari is ready to help. She used her clothing and textiles background to become a successful consultant and, in the process, created two successful businesses.

Cynthia began her career teaching flat pattern, draping, and clothing design classes at a state university. She prepared a series of workshops in which she analyzed people's hair, eyes, and skin tones with various clothing colors. "After that, friends and neighbors wouldn't stop asking me for advice on which colors looked best on them," says Cynthia. "That's when I realized the business potential behind what I was doing."

From that small start, Cynthia became a successful color and image consultant. She has worked with thousands of clients, analyzing their unique personal coloring and assembling individualized color portfolios for each. "My clients have credited me with their marriages, new careers, and increased self-esteem," says Cynthia. "Really, all I did was teach them to understand their natural beauty and how to enhance it on their own."

While developing her consulting business, she built a nationwide network of color and image consultants and created a unique color evaluation system. The system identifies more than 3,000 colors and is also used by independent color consultants. "I've been told that my materials are without equal in the field," she claims.

Organizing and assembling the color samples into individualized portfolios grew to a full-time job. Cynthia realized that a second business—a manufacturing business—was needed to assemble the portfolios. "This operation eliminated the 'busy' work that occupied too much of the consultants' time," explains Cynthia.

Her manufacturing business now prepares all the color portfolios under her label. It also purchases, cuts, codes, and stores all the fabric samples, numbering over 1,900 at present.

When a client needs customized services, she provides those, too. Her services include wardrobe management, figure analysis, and jewelry design. She also shops for clothing and accessories and recommends hairstyles, eyeglasses, skin care products, and cosmetics.

"It's flexible, versatile, challenging, and very creative," says Cynthia about her unique career. "If you enjoy working with people and are eager to see them make the most of themselves, helping individuals look their best may appeal to you, too."

Listening to Customers

Faithful customers may be a company's most valuable assets. Get to know your repeat customers, and you will learn how to reach others like them. Some businesses offer discounts or other incentives to encourage customers to return and do more business.

Staying Alert to Change

Entrepreneurs must stay aware of factors inside their industry that will affect their business. For example, fashion trends are a constant consideration for everyone in the textile, clothing, and interior decorating industries. This is an example of change occurring within an industry.

Outside the industry, factors that might cause a business to change must also be watched. Suppose plans call for constructing a major highway interchange on the other side of town. If that would direct traffic right to your competitor, you would want to stay informed on this matter.

One of the best ways to learn about changes that may affect your business is to meet regularly with others who have similar interests. Business and professional associations and the local chamber of commerce are excellent groups to explore. They inform entrepreneurs of changes in regulations, technology, business practices, customer trends, local issues, and other important matters.

◆ Entrepreneur Opportunities in Family and Consumer Sciences

The skills learned in family and consumer sciences classes can be used in a wide variety of businesses for self-employed individuals. The challenge is not in finding work, but in narrowing down the enormous list of possibilities to something that best suits you.

Self-employment opportunities are available in textiles, clothing, food products, food services, housing, and home furnishings. Other opportunities exist in human services, resource management, and communications, 19-15. In addition to the jobs mentioned in this chapter, review those discussed in previous Part 4 chapters, especially Chapter 14. Practically all the

Typical Entrepreneurship Opportunities
In Business
Antique seller
Building or clothing preservationist
Caterer
Furniture upholsterer
Kitchen designer or decorator
Tailor
Tour director
In Education and Communications
Historian
Messenger
Product demonstrator
Publisher
Speaker
Tutor
Writer
In Human Services
Babysitter
Beautician
Companion for the elderly
Drug and alcohol counselor
Housekeeper
Human development consultant
Transportation assistant
In Science and Technology
Baker
Candymaker
Dry cleaner
Health and fitness adviser
Nutritionist
Plant hybridizer
Textile stylist
In the Arts
Architect
Cake decorator
Image or color consultant
Jewelry designer
Landscape designer
Publication designer
Web designer

19-15 This is just a brief list of the many jobs open to entrepreneurs.

positions described there can be adjusted slightly to create self-employment opportunities.

The type of job you select will determine the level of experience and the educational requirements necessary. Refer to the education and training needs discussed in Chapters 14 through 18 for advice on specific jobs. Whether you work for yourself or someone else, similar jobs generally require the same training and education.

As you review the job possibilities presented in previous chapters and here, note which appeal to you. With planning, preparation, and the guidelines in this chapter, you can become an entrepreneur.

Summary

Entrepreneurs find opportunities in many types of businesses. They may harvest raw materials from nature or process the materials into more useable forms. They may focus on manufacturing products or selling them. They may specialize in providing a service. The service sector offers the most opportunity for entrepreneurs.

Most entrepreneurs enter the business world by starting their own business, although this is the riskiest way to become self-employed. When entrepreneurs buy an existing business or own a franchise, some aspects of the business are already done for them. By joining a family business, entrepreneurs experience the additional elements of family pride and family pressure. A business can operate as a sole proprietorship, partnership, or corporation.

As you develop the business and create a plan, you need to consider your interests and abilities. You also must consider a product or service that customers want, the best price or fee, a marketing plan, financial assistance, and the legal requirements.

Entrepreneurs follow a master plan to establish a business, and then refine it as needed to keep the business successful. Business-related records and documents are carefully organized and preserved for as long as necessary. They talk about the business and listen for advice. They follow customer reaction and learn how to improve the business and reach new customers. The wise entrepreneur plans ahead and watches for changes that may affect the future of the business.

Entrepreneurial opportunities can be found in all areas of family and consumer sciences. Dedicated professionals with vision, drive, and the right resources start various kinds of businesses. People of all levels of education and job experience operate business ventures. Some are more successful than others. Self-employment is a risky business, but it can be very rewarding as well.

To Review

1. Why are entrepreneurs important to the economy?

2. Name two advantages and two disadvantages of owning a business.

3. Name two qualities of successful entrepreneurs.

4. Name the five basic types of businesses.

5. List four ways you can go into business for yourself.

6. Name and describe the three legal forms of business ownership.

7. Name two factors to consider when setting a price or fee.

8. Which businesses should write out a business plan?

9. What do businesses gain by listening to customers?

10. Name five self-employment opportunities in family and consumer sciences.

To Do

1. Contact the Small Business Administration for information on starting your own business.

2. Interview your county clerk or other county government official about the necessary requirements to start a business in your community.

Glossary

A

ability. The capacity to perform a certain skill, which must be developed through training and practice. (2)

advocate. One who works vigorously to promote or support a cause. (15)

ACT (American College Testing). A college entrance examination. (4)

aggressive. Hostile and destructive; attacking as in a battle or combat. (6)

application form. A questionnaire given to prospective employees requesting personal information about education and work experience. (9)

appointed leadership. Type of leadership in which a person is designated to be in charge. (8)

aptitude. A natural talent for a certain physical or mental skill. (2)

assertive. Stating ideas in a confident and direct manner. (6)

associate degree. Certificate received after completion of a two-year program. (4)

attitude. The way a person looks at what happens in life and how he or she responds. (12)

B

baccalaureate. A four-year college degree. (4)

bachelor's degree. A four-year college degree; also called a baccalaureate. (4)

bankruptcy. A business failure that results in selling all possessions to pay debts. (19)

bid. A price estimate for a project. (18)

body language. Body movements, such as facial expressions, gestures, and posture, used to send messages to others. (6)

brainstorming. A group problem-solving technique that involves the spontaneous contribution of ideas from all members of the group. (8)

business plan. A written description of all the elements of a new business. (19)

C

CADD (computer-aided drafting and design). A computer program that can automatically draw objects to scale or exact measurements. (5)

CAD/CAM. Program using computer-generated designs to run manufacturing equipment. (5)

CAM (computer-aided manufacturing). A system in which machines set up manufacturing processes through computer commands. (5)

career. A planned sequence of work in a field, industry, or profession. (1)

career cluster. A group of jobs of similar nature or occupation. (3)

career ladder. A progression of advancement in an individual's planned sequence of work in a field. An employee generally begins with an entry-level job and progresses through a number of stages moving up to higher positions. (1)

cater. The business of providing food or service. (14)

child care. Child care programs that operate for extended hours. (16)

childless family. Couples who do not have children. (1)

children in self-care. Children who have no adult care before or after school. (16)

CIM (computer-integrated manufacturing). Using computers to control the entire factory operation. (5)

Civil Service Commission. The federal agency that hires people who work for the United States government. (9)

commission. Pay based on the number of units sold by an employee. (11)

communication. The process of interchanging thoughts, ideas, or information with other people. (6)

compromise. Reaching a mutual settlement or agreement by each person giving a little. (8)

computer. Electronic device that stores and processes information. (5)

computer literacy. Knowing how to operate a computer. (3)

conflict. A hostile situation resulting from opposing views. (8)

consignment. A selling arrangement whereby a seller displays a product, but the manufacturer maintains ownership until it is purchased. (19)

constructive criticism. Helpful suggestions for improvement in methods or behavior that do not hurt the other person. (8)

consultant. A professional who gives advice or ideas to businesses, organizations, or individuals. (14)

cooperative education. A cooperative school program that helps students gain work skills in business or industry; also called co-op. (4)

copy editor. A person who checks written materials for accuracy and clarity of meaning. (15)

copy writer. A person who prepares advertising copy for use by magazines, newspapers, or other media. (15)

corporation. A business that receives written authority from a state to form and operate. (19)

correspondent. A person who prepares and reports stories on major news events occurring in various geographic locations. (15)

cost-of-living raise. An increase in pay based on the annual rate of inflation that allows workers to keep pace with everyday living expense. (13)

counselor. Professional who helps people deal with personal, family, and social problems. (16)

creativity. The ability to make or bring something new into existence. (7)

culture. The beliefs and customs of a racial, ethnic, religious, or social group. (2)

D

database. An organized collection of information stored in computers. (5)

data communications. A process that allows computers to "talk" to each other. Information is transmitted between terminals over telephone or cable lines. (5)

decision-making process. A logical series of steps used to make a decision. (3)

demonstrator. Anyone who shows others how to perform a process. (15)

dependable. An attribute in which someone or something is reliable. (12)

dependent. A person who relies on another for financial support. (11)

destructive criticism. Remarks that focus on a person's failure or shortcomings. (8)

Dietary Guidelines for Americans. A 10-point plan for good health that applies to people of all ages. (12)

dietetics. The science of applying the principles of nutrition to food selection and food preparation. (17)

dietitian. Person that evaluates patients' nutritional needs and plans diets or eating plans. (17)

disadvantaged. A person who lacks basic resources or conditions regarded as necessary for an equal position in society. (16)

displaced homemakers. People who have stayed at home most of their adult lives and now want to earn an income. (16)

doctorate. An advanced degree requiring about two years' work beyond a master's degree. (4)

drug abuse. Deliberately taking a substance for other than its intended purpose. (12)

dual-career family. A family in which both the mother and the father are employed outside the home. (1)

E

editor. A person who reviews authors' writing for grammar, clarity, and meaning. (15)

e-mail. A message sent from one computer to another. (5)

empathy. The ability to think and act with understanding of how others feel. (8)

employment agency. An office specializing in helping people locate jobs from listings and various other job sources. (9)

entrepreneur. A person who invests time, money, and energy into starting a new business. (14)

entrepreneurship. Taking the risk of developing and managing a new business. (19)

extended family. Several generations of a family living together. (1)

F

Fair Labor Standards Act. A federal law that protects workers from unfair treatment by employers. Amendments to the law have established minimum wage, overtime pay, equal pay, and child labor standards. (11)

family. A group of two or more persons usually related by blood, marriage, or adoption who reside together in a household. (1)

family and consumer sciences. A profession devoted to improving the quality of individual and family life. (4)

family child care. Type of child care in which several children come into a caregiver's home. (16)

family life cycle. The stages of change that families pass through as they expand and contract. (1)

fashion merchandising. A broad term given to planning, buying, and selling of clothing and accessories. (14)

feedback. A response from another person that makes it possible for the sender to determine whether the message was understood. (6)

field experience. Performing or receiving first-hand information on a job related to a specific field of study. (4)

fixed expense. A business cost that occurs regularly and stays the same, such as monthly bills for rent, insurance, and water service. (19)

flexible expense. A business cost that varies according to the amount of business that occurs. (19)

flextime. A work schedule that permits flexibility in work hours. (1)

Food Guide Pyramid. A guide that helps people choose a well-balanced diet. (12)

food science. The study of the production, processing, storage, preservation, utilization, evaluation, and safety of food. (17)

food systems management. The business of preparing and serving food in an institution, such as a hospital, nursing home, retirement center, school, or other institution. (14)

formal evaluation. A written report that lets an employee know how he or she is performing on the job. (13)

franchise. A binding agreement to sell a company's goods or services in a certain area. (19)

fraud. The intentional twisting of the truth in order to get someone to give up a right or something valuable. (16)

freelance. Working independently without being employed or affiliated with one company, business, or service. (14)

fringe benefit. Any financial extra, such as paid vacation, sick leave, health insurance, and retirement plan provided by an employer. (3)

G

geriatrics. Branch of medicine that deals with the elderly. (4)

goal. The aims a person wants to reach. (2)

graduate degree. College work completed beyond a bachelor's degree. (4)

gross pay. The total amount of money earned during a pay period. (11)

group effectiveness. How well a person works with others in a group. (8)

H

hardware. The physical computer equipment consisting of four basic parts: the input device, the central processing unit (CPU), the memory, and the output device. (5)

harmony. A sense of unity achieved by the effective use of the principles of design. (18)

haute couture. High fashions created by the finest sewing. (14)

homemaker. Any person who contributes to the comfort and safety of the home and the well-being of the family members. (1)

hospitality industry. Services associated with eating, sleeping, or travel away from home. (14)

human resources. Assistance or information that comes from within a person or from other people. (3)

human services. Careers that concentrate on helping and understanding other people. (16)

I

inflection. Use of the voice to affect the meaning of a spoken message. (6)

informal evaluation. Unofficial meetings in which employee and supervisor talk about how the employee is performing on the job. (13)

initiative. The ability to start and carry out work independent of outside control or requirements. (12)

interest. A feeling that attracts special attention to an object or a matter. (2)

Internal Revenue Service (IRS). A federal branch of the U.S. Treasury Department that enforces tax laws and collects tax money. (11)

internship. A supervised learning experience in an individual's field of study. (3)

interpersonal skills. The ability to work effectively with other people. (8)

inventory. A supply of goods kept in stock for a ready sale. (19)

J

job. A task or group of tasks performed as a part of a person's work. (1)

job sharing. A work schedule in which two people split one job by dividing work hours. (1)

job simulations. Situations that are acted out or role-played, such as an on-the-job experience. (5)

journalist. A person who writes for newspapers or magazines. (15)

L

lateral career move. Advancing from one job to a different but related job at the same level, rank, or status in the company. (13)

leader. Any person who plans, directs, or guides the activities of others toward a shared goal. (8)

leadership skills. Ability to plan, direct, or guide the activities of a group. (8)

learning style. A person's preferences and tendencies that influence learning. (5)

letterhead. Stationery with a company or organization's name and address printed on it. (5)

letter of application. Letter written by a job applicant to interest an employer in his or her qualifications for a position. (9)

letter of resignation. A written notice that an employee is leaving his or her job. (13)

lifestyle. The way an individual or group of people chooses to live. (2)

M

management. Using resources to get what an individual wants and needs. (1)

marketing research analyst. A person who researches the size, location, and makeup of a product market. (14)

master's degree. Advanced degree received after two years of study beyond a bachelor's degree. (4)

mediation. A conflict-resolution technique in which opposing sides are brought together by a neutral person to discuss a fair settlement to a dispute. (8)

memorandums. Informal messages written from one person or department to another in the same company. (5)

merger. The absorption of a company or business by another company, or the combination of two or more companies. (13)

merit pay raise. An increase in pay based on employee job performance. (13)

minimum wage. The lowest amount per hour that employers can pay workers. (11)

motivation. The strong desire to achieve a goal. (7)

N

nanny. A person who lives with a family to care for their children. (16)

net pay. The amount of money left after all deductions are taken from gross pay. (11)

networking. Computer terminals wired together for in-house communication. (5) Sharing ideas and information with others of similar interests. (8)

nonhuman resources. Available material means for assistance or information. (3)

nonverbal communication. Communication that involves factors other than words. (6)

nuclear family. A unit made up of a father, mother, and their children living together. (1)

nutrition. The study of how the body uses food. (17)

nutritionist. A nutrition educator who teaches people how food affects the body and how to eat well for good health. (17)

O

OSHA (Occupational Safety and Health Administration). Organization that enforces job safety and health standards for all workers. (12)

overtime. Work on a job more than forty hours per week. (11)

outsourcing. Hiring workers to perform tasks for the business outside the business environment. (1)

P

paraprofessional. A trained aide who assists or works under the supervision of a professional. (16)

parliamentary procedure. A method of conducting meetings in which work is carried out according to certain laws and guidelines. (8)

partnership. A business owned by two or more persons. (19)

payroll deduction. Money that is subtracted from a paycheck for taxes, insurance, savings plans, Social Security, or other benefits. (11)

peer. Person of the same age and social group. (2)

performance test. Test requiring a job applicant to perform a certain skill. (10)

personal data sheet. Important facts about a person, including education, work experience, organizational experience, and awards. (9)

personality. The total combination of an individual's behavioral and emotional characteristics. (2)

personal management skills. Ability to use one's knowledge and attitude to obtain and hold a job. (7)

personal priorities. Objects, beliefs, and principles that are important to each individual. They give direction to actions, thoughts, and feelings. (2)

personnel policies. Company rules and regulations that outline the behavior expected of all employees. (11)

placement office. A postsecondary or college job service providing assistance in finding professional work. (9)

portfolio. A collection of information that highlights an individual's education, expertise, and achievements. (9)

practicum. A work experience related to a specific field of study. (4)

preemployment test. A means of assessing a job applicant's skills and abilities. (10)

prejudice. Opinions that are generally negative in nature and usually based on false or insufficient information. (8)

premium. The amount of money paid to cover a certain period of an insurance policy or plan. (11)

probationary period. A trial period during the first few weeks or months of employment to see how well a new employee performs on the job. (13)

productivity. The amount of work employees do. (7)

promotion. Moving to a higher position with more responsibilities within the same company. (13)

prototype. A working recipe for a potential food product. (17)

punctual. Able to be on time. (12)

R

Random Access Memory. (RAM) Information temporarily stored as it is being entered into the computer and processed by the central processing unit (CPU). (5)

Read Only Memory. (ROM) Information that has been permanently stored in the computer at the factory. (5)

real estate broker. A person who helps people buy and sell buildings and land. (14)

references. People who know a person well and could give information regarding his or her character and abilities. (9)

reporter. A person who gathers information and prepares stories that inform their audience about different events and issues. (15)

resources. Material and nonmaterial items that help individuals reach goals. (1)

responsible. An attribute in which someone is capable of being trusted to carry out a job or duty. (12)

resume. A brief outline of a person's education, work experience, and other qualifications used to apply for a job. (9)

retailer. A business that sells products directly to consumers. (19)

S

sabbatical. A leave of absence from a job, usually taken for more schooling or training. (10)

salary. Pay for work that is a fixed amount for a period of time, usually a year. (11)

salutation. The greeting used before the body of the letter. (5)

SAT (Scholastic Aptitude Test). A college entrance examination. (4)

seasonal. Employment in which workers only work during a particular time of the year. (13)

self-actualization. The need to be everything one is capable of becoming. According to Maslow, it is the highest level of need. (2)

self-concept. The ideas and impressions a person has about himself or herself. (7)

self-esteem. The feeling that an individual has of self-worth; a feeling of being needed and valued. (1)

self-motivation. Inner urge to achieve and succeed. (12)

seniority. The status of having worked a long time in a company or business. (11)

severance pay. Pay to an employee who is permanently laid off due to reasons that are not the fault of the employee. (13)

sexual harassment. A form of employment discrimination including any unwelcome sexual advances, requests for sexual favors, or other sexual conduct. (11)

shareholder. Part owner of a corporation. (19)

single-career family. A family in which only one parent is a wage earner. The other parent has the responsibilities of caring for the home and family. (1)

single-parent family. A family with only one parent available as head of the household. (1)

software. Set of instructions that directs and guides a computer. (5)

sole proprietorship. A business owned by only one person. (19)

stalemate. A standoff during which no solution satisfies the disputing parties. (8)

standard. A means to determine if goals have been reached. (2)

standard of living. The lifestyle or type of living that people have due to the quantity and quality of services they can afford. (2)

stepfamily. A family formed when a single parent marries someone who may or may not have children. (1)

stereotype. A belief that all members of a group share the same common characteristics. (1)

stewardship. The careful and responsible management of something entrusted in one's care. (15)

stress. Any emotional, mental, or physical tension people experience. (7)

support system. Any group of people who help with the care of the family, especially in difficult times. (1)

syndicated. Published in newspapers throughout the country. (15)

system. An independent group of parts or members forming a unified whole. (8)

T

teamwork. Working together to reach a common goal. (8)

technical writer. Person who composes scientific and technical information into words the average person can understand. (15)

technology. The use of ideas, methods, tools, and materials to get things done; the application of knowledge to solve problems and improve and extend human capabilities.(3, 17)

Tech Prep (Technical Preparation Education). A combined secondary and post-secondary program integrating academic and technical courses toward career preparation. (4)

terminals. The output and input devices such as the printer, screen, and keyboard. (5)

textiles. Fibers and yarn made into cloth. (14)

tip. A certain percentage of money that customers leave for the person who served them. (11)

trade apprenticeship. A type of specialized education in which skills and knowledge are learned by working on the job. (4)

trade association. An organized group of people involved in similar interests or lines of work. (15)

transferable skills. Skills that are useful in different work settings. (3)

U

unemployment compensation. Paychecks given for a limited time to an employee for unemployment through no fault of the employee. (13)

unlimited liability. A legal obligation that makes a business owner responsible for all business-related debts. (19)

V

venture. An entrepreneur's new business. (19)

verbal communication. Communication that involves words. (6)

vintage. Refers to items from a past era. (18)

visual merchandising. The promotion of a store's image through its storefront, interior decor, and merchandise displays. (18)

volunteer leadership. Type of leadership in which a group member volunteers to be in charge of a committee or function. (8)

volunteer work. Work that is done without pay. (3)

W

wage earner. A person who is paid for the work he or she performs. (1)

wages. Pay received for hourly work. (11)

webmaster. A title used by technology specialists who create the appearance and content of company Web sites. (15)

wholesaler. A business that sells products to retailers. (19)

word processing. Typing words on a keyboard, viewing and rearranging them on the screen, and printing a hard copy. (5)

work. Any activity that produces something of value. (1)

work ethic. An individual's or society's attitude or belief about work. (1)

writer. A person who develops original fiction and nonfiction work. (15)

Index

science and technology, 314-321
Food production in services, high
school courses, 72
Food science, 317, 318
Foodservice, 239, 240
Food stylists, 351
Food systems management, 239
Food technologists, 317, 318
Formal evaluations, 222
Foster, Pat, 296
Franchise, 366, 367
Fraud, 297
Freelance, 259
Fringe benefits, 51
child care provisions, 182
educational opportunities, 182
evaluating job offers, 181-183
insurance, 181
investment opportunities, 181
parental leave, 182
retirement or pension plans,
181
vacation, sick leave, and personal leave, 182
Furniture designers, 350
Future Business Leaders of
America–Phi Beta Lambda,
148
Future job trends, 55-58
aging population, 56
art careers, 355
business and marketing
careers, 261, 262
economic factors, 58
education and communications
careers, 285
effects on occupations, 57
emphasis on healthy living, 56
family and consumer sciences,
83, 84
human services careers, 307
knowledge and information, 55
more time at home, 55, 56
population trends, 57
project-by-project work, 56
science and technology
careers, 334

G

Geriatrics, 74, 292, 293
Goals, 43-46
career, 45
definition, 43
lifestyle, 45, 46
prioritizing, 29
reaching, 131, 132
retirement, 45, 46
Goal setting, 129-132
Government's role in safety, 213
Graduate degree, 83
Graduate schools, 83
Griepentrog, Linda Turner, 249
Grooming, 188
Gross pay, 194
Group effectiveness, 134-143
communication, 142, 143
conflict resolution, 143
creative-thinking skills, 140-142
definition, 134
interpersonal skills, 135-138
problems in the workplace,
138-143
Guide for Occupational Exploration,
54

H

Harassment, 193
Hardware, 100
Harmony, 340
Haugh, Bridget, 339
Haute couture, 246
Head housekeeper, 306
Health and fitness, 40, 41, 213-219
Dietary Guidelines for
Americans, 213-216
drug and alcohol abuse, 217-219
Food Guide Pyramid, 215, 216
maintaining, 127
mental health, 219
rest and sleep, 217
tobacco, 217
Health Occupations Students of
America, 148
Healthy living, effect on future
job trends, 56

Heeb, Gail, 252
High school family and consumer sciences courses, 70-74
Hobbies and activities, 33
Home furnishings merchandising, 250, 251
Home health aide, 294, 295
Homemaker, 16, 294
as a career, 16, 17
Home management consultant,
255, 256
Home-study, family and consumer sciences, 79
Honesty, 208
HOSA, 148
Hospitality and tourism services,
high school courses, 73
Hospitality industry, 242, 243
Hospitality, tourism, and recreation careers
arts, 353
business and marketing, 242-
245
education and communica-
tions, 282
human services, 303-306
science and technology, 332
Hostile environment harassment,
193
Hotel management, 243, 244
Household products and furnishings manufacturer, 251
Housekeepers, 295
Human assistance careers, 292-
297 *See also* Family studies
and human assistance
careers
Human resources, 63
Human services, definition, 287
Human services administration,
301
Human services careers, 287-309
business and marketing, 255,
256
child development and early
childhood education, 288-292
consumer and resource management, 297-303
education and training needed, 307

W

W-2 form, 196, 197
W-4 form, 195, 196
Wage earner, 16
Wages, 194
Want ads, 159
Wardrobe consultants, 344
Webmaster, 275
Wellness careers *See* Food, nutrition, and wellness careers
Wholesaler, 363
Word processing, 102
Work, 15-27
    balancing family and, 28-30
    definition, 16
    impact on the family, 25-27
    meaning of, 15-17
    reasons for, 17-20
Work-based learning programs, 74-78
    cooperative education, 74
    tech prep, 75-78
Work ethic, 18
Writers, 278
Writing skills, 93-98
    business reports and memos, 96, 97
    e-mail, 96, 97
    improving, 97, 98

Z

Zieman, Nancy L., 277